BRIGHT NIGHTS

BRIGHT NIGHTS

PHOTOGRAPHS OF ANOTHER NEW YORK

TOD SEELIE

PRESTEL

MUNICH · LONDON · NEW YORK

CONTENTS

7   Introduction Jeff Stark

11   Grotesque Seduction Carolina A. Miranda

33   Your Fear of Looking Stupid Is Holding You Back Caledonia Curry

53   Crowd Surfing Past the Camera Joe Ahearn

73   The Only Photographer at Bike Kill Conrad Carlson

93   F-Stop G Ian Vanek

113 A Feral Underground Paradise Colin Moynihan

133 Brooklyn Was More Fun Sto Len

153 The City Askew Benjamin Shapiro

171 Portals to Another World Evan Pricco

190 Captions

192 Acknowledgements

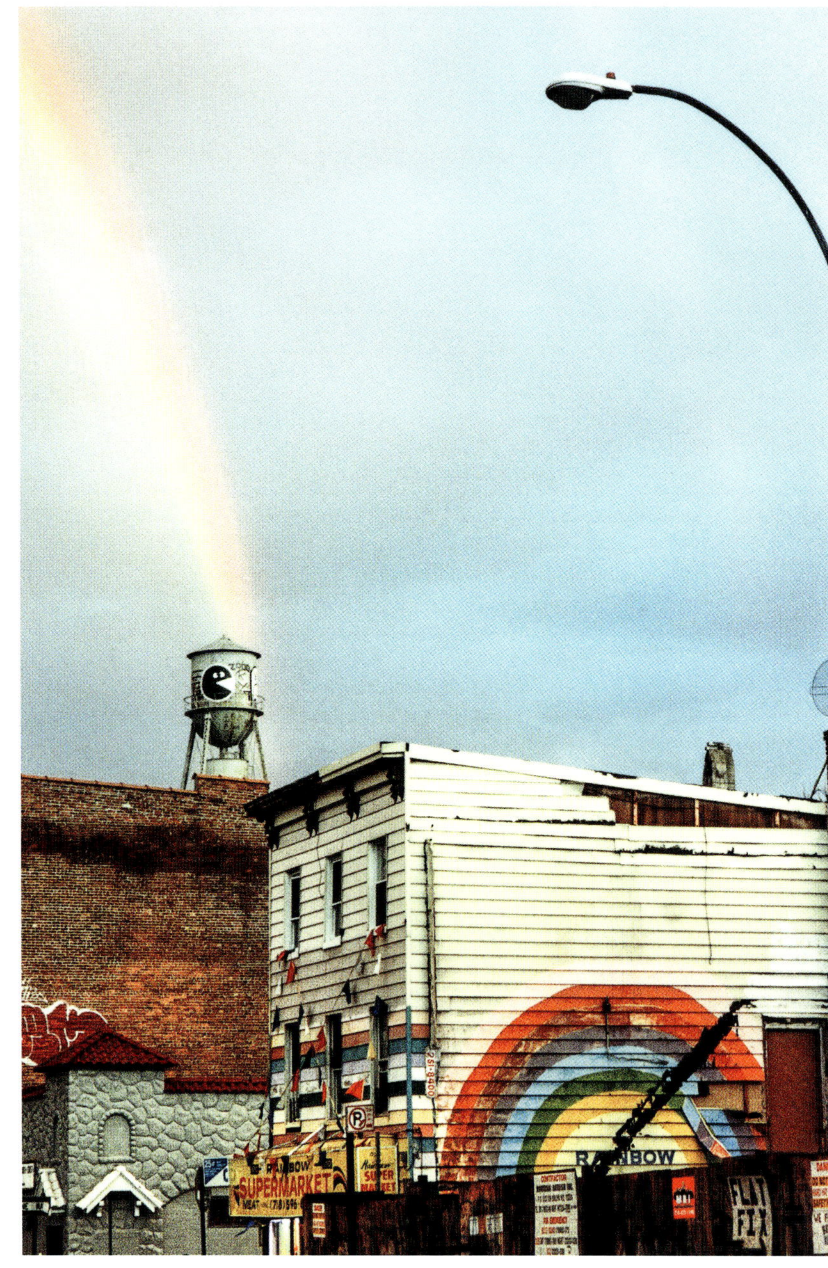

RAINBOW
SUPERMARKET
RAINBOW
FLAT
FIX

INTRODUCTION
JEFF STARK

We love telling stories about New York.

We love it so much, we tell stories that are not even true.

Here is one of those stories: New York has lost its edge.

It's a story we've been telling ourselves for the last 20 years, and it goes like this: New York used to be a thriving pisshole. It was dirty and dangerous and unspeakably cool, just a few years before you or I got here—whenever that was.

But now, the story goes, New York is dead. Bankers and tourists have overtaken Manhattan. The rent is going up in Brooklyn. Artists are choked out and headed for Berlin. CBGB is gone, and there's an Applebee's on 42nd Street.

What was once the city of Patti Smith and Robert Mapplethorpe, of William S. Burroughs and Allen Ginsberg, of Jackson Pollock and Lee Krasner, of Bob Dylan, Jim Jarmusch, Marcel Duchamp, Andy Warhol, and Jean-Michel Basquiat has been reduced to a set piece for morning TV shows and candy-coated romantic comedies.

Safe. Lame.

Tod Seelie's photographs say this story is a lie. Or, maybe, if it's not a lie, it is certainly not the truth—because New York is alive in these pictures. In his photographs, people swim in the East River. They take over the Manhattan Bridge on bikes. They smash cars in the street.

This New York is not simply made of glass condos, or a boring playground for creative professionals. It's a celebration of something else entirely. It's a dense place: complicated, contradictory, confusing...and so, so awesome.

* * *

I started hanging around Seelie and other kids from Pratt Institute in 2001. He was fairly new to photography back then (he'd studied sculpture in school, then switched). Honestly, I don't really remember him that well. It's not that he was forgettable or dull. It's just that he was a modest Midwestern guy from Ohio, surrounded by people with Roman candle eyes.

Wow, were they fun. They threw dance parties in the middle of the street, and late at night they'd strip all of the advertisements out of subway cars and replace them with their own artwork. No one had convinced them that New York was dead. They'd dreamed of the kind of city they wanted to live in, and were in the process of making it themselves.

Who was around at the time? A bunch of people who broke out of their own subcultures, skipping across the edge of the mainstream. Back then, Japanther were becoming a band because Ian Vanek had an idea for a T-shirt. Swoon was just starting to experiment with street art. The band Matt & Kim were there, not playing together yet. There were a dozen more kids in that group too, like Polina the muralist, and Hubert, who became a farmer.

At the time, Seelie was mostly shooting empty landscapes with a side of portraits. But he was also hanging out with all these people, and his camera started to come out when things got good. Sometimes he was asked to document art projects that he was working on with everyone else. Other times, he just shot.

It wasn't obvious at first, but the life he was living started seeping into his pictures. You started to see his friends. You started to see the places they lived and the things they made. And, eventually, you started to see him.

* * *

Most of Seelie's photographs make me ask two questions:

1. What am I looking at?
2. How the hell did he get that photograph?

I usually don't have an answer for the first question, even though, sometimes, it's pretty clear that I'm looking at a picture of two people on homemade tall bikes jousting with PVC pipes. That, of course, still doesn't explain what the fuck I'm seeing.

Seelie's photos take us inside subcultures we might never have known existed. Subcultures are insular and coded by definition. They have razor-thin distinctions that don't make a lot of sense if you're not immersed in them yourself. Though there are other photographers who show us these worlds, Seelie's images make them look like alternate ways to create a life. This is partly because the people in his photos don't look like they're performing for the camera—they are living passionately. He manages to capture their lives in a way that is honest and special, without compromising their integrity.

This trick is pulled off because Seelie belongs to several subcultures himself—many of which are unnamed, all of which appear in this book. As it happens, these subcultures offer real alternatives to the mainstream creative industries of New York (not to mention the uncomfortable police state encouraged by a 20-year reign of two conservative mayors). These groups are supportive, nourishing, and generous. Collaboration is almost a given, and everyone pitches in to help realize projects.

It's the reason why Seelie has the best pictures from Bike Kill, the annual Halloween block party put together by members of the Black Label Bicycle Club. Or why he was on the boat with the Swimming Cities crew, which piloted rafts down the Hudson River and around the Battery of Manhattan. People trust him—not just as a photographer, but also as a person. I'd argue that because he understands his own subcultures, he easily breezes

into others. When he ends up at a basement dance party in Harlem, he captures the chaos and sex in a way that's messy and weird, rather than skanky and simple. He might not be at home, but he's not just a tourist.

* * *

Seelie's photographs connect us to what we think is great about New York, and to what we think *was* great about New York. But they're not nostalgic. They don't look back. The people in them don't seem like they're copying poses they've seen before. Consequently, the pictures look immediate. Now—in the sense that someone just spilled beer on you, and there's a foot in your face. That kind of now.

In a way, all of the work in this book is of a single subject—New York. However, the photographs are connected in a way that makes sense when you look at how Seelie moves through the city (which, incidentally, is usually on a bicycle).

There are pictures of friends of course. Sometimes, those photographs are about hanging out, making out, or exploring abandoned buildings. There are also images shot on assignment for magazines or websites—mostly bands, but also assorted randomness, like amateur strip contests.

Then, there are the almost incidental photographs, often captured with the point-and-shoot camera in his pocket. These come from living in Brooklyn, being on the street, and knowing where to look: dead rats, cars on fire, double rainbows. For me, they are connected to the work of photographers like Lee Friedlander, who created a sort of romantic aesthetic of American decay, showing what things actually look like rather than what we want to think they look like.

Finally, there are photos that document art projects and events, mostly put on by friends and co-conspirators. Seelie often documents performance artists, weird theater, site-specific installations, and any multitude of sweaty gigs. With his SLR (a common digital camera with a nice lens), he makes these events look better than just about anyone else, from the practiced pros to the amateurs with their endless snapshots.

There is a certain filthy glamor in some of these images, but to be clear, it's not like Seelie's subjects tolerate him because he takes great pictures. Not at all. He's invited because he's good to be around. Because he always washes his own dishes. Because he carries the heavy part up the stairs. And because he always shares his pictures.

That last one is a big deal. Professional photographers regularly keep photos to themselves. Others lurk like voyeurs at a peep show, furtively snapping pictures and disappearing at the end of an event. I've never once wondered what happened to all the photos Seelie shoots; if they're any good, they'll be on one of his websites. I know he's not building a secret stash to unleash into the world in case everybody gets famous.

At times, I think the way he shares photos is a radical act of community. The pictures are there, online or in small galleries, posted in a way that lets us develop a narrative about who we are based on how we appear through his eyes. It's a rare thing.

It's a pleasure to watch Seelie work, in part because his method is so matter-of-fact, so relentless. He doesn't rush into the center and shoot what everyone is looking at; he's not a quick draw. He looks first, and then he marches in for his first set up.

He shoots, checks focus, and then moves on to his next spot. There's craft in his pacing.

This would be less remarkable if everyone around him wasn't in the midst of complete chaos, actually hanging off the rafters, which I've seen at more than one show he's photographed. I've also watched him get kicked in the head in a mosh pit, and circle a swim party in a small boat to get an alternate perspective on the scene, rowing himself with little splashes in between shots— working while everyone else is having fun. Seelie always says that his goal is to make an event look like it *felt* to be there. It turns out that you don't achieve that by accident. It takes work.

* * *

The flipside to Seelie's images of chaotic nightlife are the wide, still landscape shots. These were first created on a medium format camera and became part of an early series called *Of Quiet*. You can still see traces of that work in his New York pictures of abandoned spaces, lit by moonlight or metal halide streetlamps.

Related is his series that I could call *All Alone at the Party*, which are photos of people experiencing a solitary moment amid something far larger and louder than themselves: a sweaty dancefloor, a passing train, a crumbling building. I find them incredibly touching. It's these pictures that connect his work to photographer Nan Goldin, one of his primary influences. Here's Matt from Japanther with a black eye on a couch. There's some guy standing in his underwear, not entirely there. There's a girl, hovering over a crowd, lost.

These images have a way of wiping away subculture and connecting to anyone who's felt the weight of loneliness.

I love looking at pictures of people being young and alive, but they don't mean as much if you never see the melancholy on the flipside of that decadence. Goldin showed us the sadness of intimacy with one other person. Seelie does it in a crowd.

* * *

Most of the photographs in this book were taken in the first decade of the new millennium. While you're looking at them, it can be easy to forget that you're seeing what happened just after September 11, what happened while bankers ripped apart the economy from their perch on Wall Street, what happened while the country supposedly couldn't turn off reality television or look away from social media.

We told ourselves all kinds of stories about this period. It was a bad time.

And yet, you wouldn't know it to look at these photos; the people in them are often having the time of their lives. It's important to remember that what is going on in them is true. A true story. We often think that subculture is just another thing to buy—that you can put a patch on your jacket and call yourself a punk. But, at its best, the subculture you create for yourself and your friends is something more. It can be an active rejection of a poisonous culture, a rejection that is both life affirming and liberating in a city where people tell you that everything worth doing has already been done.

Tod Seelie's pictures remind us that we don't have to live in a boring city, but his critique is even deeper. In a way, the photographs challenge the notion of boredom itself—that modernist disease—and show it banished by the ecstatic joy of living life on the margins of New York City. There are still surprises here, even in dark times, and they make life worth living. They show us maybe the remedy is not to make more money, but to spend less and live more. They show us you can create art, dance with your friends, set off on a raft, or take over the whole building.

Don't ask for permission. Just do it yourself.

That life is way too awesome not to live it.

Jeff Stark is the editor of Nonsense NYC, a weekly e-mail list about independent arts and culture. He also makes large-scale installations and creates theatrical events in unusual places.

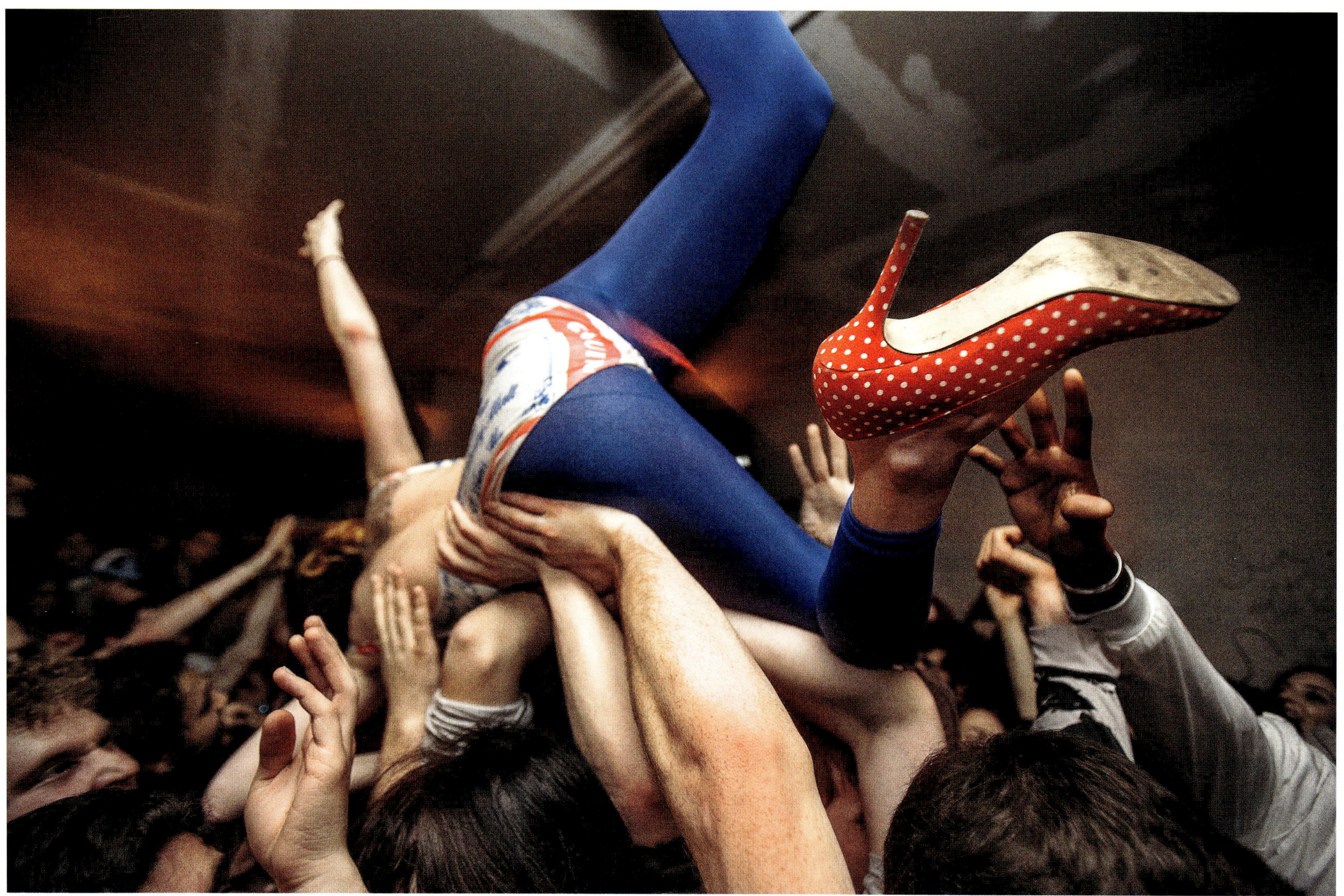

GROTESQUE SEDUCTION

CAROLINA A. MIRANDA

It's the middle of a concert. There is an explosion of drums and guitar and screaming and rhyming in the sardine-can confines of a dilapidated former grocery stand somewhere in the middle of Brooklyn. The atmosphere is equal parts mosh pit and sauna. In the middle of this, there is a woman. She is attired—quite remarkably—in a pair of electric blue leggings and polka dot pumps. And she is floating, ecstatically, on the outstretched palms of a roiling crowd, one heel pointed at the sky, one arm reaching upwards in a gesture of abandon. It is precisely at this moment that Tod Seelie takes his picture.

High Heels Crowd Surf (page 10) is interesting for a number of reasons. For one, there is its color and texture, from the synthetic sheen of the woman's cobalt leggings to the cherry-colored daintiness of her cloth high heels. There is also its depth. Her body points into the picture, away from the viewer, a scrum of hands delivering her to the rear of the room. We can't see her face, nor can we see the faces of most of the crowd. But we can feel them—and practically smell them (most likely somewhere on the continuum between hot armpit and stale beer).

Seelie has been taking pictures of basement rock concerts, bike jousting tournaments, protests, bar fights, illicit tunnel dinner parties, and even extended bouts of Jell-O wrestling for more than a decade. During this time, a lot of other people have taken pictures, too. Chances are you'll find images of these same events warehoused somewhere online, on music sites and personal blogs. However, when faced with a flood of images from a Japanther concert, it's pretty easy to pick out the ones taken by Seelie. The reverie is apocalyptic. His framing provides glimpses of odd angles and lost moments, leading the viewer's eye to places it wouldn't ordinarily go first. His sense of color and texture can make you practically taste the bloody noses. A lot of photographers can take a picture of someone screaming. Few of them can make it seem as if that person is screaming at you.

Since the invention of the camera, photographers have spent their waking hours chronicling urban subcultures. In the early 1930s, Brassaï made deeply cinematic portraits of prostitutes in his adopted city of Paris. In the 1930s and 1940s, Weegee turned his flash on the tenement dwellers and flamboyant mobsters of New York's Lower East Side. Diane Arbus spent the 1950s and 1960s chronicling circus habitués and the dwarves and sword swallowers who headlined Times Square freak shows. Certainly, Seelie draws from these traditions. He expresses a deep connection to the lives of the people he photographs.

Even as he displays a profound empathy toward his subjects, Seelie nonetheless remains an unblinking observer. These are not mannered portraits set in perfectly lit studios, or images that creak under the weight of moody filters and excess saturation. In a Seelie picture, what you see is what you get. A singer wails from a sticky-dank concrete floor (page 175). A man in a pair of tighty-whities displays a pale basketball stomach tattooed with the words *Hug Life* (page 13). There are wild gesticulations, twisted poses, and contorted facial expressions—a kind of punk ballet—of the sort recorded by the late conceptual artist Bruce Conner, who in the 1970s spent a couple of years taking pictures at a San Francisco punk club. In his images, Conner recorded moments of rage, joy, and recklessness. Seelie works in the same vein. In 2012, he attended a vogue dance battle at a Manhattan nightspot. The event produced one of his most remarkable pictures, of a vogue dance battle at the nightclub Escuelita (page 22). In it, a performer in slim jeans and a cropped bright T-shirt bends backward in an acrobatic flip, exposing a length of taut belly and ridges of straining neck muscles. The floor is scuffed and dim; the horizon is lined by a row of blurry legs. It is an erotically charged moment. The dancer gazes right at the lens, lips parted, back arched. But her eyes reveal that she is elsewhere, her mind lost in the mechanics of this extravagant display.

Seelie manages to capture moments such as this with a regularity that defies explanation. He is not a street photographer in the literal sense. He does not tool around New York City looking for random moments to snap. However, his instincts certainly draw from that tradition. He understands the exact moment when someone in a public space has let down their guard and done something extraordinary. There is also a distinct rawness to his imagery that evokes the work of street shooters such as Helen Levitt and Leon Levinstein, two artists who could create a visual sucker punch out of a simple gesture or look. Levitt documented a certain feral quality in the children she photographed—one that was not conventionally charming or cute. Levinstein, in turn, reveled in the rumpled forms of fat, wrinkled bodies. Seelie finds his poetry in moments of high creativity, when creation and destruction seem to be occurring in equal amounts: banged up men on hand-built bikes, screaming lead singers, and the sight of a man in a hand-sewn mask (page 118), rolling his eyes to the ceiling in ecstasy (or is it pain?).

It can be easy to get distracted by the sheer pandemonium in many of these images. Seelie's subjects often look as if they're about to lose a limb. But give his work a more thorough inspection and you'll find a world that exists in shocking, ebullient color. In one classic shot, a tangerine sky hovers over a crowd going nuts at a rock concert (page 14). In another, a man in a crimson-colored Santa suit rides a tall bike along a snow-covered road (page 155)—an image that is sublimely absurd, and provides an extreme juxtaposition of tones. Other photos contain emerald green skirts, crisp denim jackets, and the icy blonde hair of a solitary figure sitting primly in a black leather room (page 23). It's a palette inspired by the drama of William Eggleston, the pioneering American photographer who could turn the mundane (think chartreuse curtains and floral polyester) into practically tactile color-field experiences. The work of lens men Martin Parr and Joel Sternfeld is also instructive—two photographers with a knack for capturing the lurid qualities of things like strawberry cottage cheese and wood paneling.

Seelie has countless photos splashed with these wild bits of color, but there is one in particular that reads like a playful tribute to Eggleston: three women in red blouses and covered in red body paint, sit before a wall that is the same deep shade of red (page 154). The angle is not a traditional one. The figures are marginal, seated at the bottom right of the photo. The rest of the frame is occupied by the blood red wall, which bends into a corner at the left. In its tone and content, Seelie's snap echoes an iconic 1973 picture by Eggleston, in which a bare light bulb descends from a crimson ceiling, the wall folding into a corner in the distance. Seelie's picture, however, isn't simply a mindless copy. In his image, the three women stare animatedly to the right. The viewer is left to imagine what sort of madness might be occurring just out of frame.

At a time when a lot of urban photography feels indistinguishable, preoccupied with empty architectural landscapes or stagey portraits that use the city as set dressing, Seelie's work feels wondrously alive. In sweaty basements and garbage-strewn lots, he has found creativity in the midst of messy delivery. He absorbs and synthesizes the traditions of artists who came before him, but has a voice that is distinctly his own. The pictures in this book are bubbling cauldrons of insanity and confusion and joy and pain. They are grotesque yet seductive: never pretty, yet filled with beauty.

Carolina A. Miranda is a freelance writer and radio reporter who has produced stories on culture and travel for TIME, ARTnews, Art in America, Fast Company, *"All Things Considered", and "Studio 360". She has also served as a contributing art critic and reporter for New York Public Radio.*

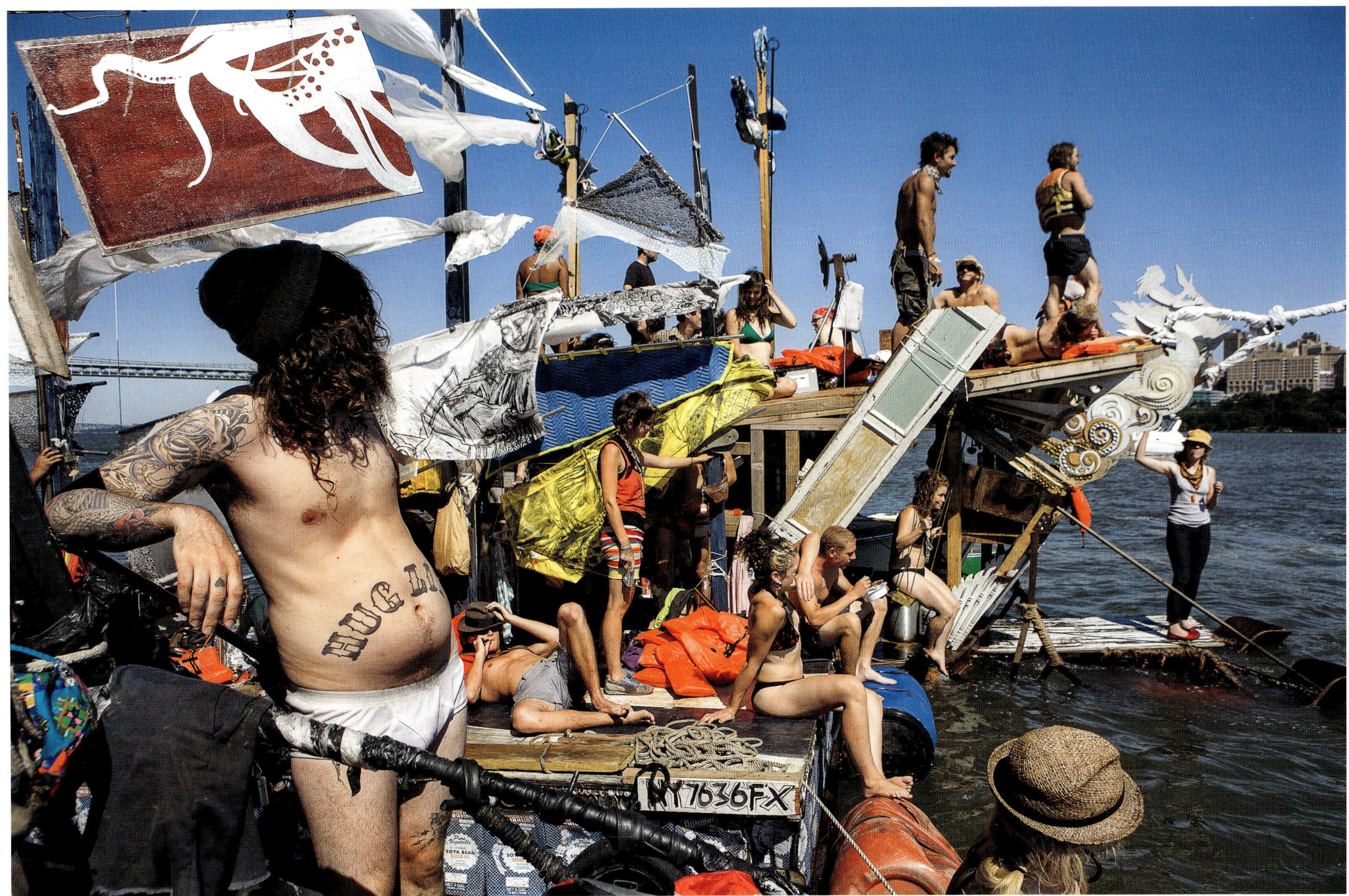

Y7636FX

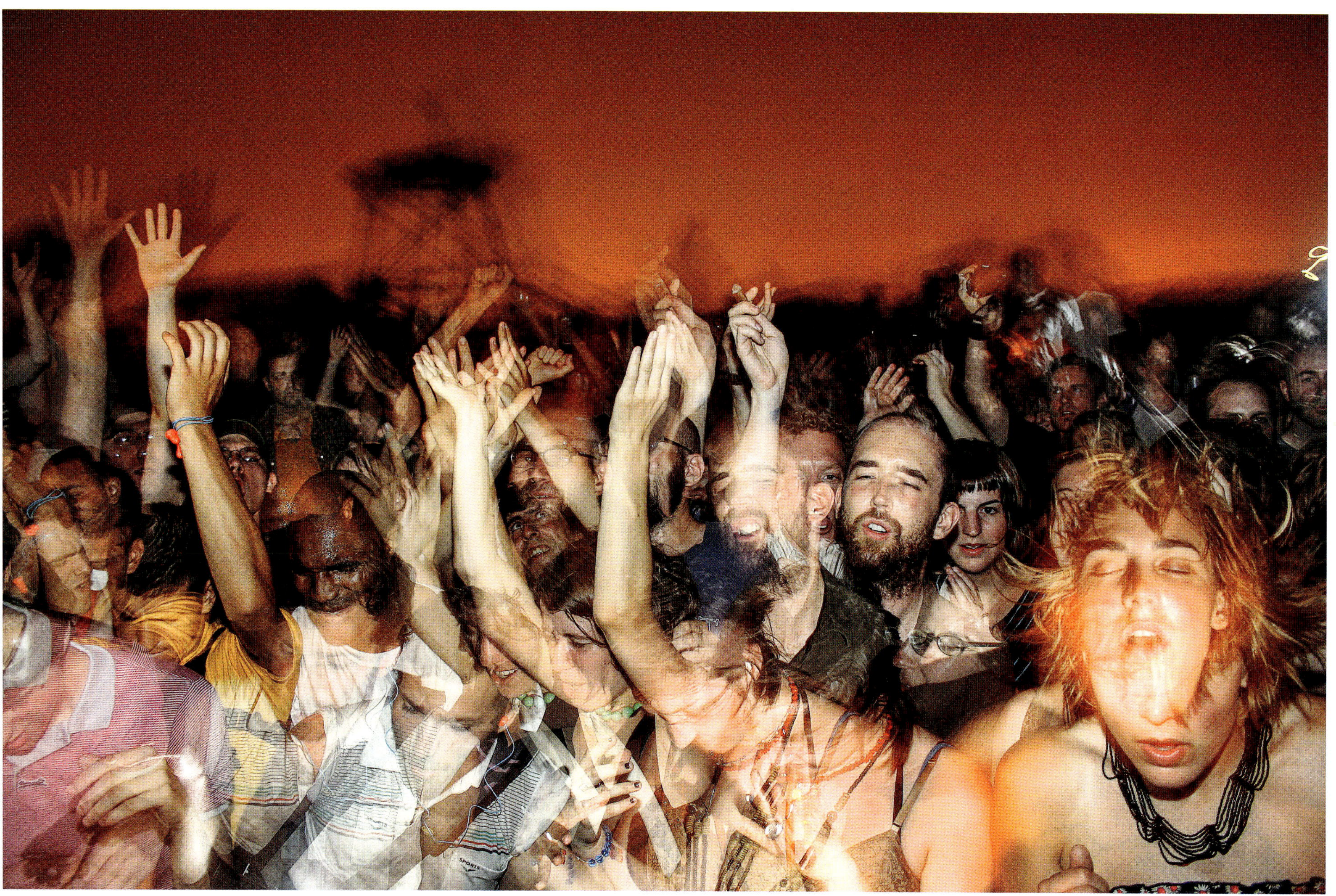

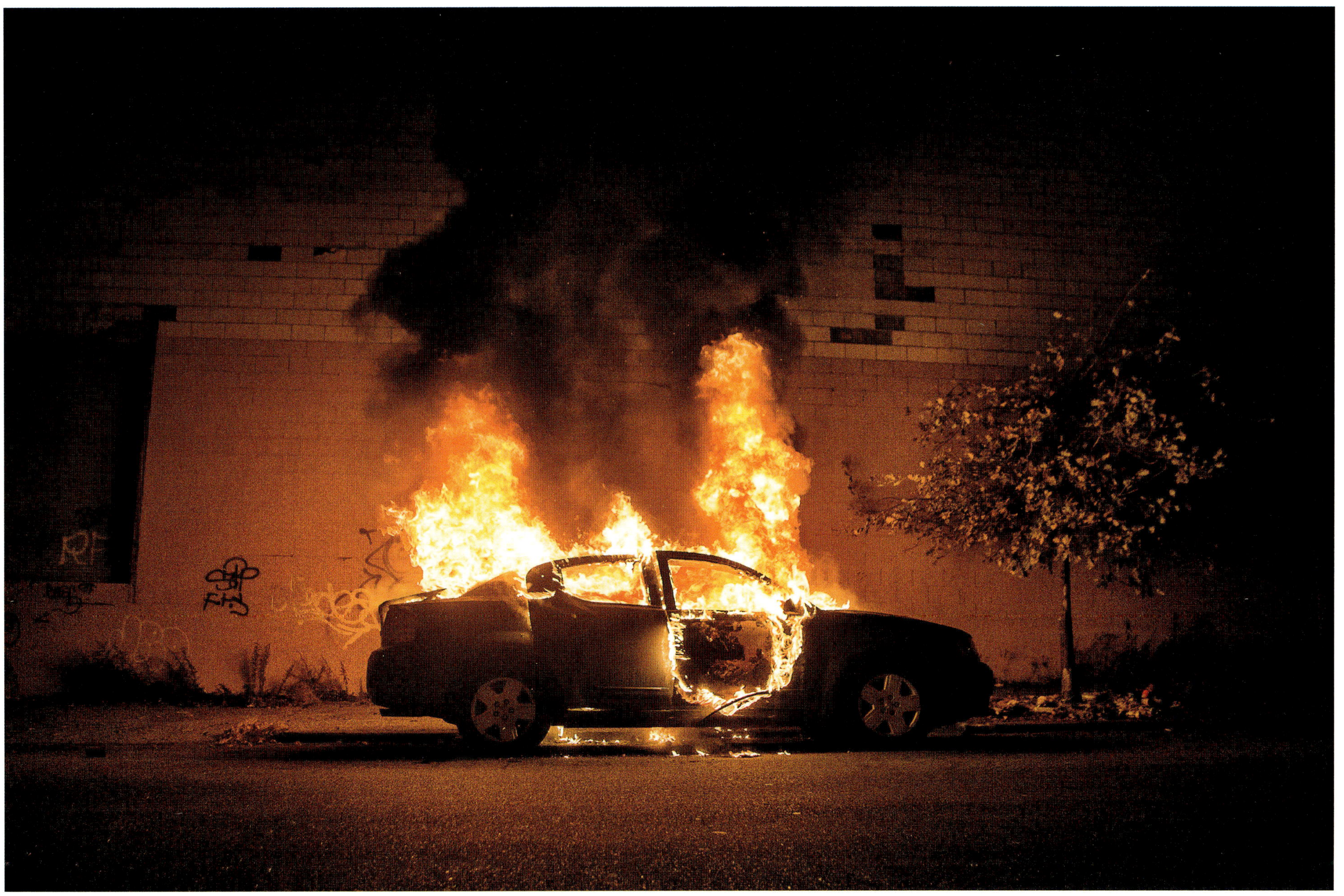

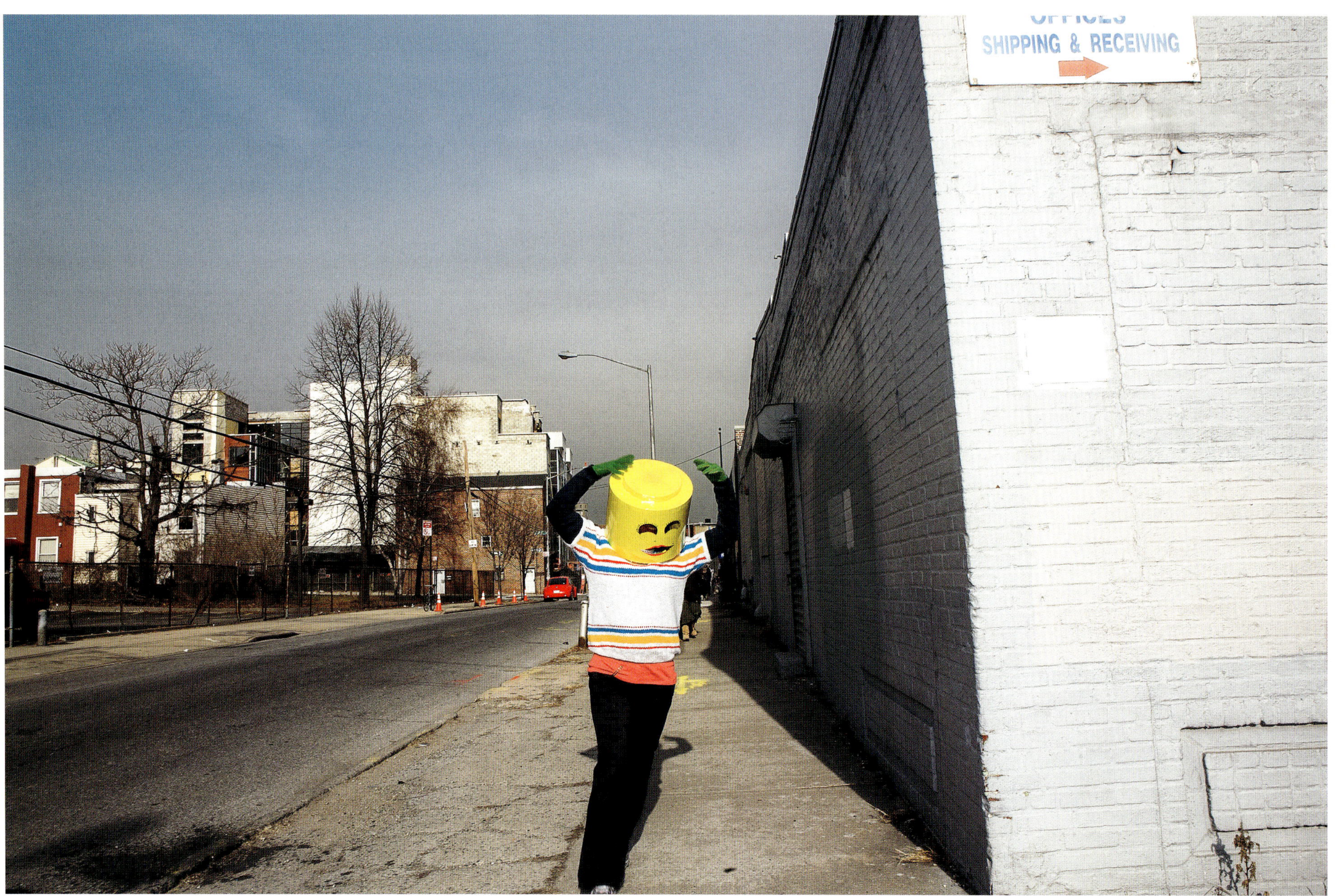
OFFICES
SHIPPING & RECEIVING

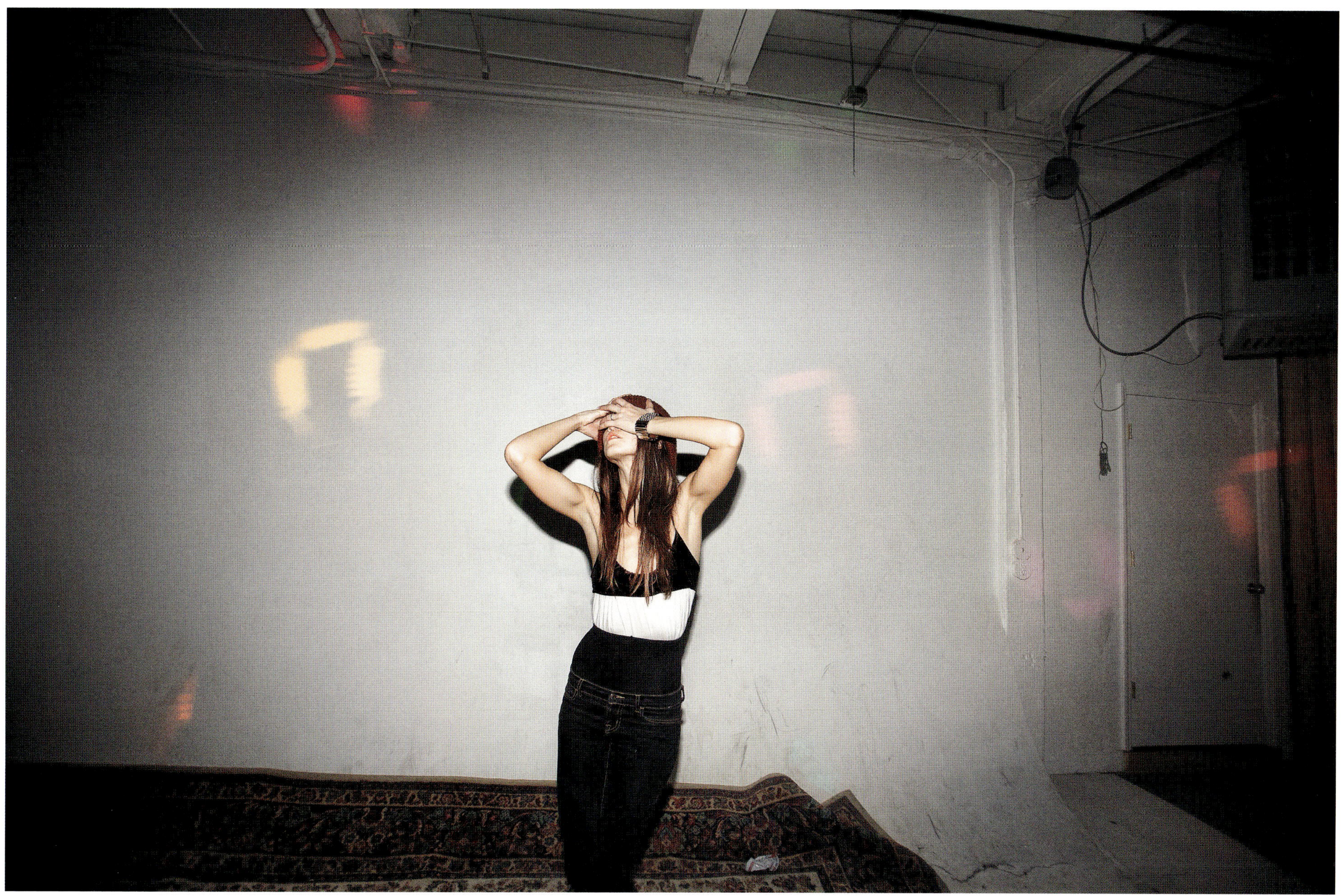

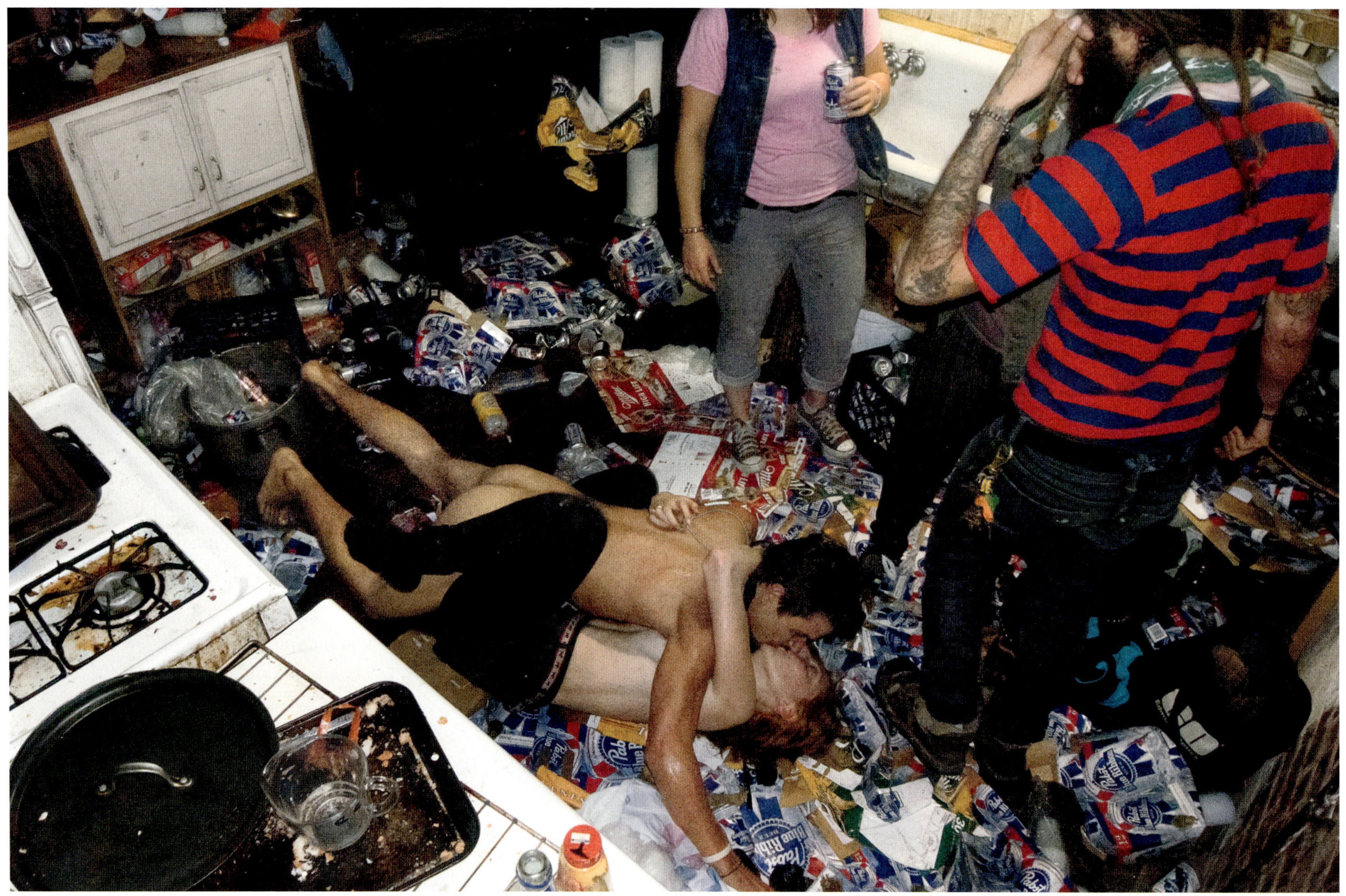

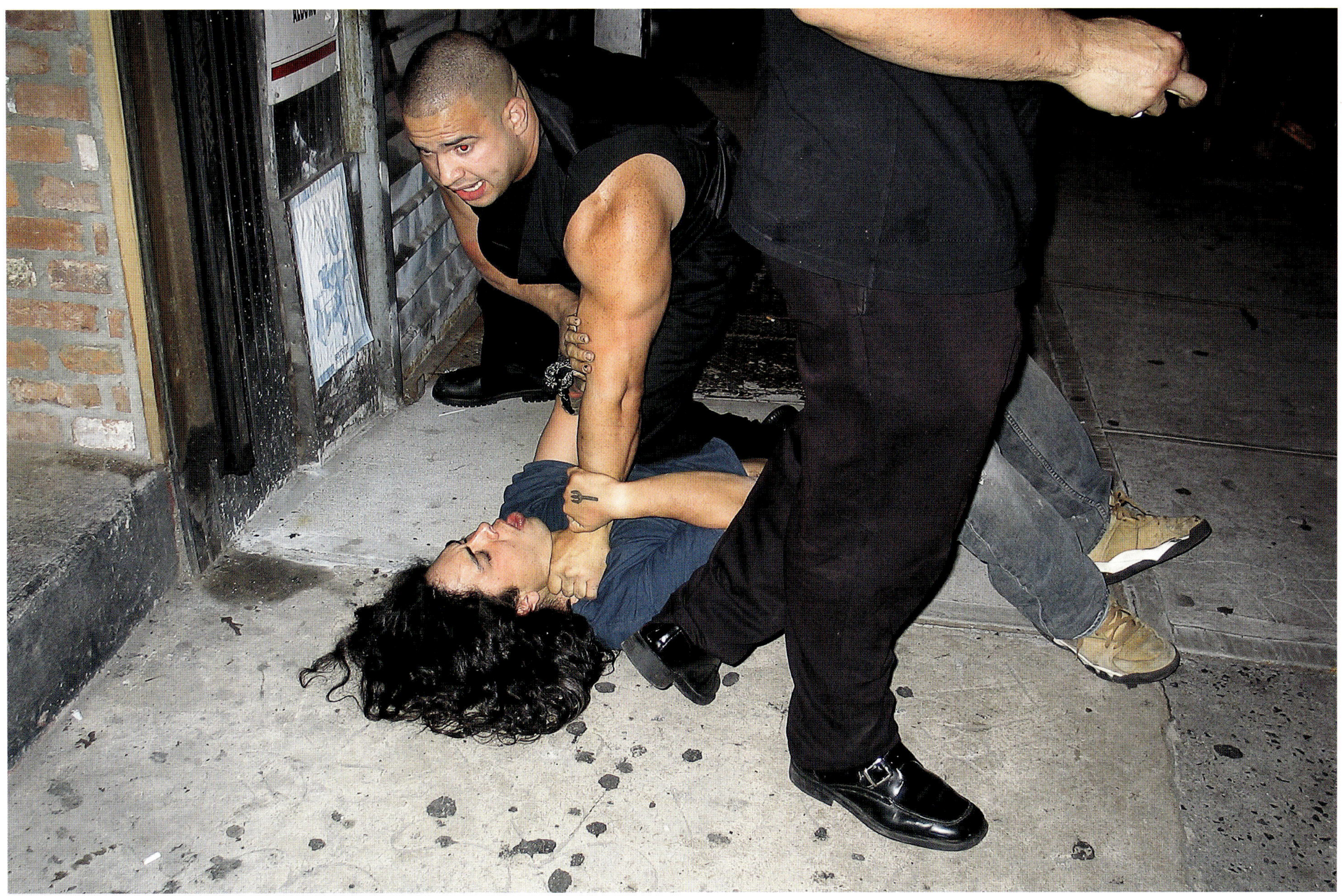

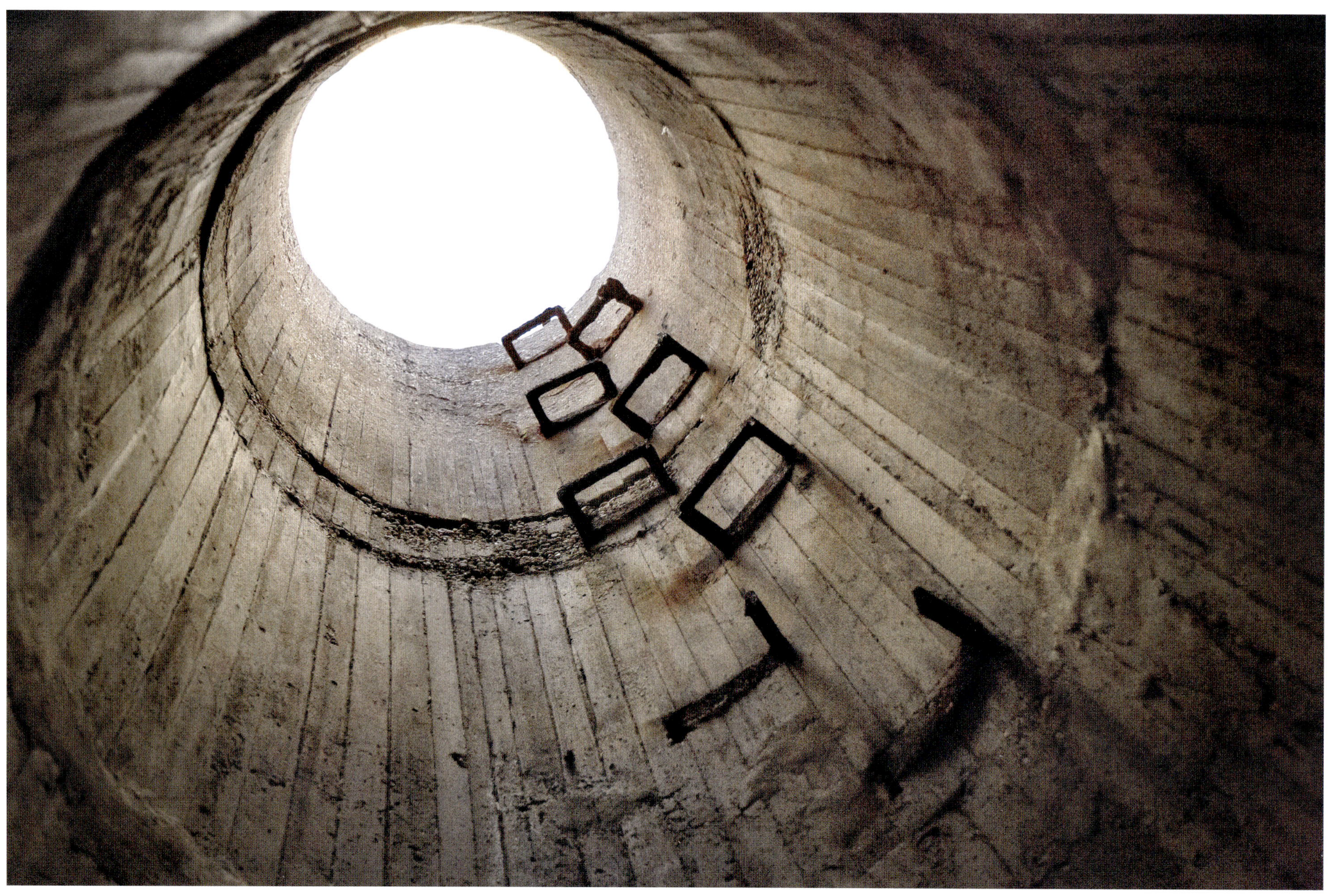

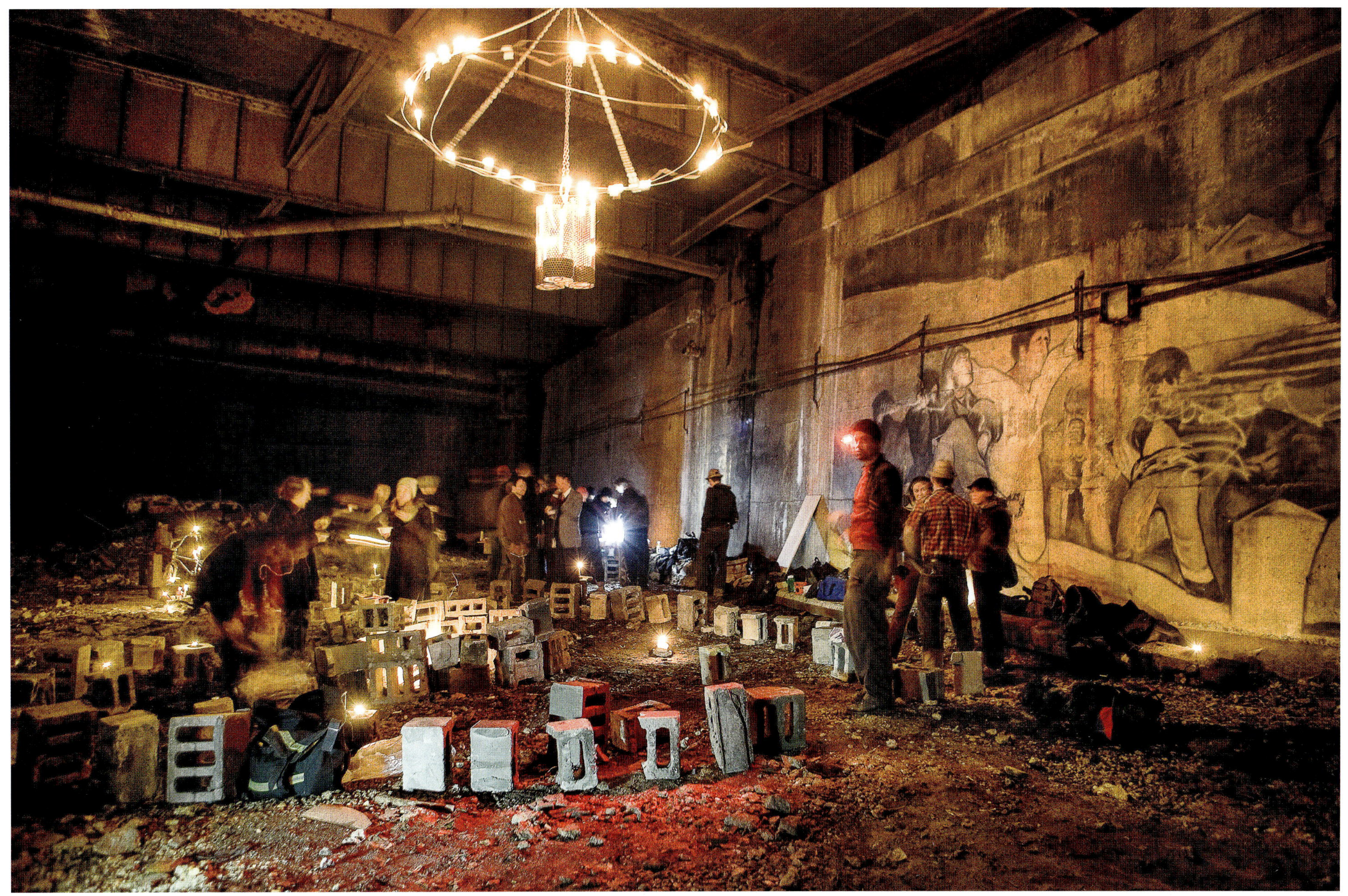

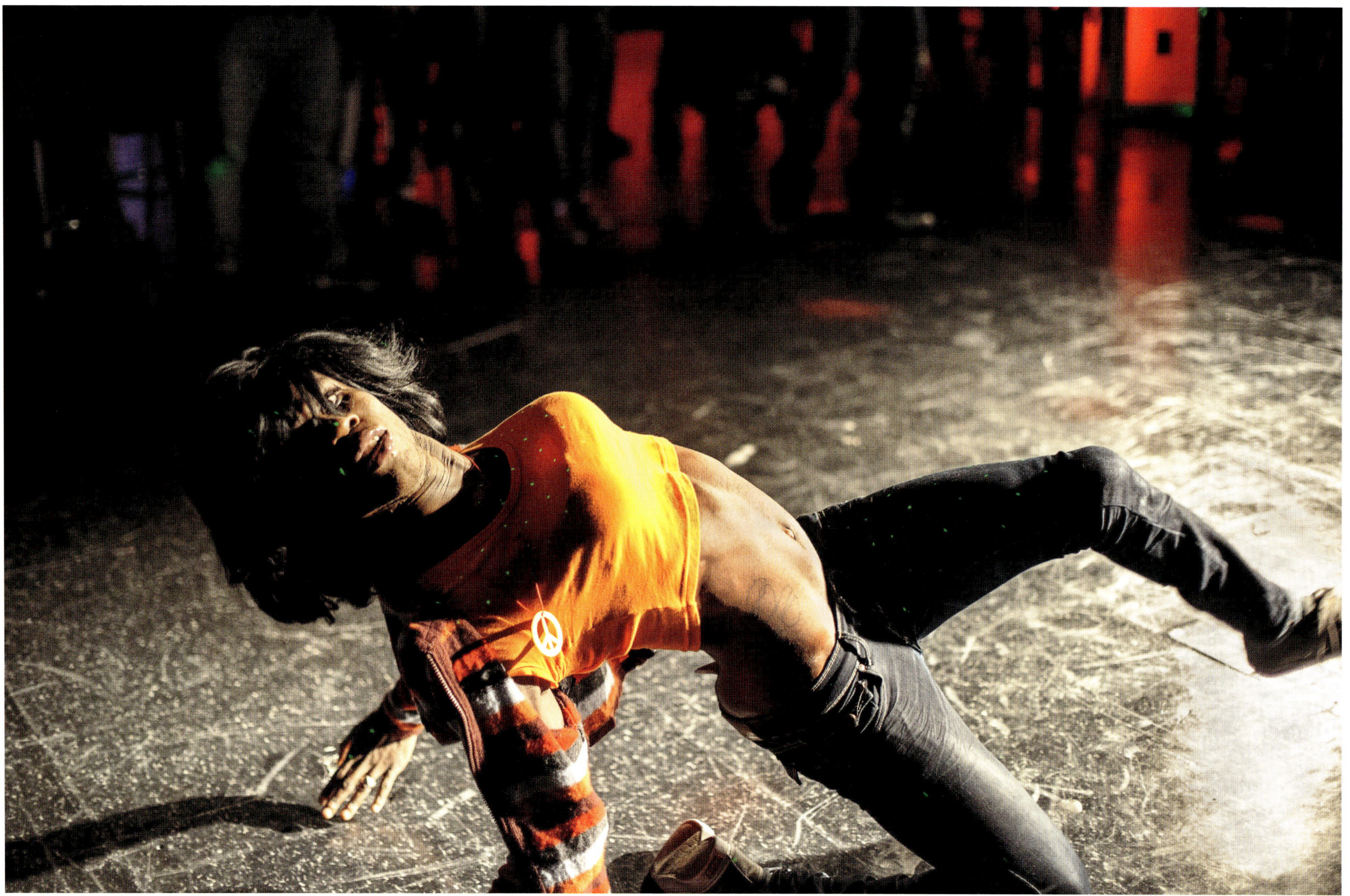

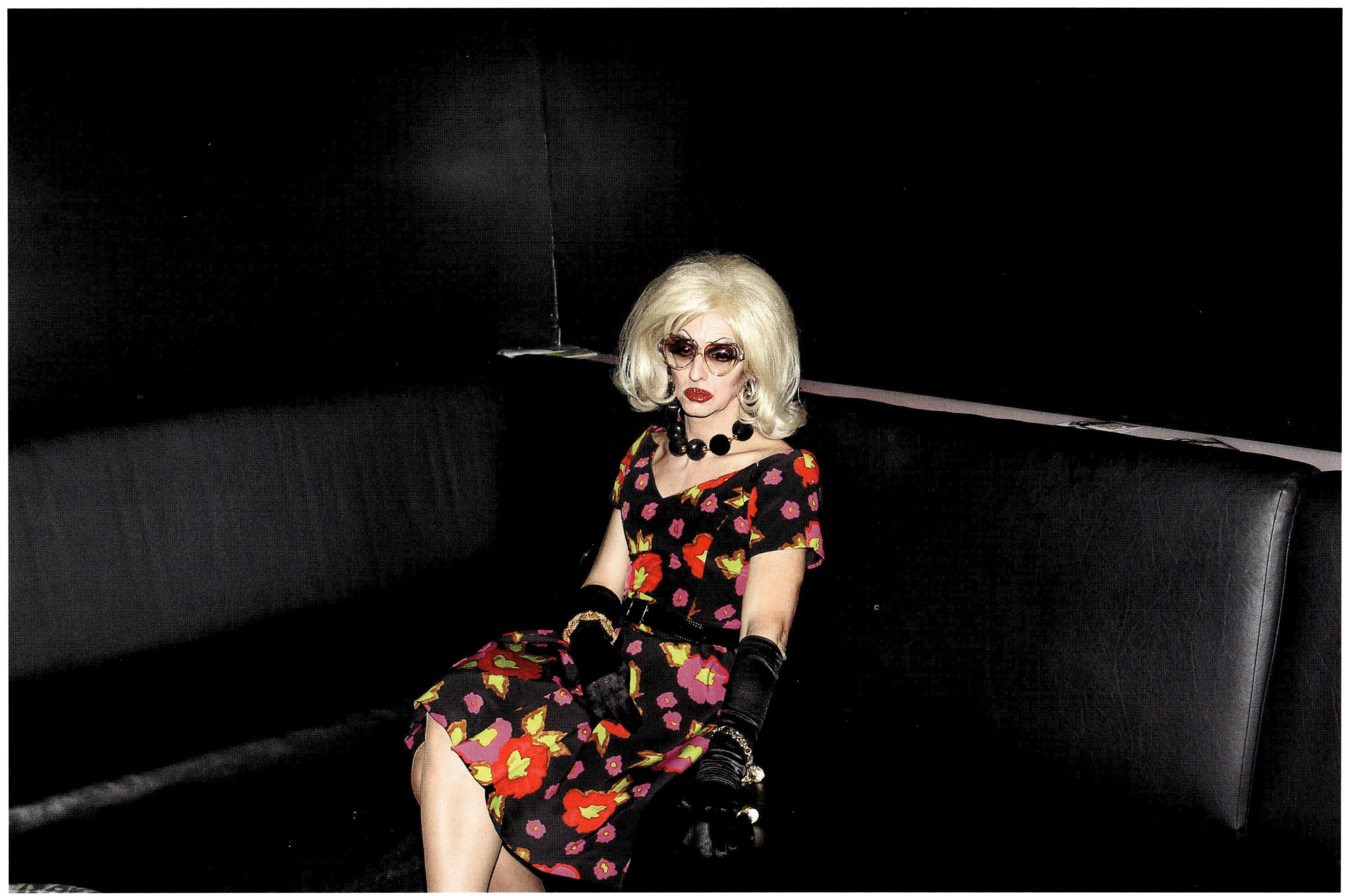

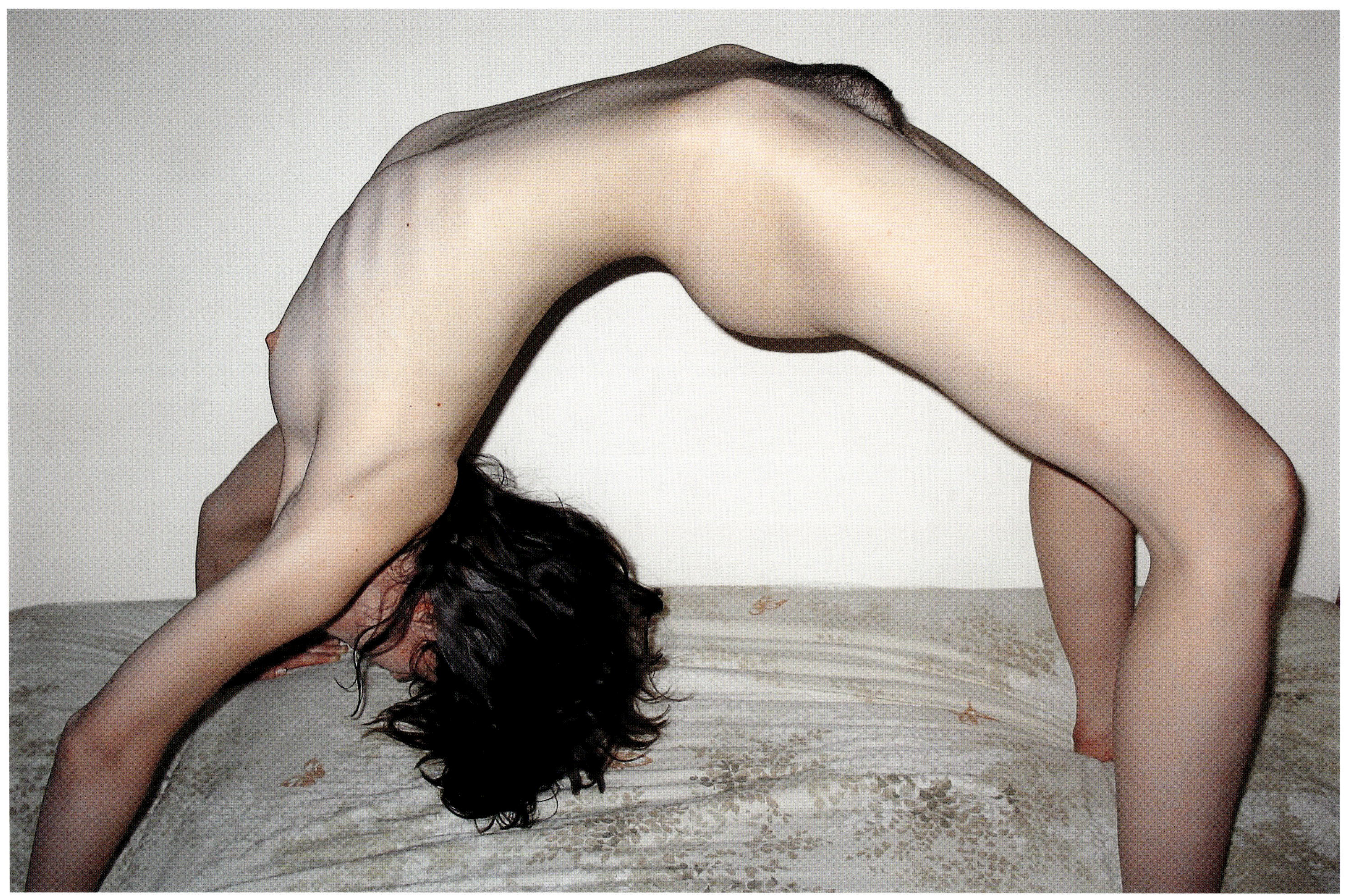

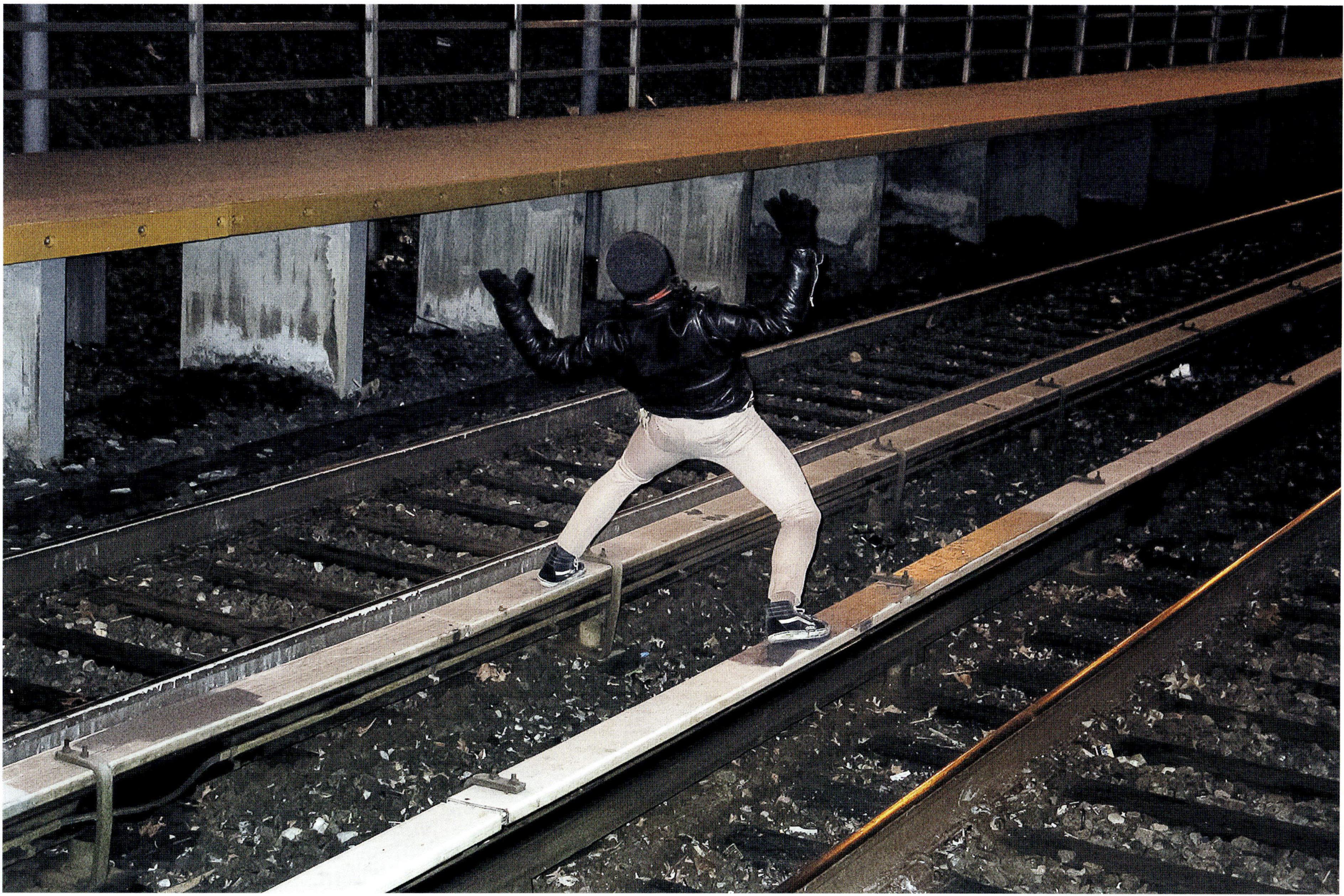

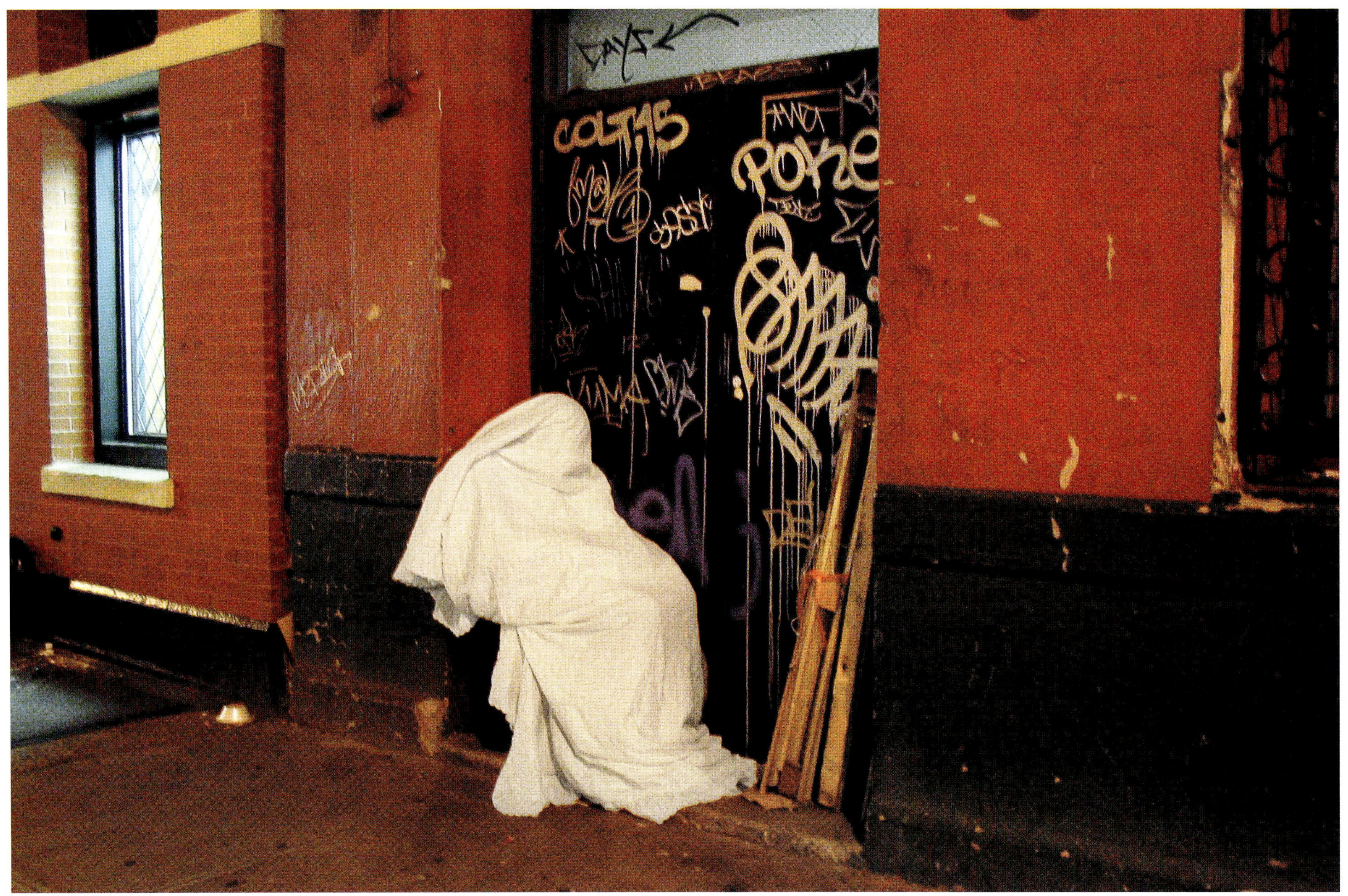

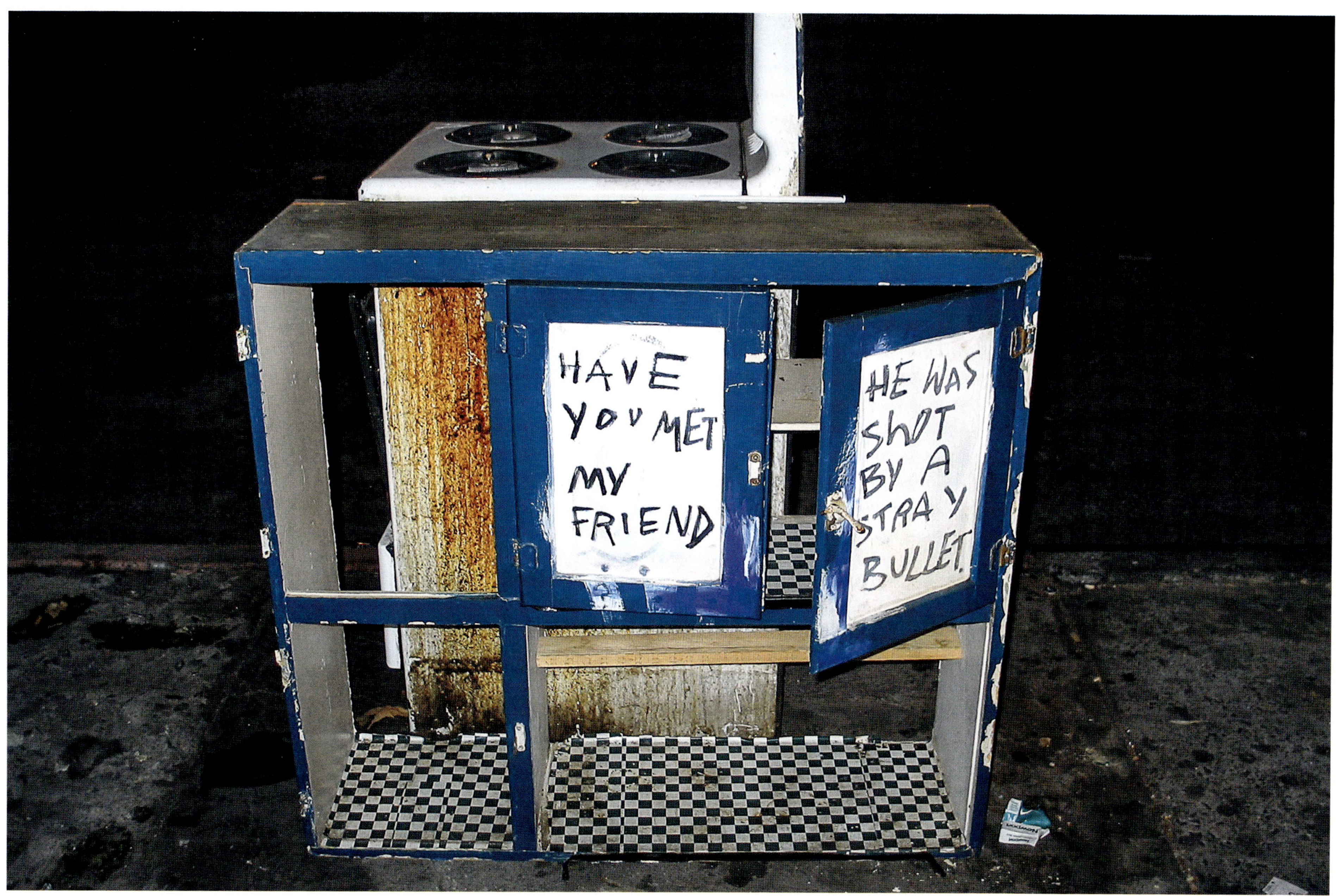
HAVE YOU MET MY FRIEND
HE WAS SHOT BY A STRAY BULLET

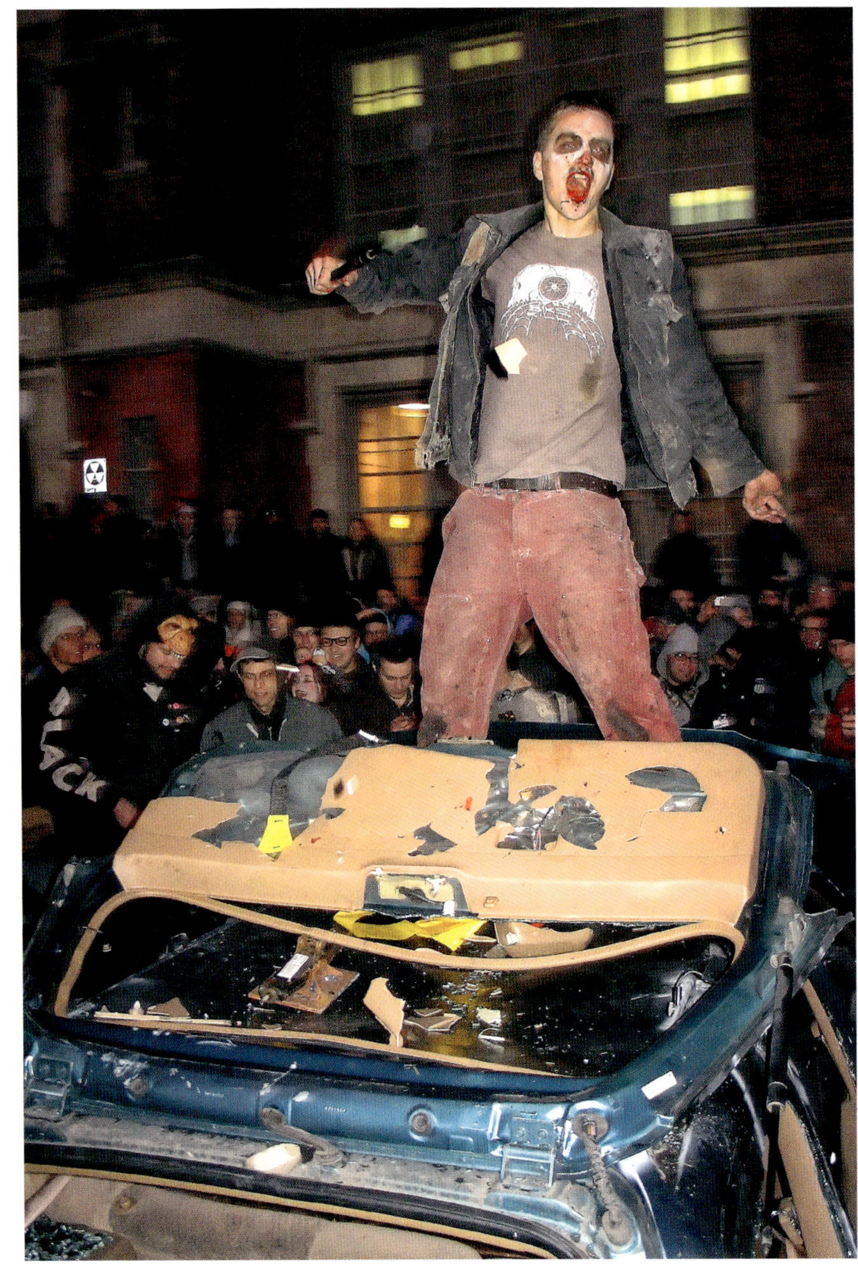

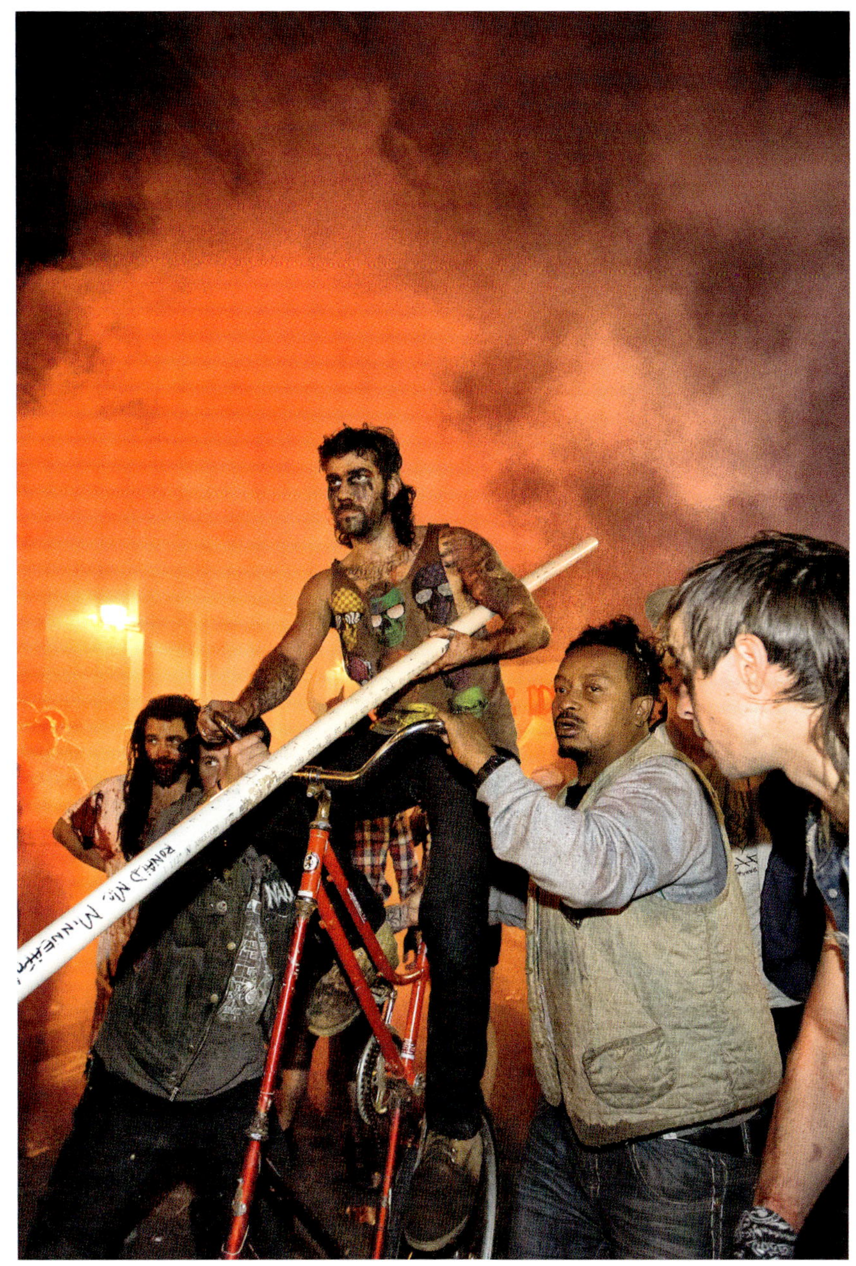

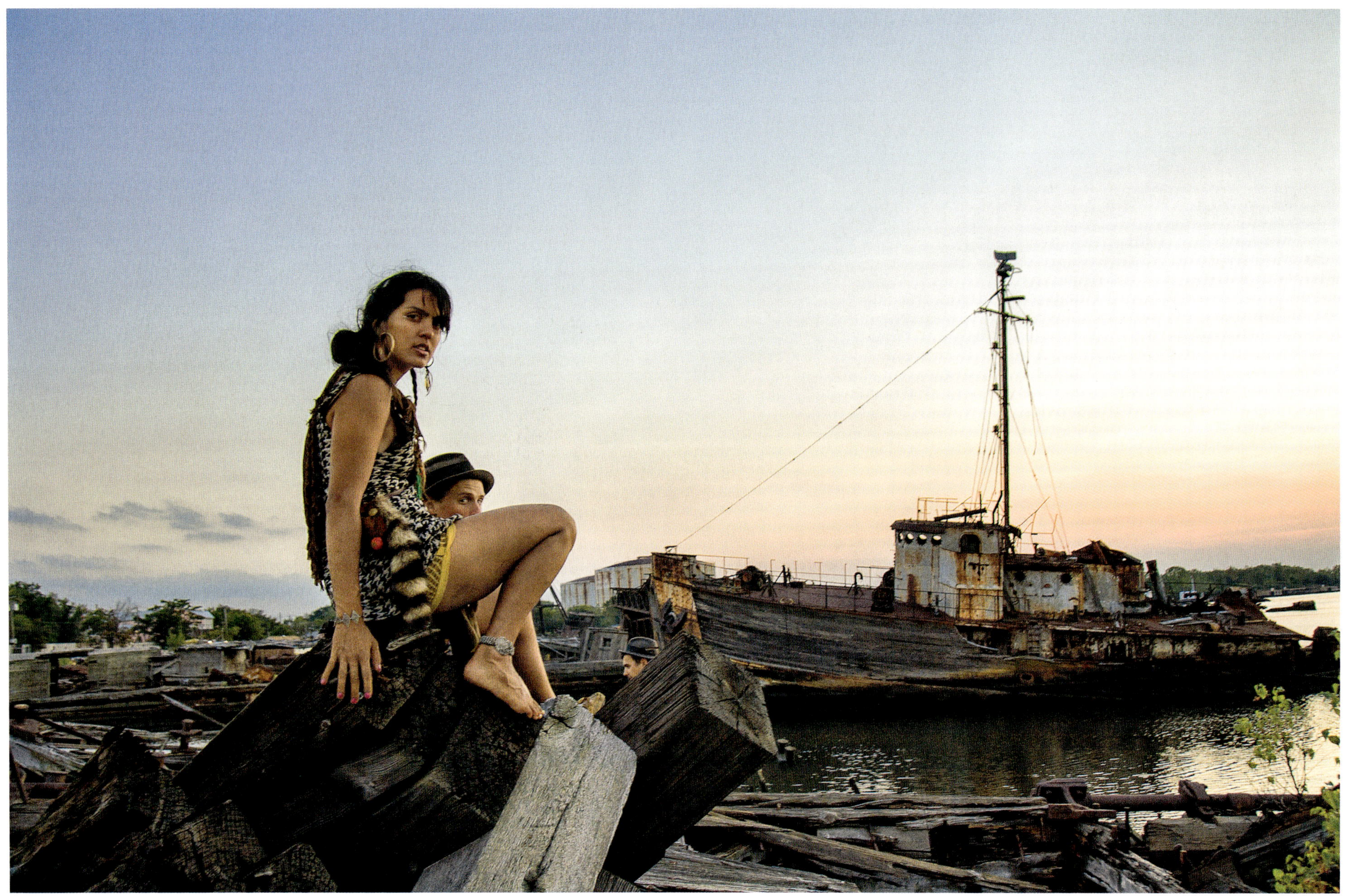

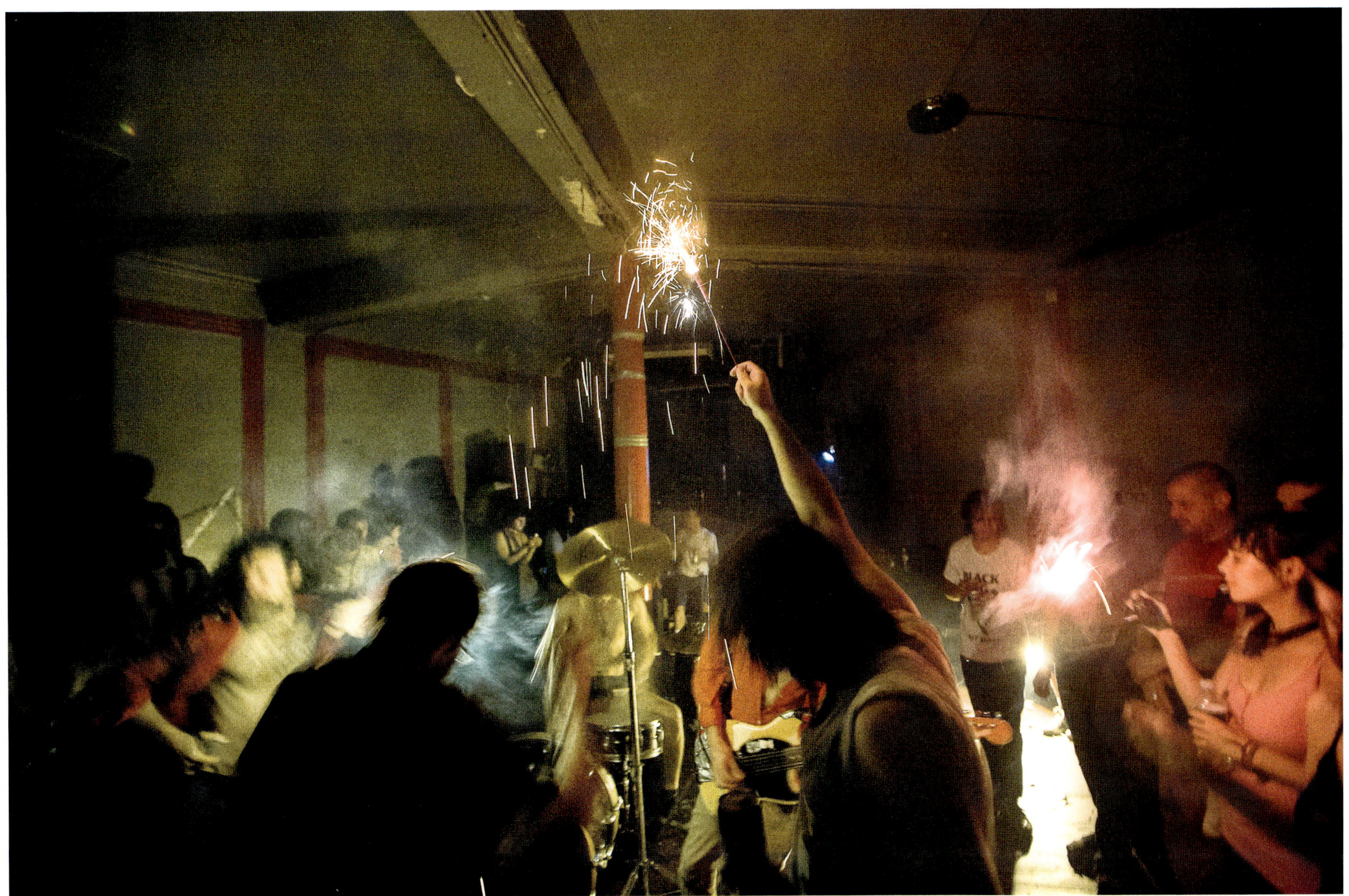

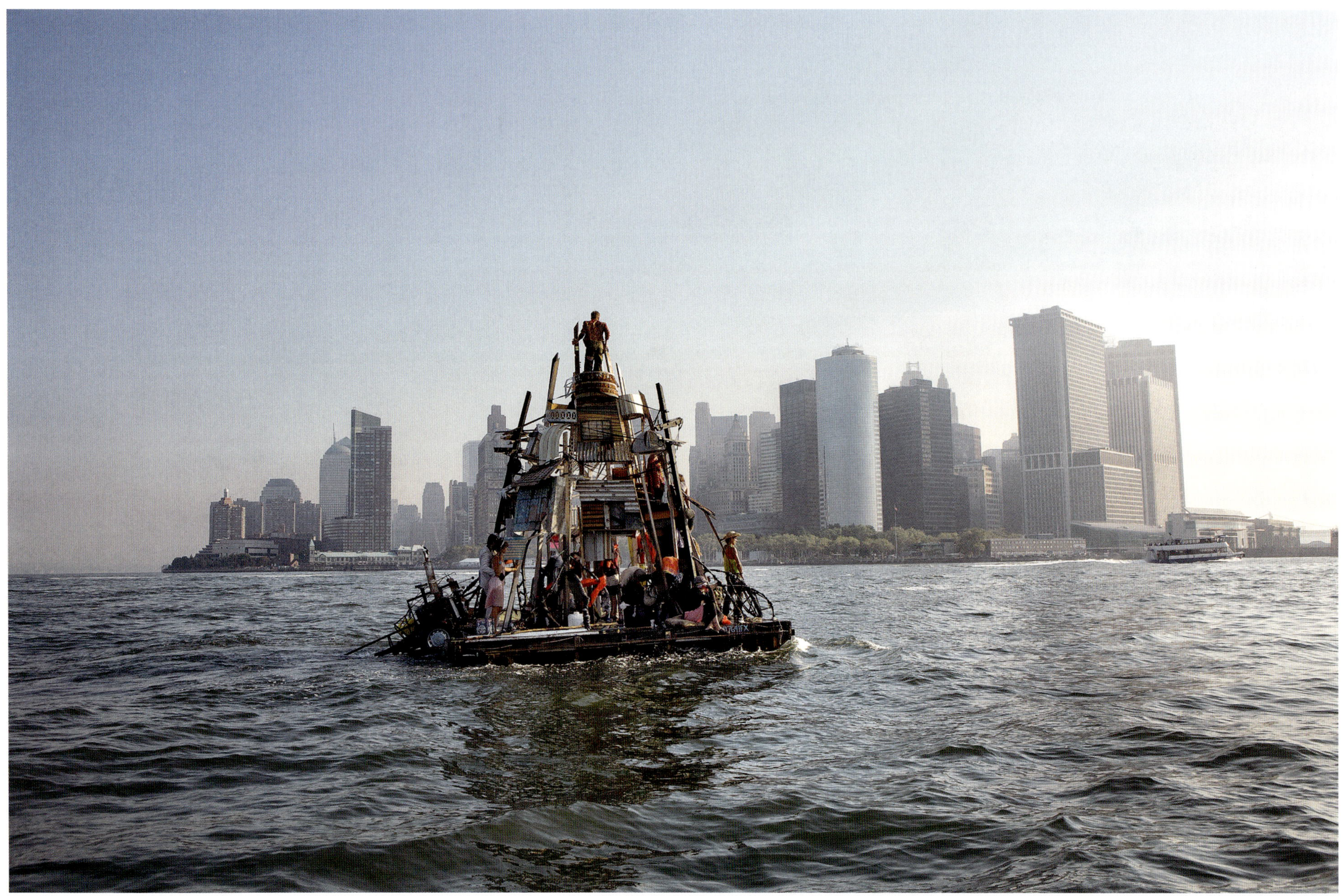

YOUR FEAR OF LOOKING STUPID IS HOLDING YOU BACK
CALEDONIA CURRY

Part of me thinks if Tod Seelie didn't see something, and capture it, it didn't quite happen. It's not that I invest in him the power of God and the Internet and the media and the all-seeing eye reflecting our world back to us, but...well...yes, maybe something close to that. Tod is our eyes. He is our memory.

Yes, there are endless raunchy photos of sweaty, bloody rock shows, people flying through the air, kicking things that are exploding into flames, and lots of compound bone fractures in progress. But that's not the secret of why Tod is an instrument of our living memory. There is something quieter, lighting the images as if from within. I notice it most startlingly when he has photographed something I've been involved in making. There is always a moment when I first see Tod's photos and am overcome with the realization of how much would have been lost without them.

In the first few years of the millennium, we could feel New York closing in. The grief that followed September 11 had ground down into an endless war. We watched gentrification calcify into condos as the city paved over wild spaces, and felt like it was now or never. So we came together for street parties featuring homemade junk bands, food fights, dumpster dinner parties, and dangerous jerry-rigged public sports. Were we making a last-ditch attempt to draw a line, to redefine what was public, and insert a space for participation in the creation of the city at street level? Or were we simply reveling in it while it still existed? So many things that I have seen and felt, Tod saved for us.

We're in Walter De Maria's Earth Room in SoHo. There are so many rules in this white room gallery installation: no photos, no touching, no breathing. It is so quiet. But we are ready. We have on bikinis under our winter clothes. A tiny boom box is doing its best to blast Japanther, while Dana distracts the gallery attendant with fresh cookies. Suddenly, the room is full of squeals and grunts as we mud wrestle in the middle of the installation.

It's summer. I'm running over the Williamsburg Bridge because the cops have kicked us out of a public park in Manhattan.

WE WATCHED GENTRIFICATION CALCIFY INTO CONDOS AS THE CITY PAVED OVER WILD SPACES, AND FELT LIKE IT WAS NOW OR NEVER. SO WE CAME TOGETHER FOR STREET PARTIES FEATURING HOMEMADE JUNK BANDS, FOOD FIGHTS, DUMPSTER DINNER PARTIES, AND DANGEROUS JERRY-RIGGED PUBLIC SPORTS.

WE WERE POISED ON THE EDGE OF THE WORLD FOR A MOMENT.

I am wearing clothes made out of newspaper, and am hoping they don't fall apart before I get to the other side of the bridge and add public nudity to our list of possible charges. Jeff is hauling the smoking grill that Leslie and I built into a shopping cart. Polina's pipe xylophone on bike wheels is clanging gloriously. People are whooping and screaming and skipping, and someone is carrying a banner that says, "Your fear of looking stupid is holding you back." "These are my friends," I think. "This is what we do for fun."

Rounding the tip of Manhattan that September day in 2008 on wooden rafts we had made ourselves, seeing the southern bend of the city churn past us on the way back, gliding toward the relative safety of her immense bridges—I will never forget how that felt, how we were poised right on the edge of the world for a moment. And, until I saw Tod's photographs of it, I never would have imagined anyone else would be able to understand it.

All this time Tod is there, building and hauling and playing. Then, he quietly slips just outside of it, recognizing the wild beauty in the faces, events, and dark streets on the way home from whatever we got up to that night. He gets the fireworks at center stage, and he also gets the lonely city, its streets captured as canyons and basins of pre-dawn light, as mournful as the day was joyous. He has found a way to know life in that flesh-and-bone way he yearned for back in the day when we were still kids wondering how we would do it, and to hold it long enough so that, later, we may remember who we are and where we have been. For this, a tiny generation is deeply grateful.

Caledonia Curry is Swoon, a Brooklyn-based artist whose life-sized woodcuts can be found on walls in cities around the world. Her work is in the permanent collections of institutions including the Museum of Modern Art, the Brooklyn Museum, and Tate Britain.

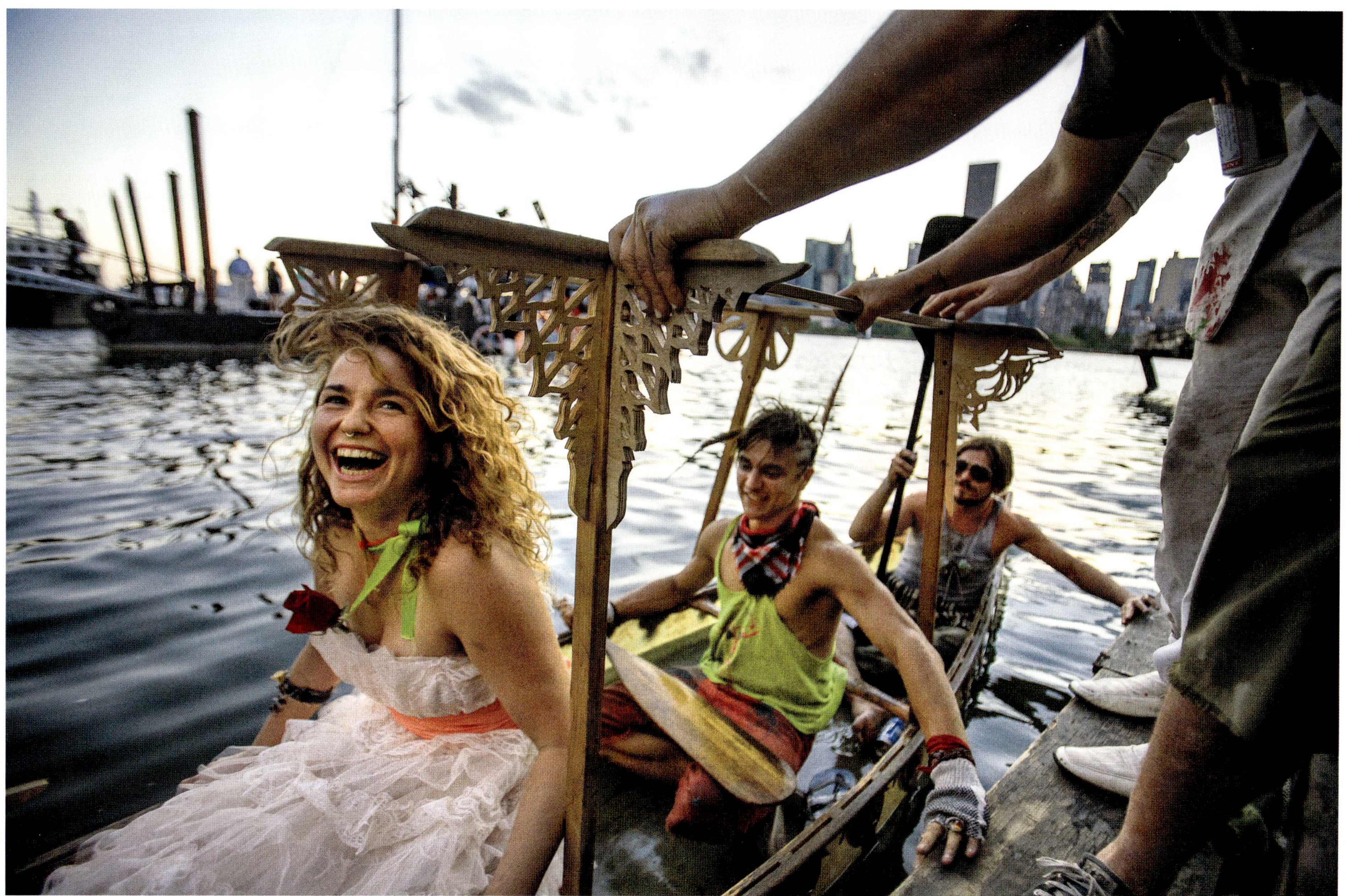

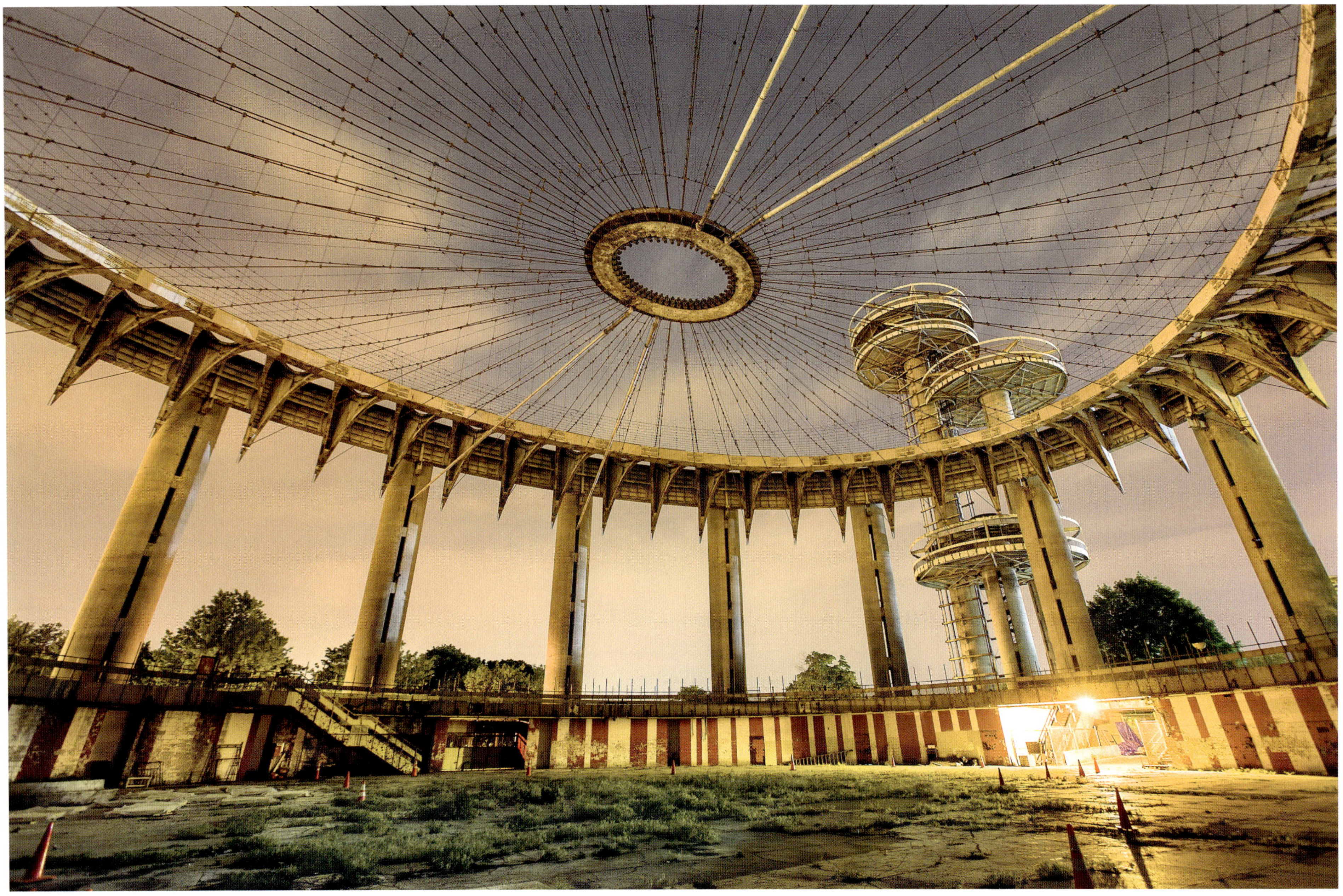

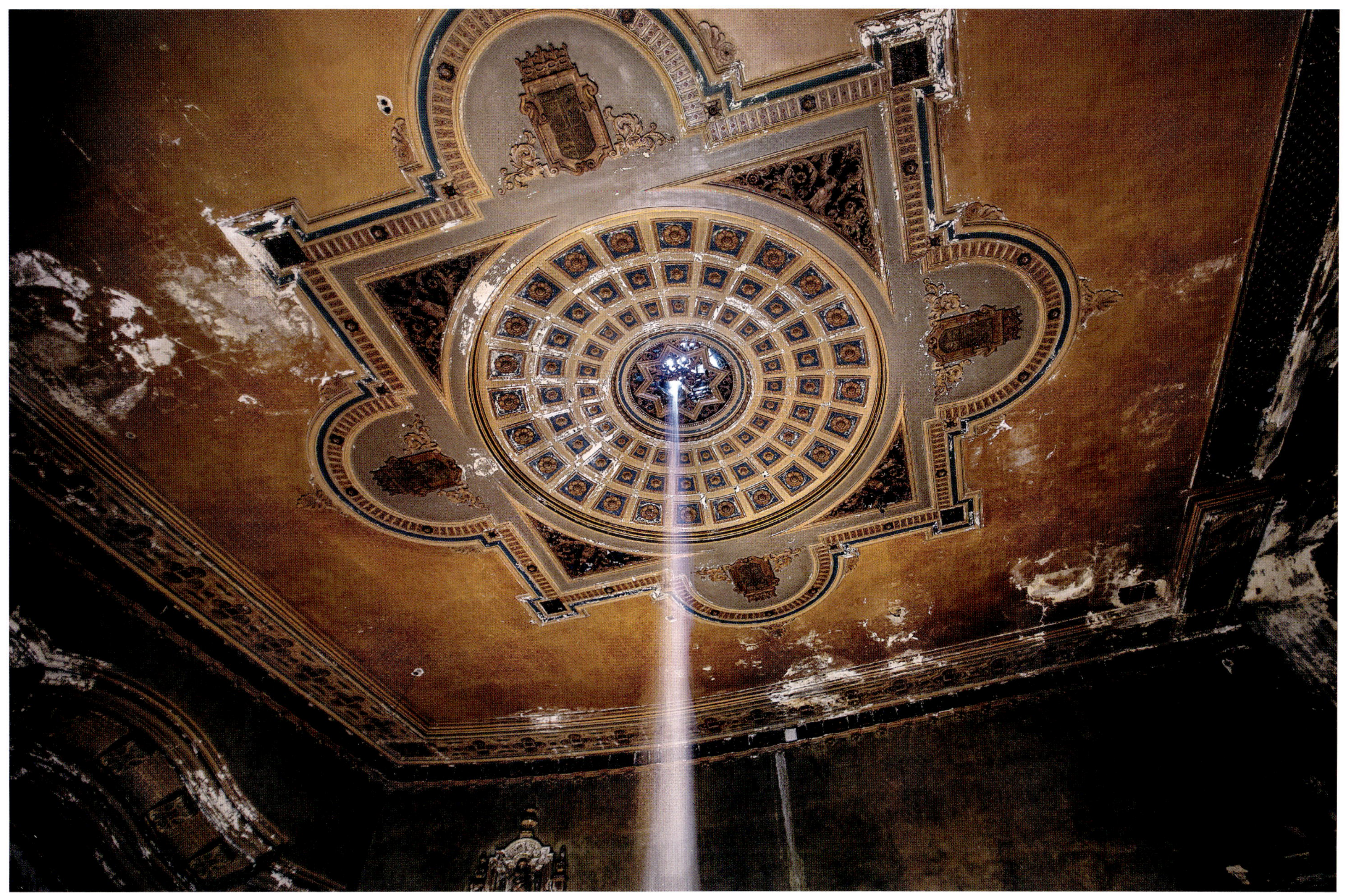

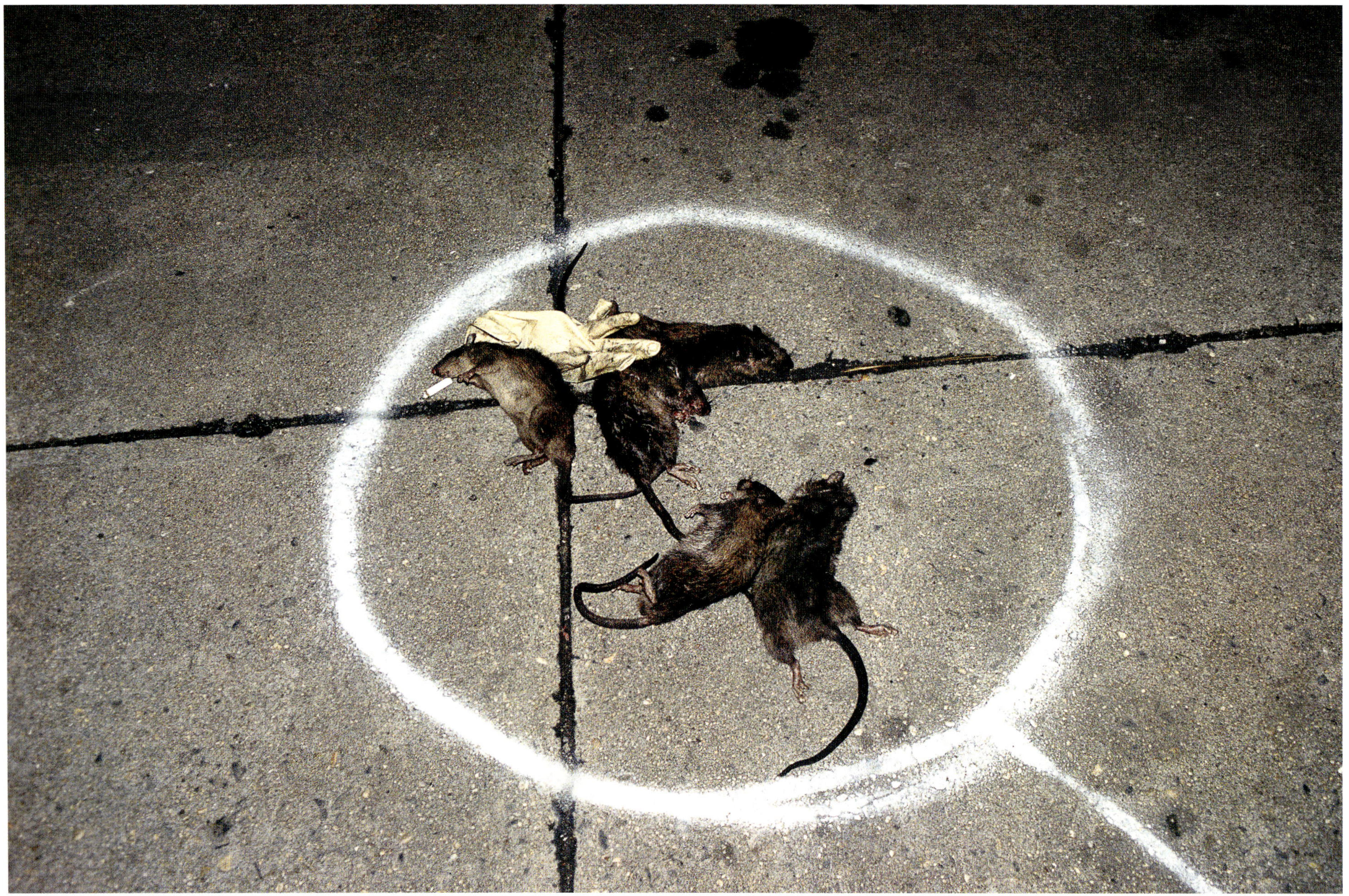

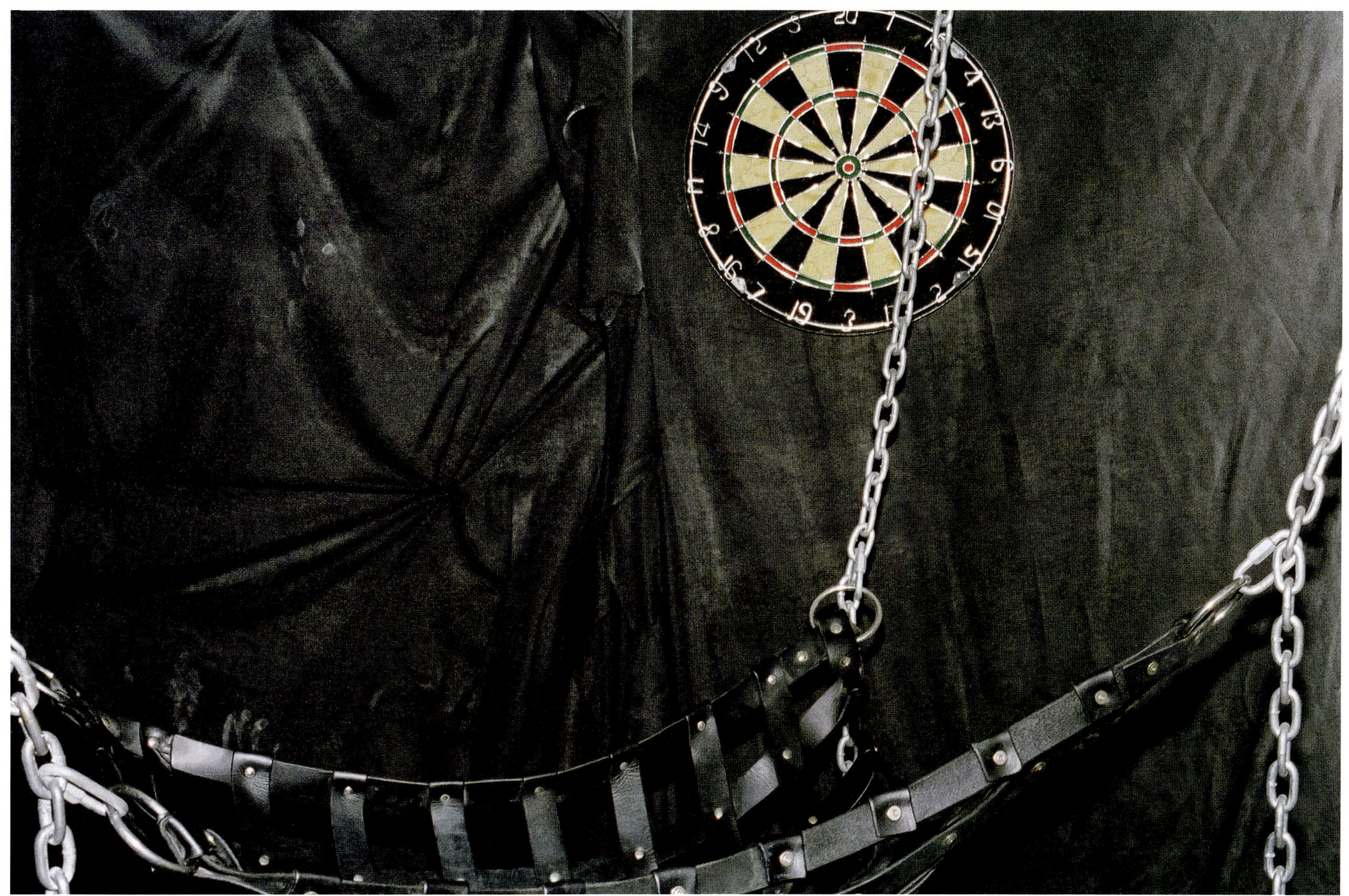

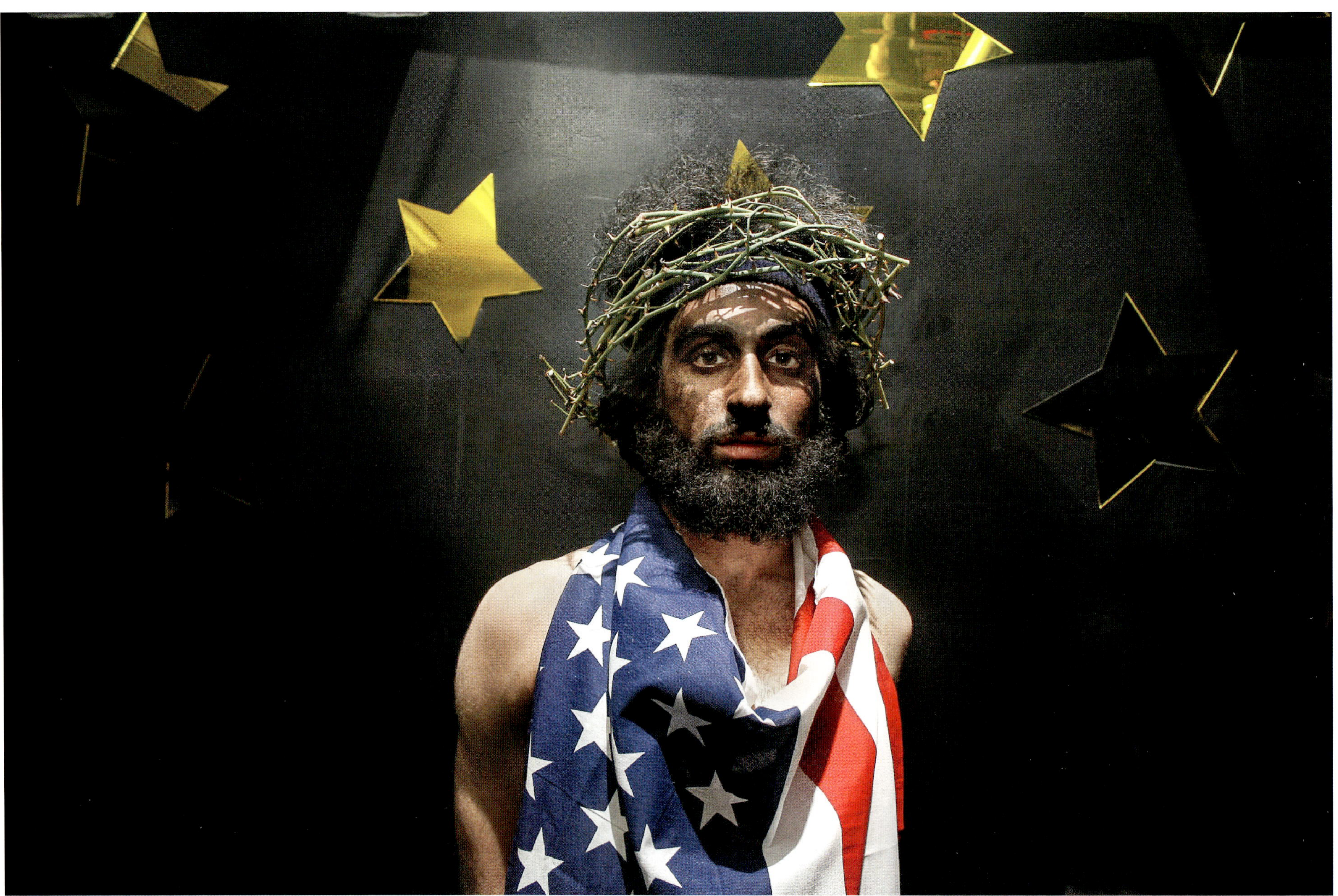

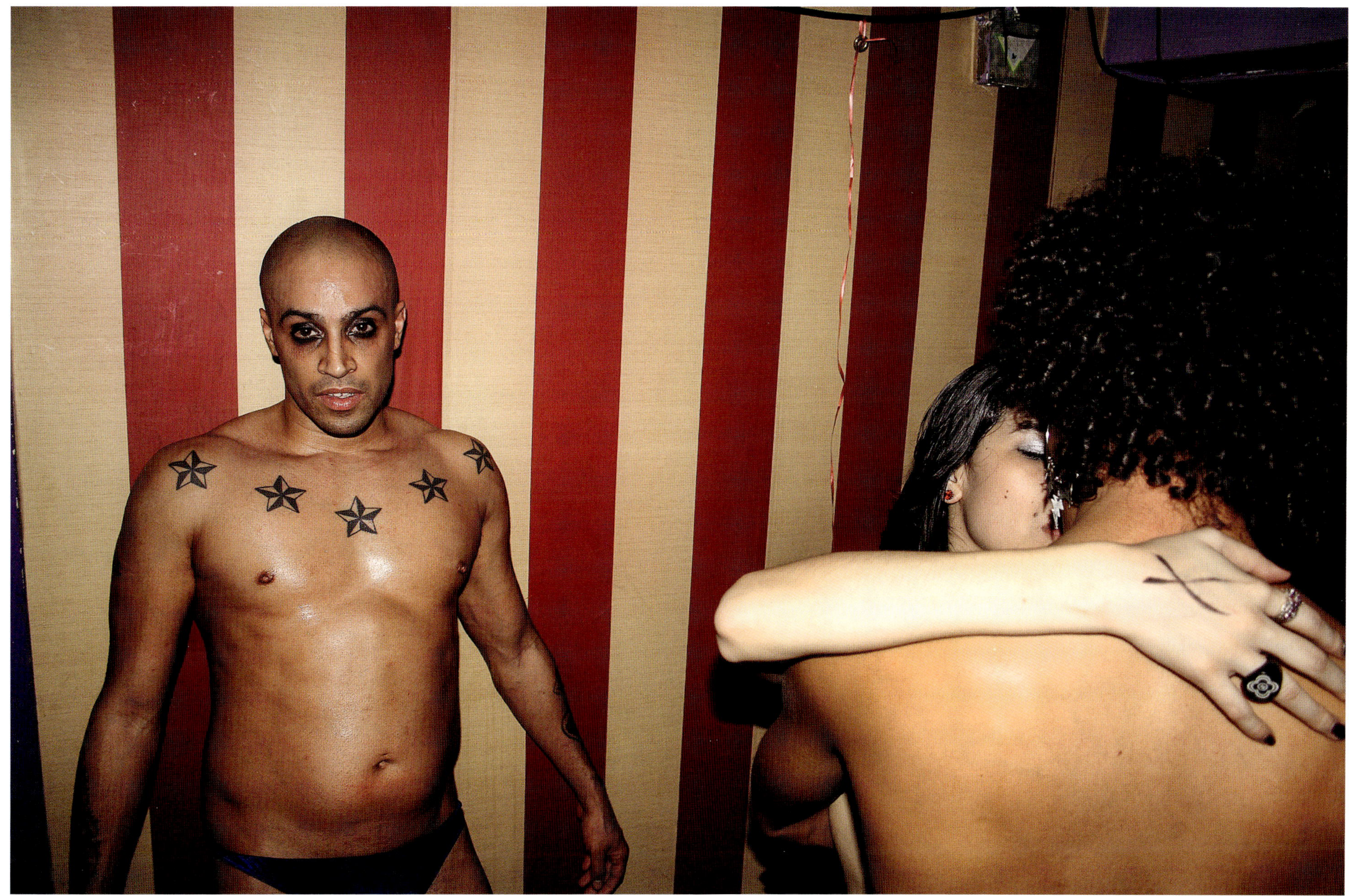

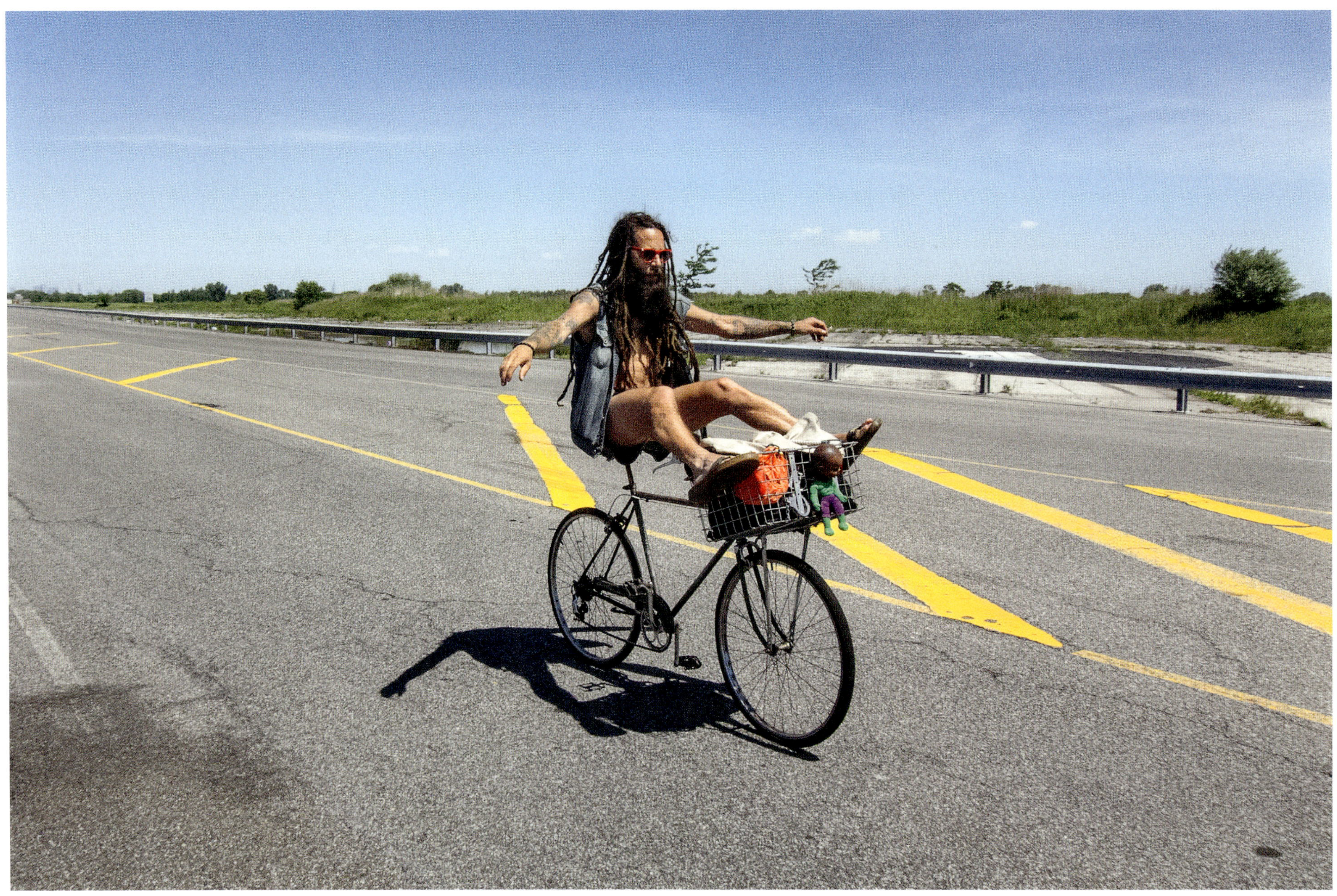

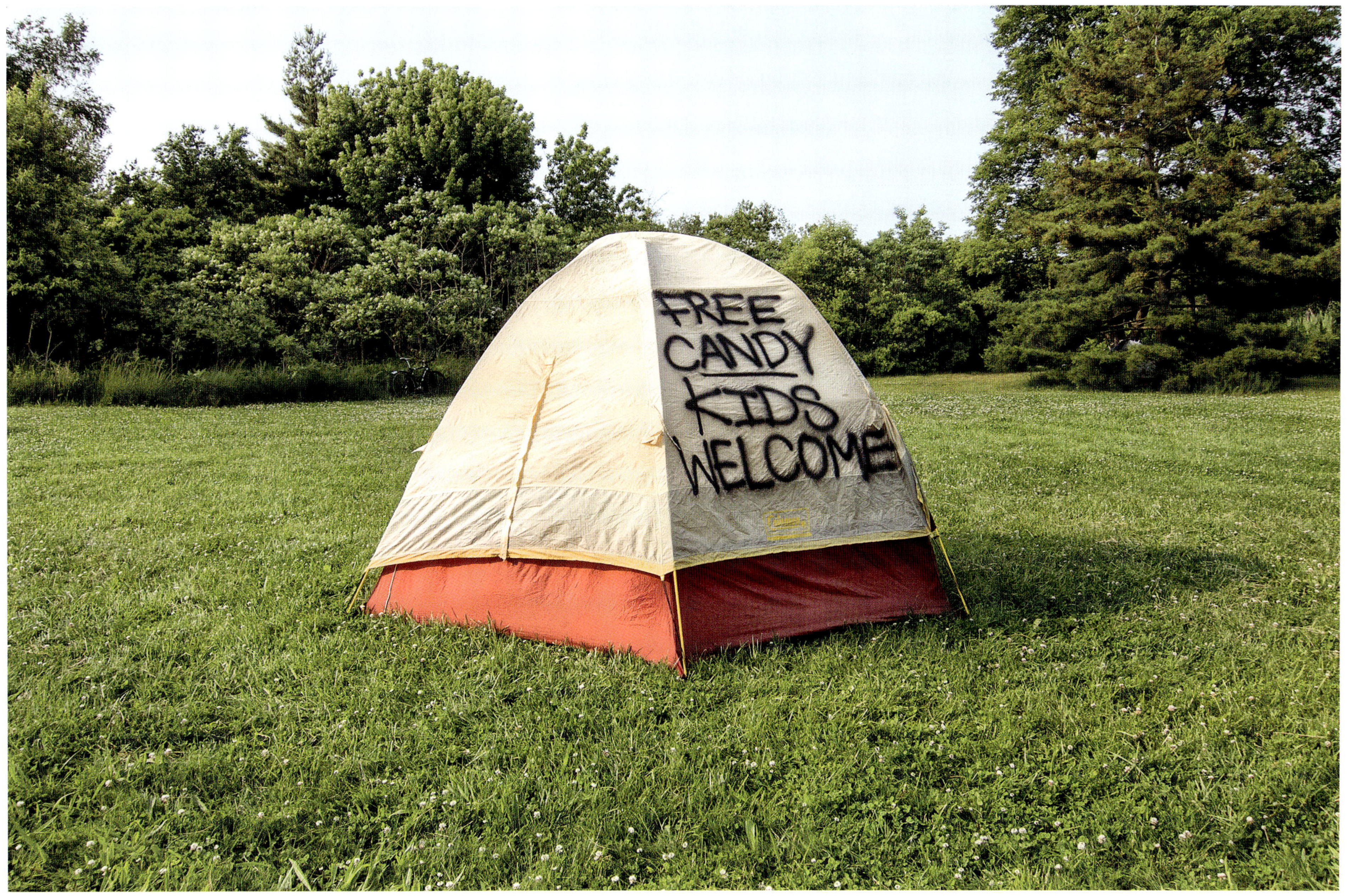
FREE
CANDY
KIDS
WELCOME

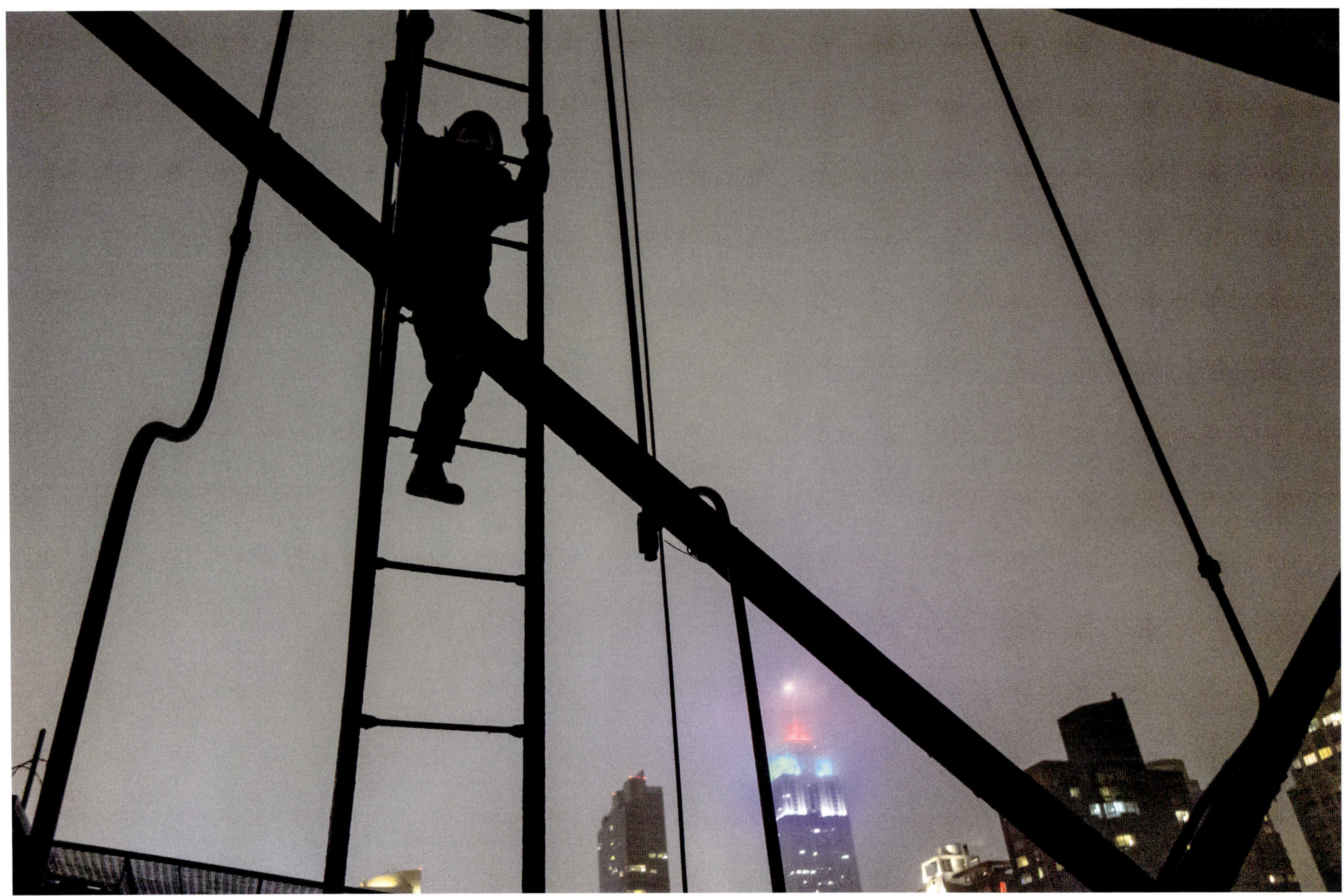

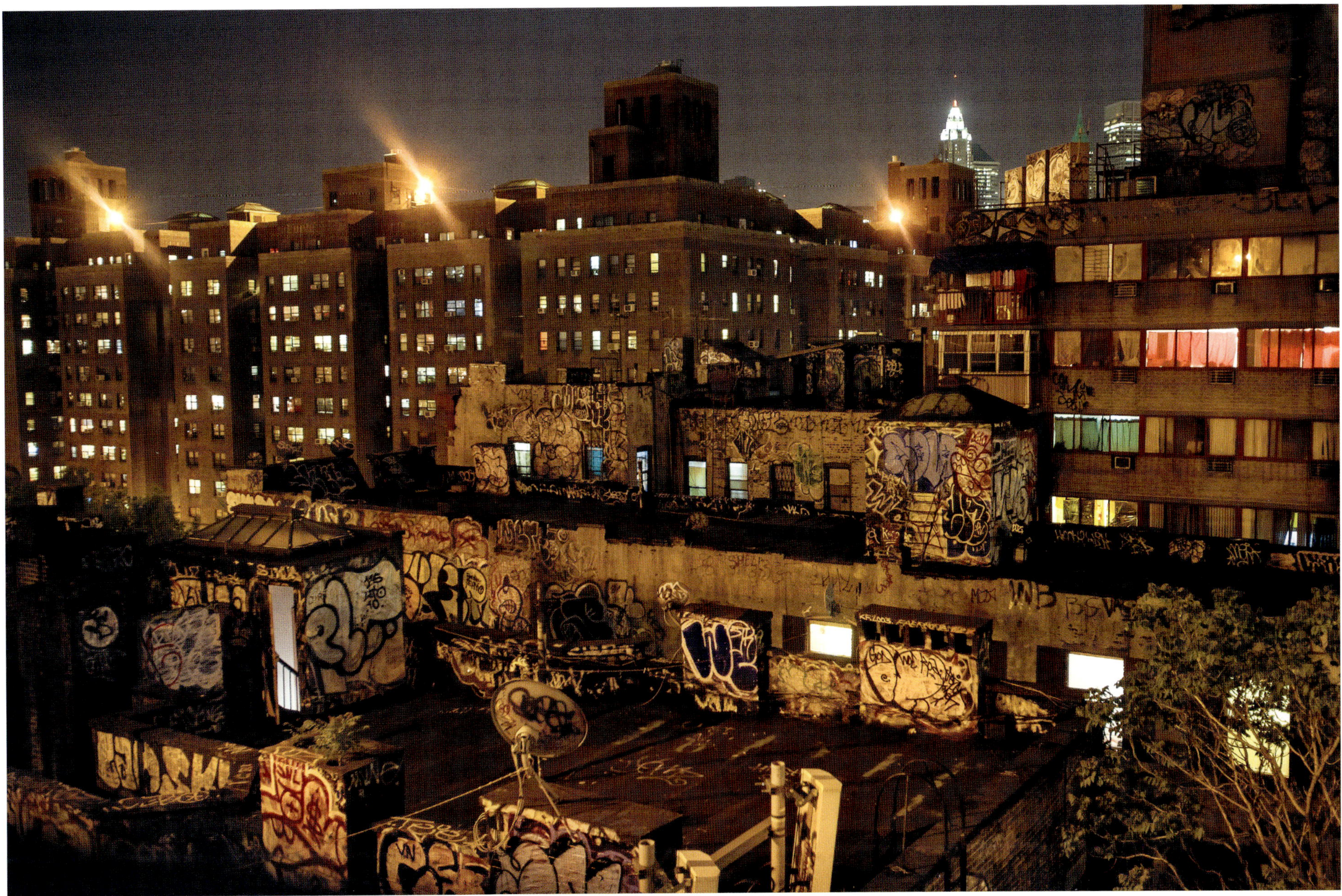

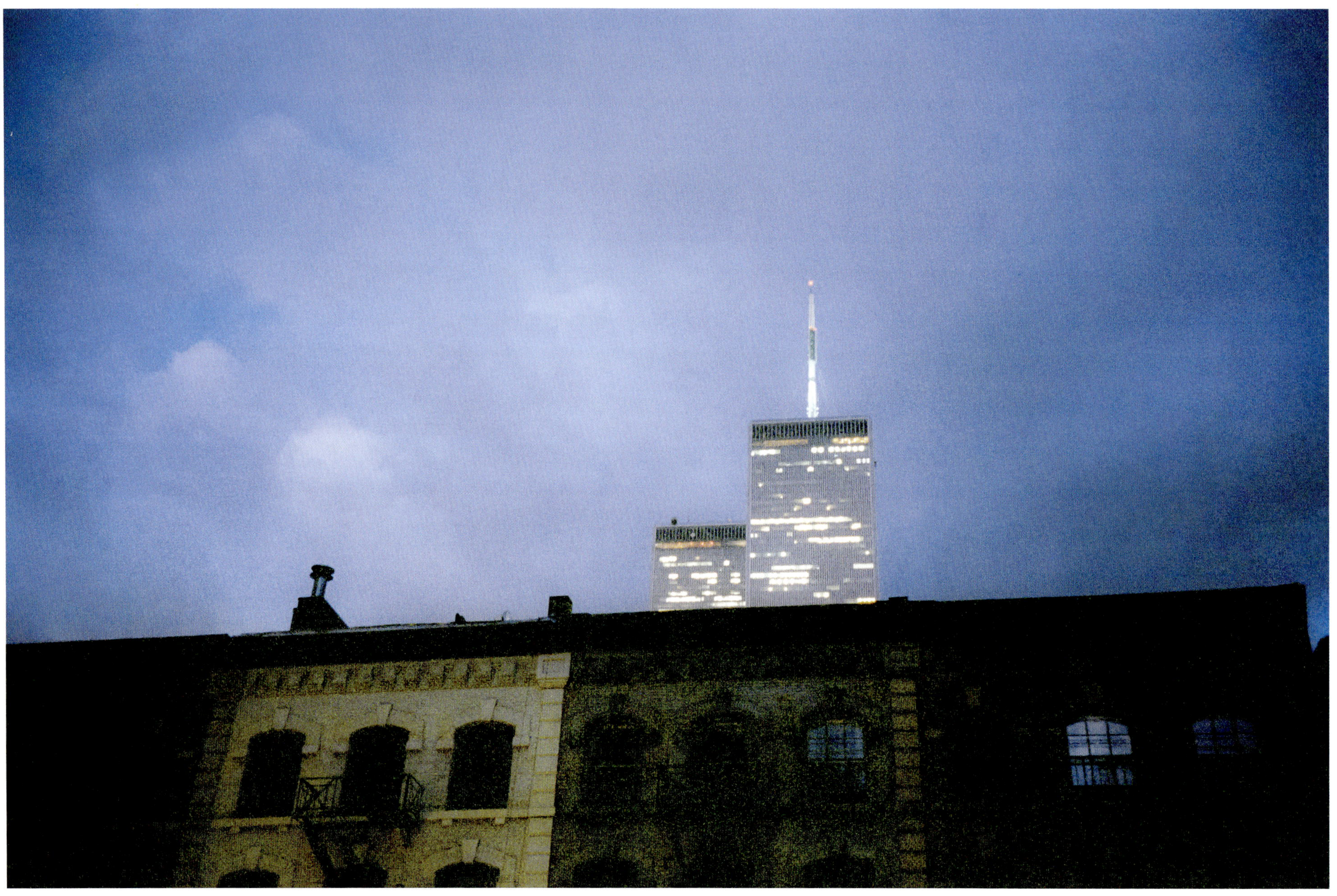

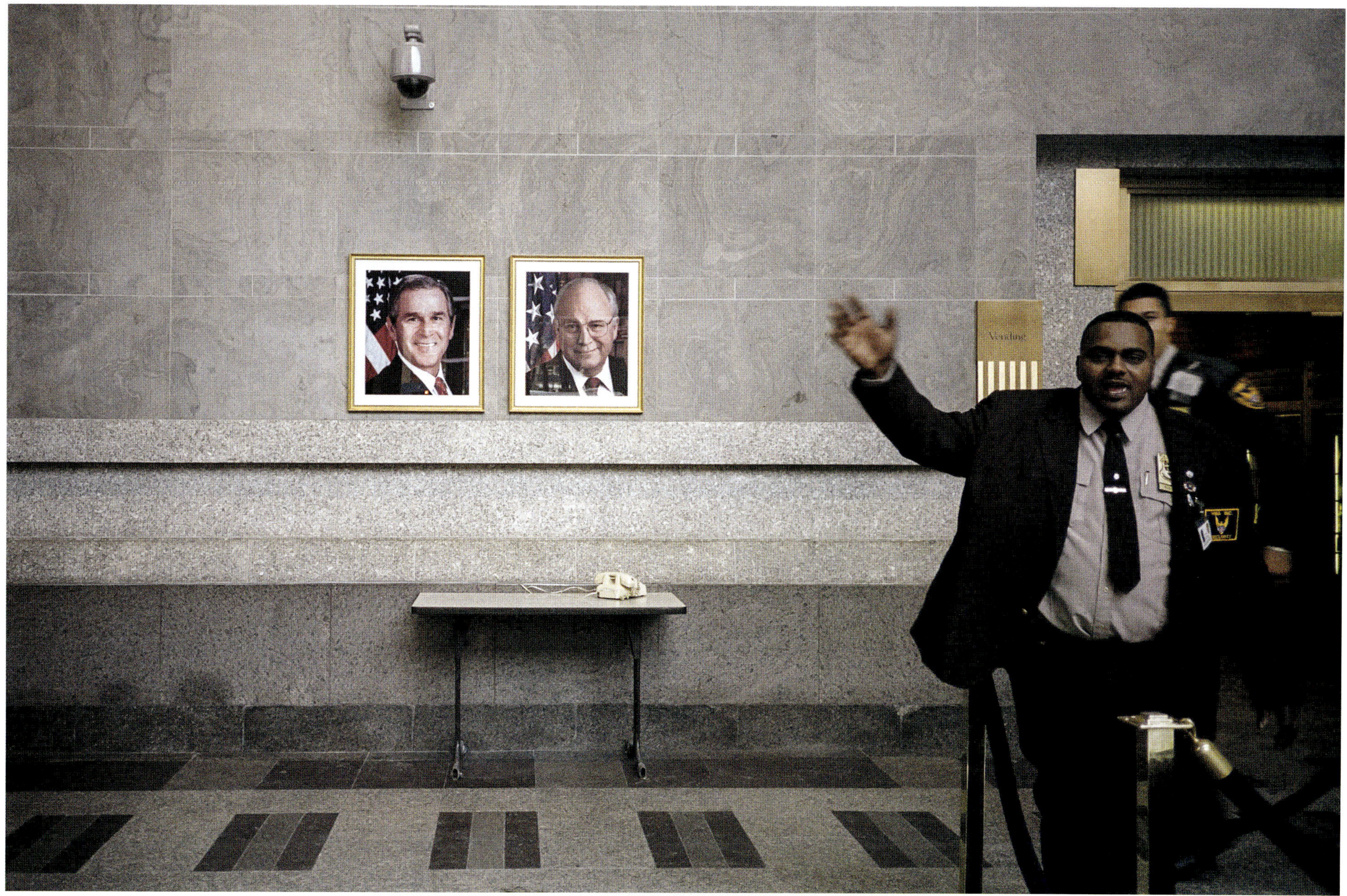

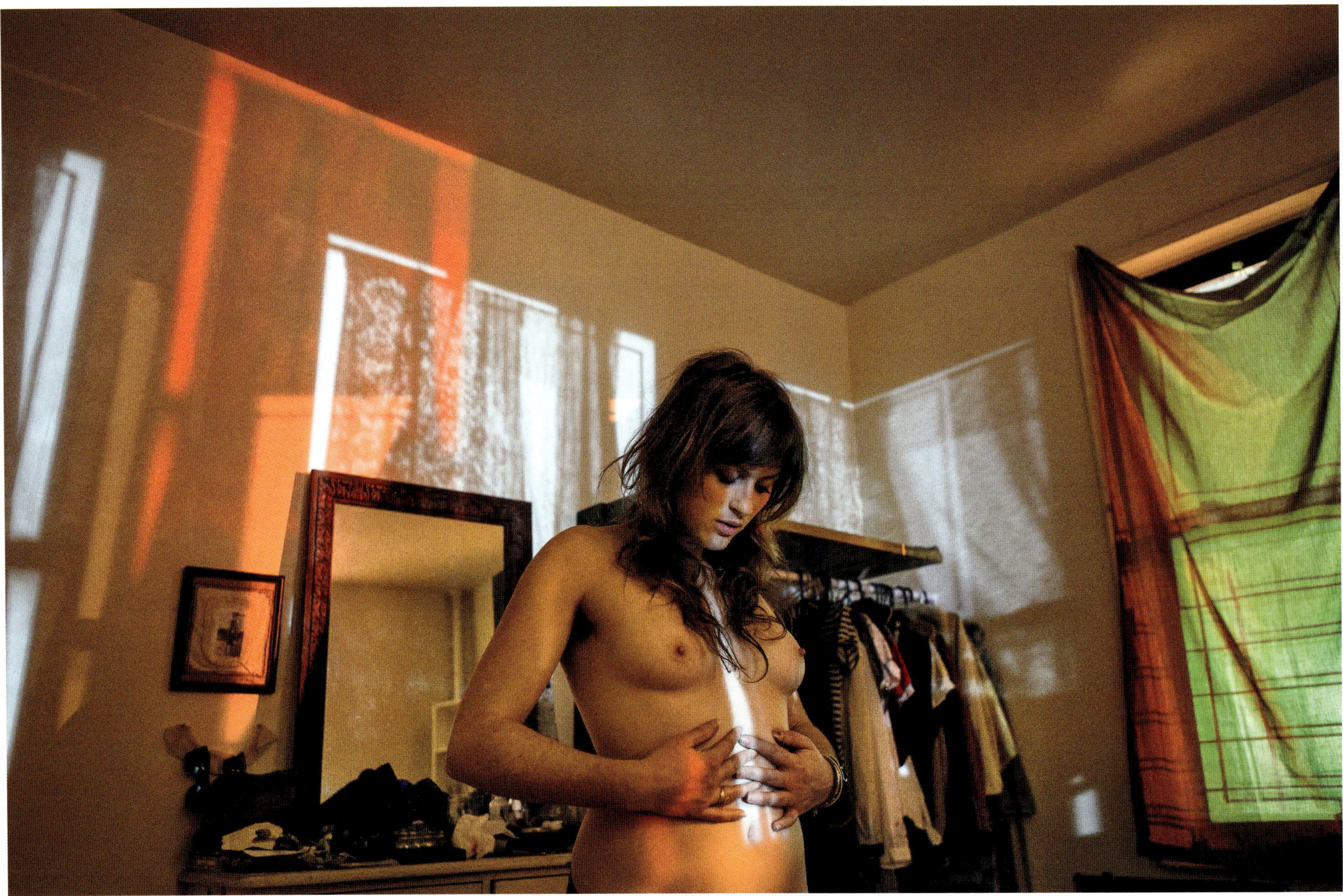

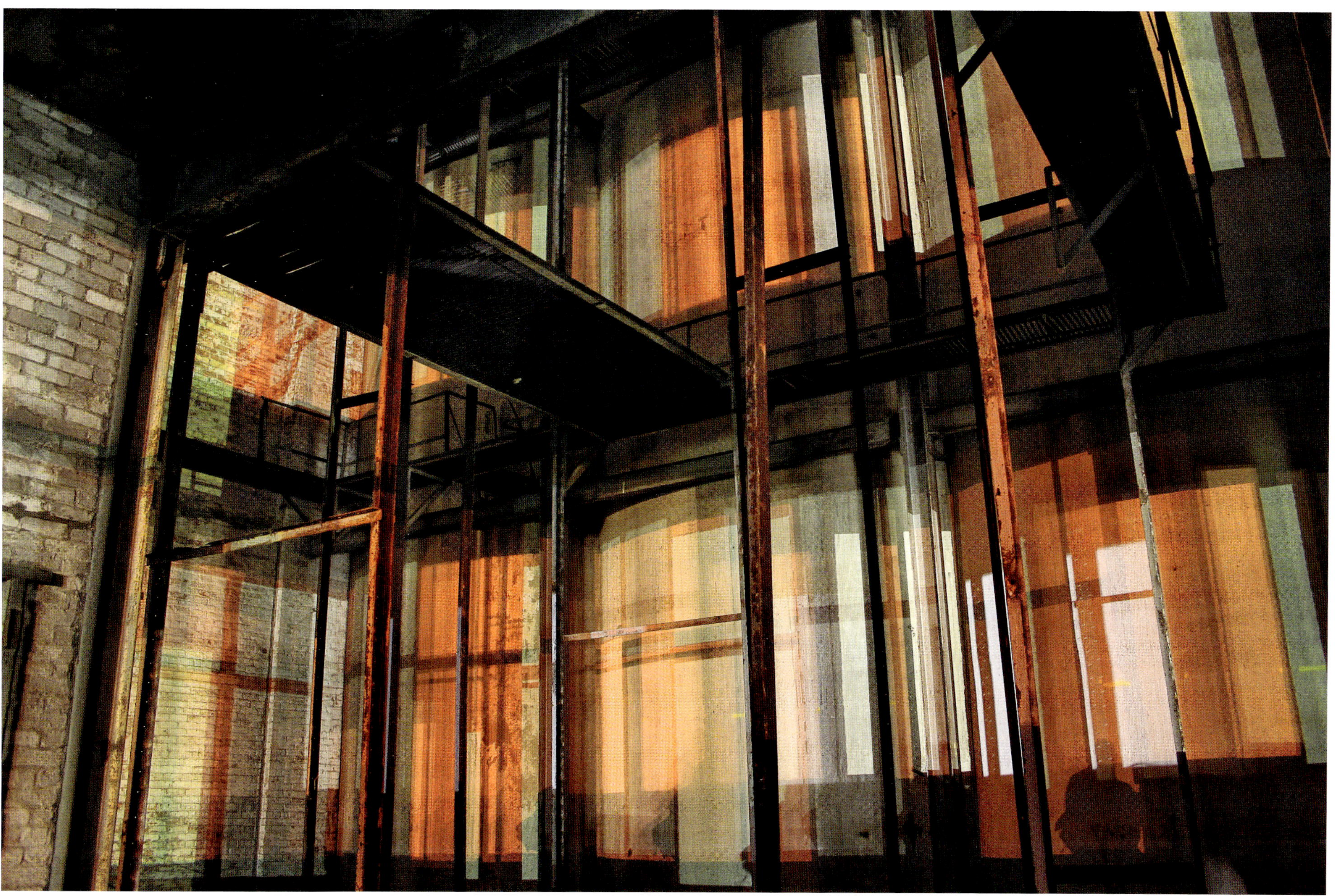

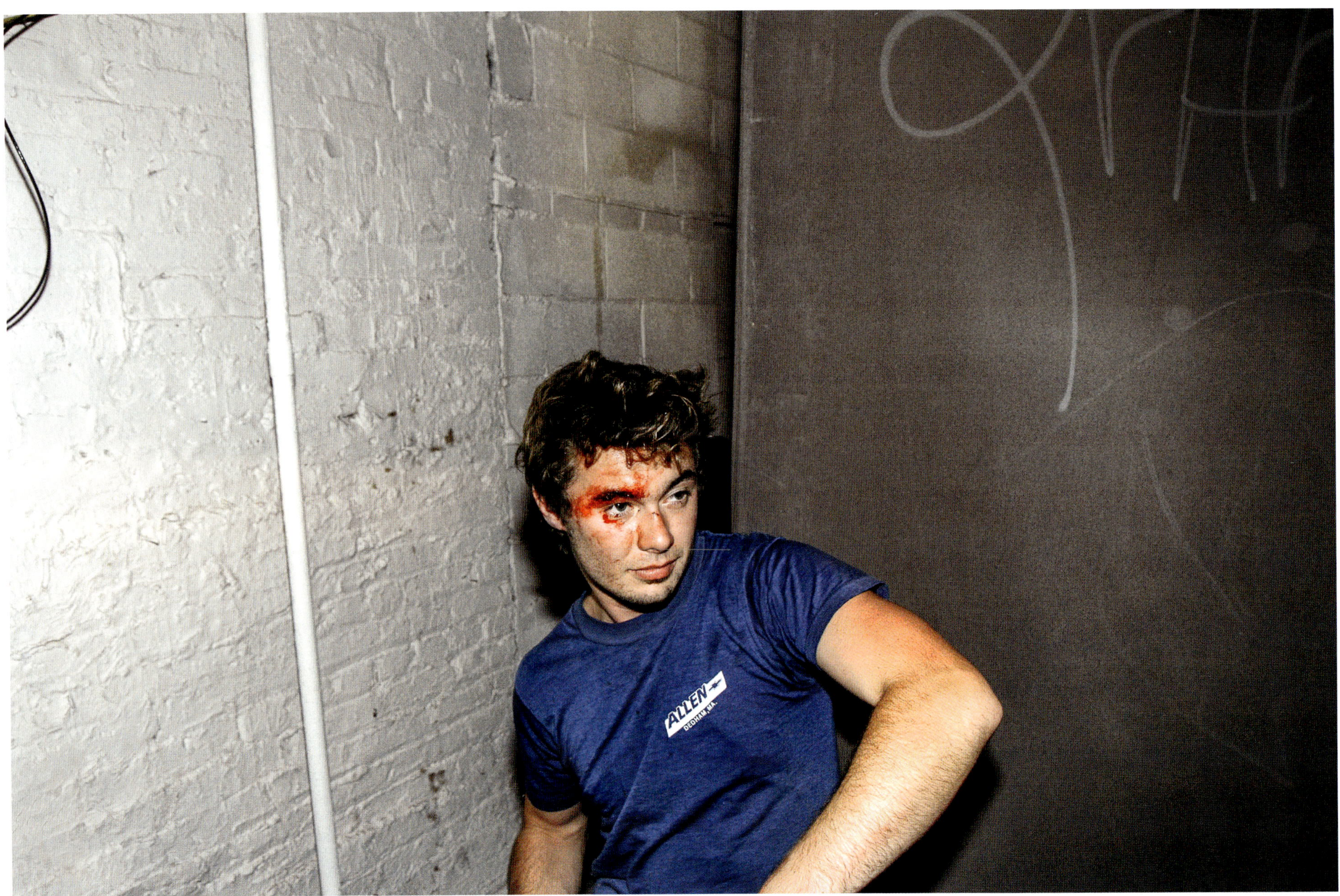

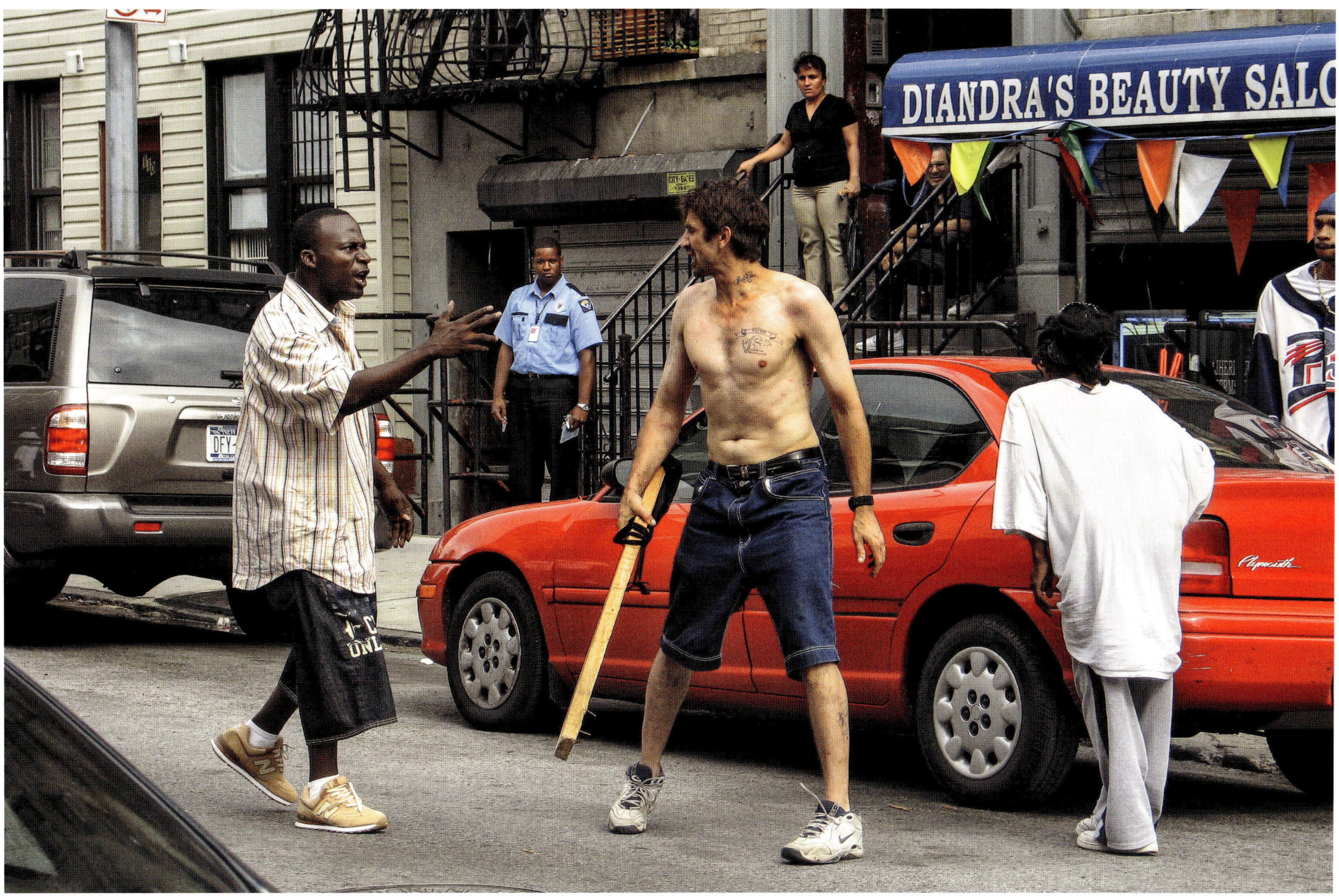

DIANDRA'S BEAUTY SALO
Plymouth

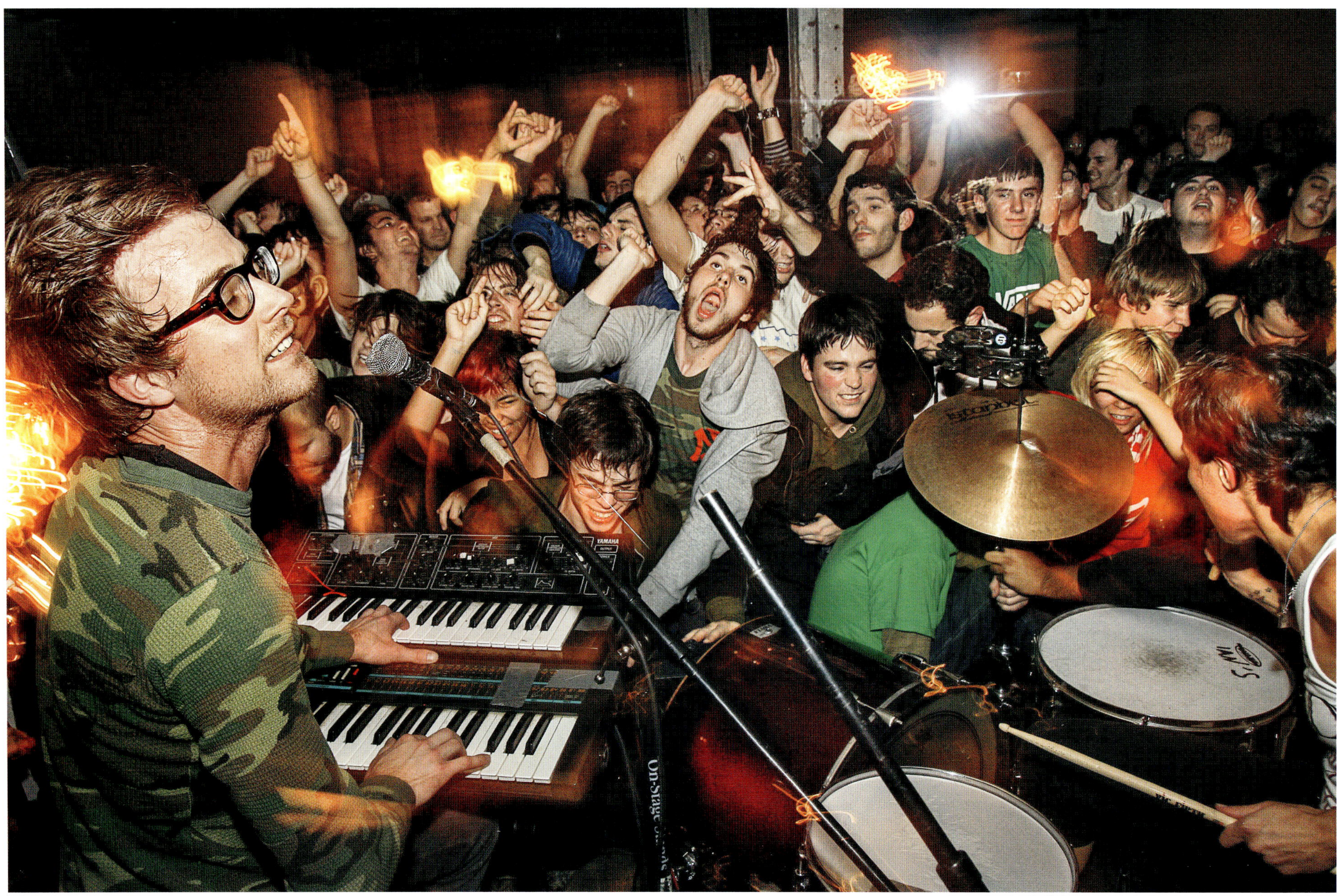

CROWD SURFING PAST THE CAMERA
JOE AHEARN

I grew up in Times Square, on 43rd Street and 8th Avenue. I have distinct memories of muggings and street fights in broad daylight. This is mostly thanks to my father, the filmmaker Charlie Ahearn, who dutifully recorded our surroundings from the windows of our apartment. He compiled a perverse mix of New York mayhem and home movies that help guide my memories, now that the building has been torn down and Midtown has been re-skinned. My family then moved downtown to a coffee and tea warehouse in Tribeca, where I spent middle school and high school breaking into construction sites and abandoned buildings. I learned about long-exposure photography to try and capture those moments. Upon returning from adventures a few years later that served as a temporary replacement for college, I found most of those building projects completed and the neighborhood unrecognizable.

For the past several years, I've done almost nothing besides go to shows, run shows, and plan shows—but these are ephemeral accomplishments. Most of the venues have new names, and most of the bands have broken up or gotten so big I never see them anymore. I walk into Roberta's, a pizza place in Bushwick, and remember the gutted concrete pit it used to be—the one that hosted a Parts & Labor record release show years ago, where Matt & Kim headlined on a stage that was actually a giant saw table. It seems like a weird vision I had.

New Yorkers have a habit of swallowing their history, maybe because of their compulsion to stay busy with a million projects. But Tod Seelie's photographs are reminders. I remember wandering the World's Fair grounds in Queens, looking for a space to set up the finale for a subway performance I was planning on the 7 train. The entire time, my vision was colored by photos I'd seen of secret dinners that Tod took from the towers next to the globe. Or, I remember waiting with my family beside the Hudson River near my grandmother's house in upstate New York, watching him disembark with the rest of the Swimming Cities fantasy crew.

I've crowd-surfed past Tod's camera more times than I can count. I've followed strangers into subway tunnels, only to find Tod beneath a steel chandelier. And after four years in a row spent battling the hordes in Austin, Texas, and finding Tod on every corner, every night, I decided to finally skip South by Southwest to attend a much smaller festival in Monterrey, Mexico, only to find him there too.

Tod captures the most surreal edges of a dream that I want to live inside. Looking at his photographs is like waking up from that dream and finding a strange creature's hat under your pillow. The dream was unreal, but here's the proof: It must have happened. It must be possible.

Joe Ahearn is a curator for the Clocktower Gallery. He helps run Showpaper, *a bi-monthly all-ages music listings newspaper that features a full-color print by a different artist in each issue. He also organizes events at Silent Barn, a DIY art and music space in Brooklyn.*

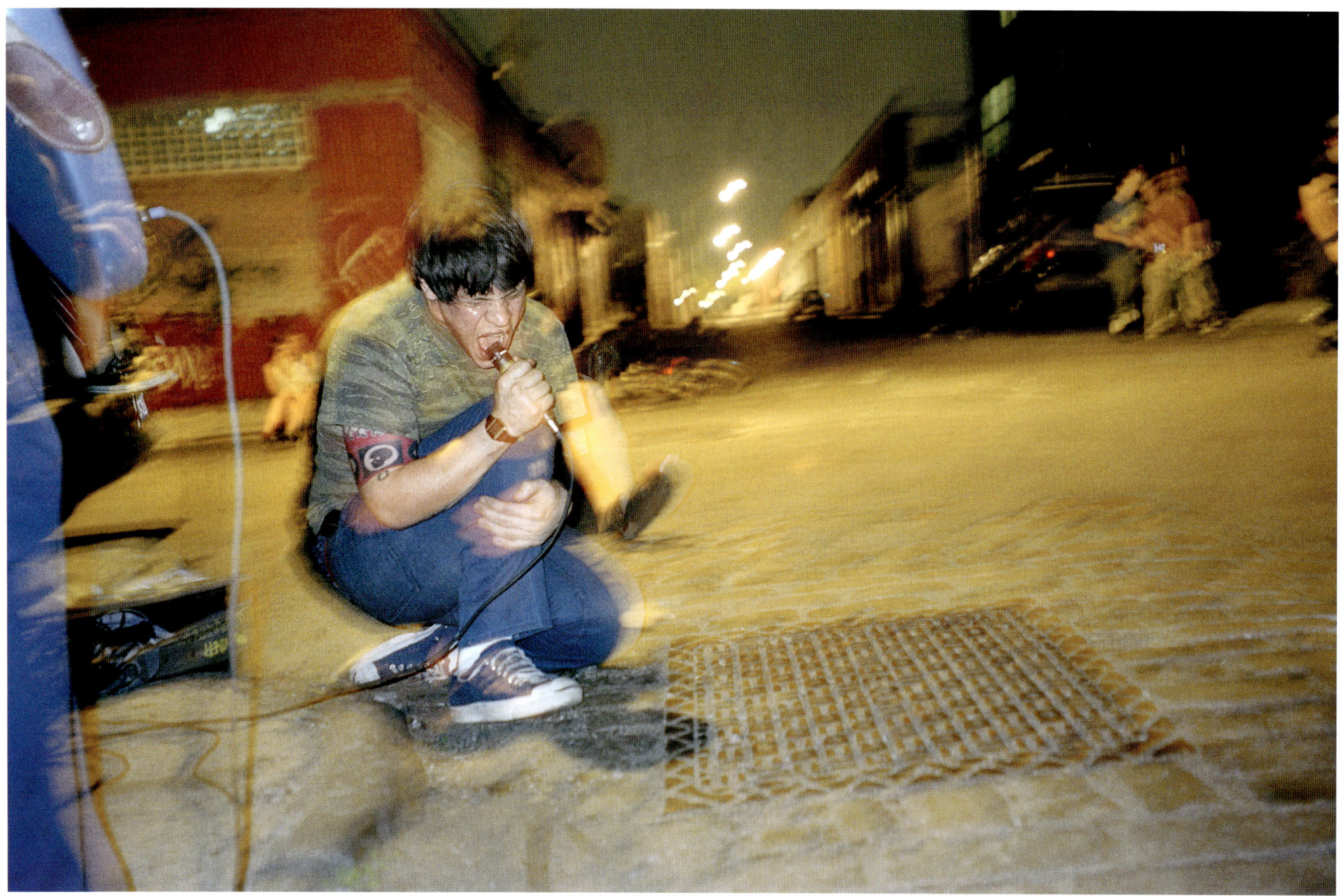

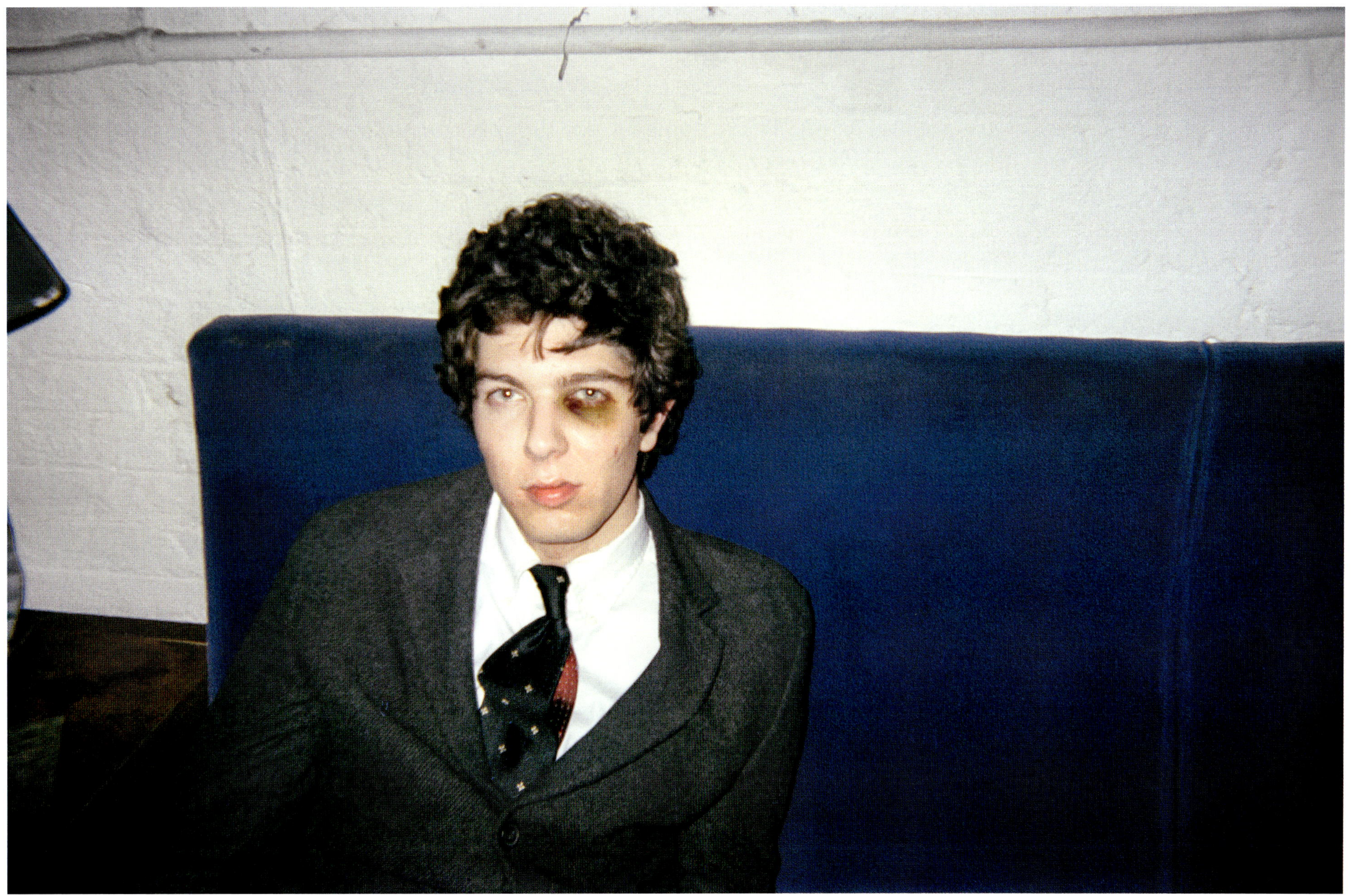

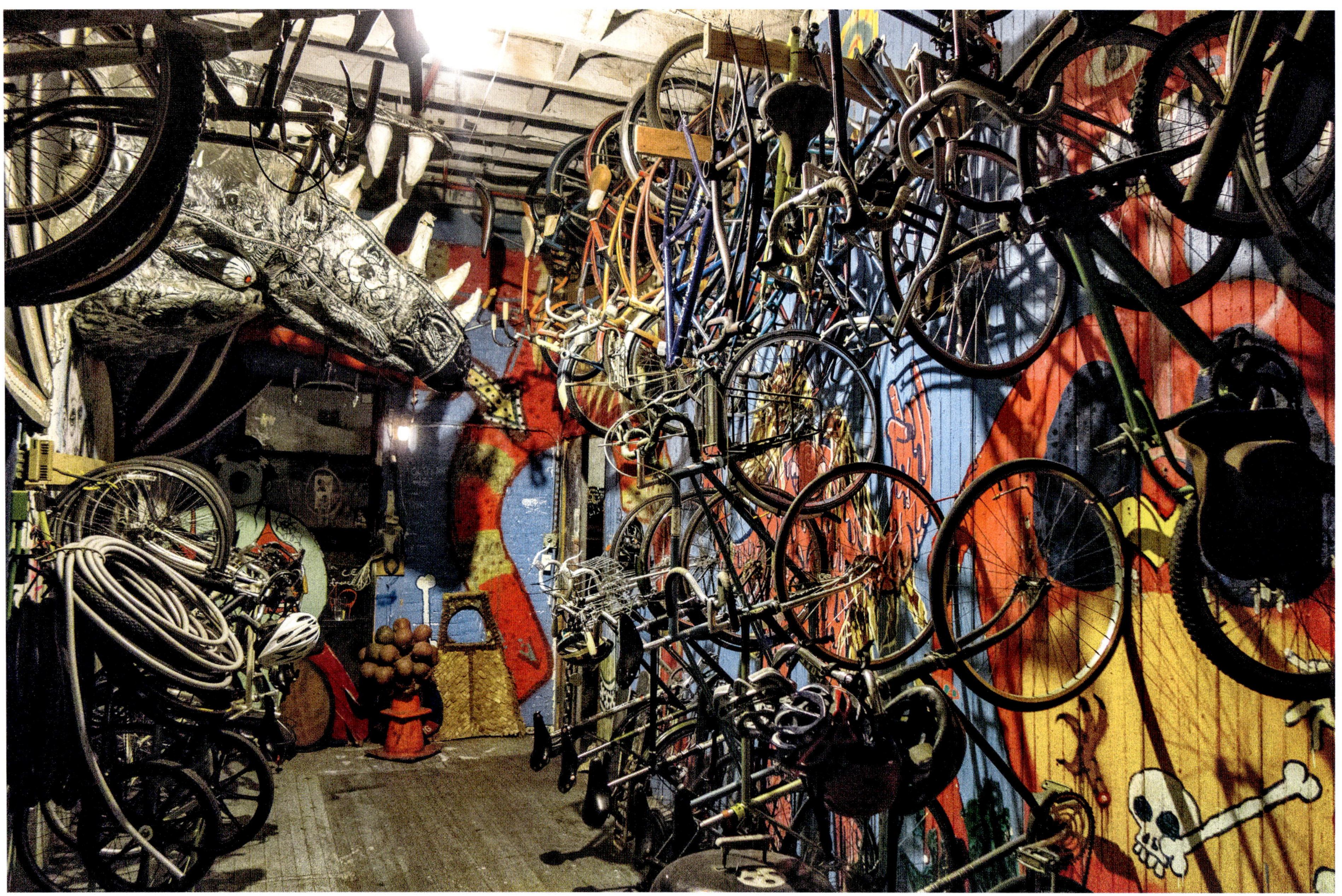

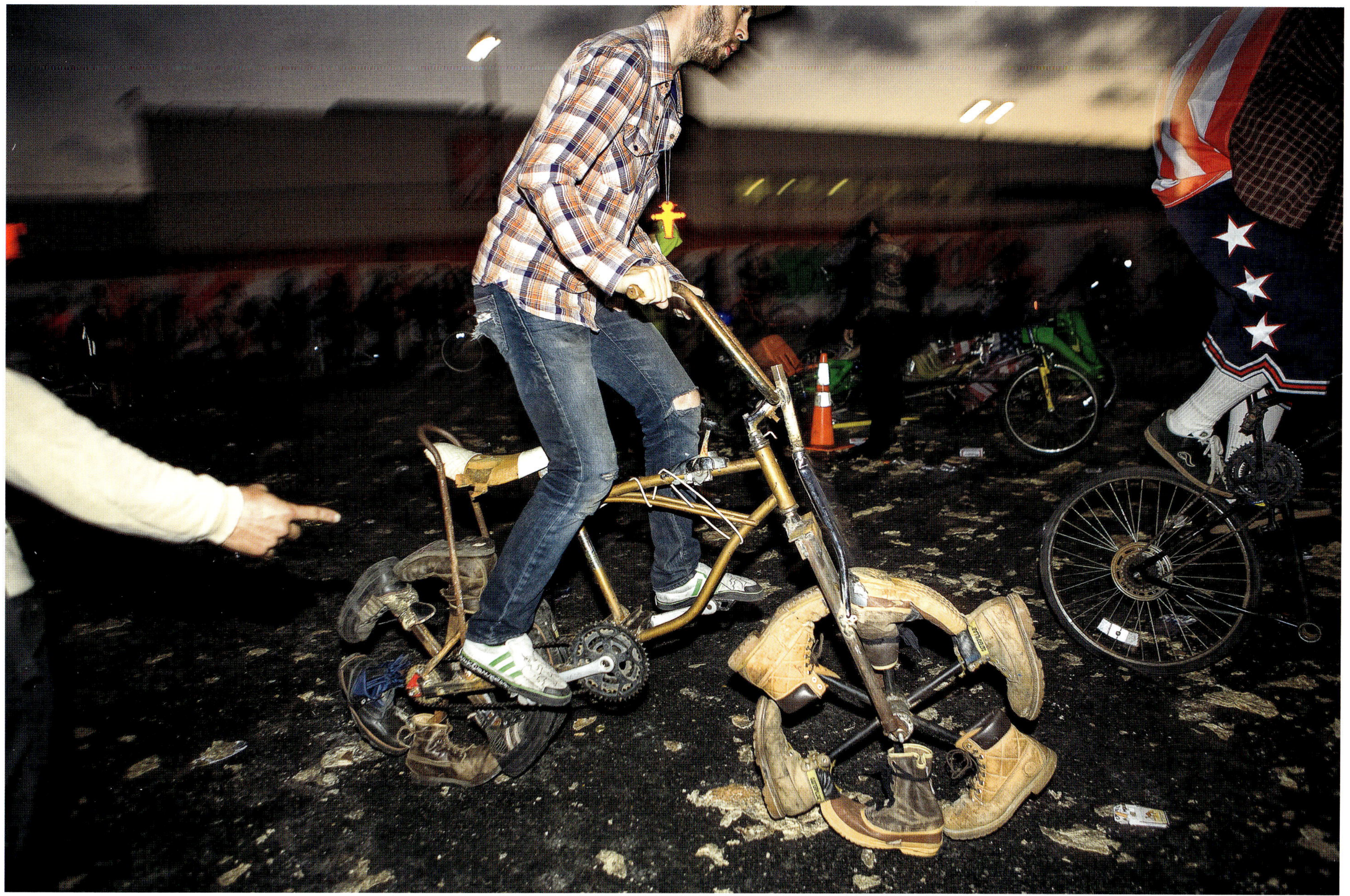

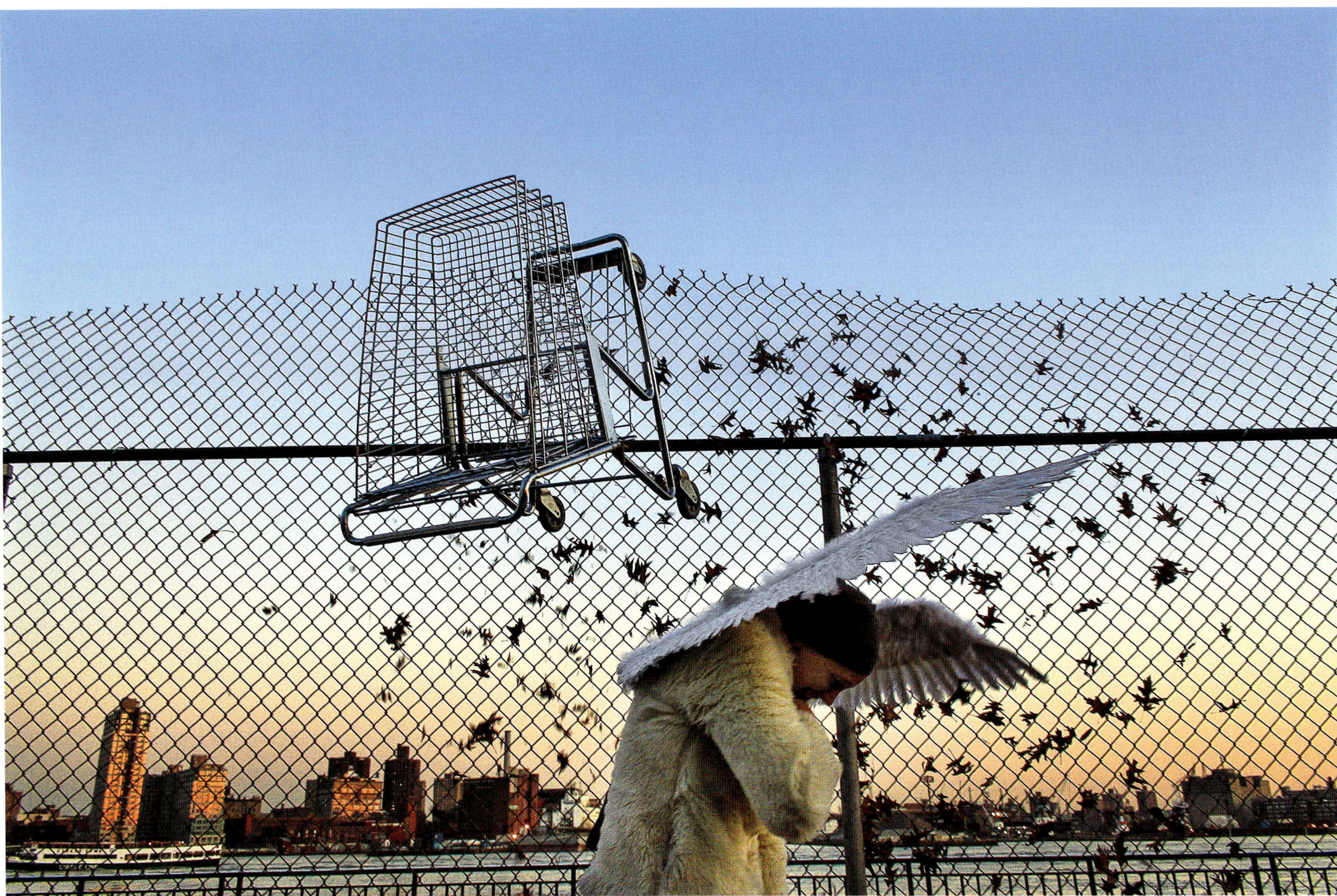

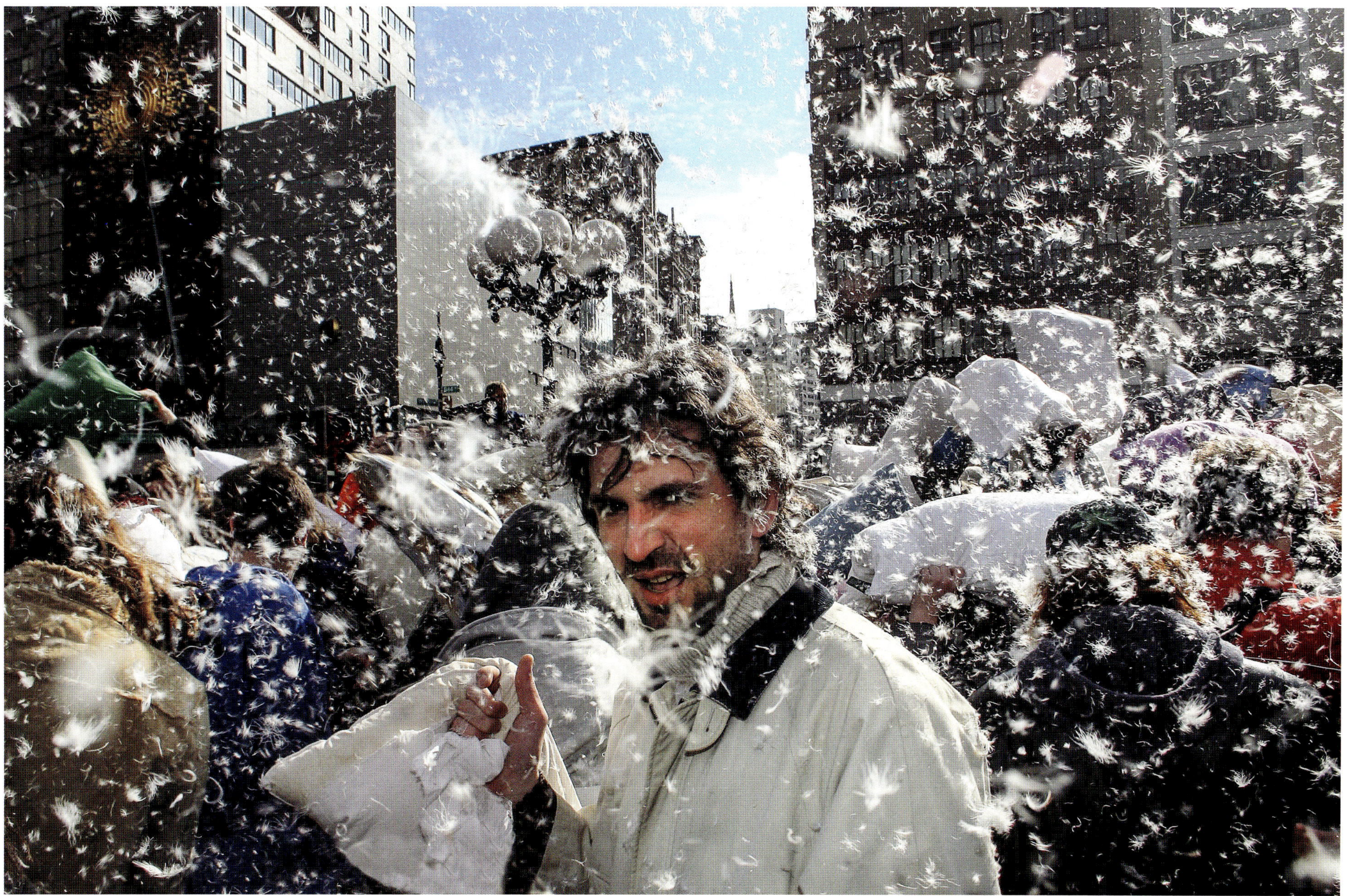

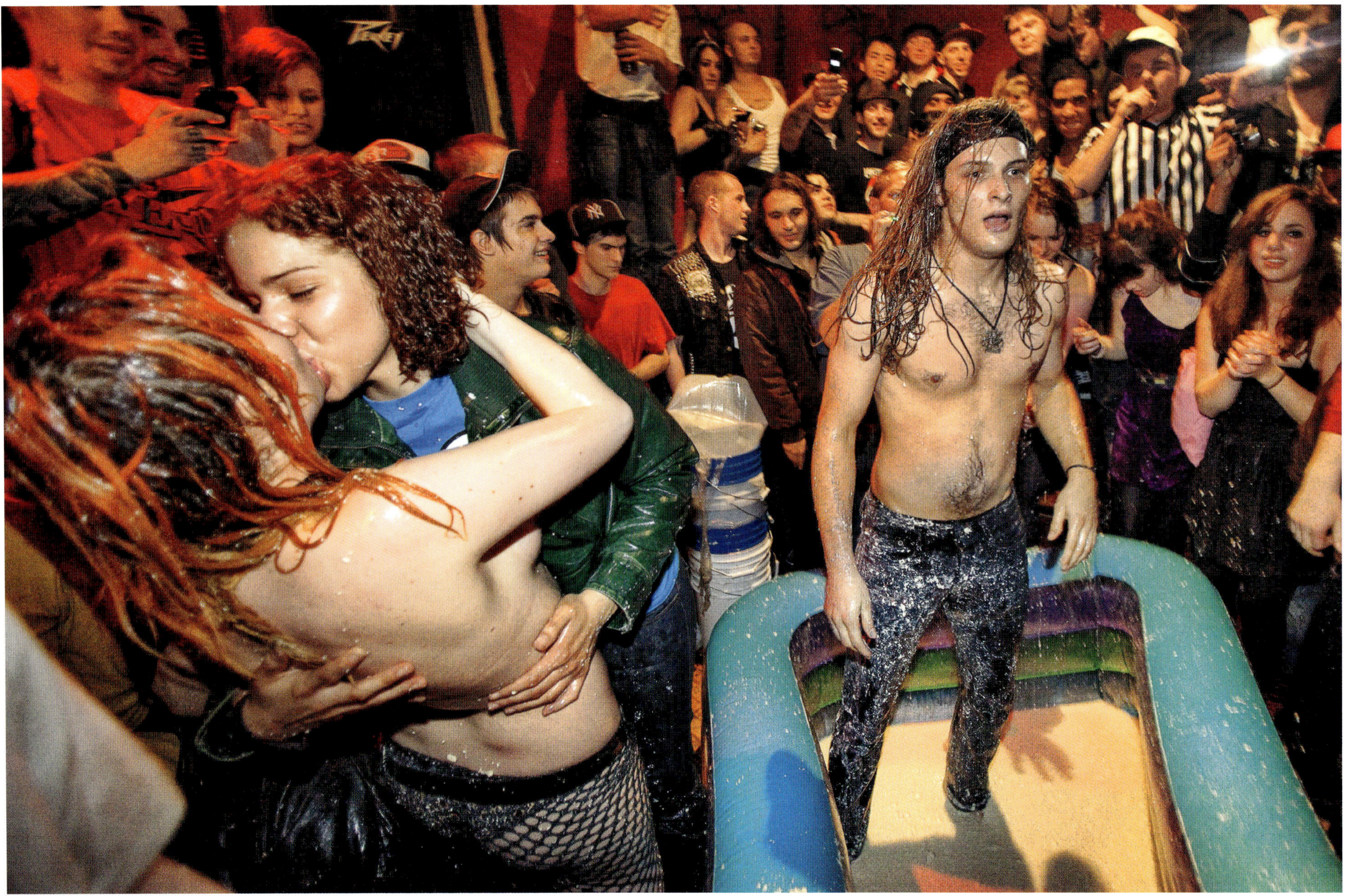

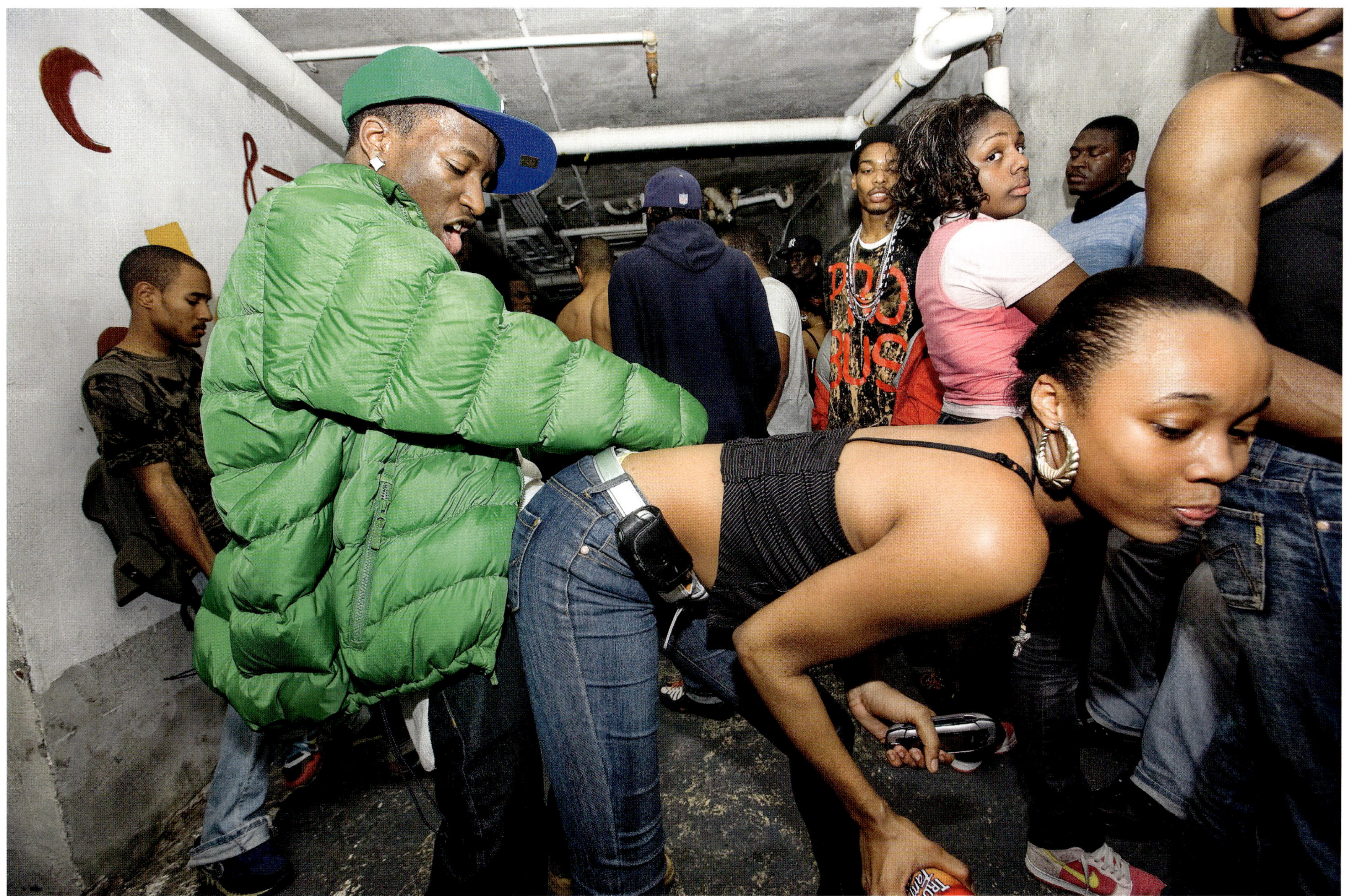

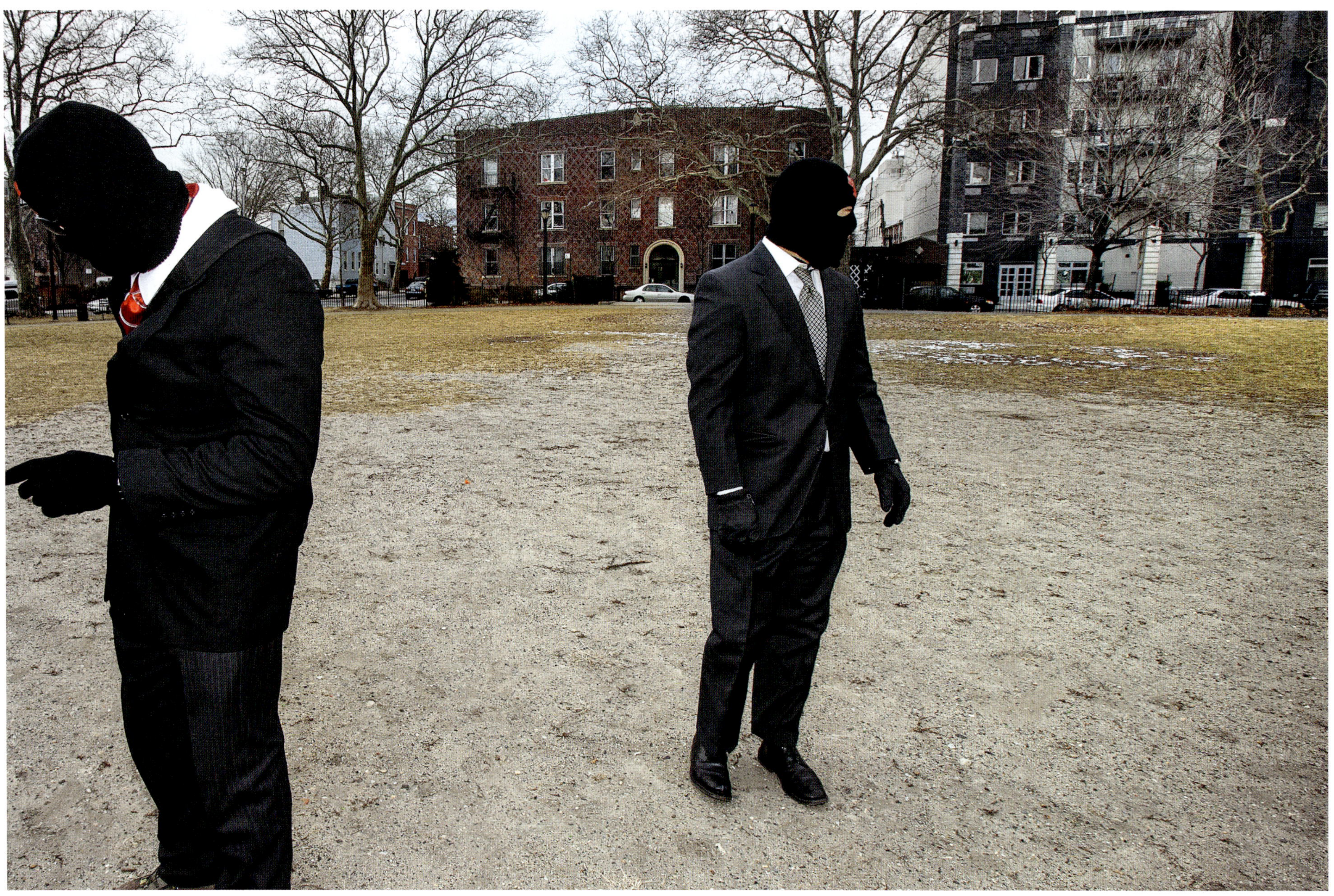

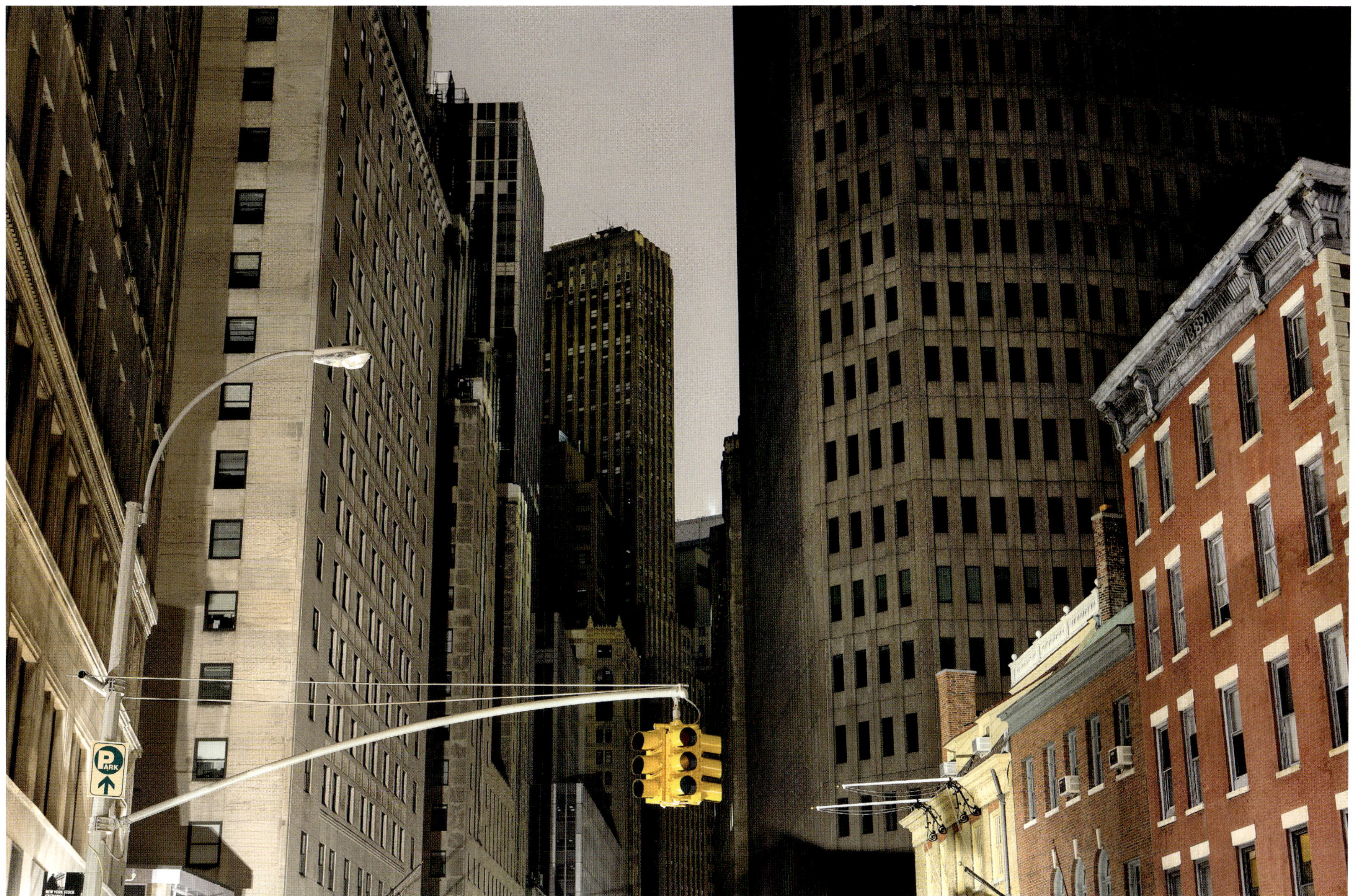

P
ARK

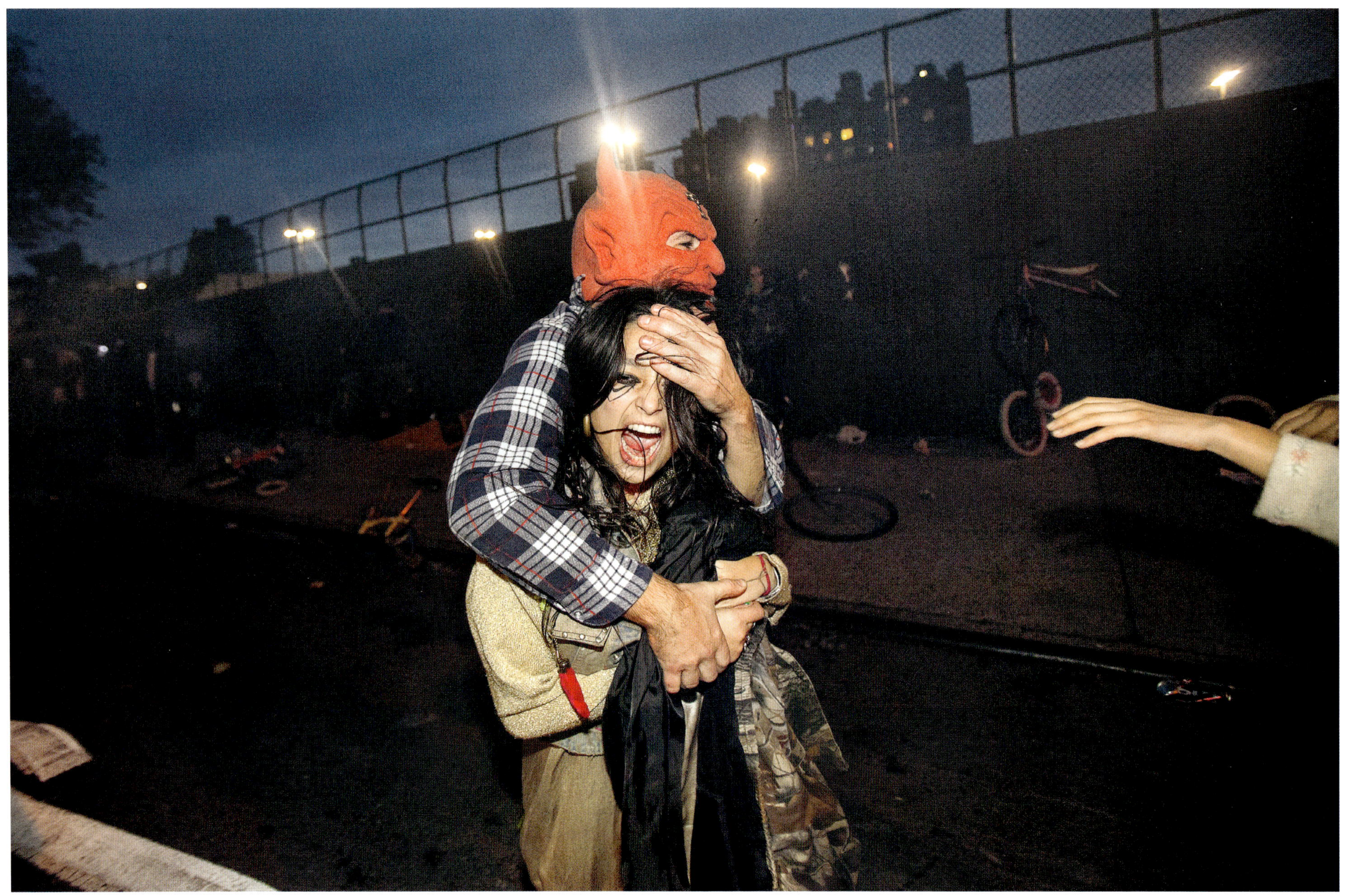

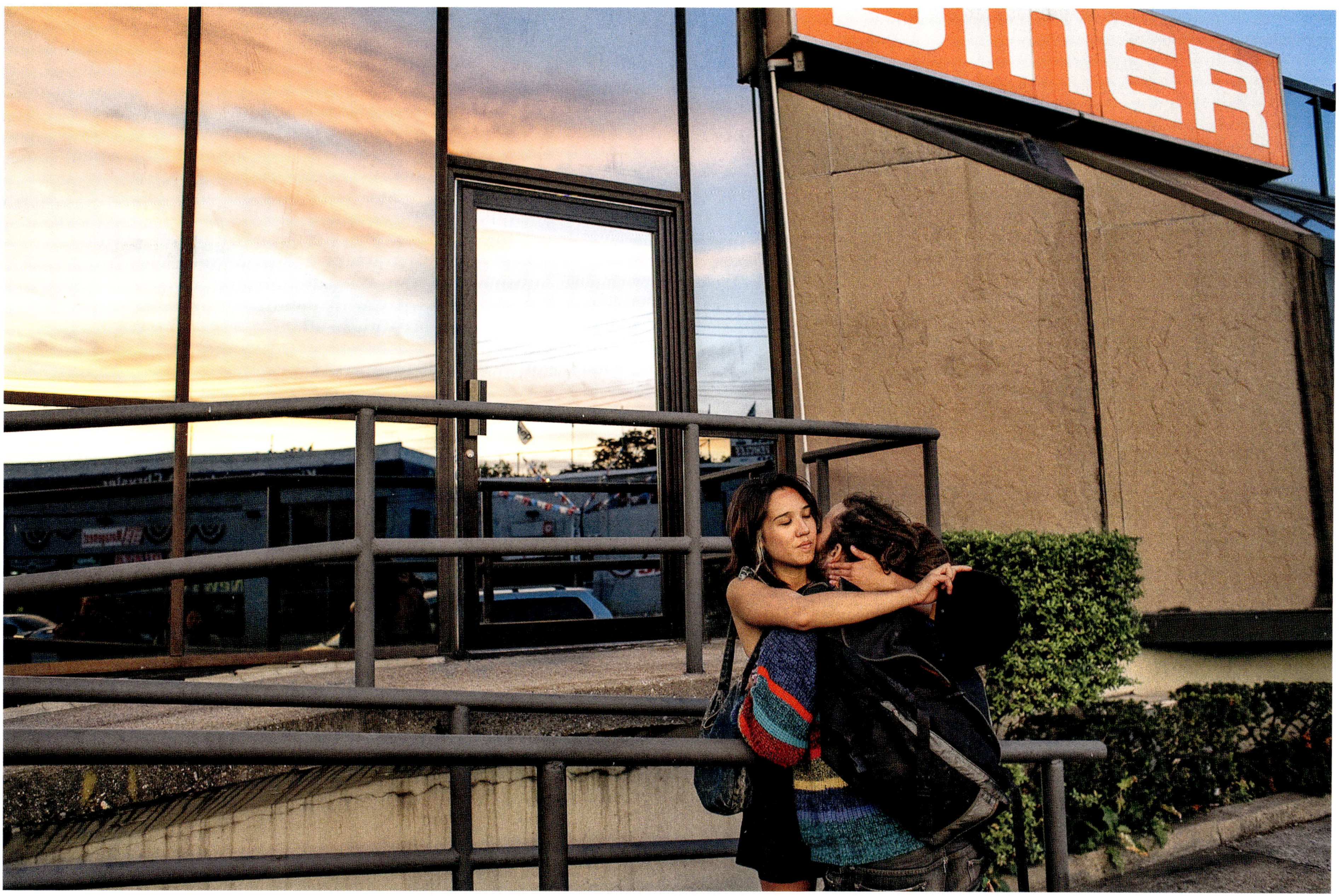
DINER

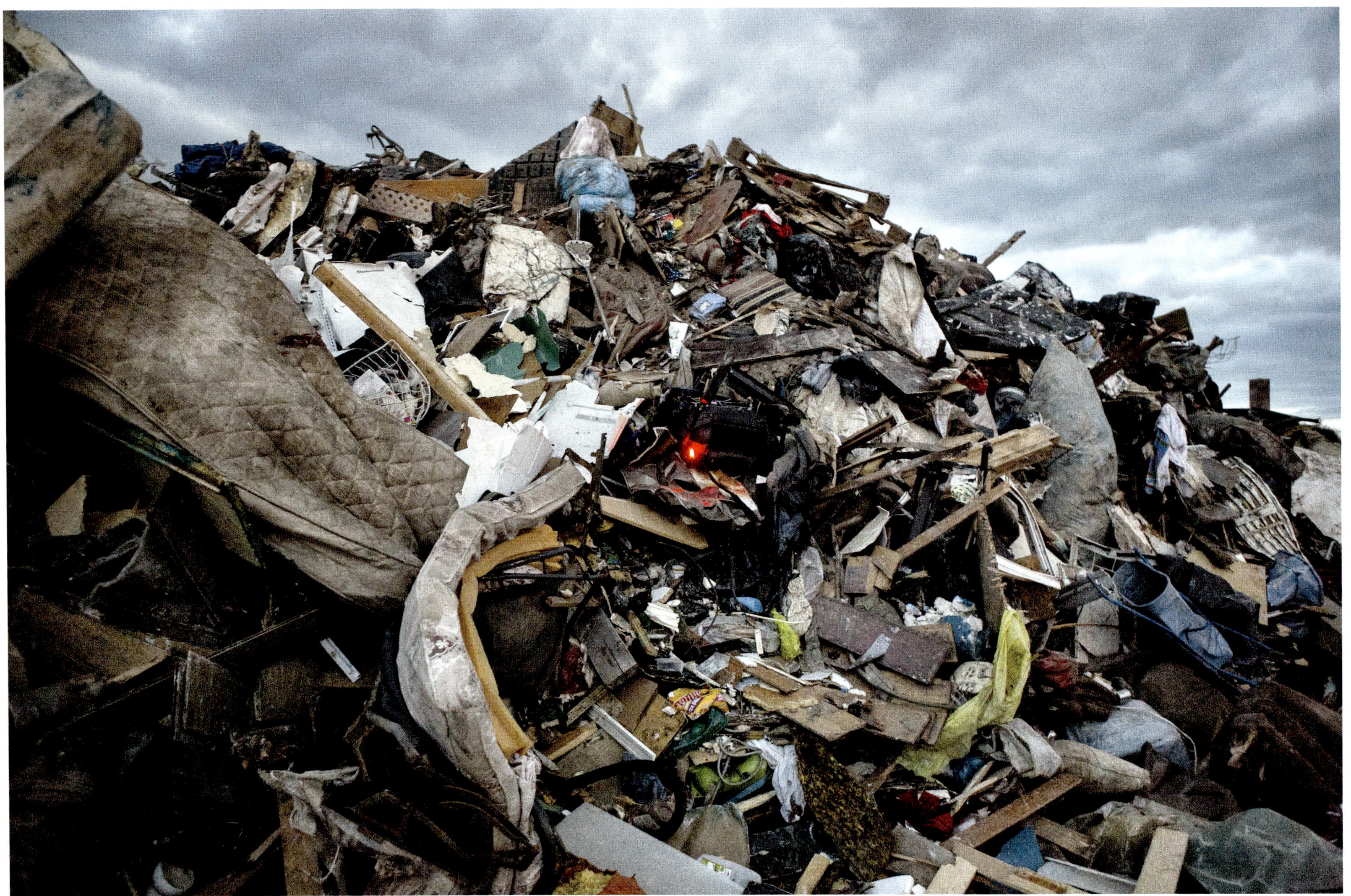

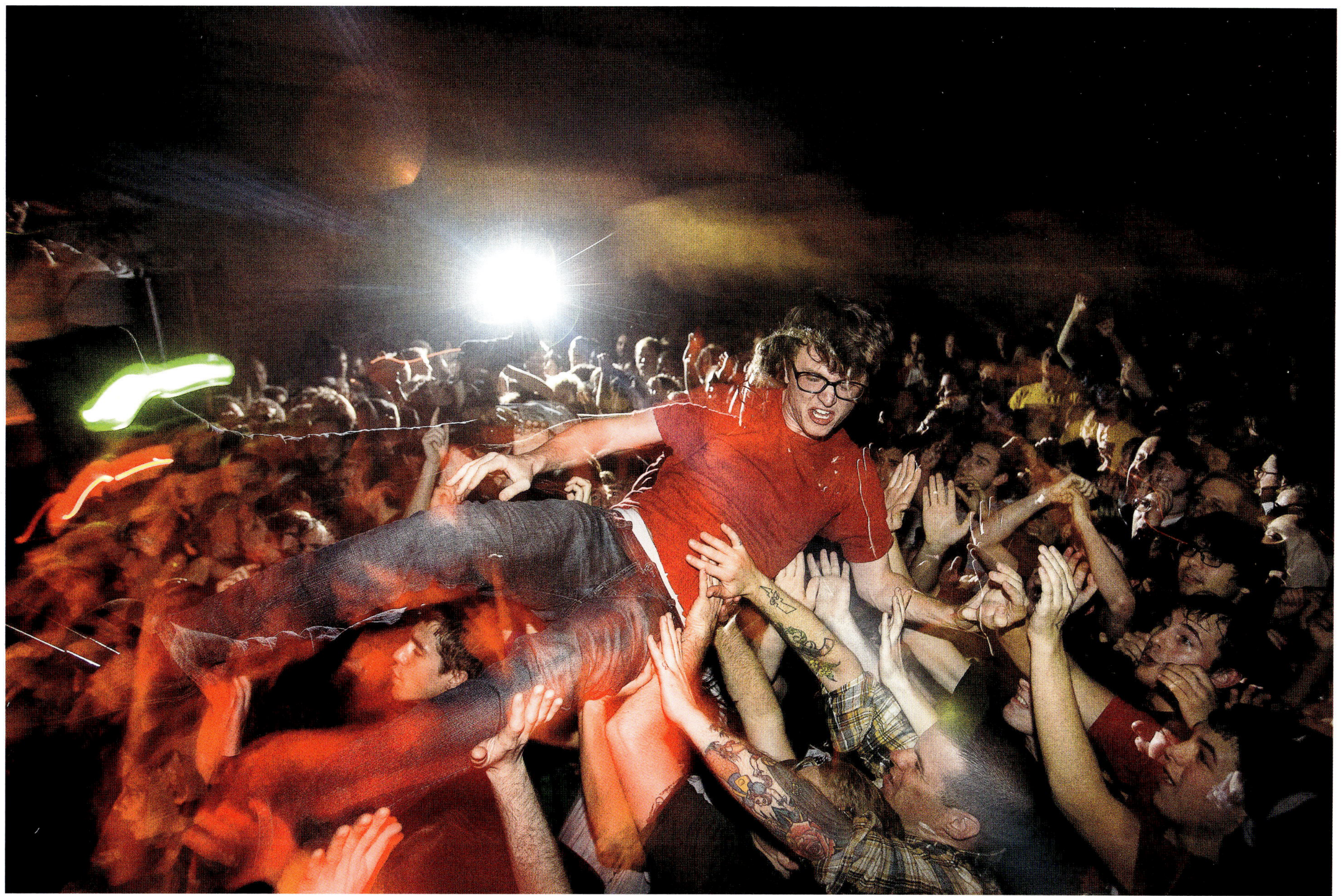

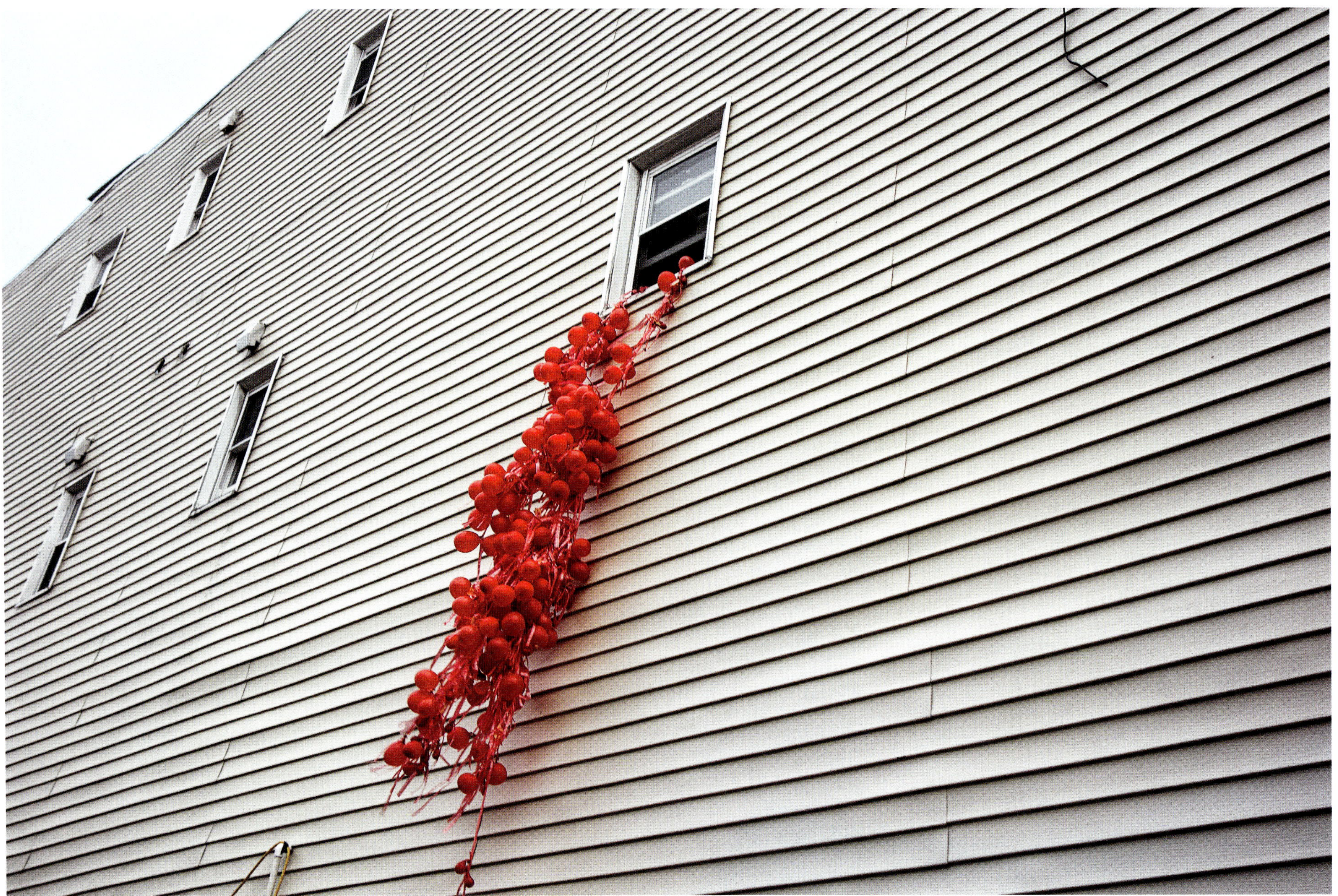

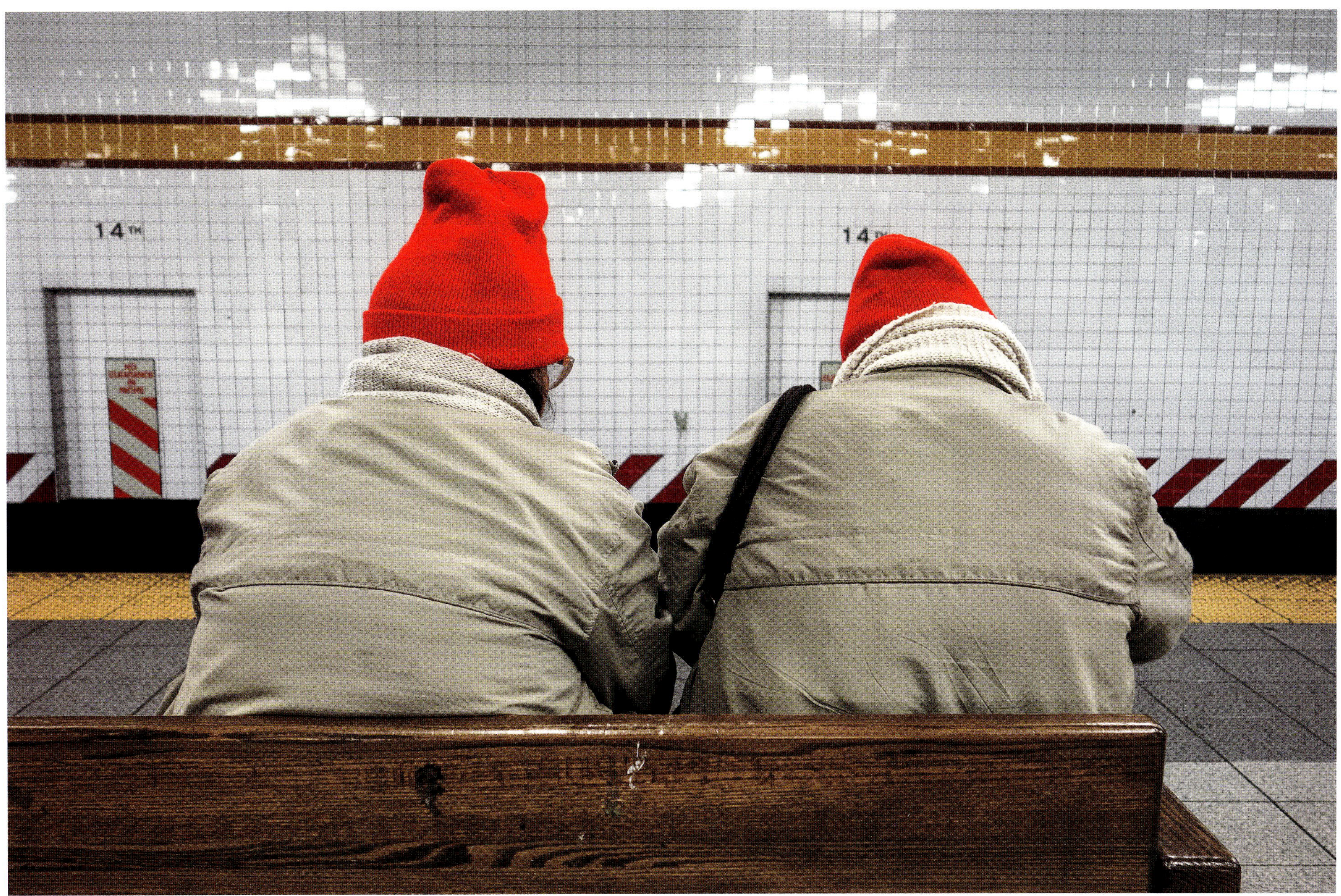

14 TH
14 TH

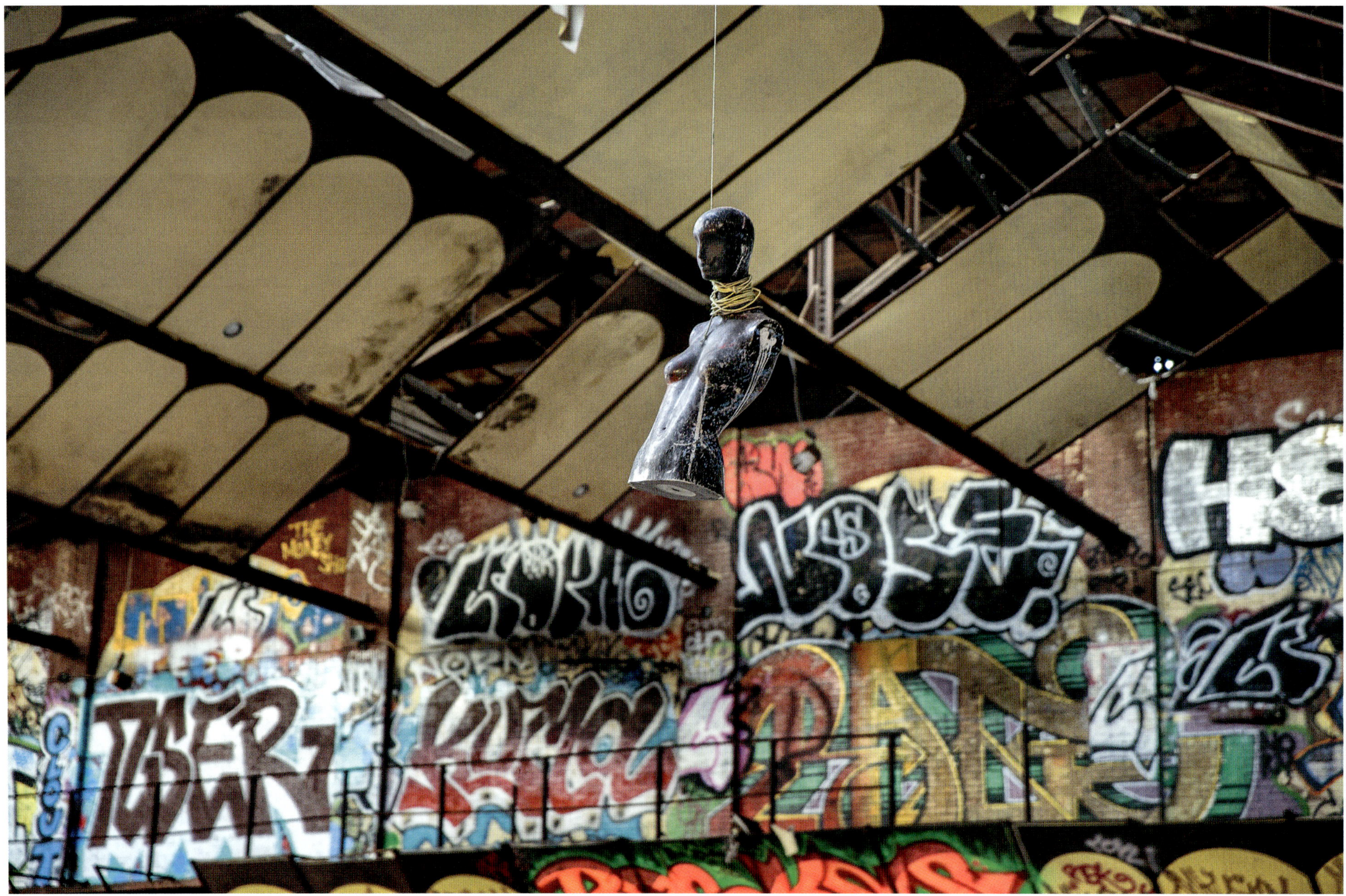

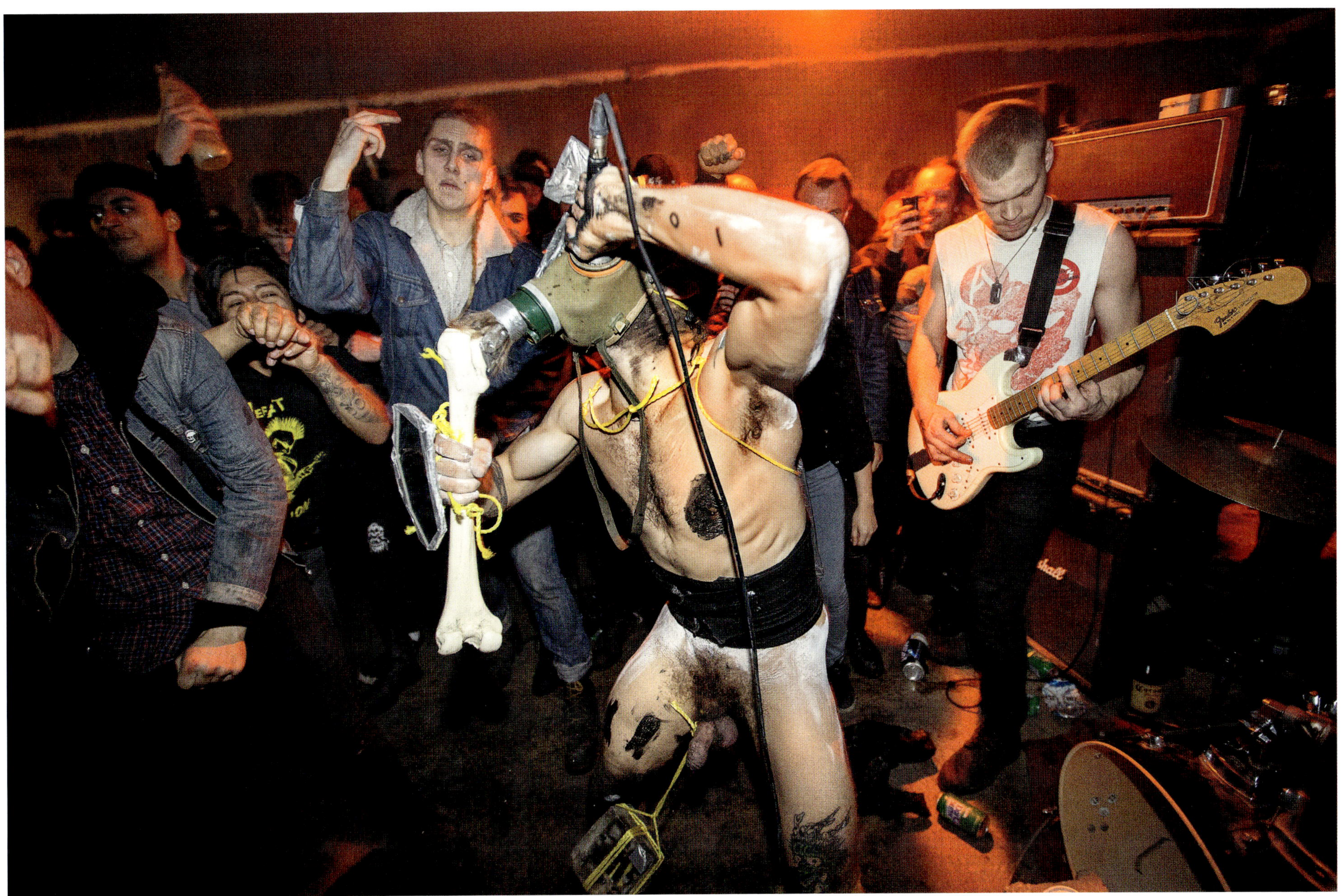

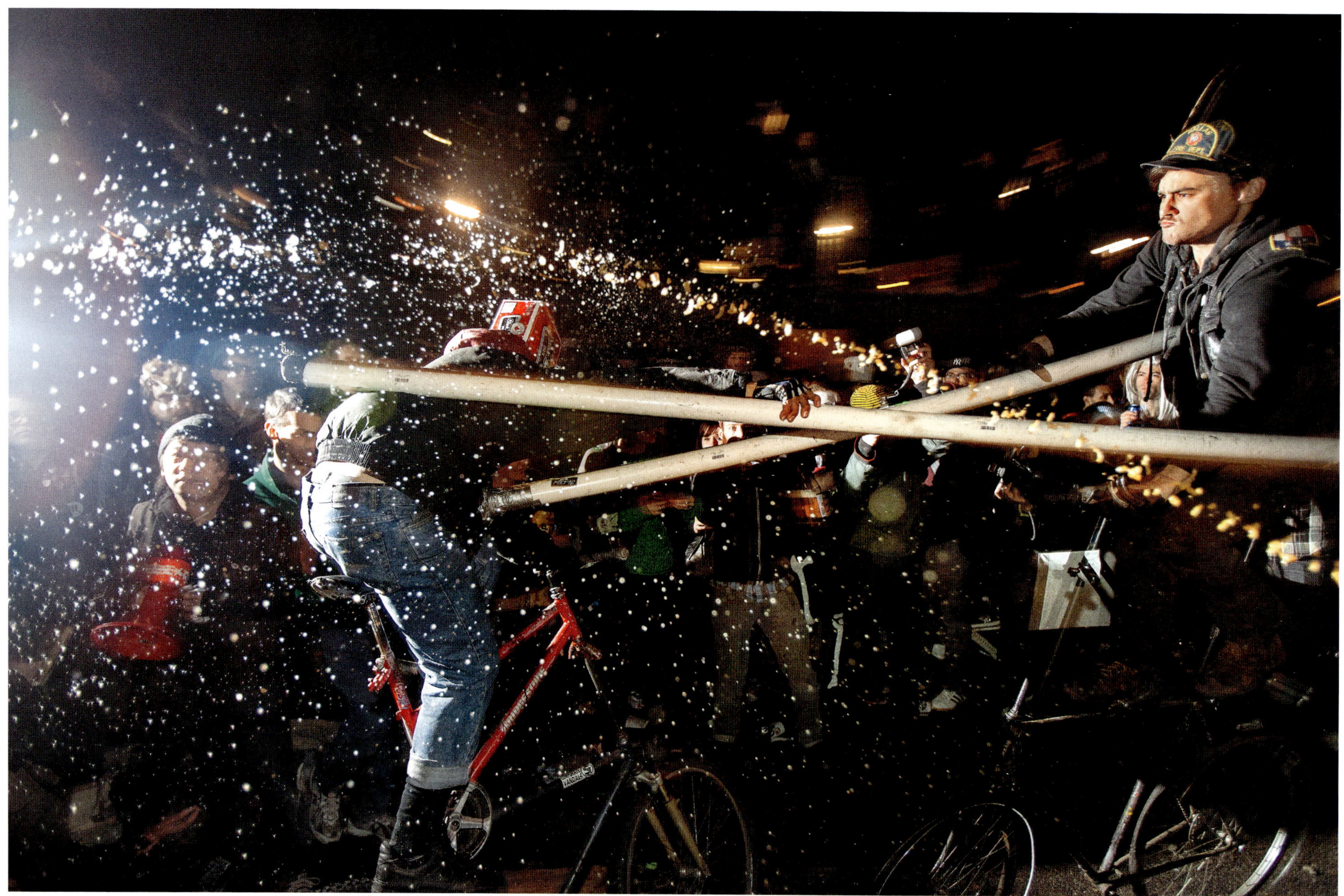

THE ONLY PHOTOGRAPHER AT BIKE KILL
CONRAD CARLSON

Around the time the Republican National Convention came to New York City in 2004, there was a ton of momentum relating to bikes. A community was being formed because of how crazy and political it all was. The activist group Time's Up was effective in terms of organizing. Critical Mass was big. Black Label was just getting started in New York, and so were some other bike clubs. Alley cat races were exploding. The Internet made it all seem important, like it was affecting everyone. To me, that moment was about people having their own voice and creating their own media outlets.

In 2002, Tod Seelie was at the first Bike Kill, Black Label's day-long block party of mutant bicycles. I think he's been to all of them since. He always comes early and stays late, so he has a lot of portraits of bikes and people riding them during the day, and then, he knows where to be when things get really crazy at night. He's good at capturing the intensity and raw emotions. His photos are proof of things that happened so fast you forgot; details you can't remember after the blur of the day.

At Bike Kill, most photographers focus on one event, or one person on a bike. However, Tod understands the way that everything happens at once. A lot of times his images are really dark, when in fact a lot of Bike Kill is about having fun in the face of danger—but you always know it's going to result in an epic photo.

A few years ago, we thought there were too many photographers hanging out at Bike Kill. You would see all these people who would never ride bikes or participate in any way, people who would rather take a picture of the crazy thing they saw instead of actually being part of the event. So we decided to make it smaller. We told people to bring their bikes, not their cameras. But we never said that to Tod.

It's a given that he will be present at all kinds of events, which is pretty lucky. People will often not make plans to document their own event because they know Tod will show up. I'm so glad he was there at Bike Kill, at the first parties I DJed at the Chicken Hut, and on a junk raft with all our artist friends as part of Swoon's Swimming Cities project.

Early on, he was one of the few photographers around. He knows everyone, and wants to capture everyone. He is always there.

Conrad Carlson is a visual artist, President of the New York chapter of the Black Label Bicycle Club, and a DJ who plays under the name Dirtyfinger.

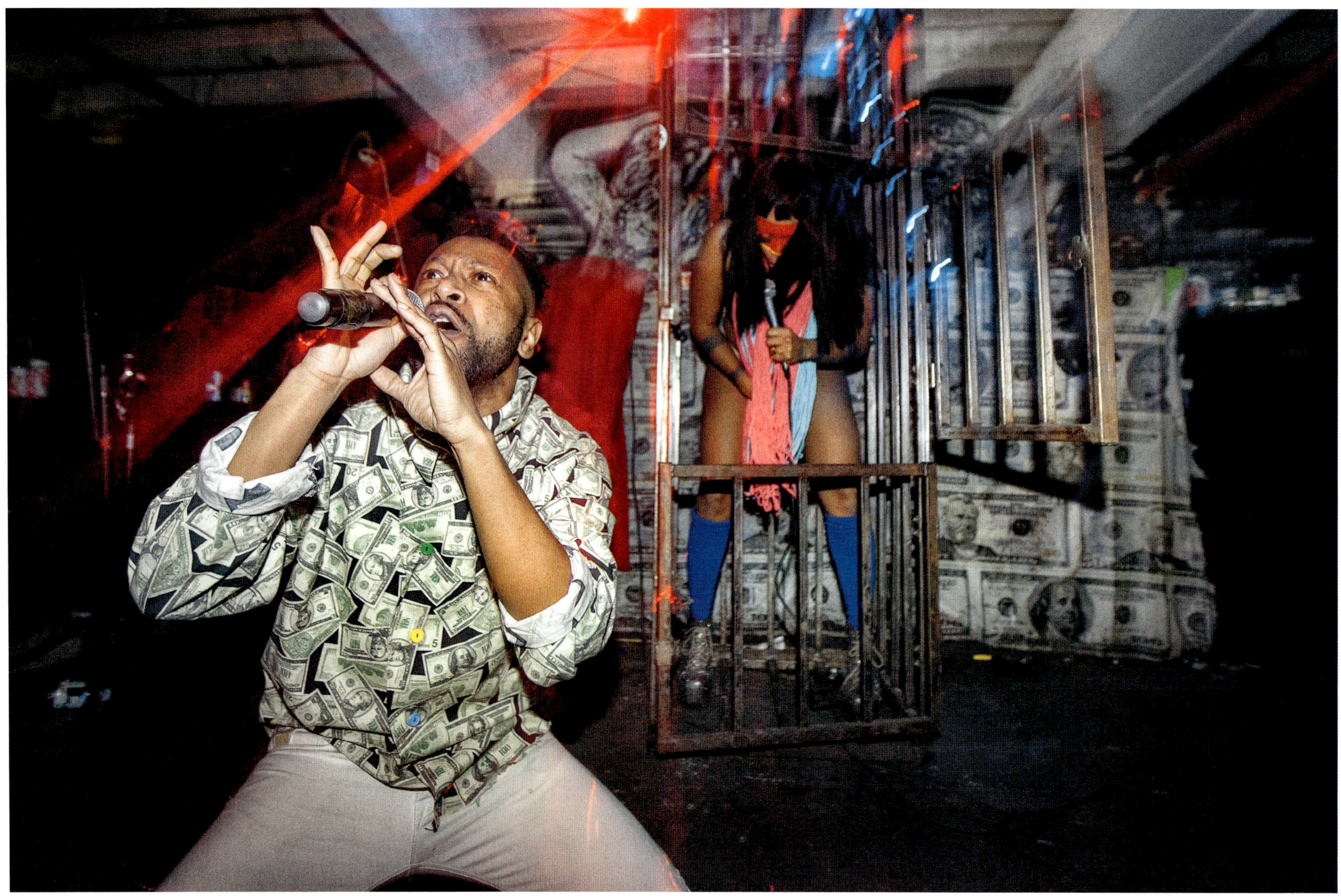

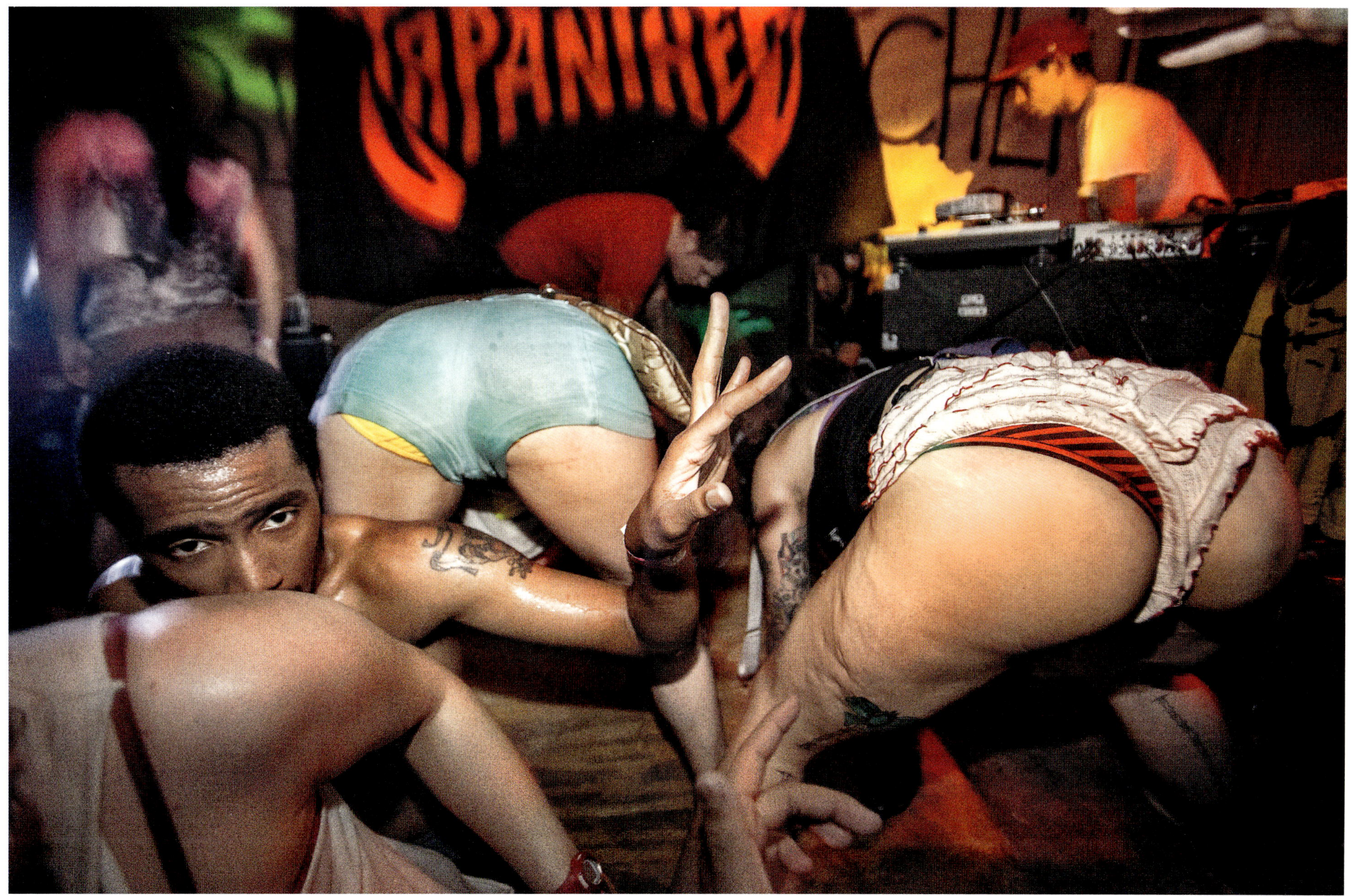

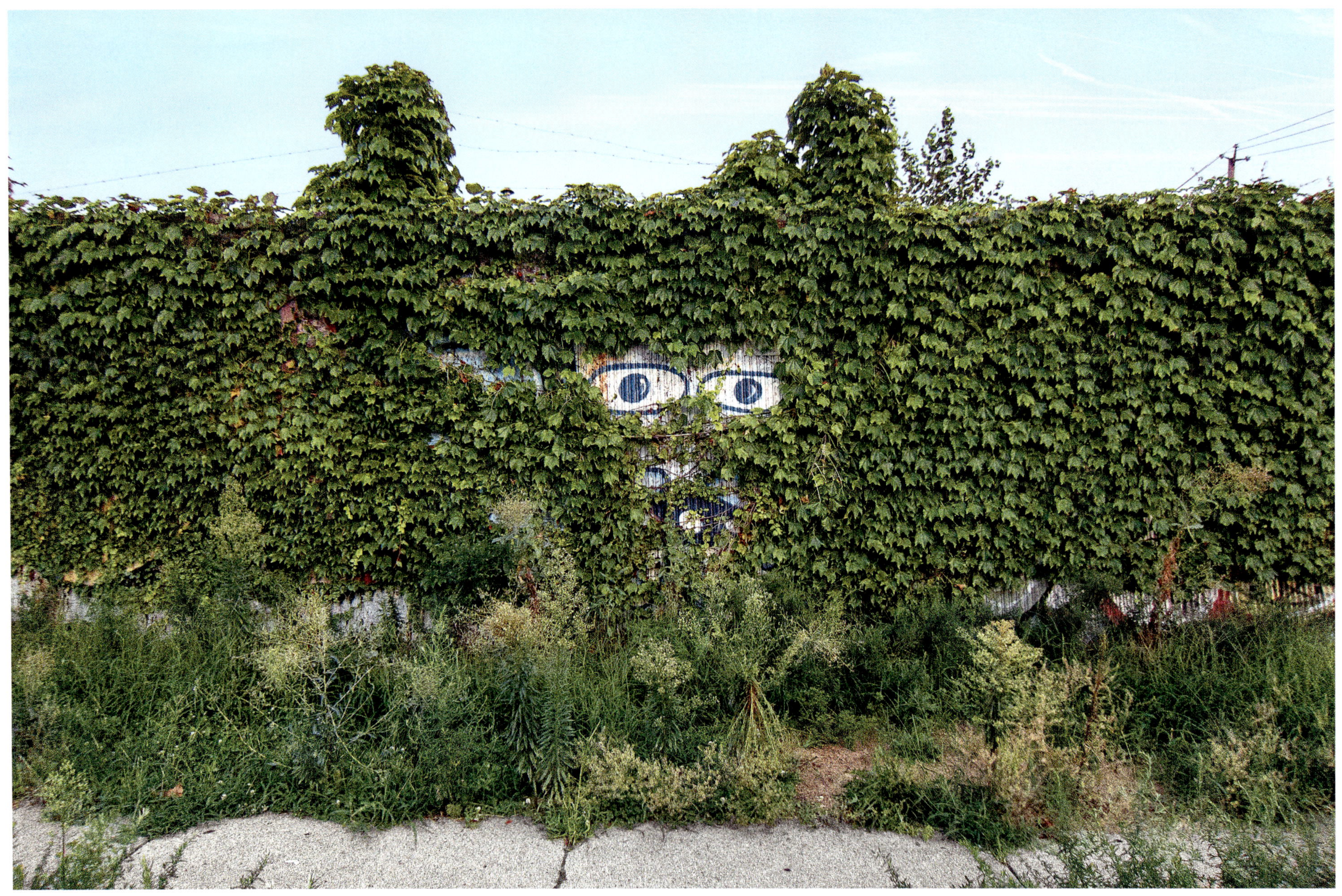

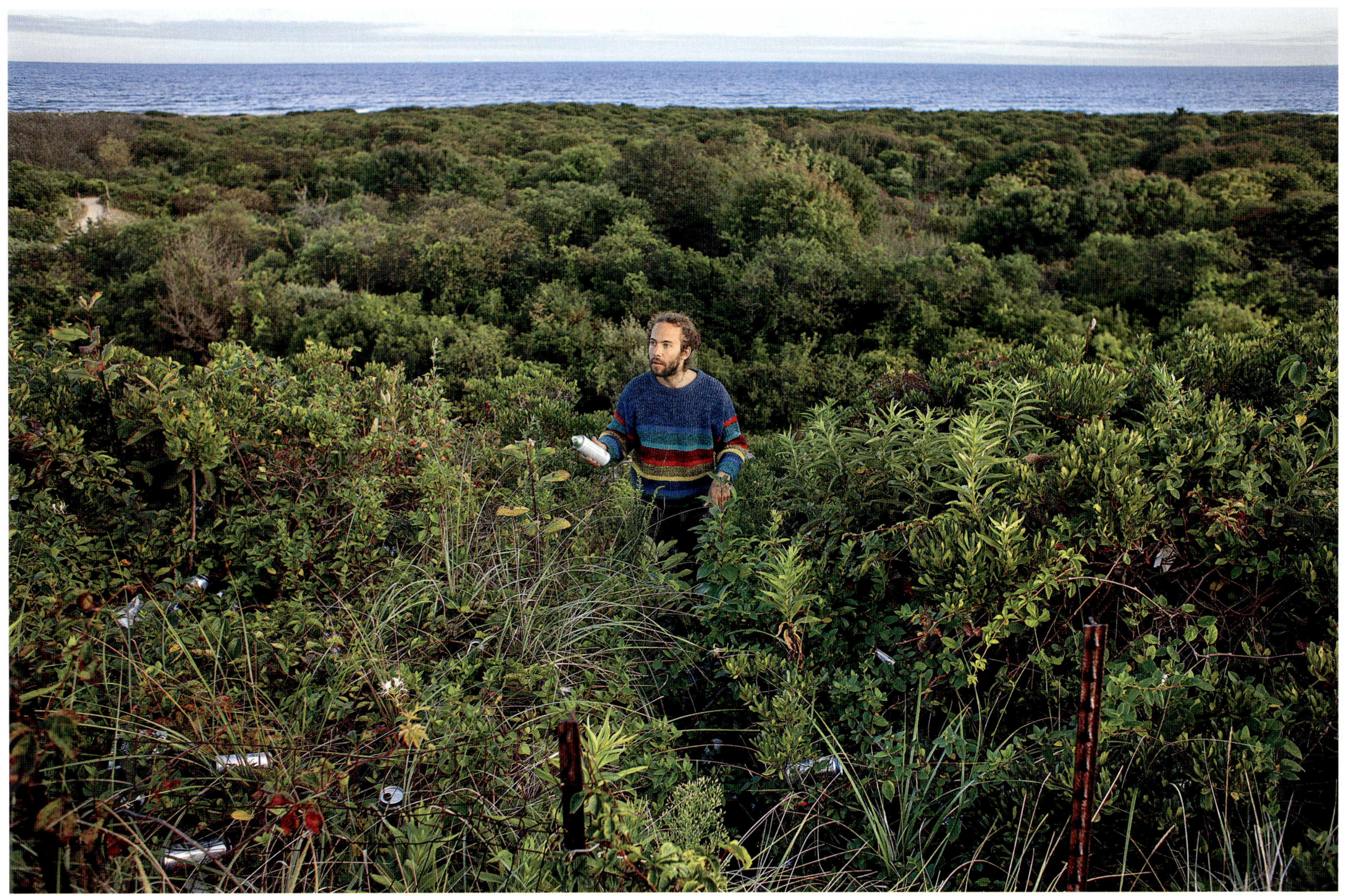

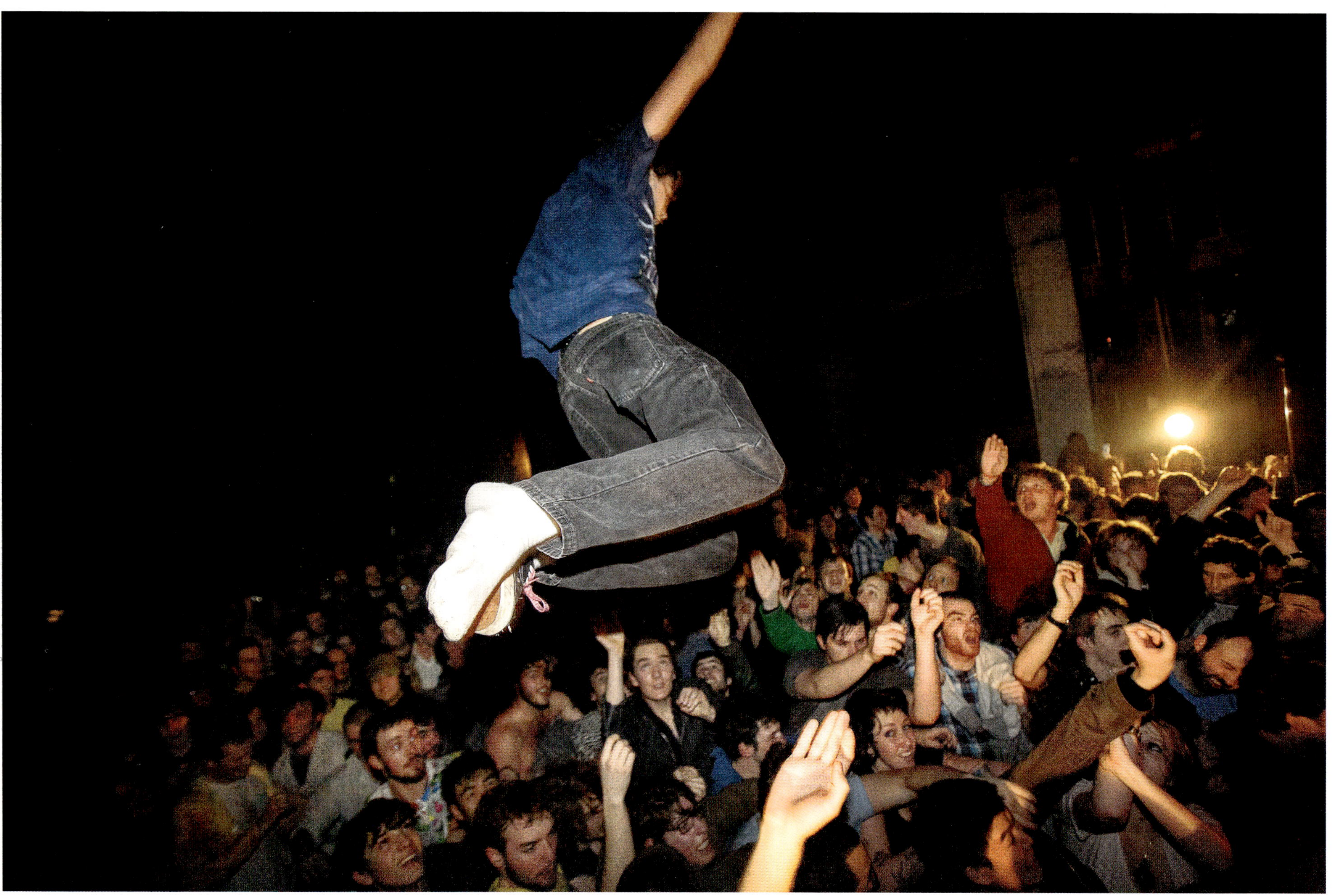

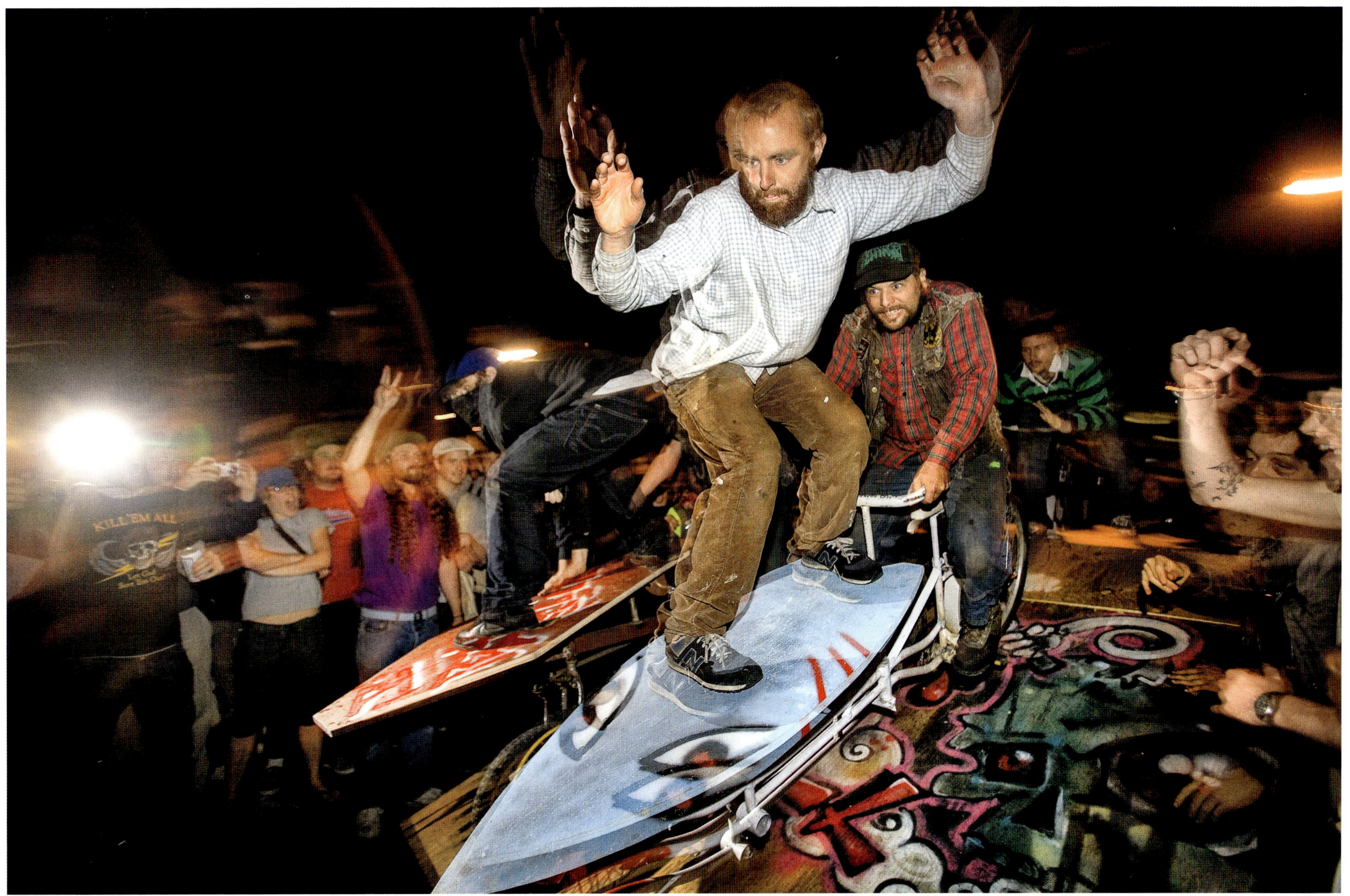

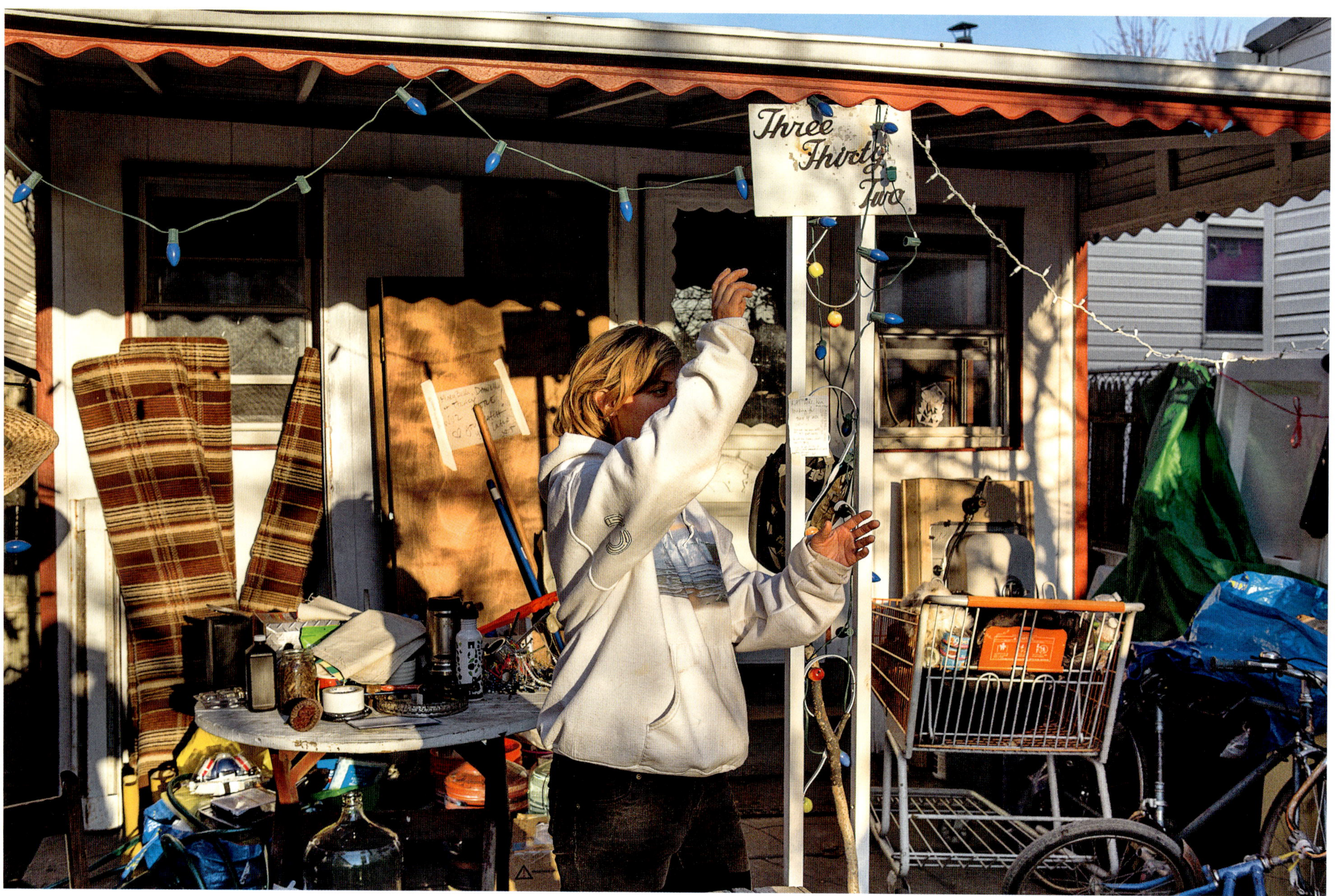
Three
Thirty
Two

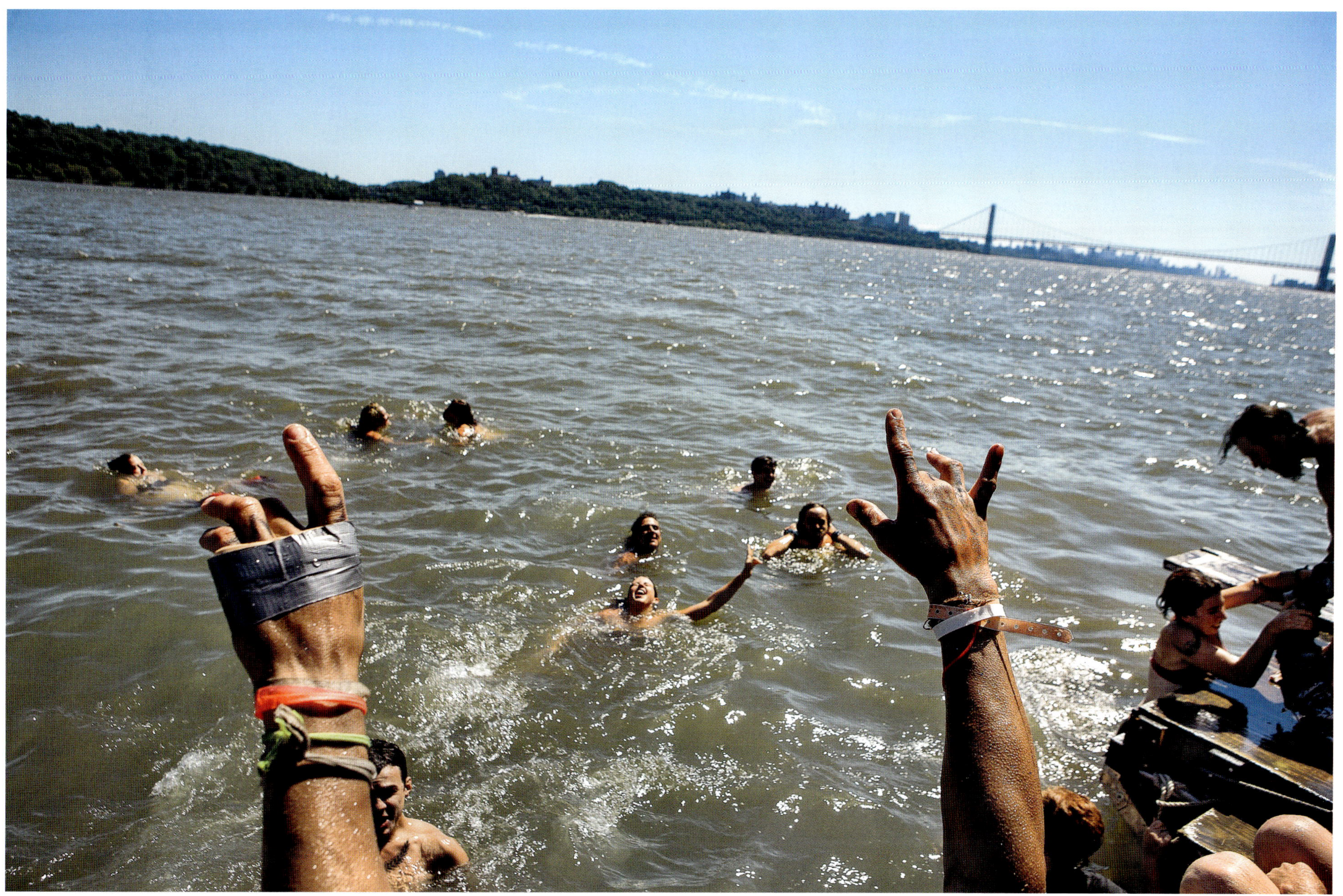

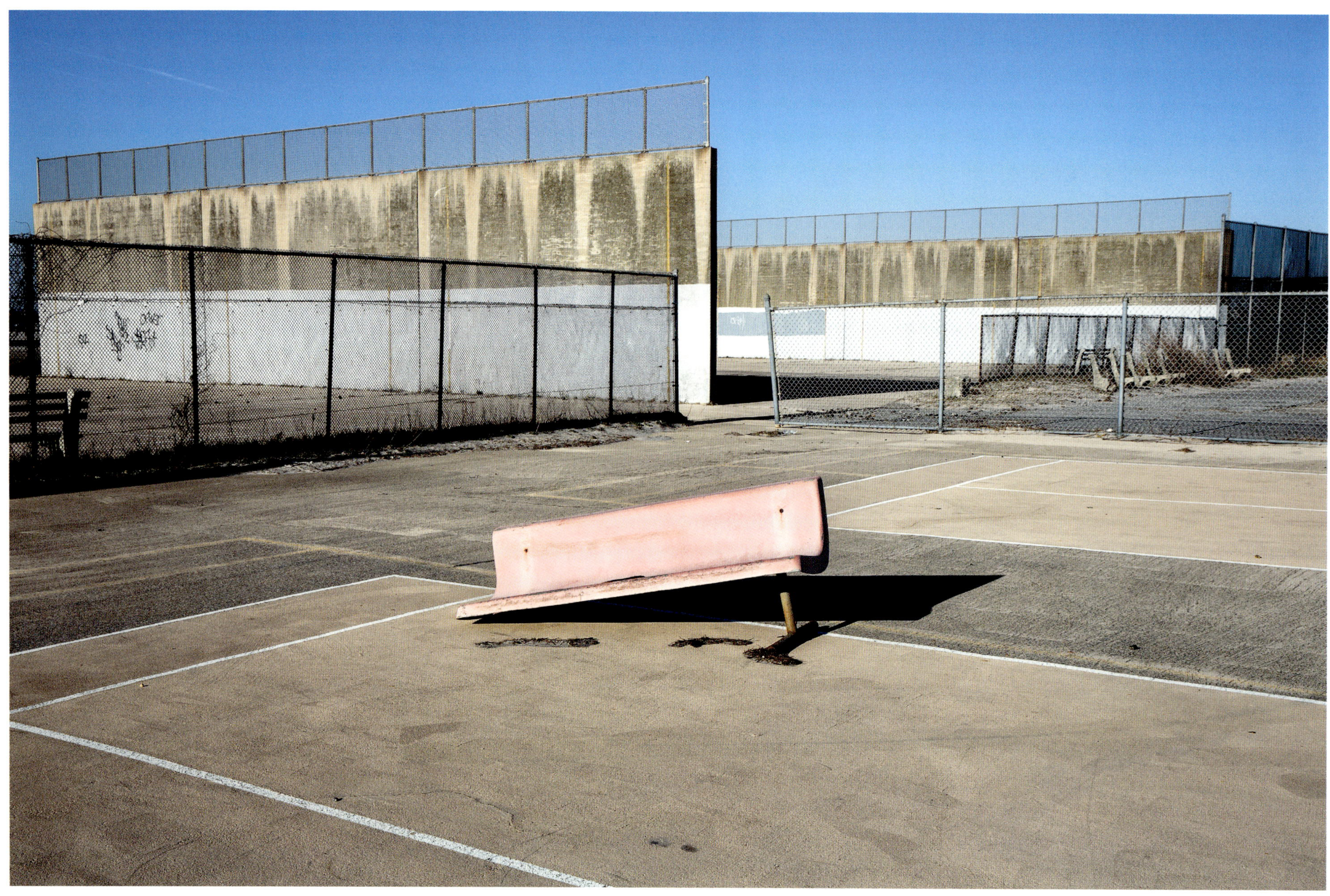

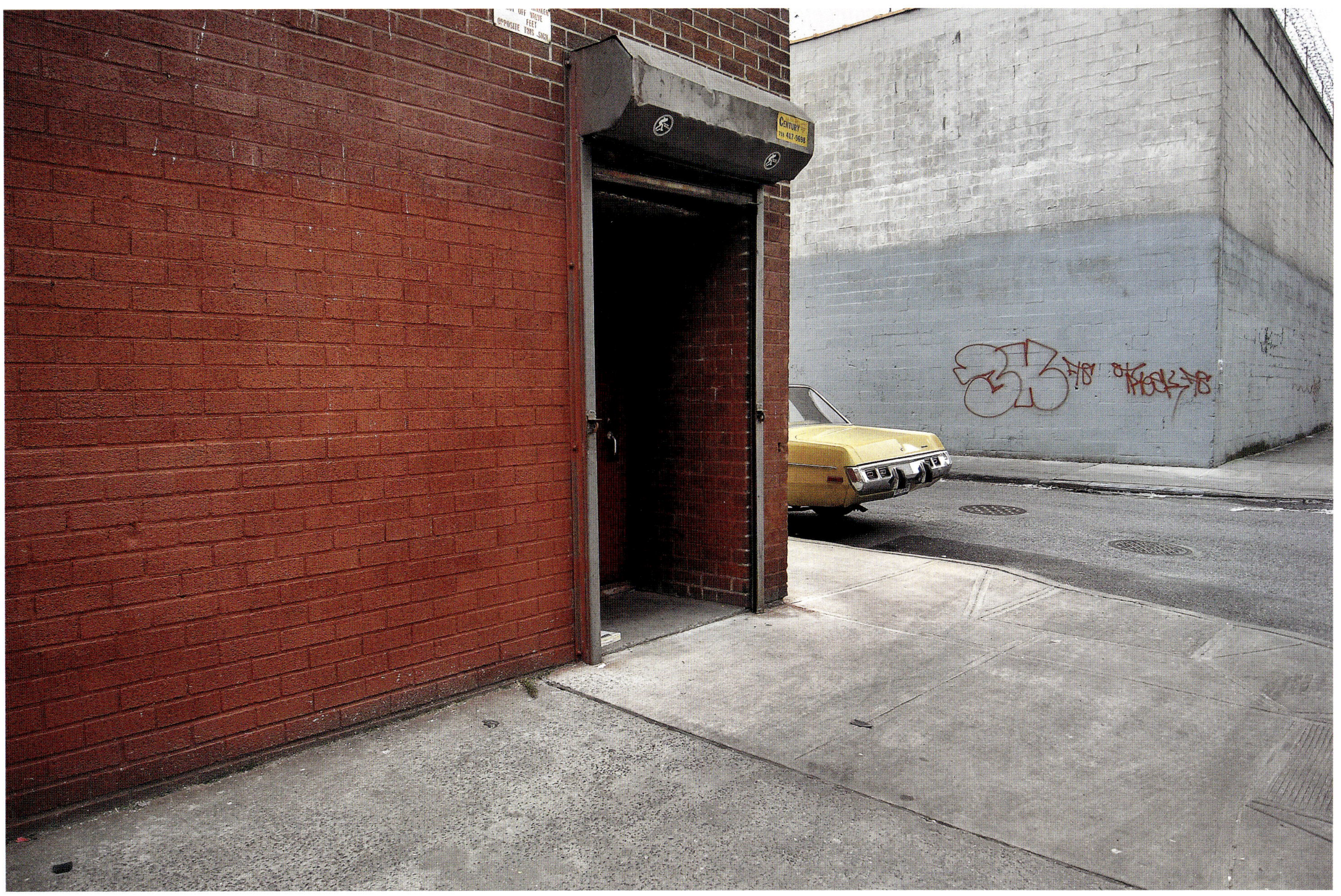

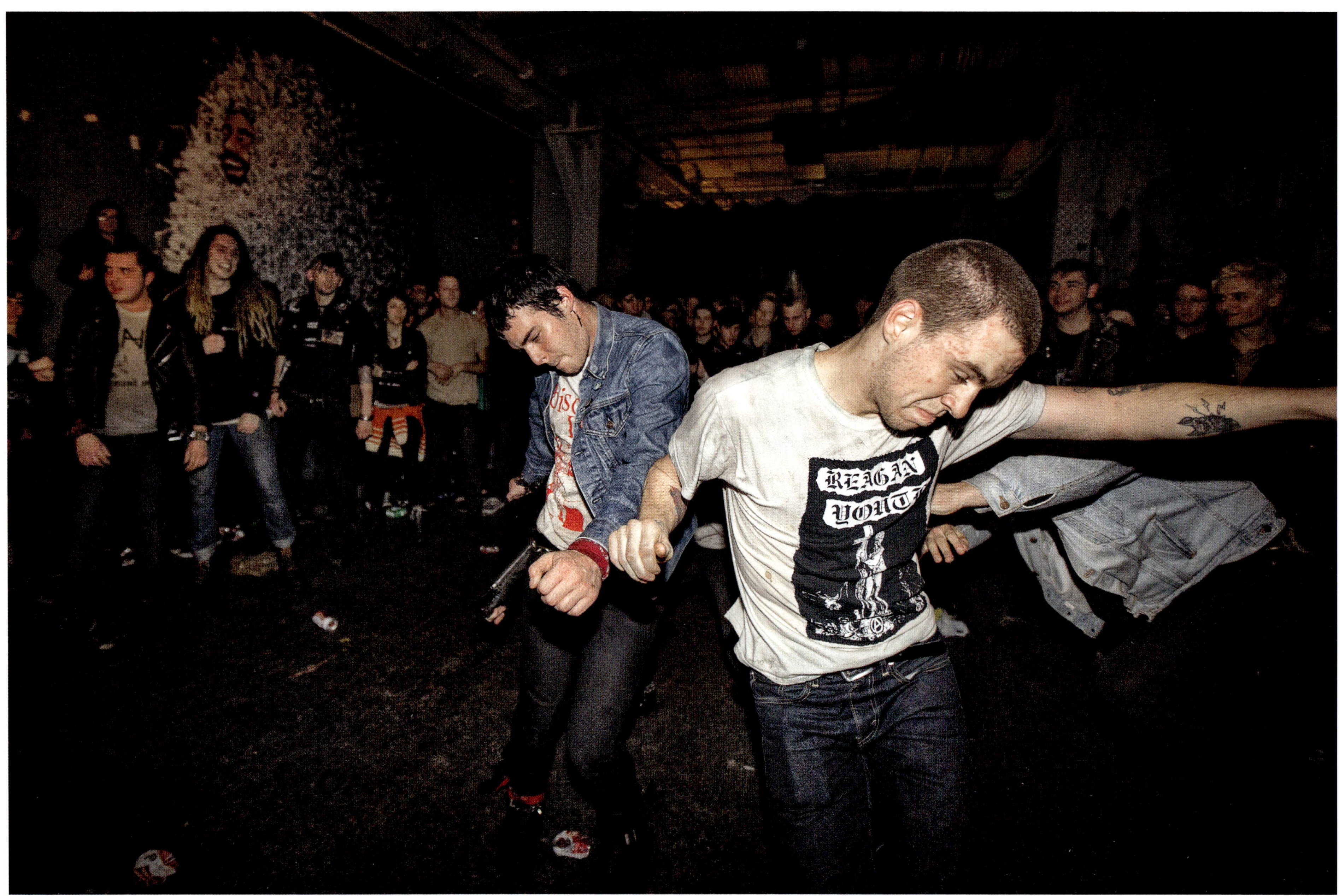

REAGAN
YOUTH

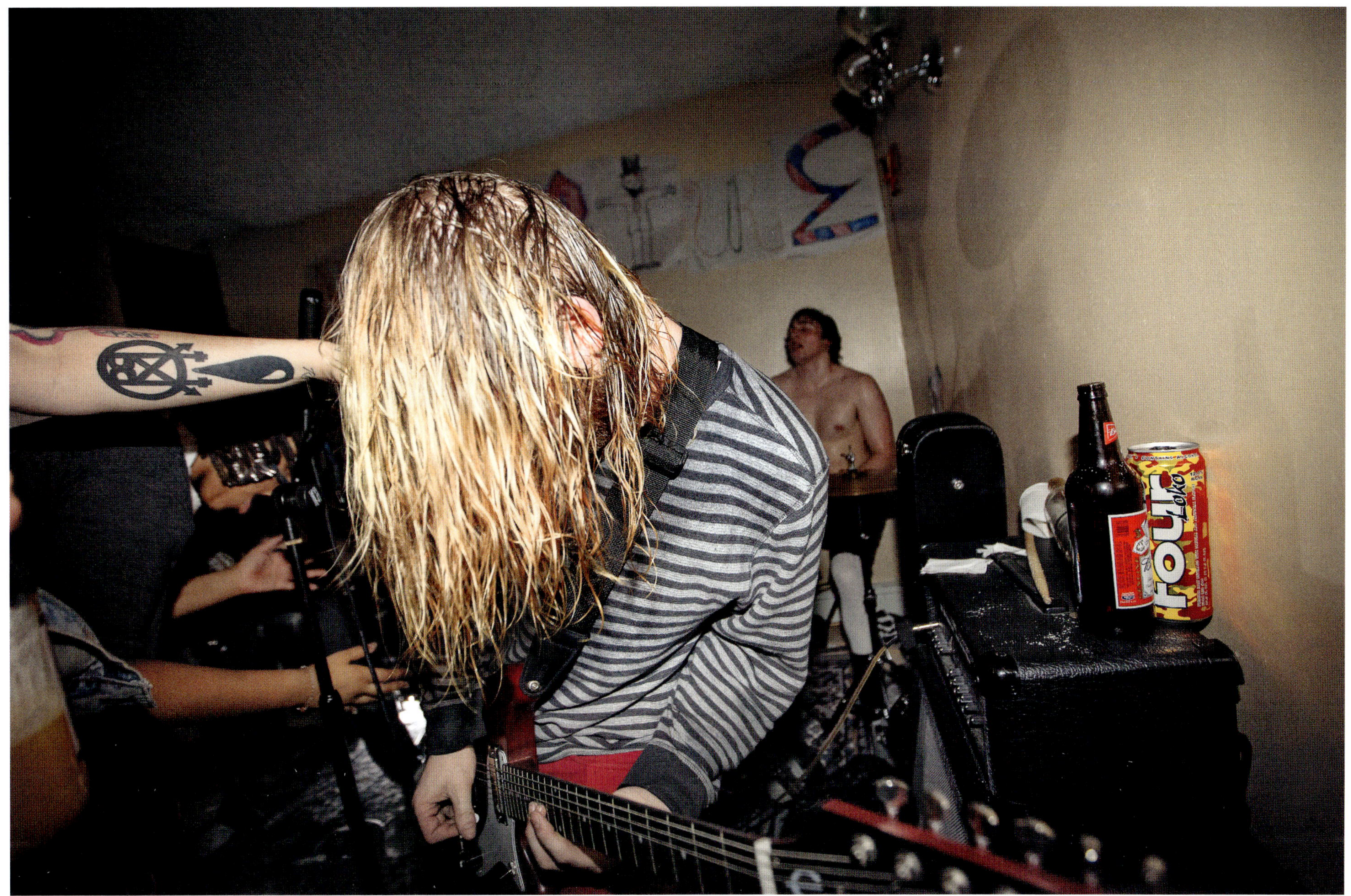

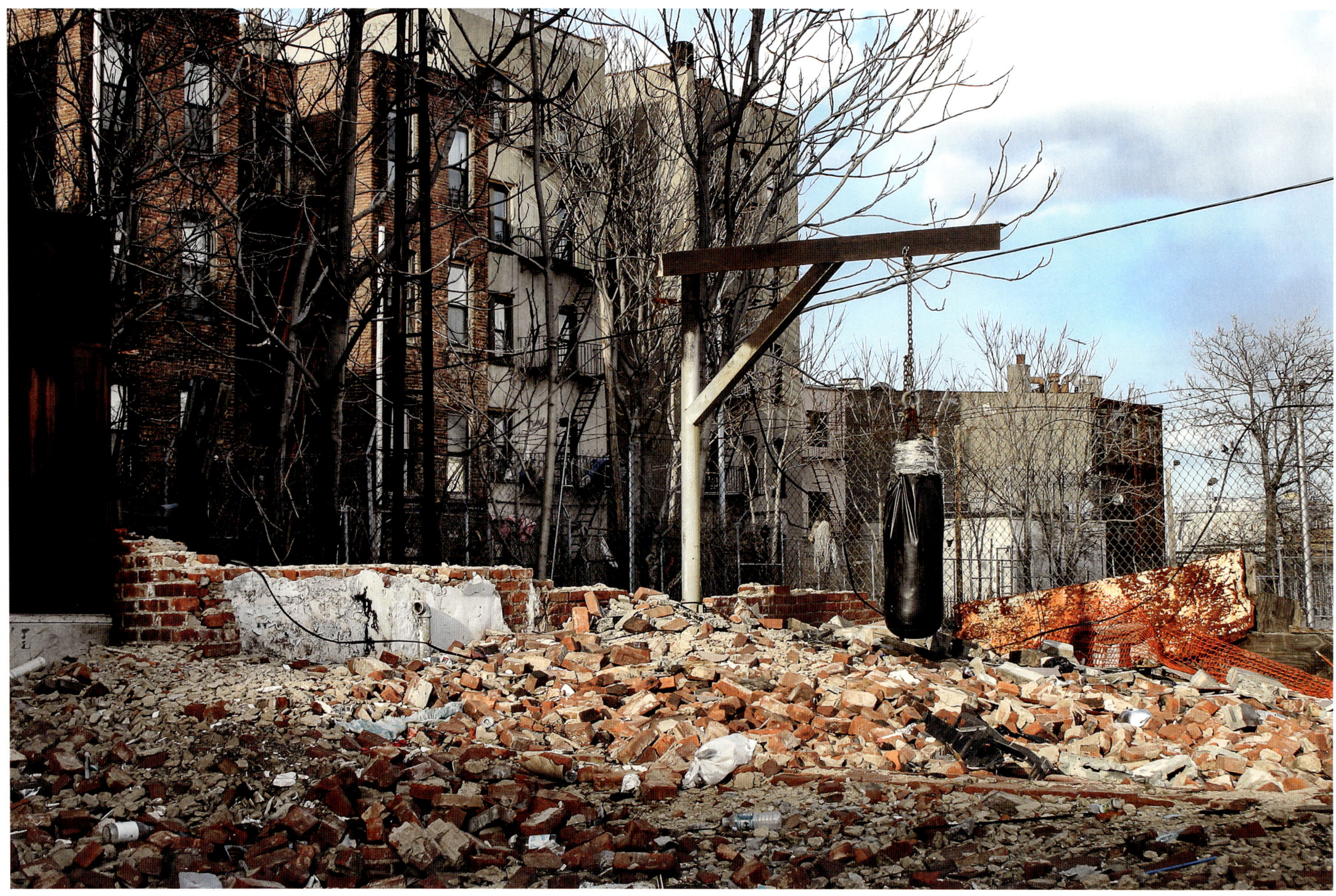

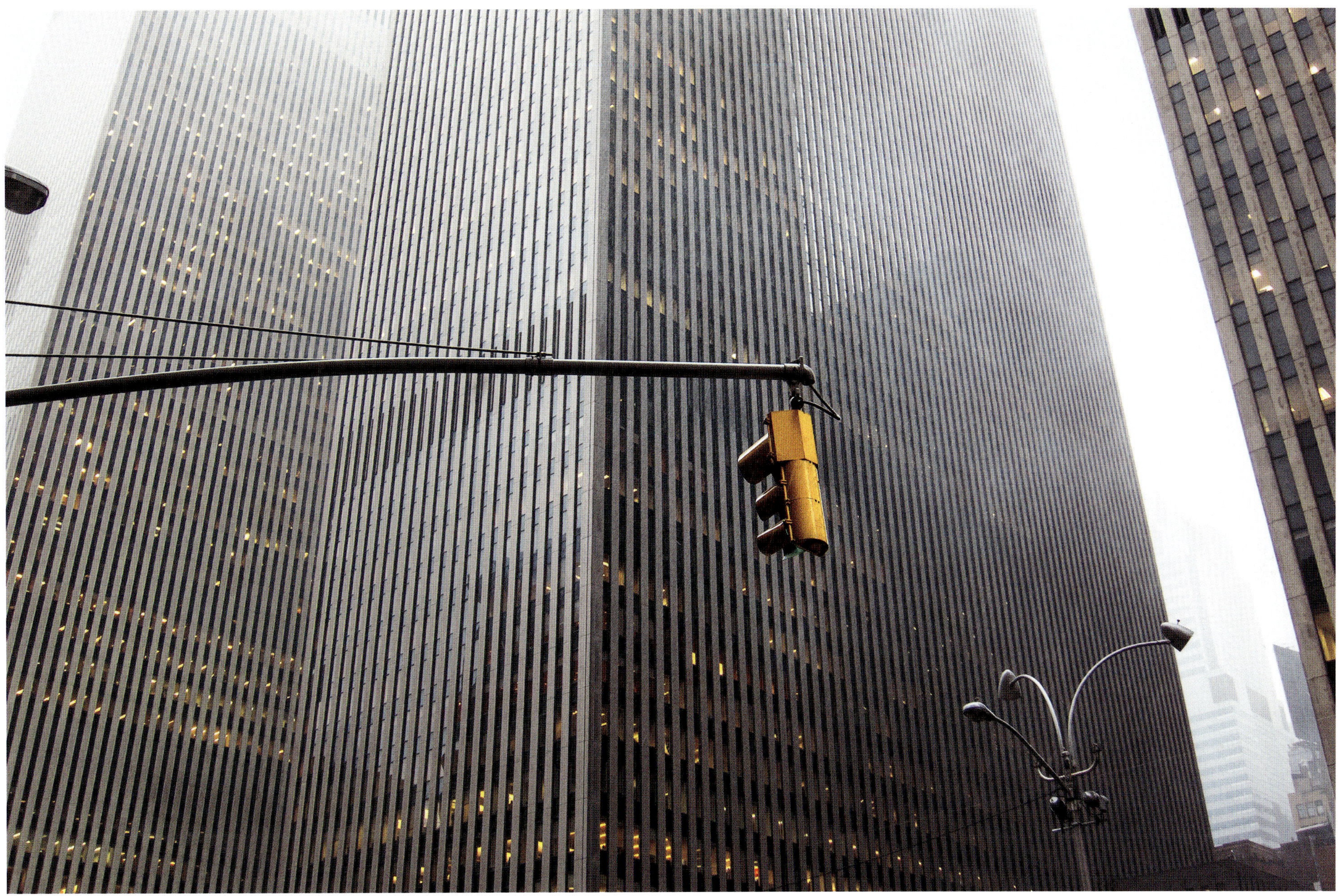

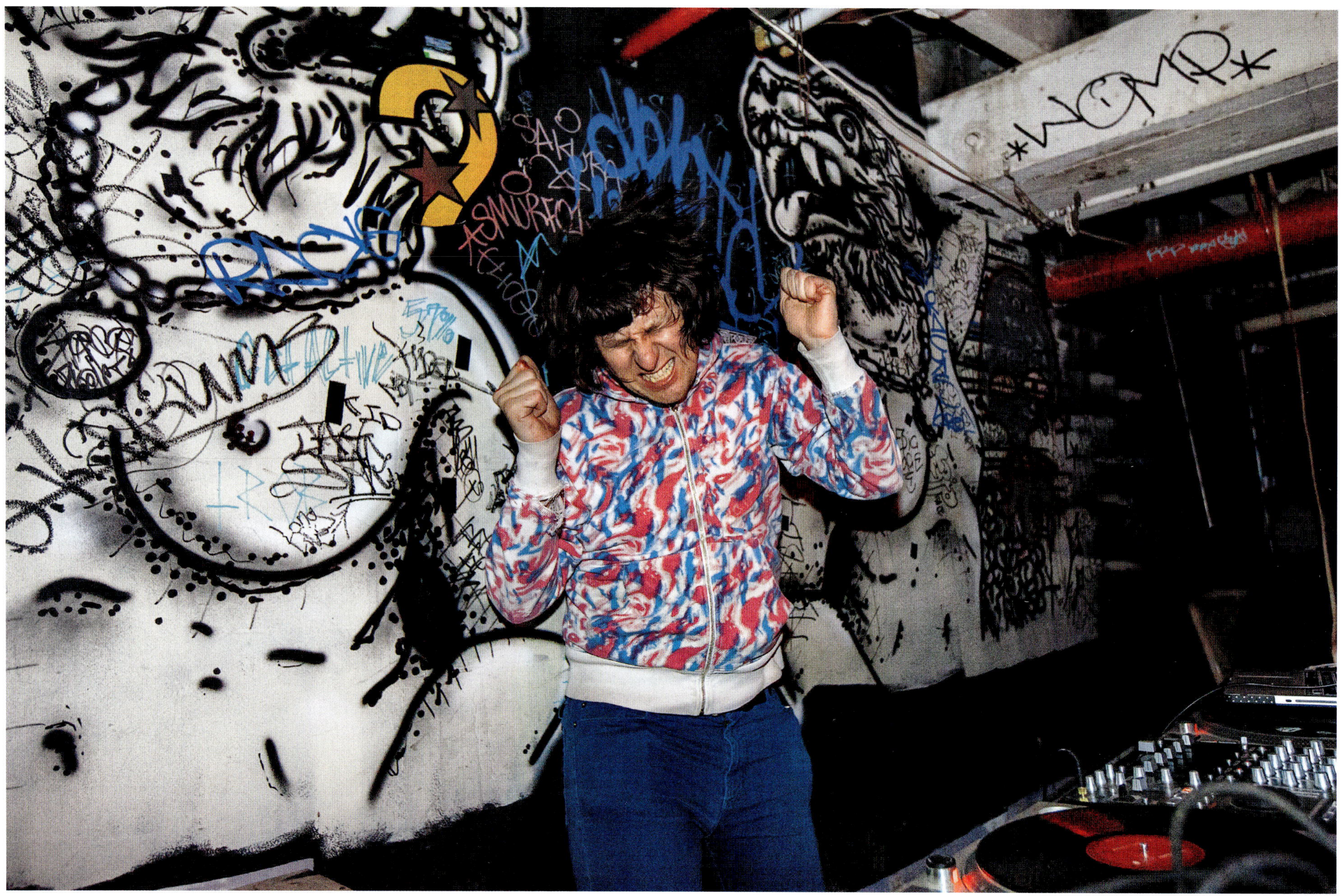
WOMP

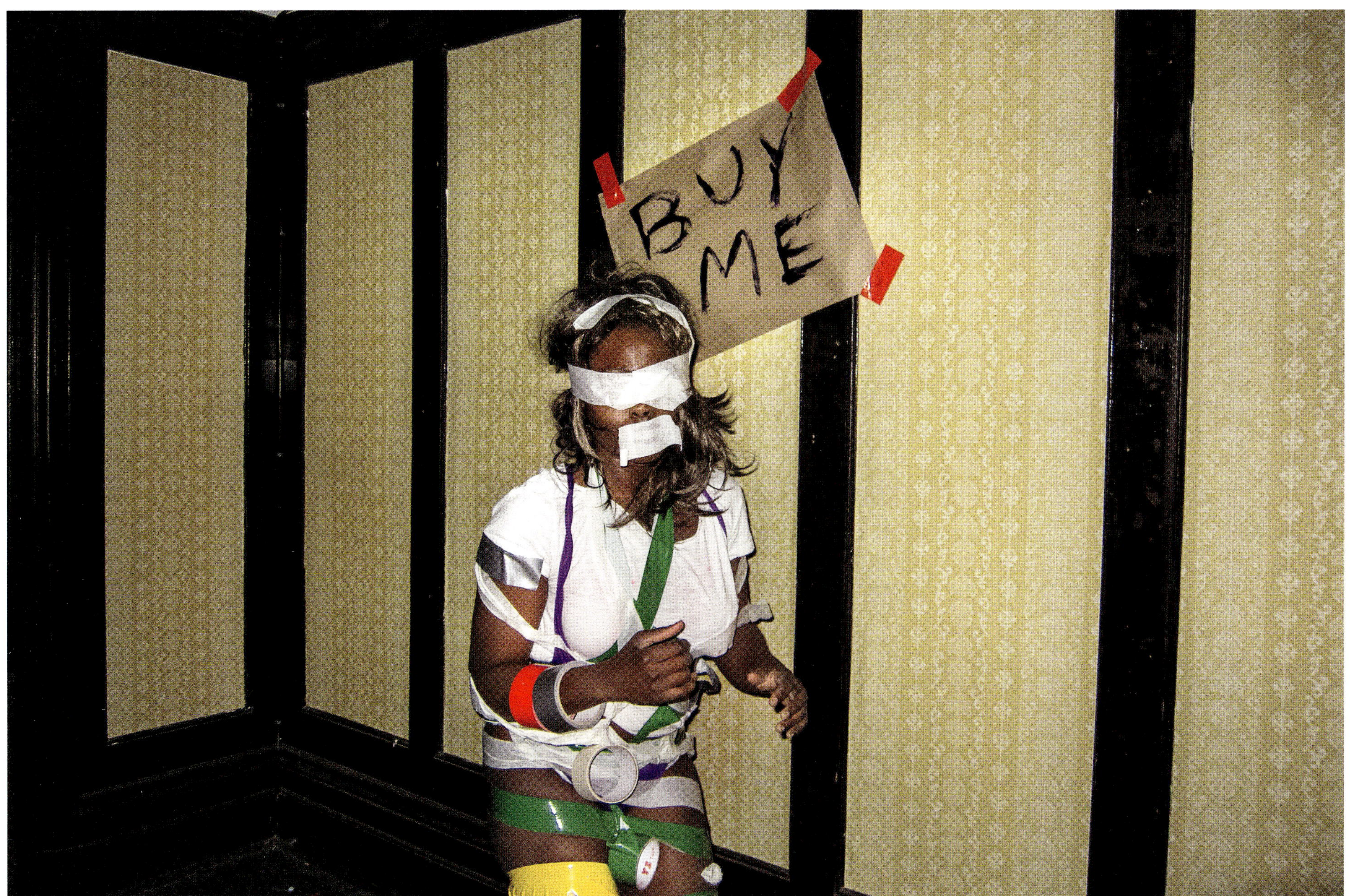
BUY
ME

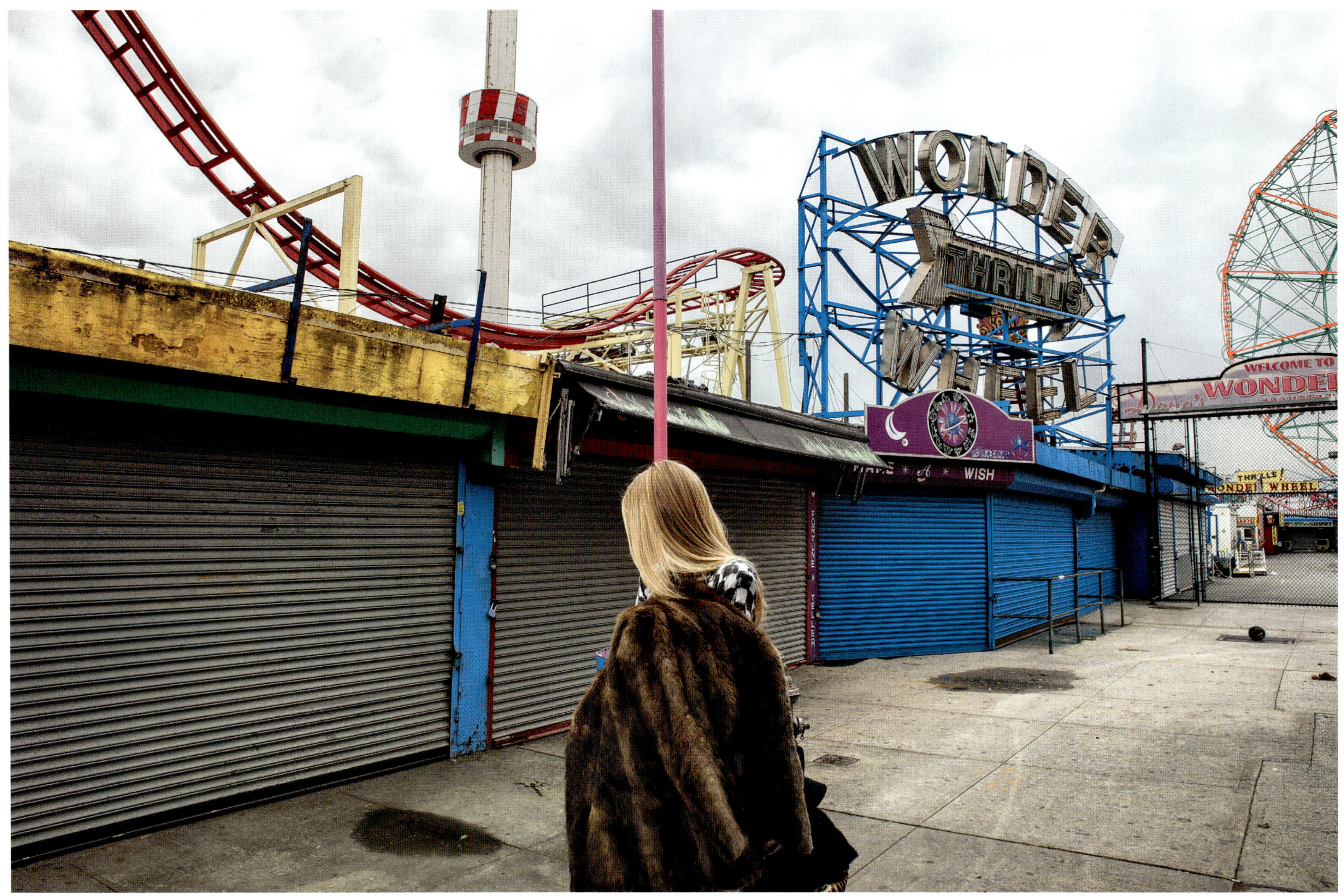

WONDER
THRILLS
WHEEL
MAKE A WISH
FORTUNE TELLER
WELCOME TO
WONDER
Deno's
THRILLS
WONDER WHEEL

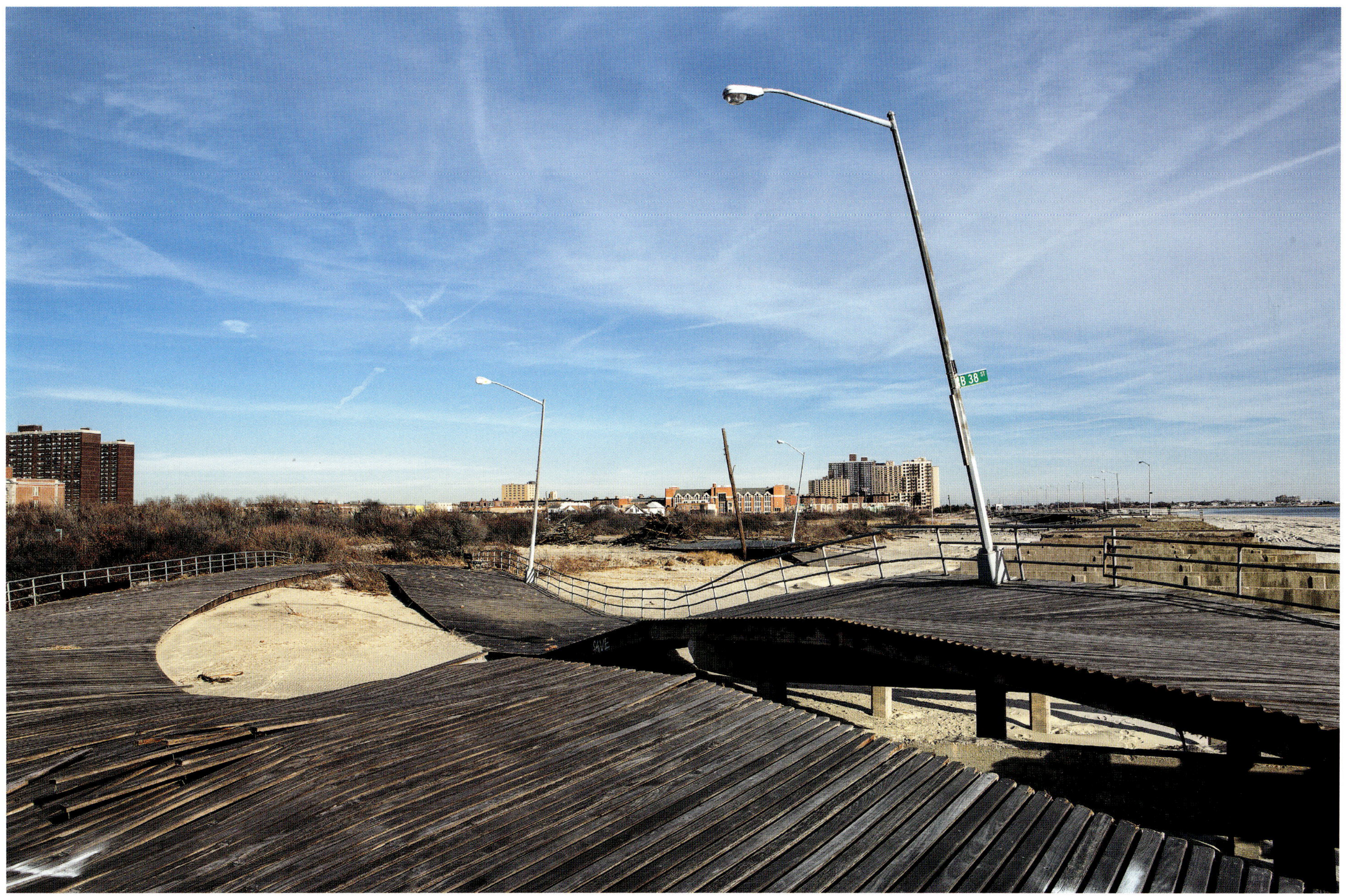
B 38 ST

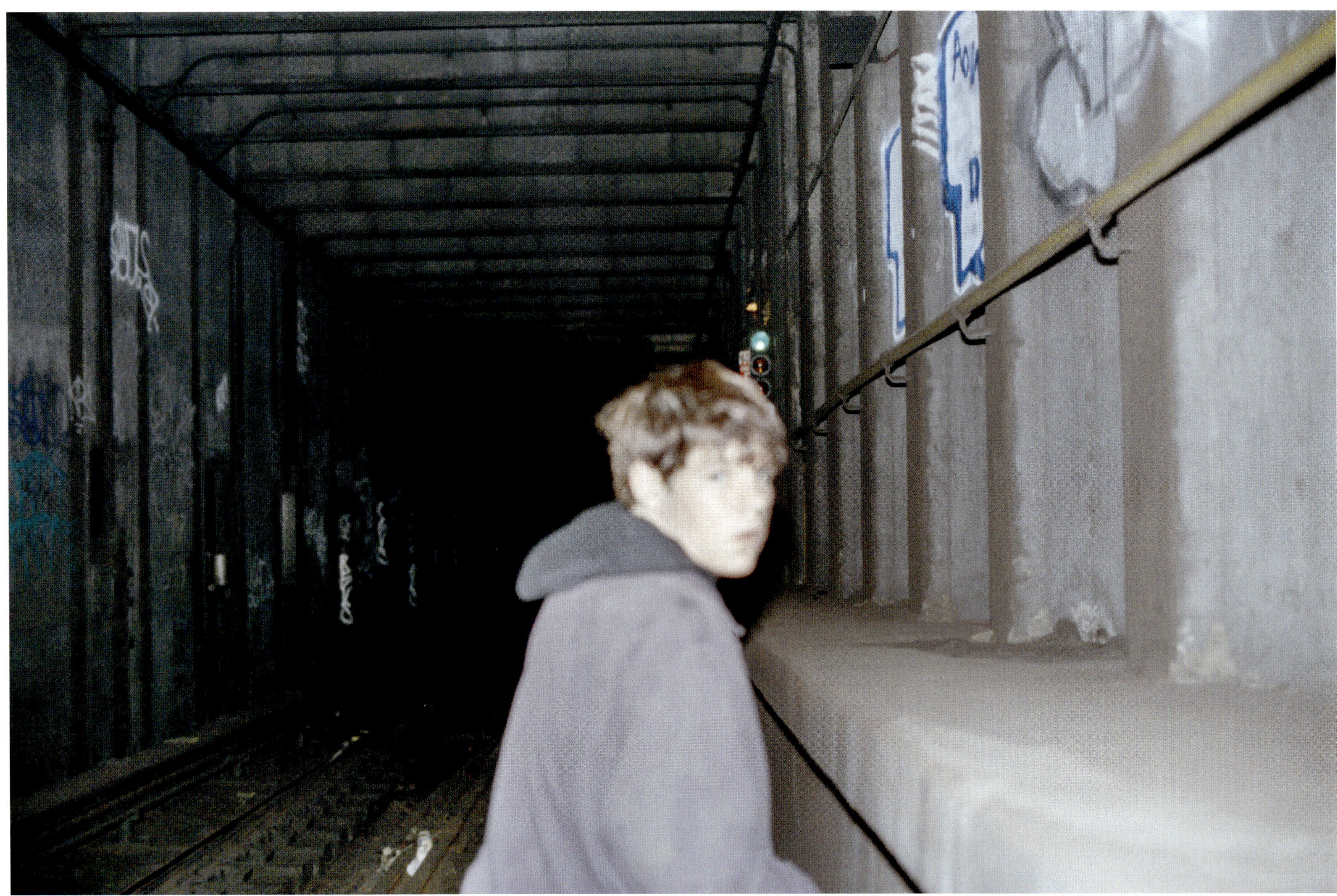

F-STOP G
IAN VANEK

Circa 1999, the bulletin board in the science building at Pratt Institute advertised a room on Kent Avenue off of Myrtle Avenue in Brooklyn. In my short dormitory career I had thrown a pretty great rager, and already managed to attract the attention of the FBI thanks to an out-of-town guest's conspiracy case. Having rapidly scorched my tiny environment, I set out on a quest to find the cheapest shithole I could rent. First stop: Tod Seelie's $300 storefront apartment.

The *zip zip zip zip* of an air compressor tightening and loosening car tires sang out at all hours. Boys headed to elementary school screamed wrestler's names at 7 A.M. The girls just screamed. Our apartment wasn't without charm though, and meeting Tod seems a great gift today. I would borrow his scanner to make issues of my zine, and he even taught me how to scan slides.

Our friendship has had ups and downs since then, but Tod's unwavering vision is ever-expanding. His photos of early Japanther tours no doubt lent us great credibility, and for that we are forever thankful. Those shows were held in sweaty bars, alleyways, and basements. They all had a kind of wild, soulful energy—even the empty ones. Anything could happen and anyone could attend. Of course, our friends would come. Having a photographer present was never my choice in these situations; I thought it would change the shows in some way. But Tod took really beautiful, chaotic photos because he lived and walked many of the same paths we walked. He, too, was (and is) performing, in a way.

Ian Vanek is one half of Japanther, a collaborative sound and visual art project with Matt Reilly. The band formed at Pratt Institute in 2001, and was featured in the 2006 Whitney Biennial, the 2011 Venice Biennale, and the Museum of Modern Art in 2013. He has collaborated with a diverse pool of artists such as Gelitin, Dan Graham, Raymond Pettibon, Aïda Ruilova, Kelly Nipper, and Spank Rock.

THOSE SHOWS WERE HELD IN SWEATY BARS, ALLEYWAYS, AND BASEMENTS. THEY ALL HAD A KIND OF WILD, SOULFUL ENERGY—EVEN THE EMPTY ONES.

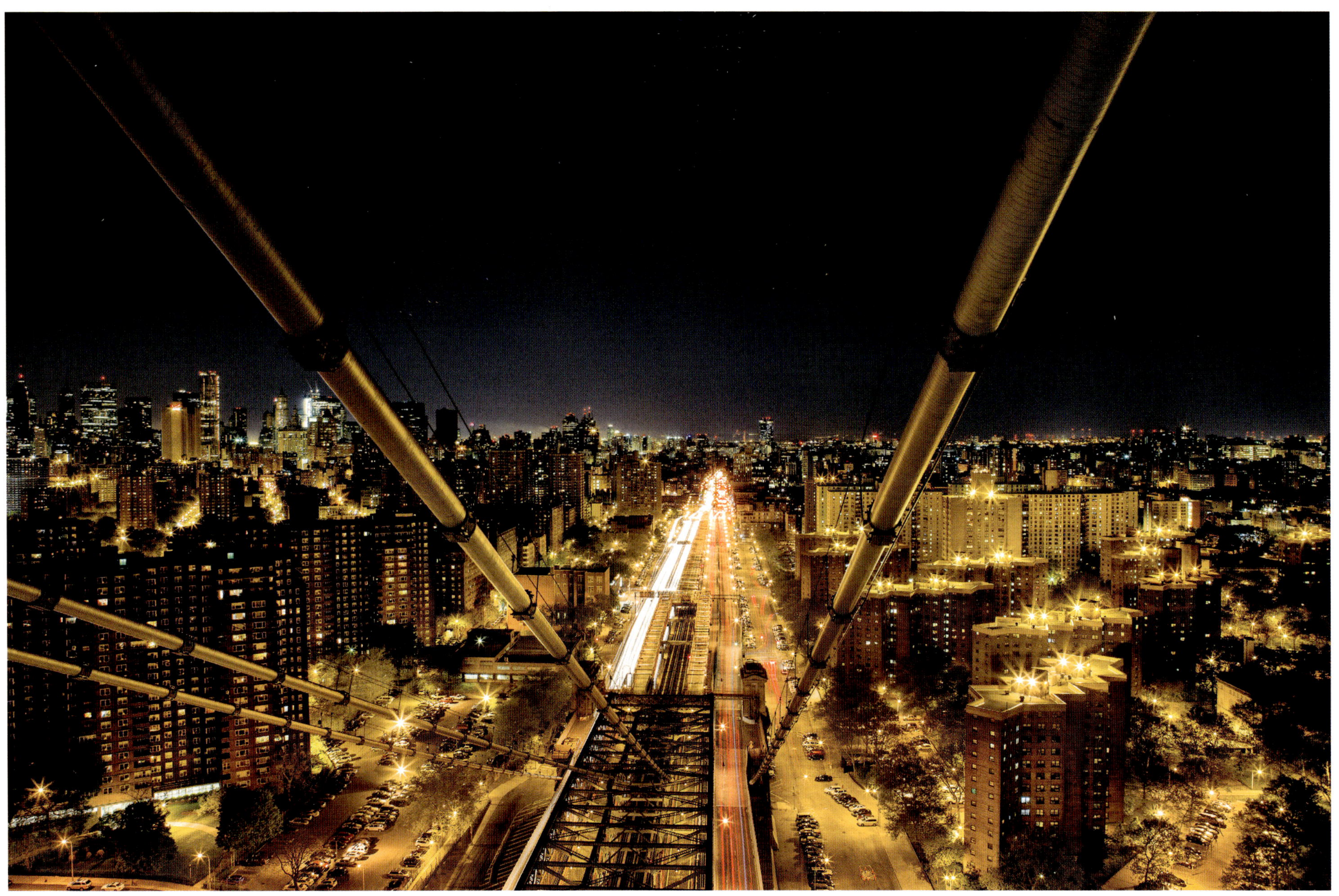

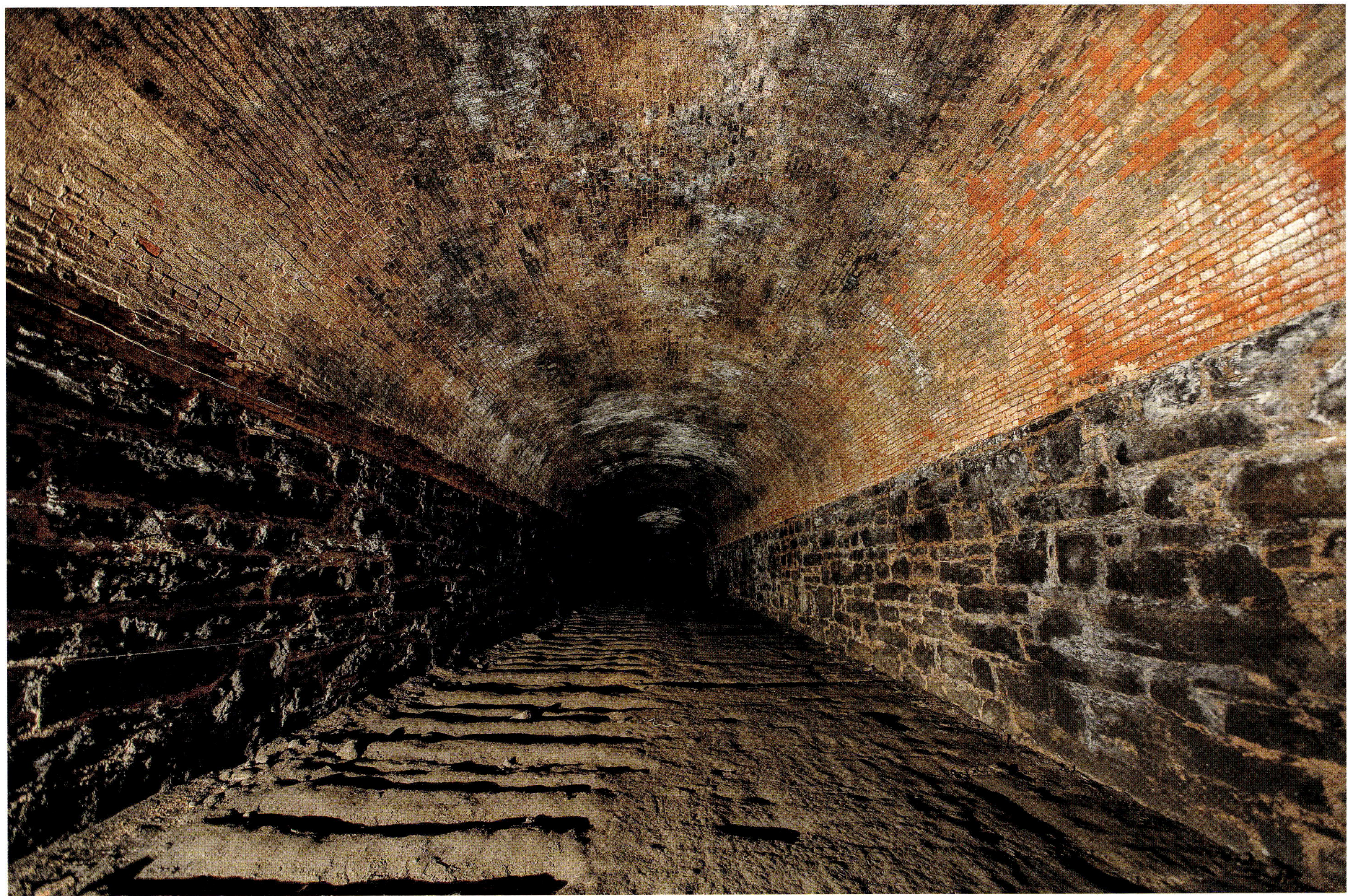

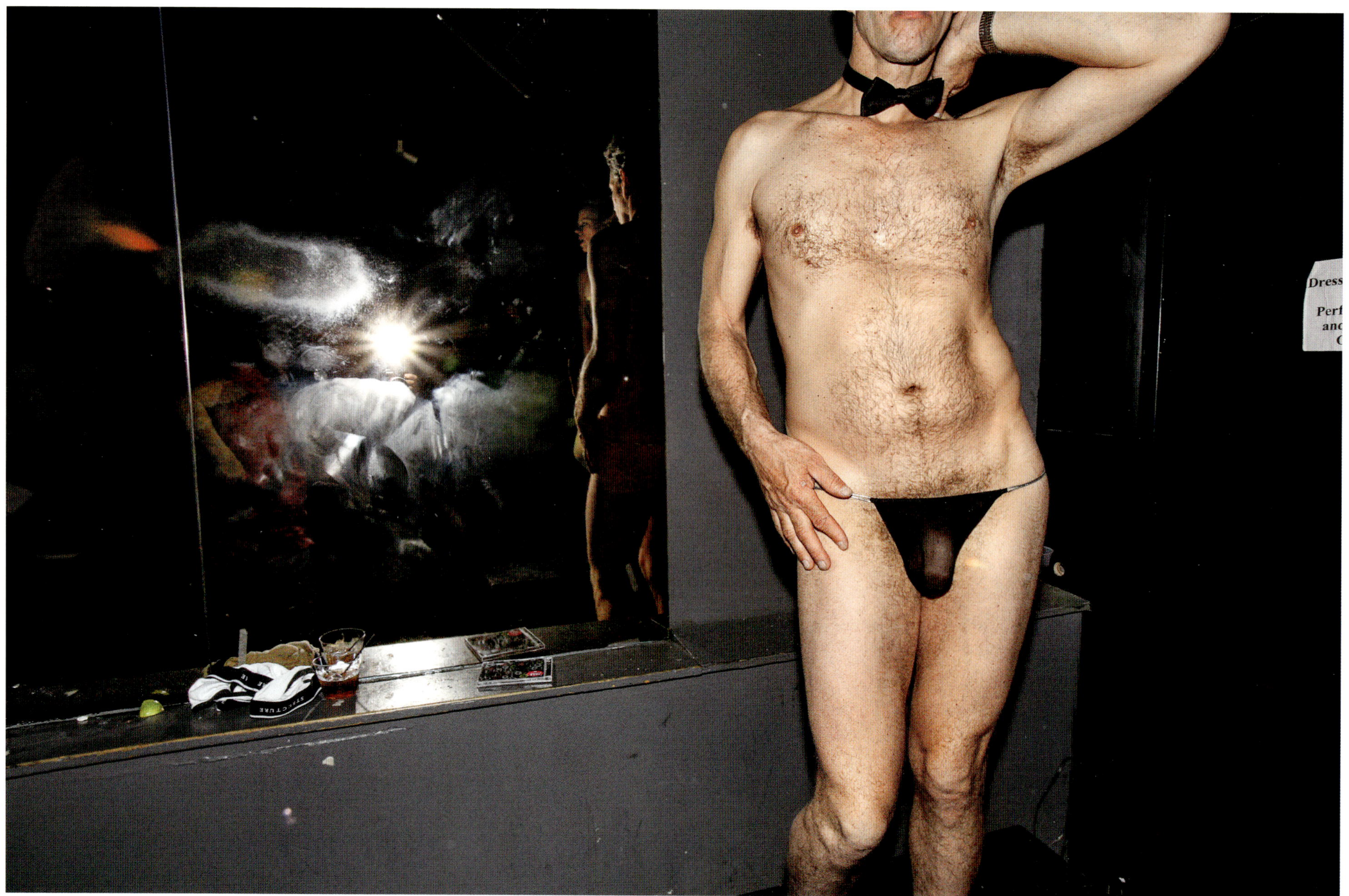

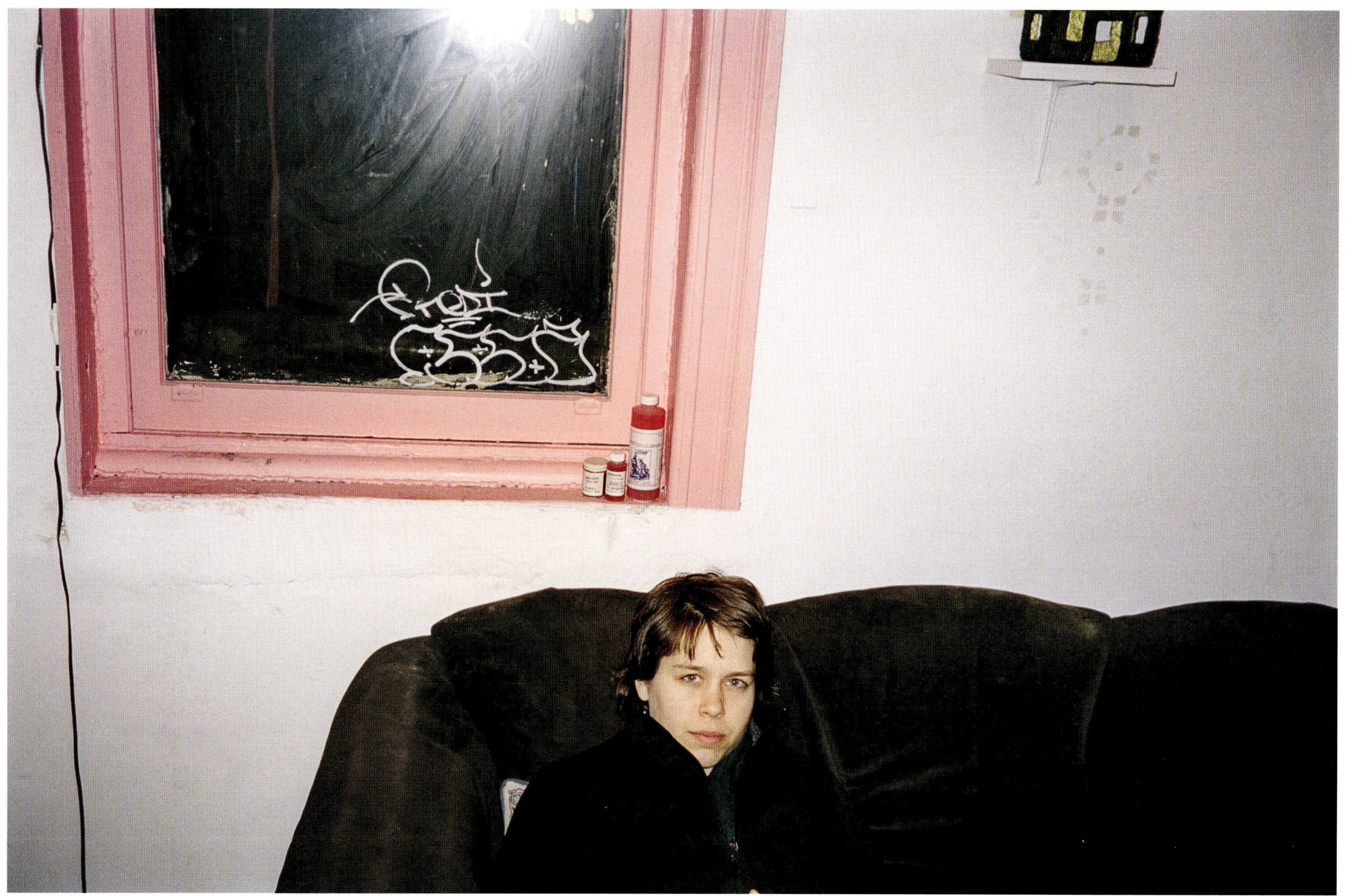

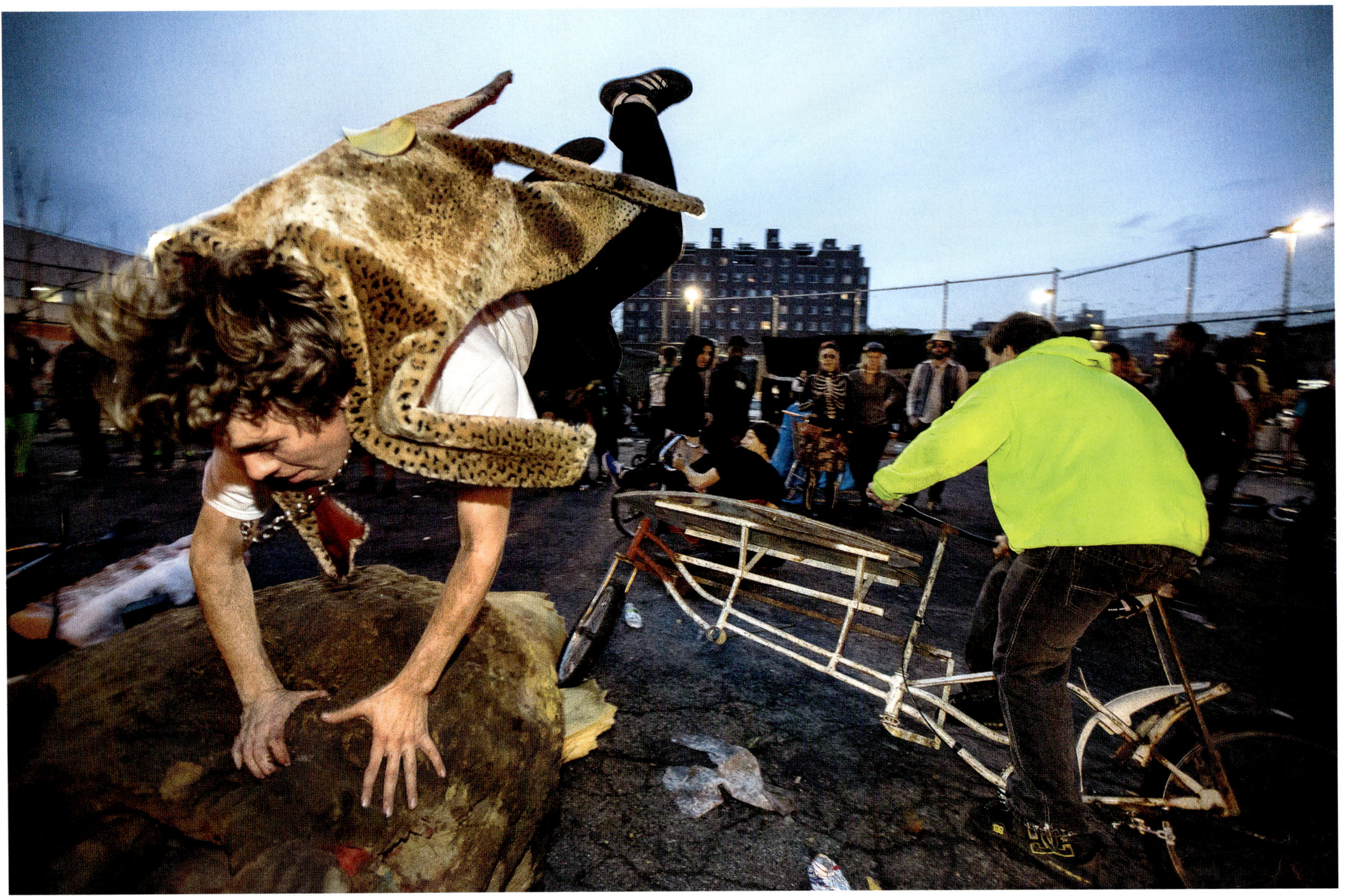

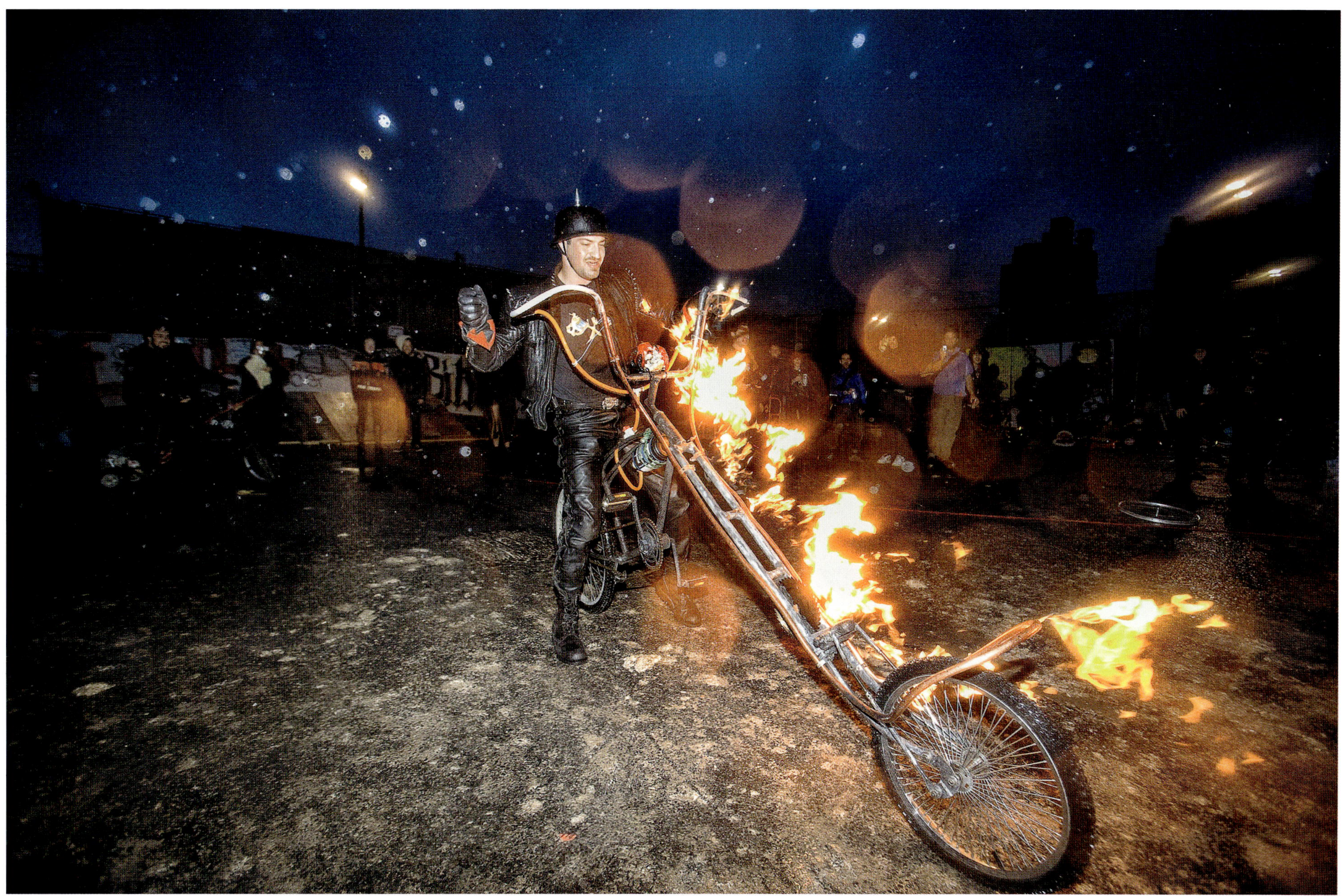

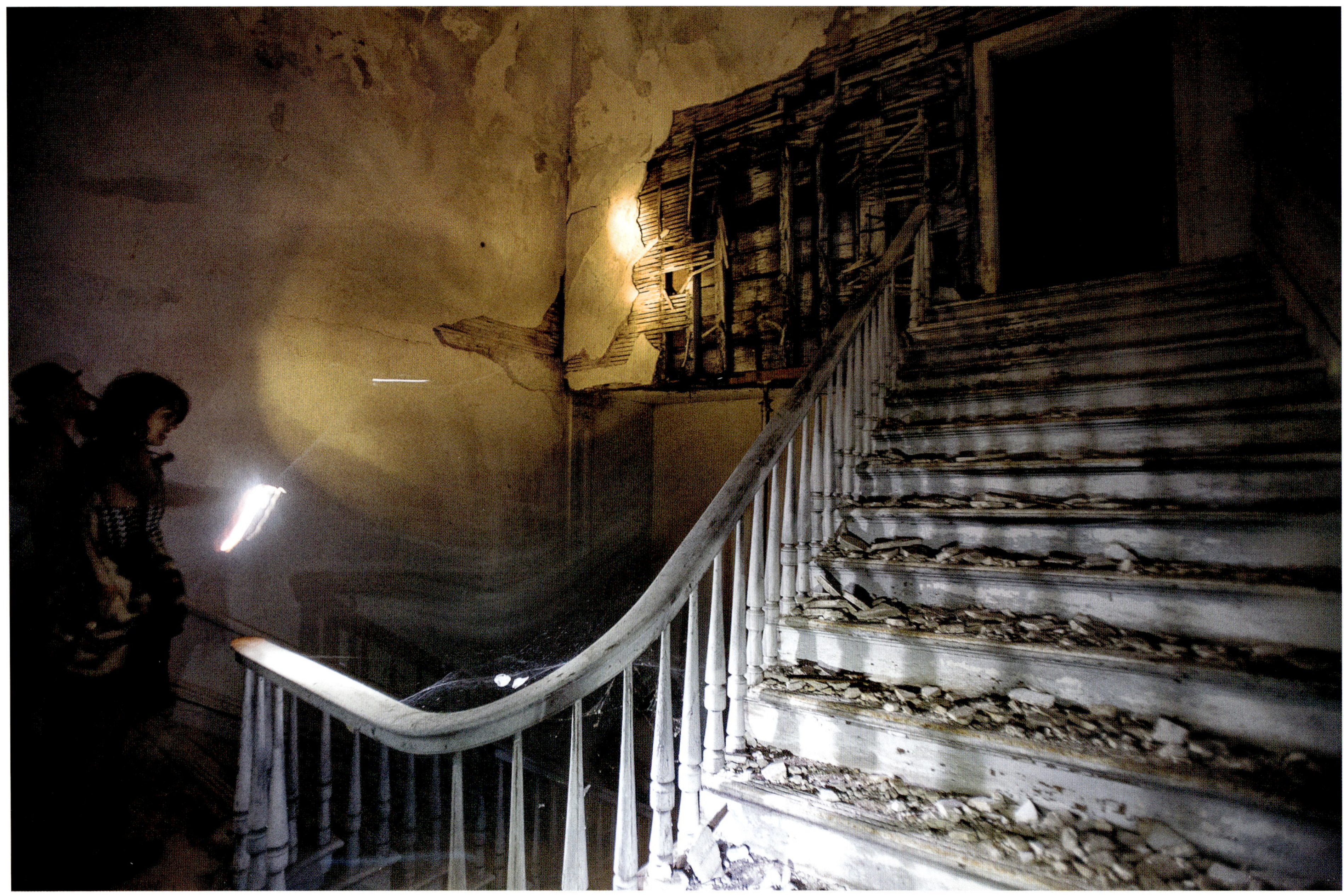

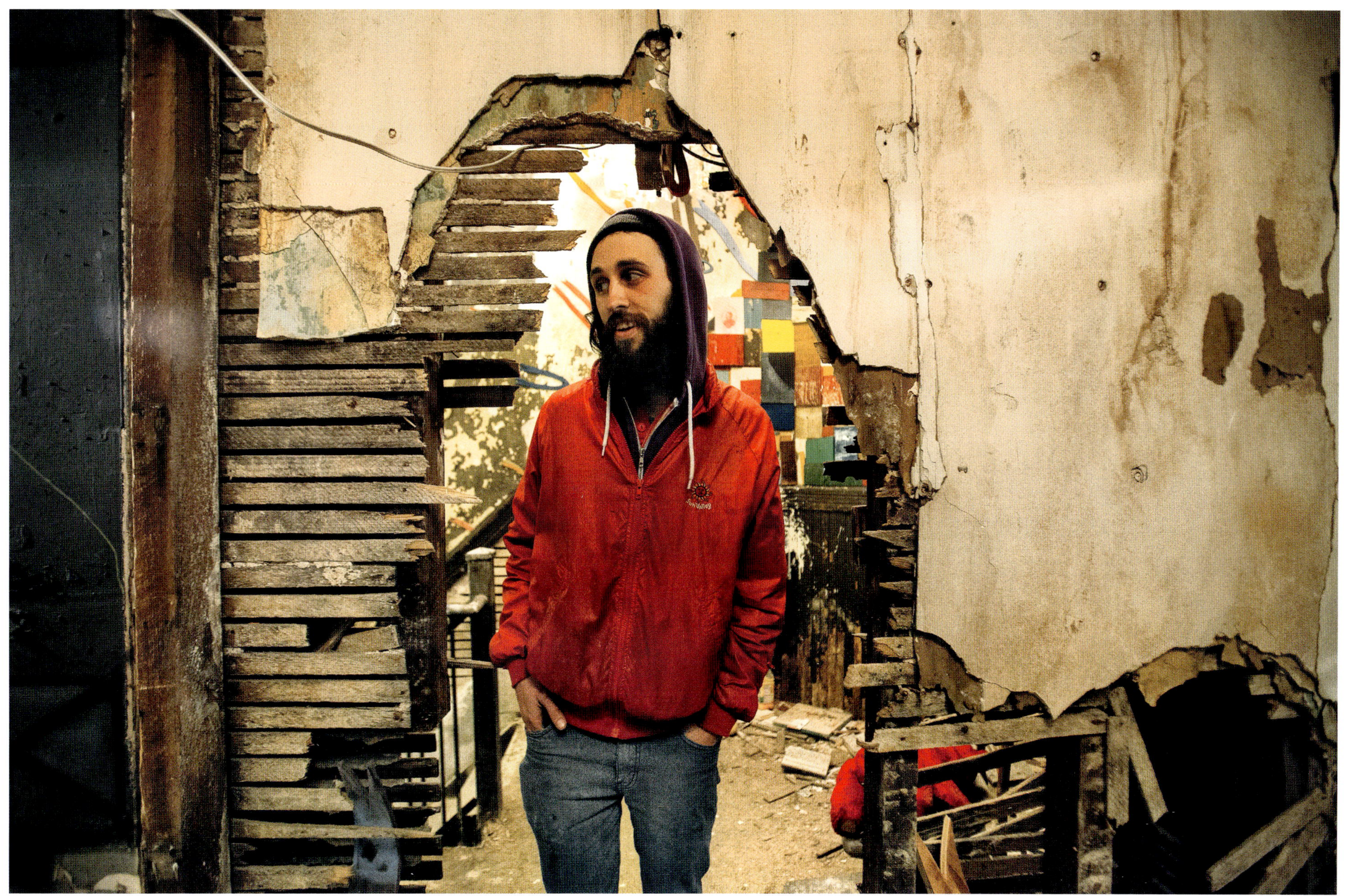

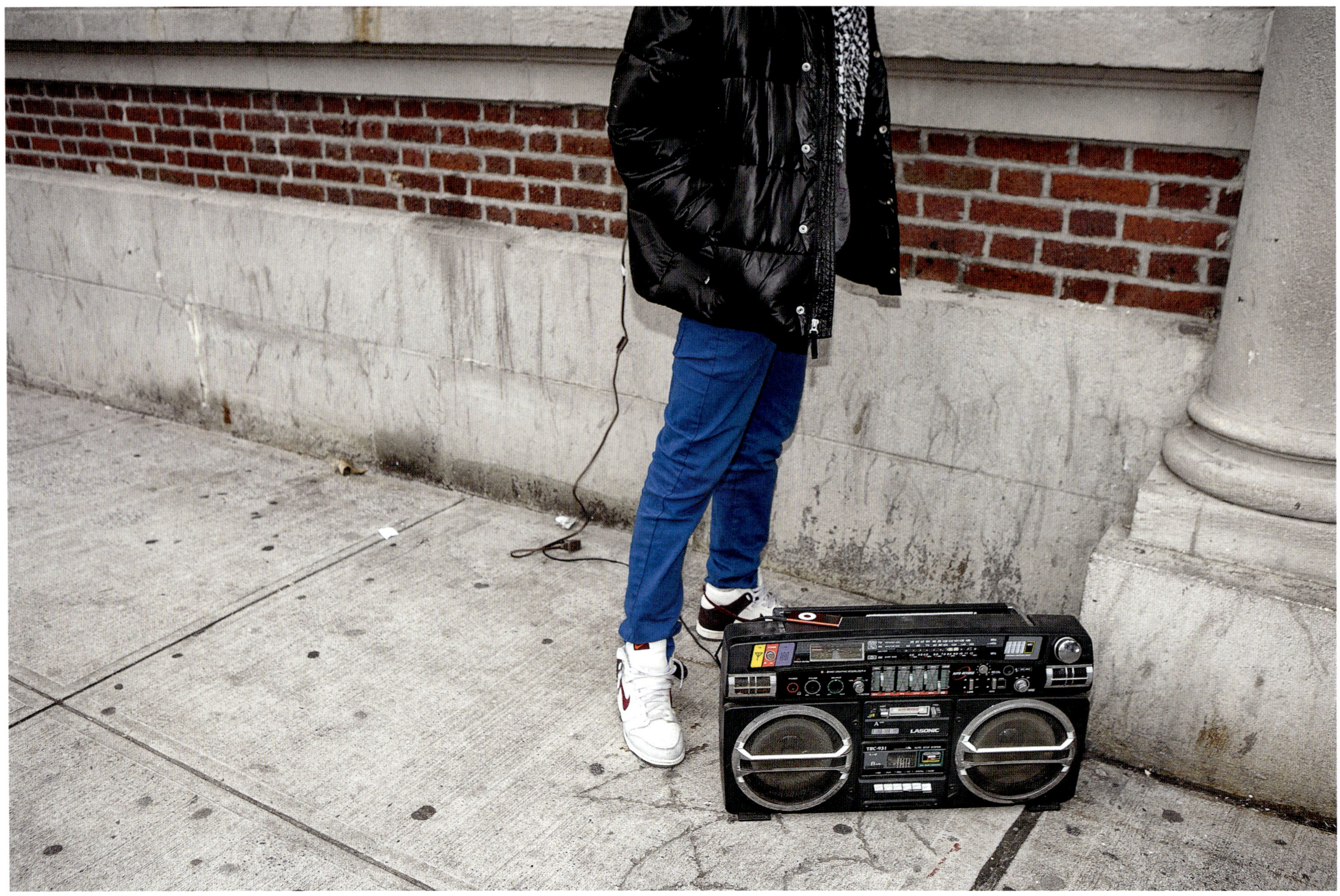

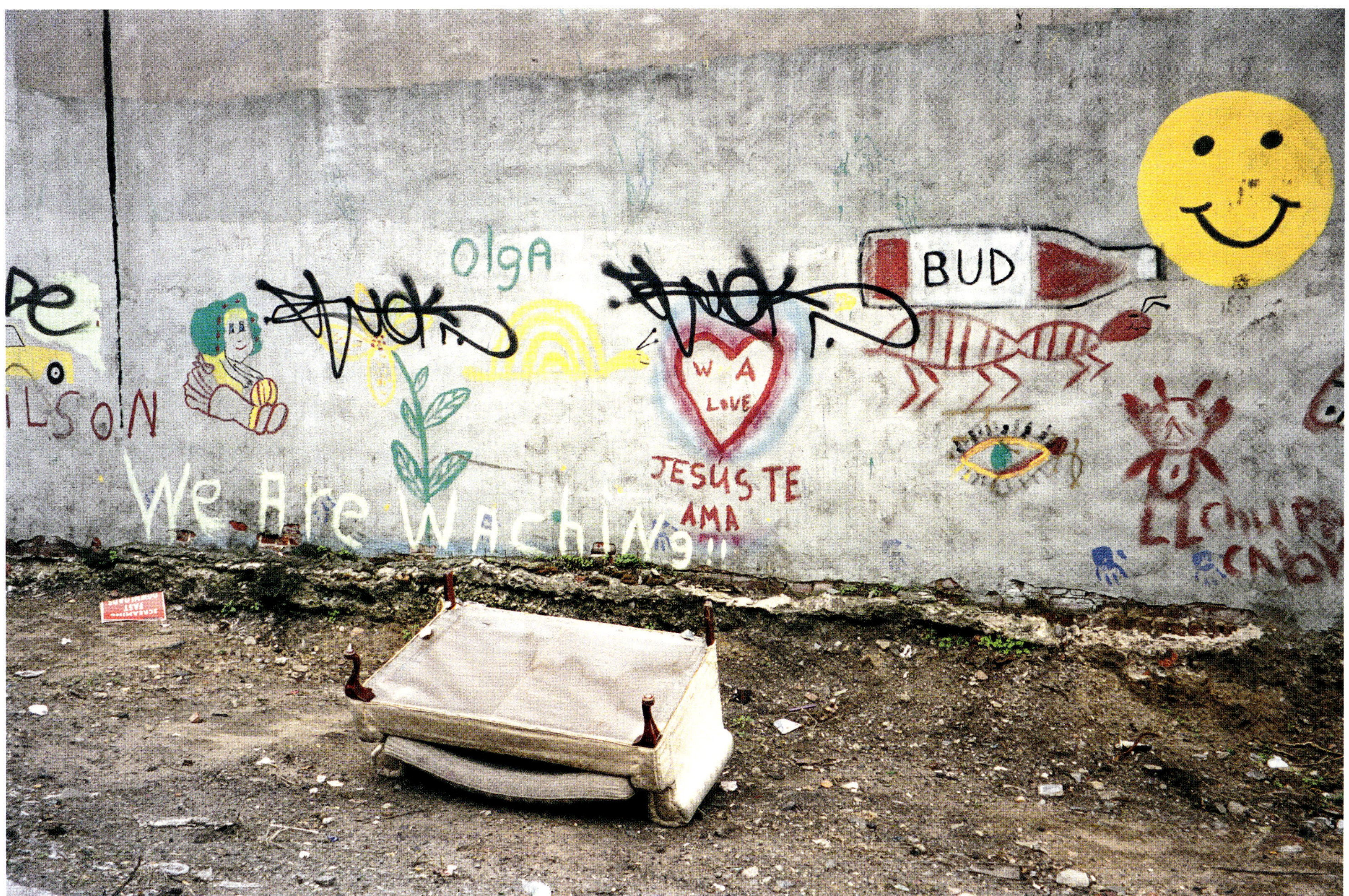

Olga
BUD
WILSON
W A LOVE
JESUS TE AMA
We Are Waching!!

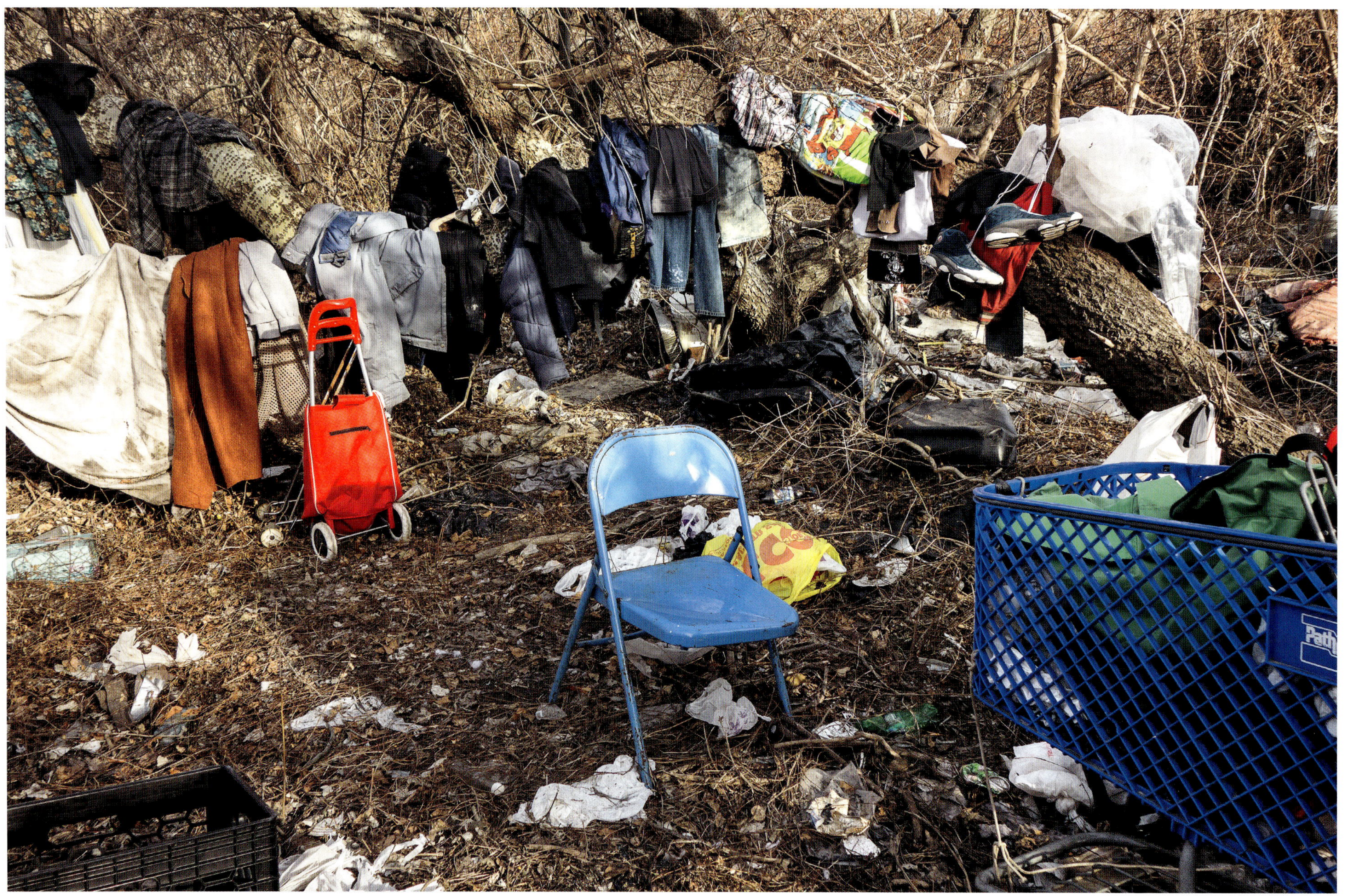

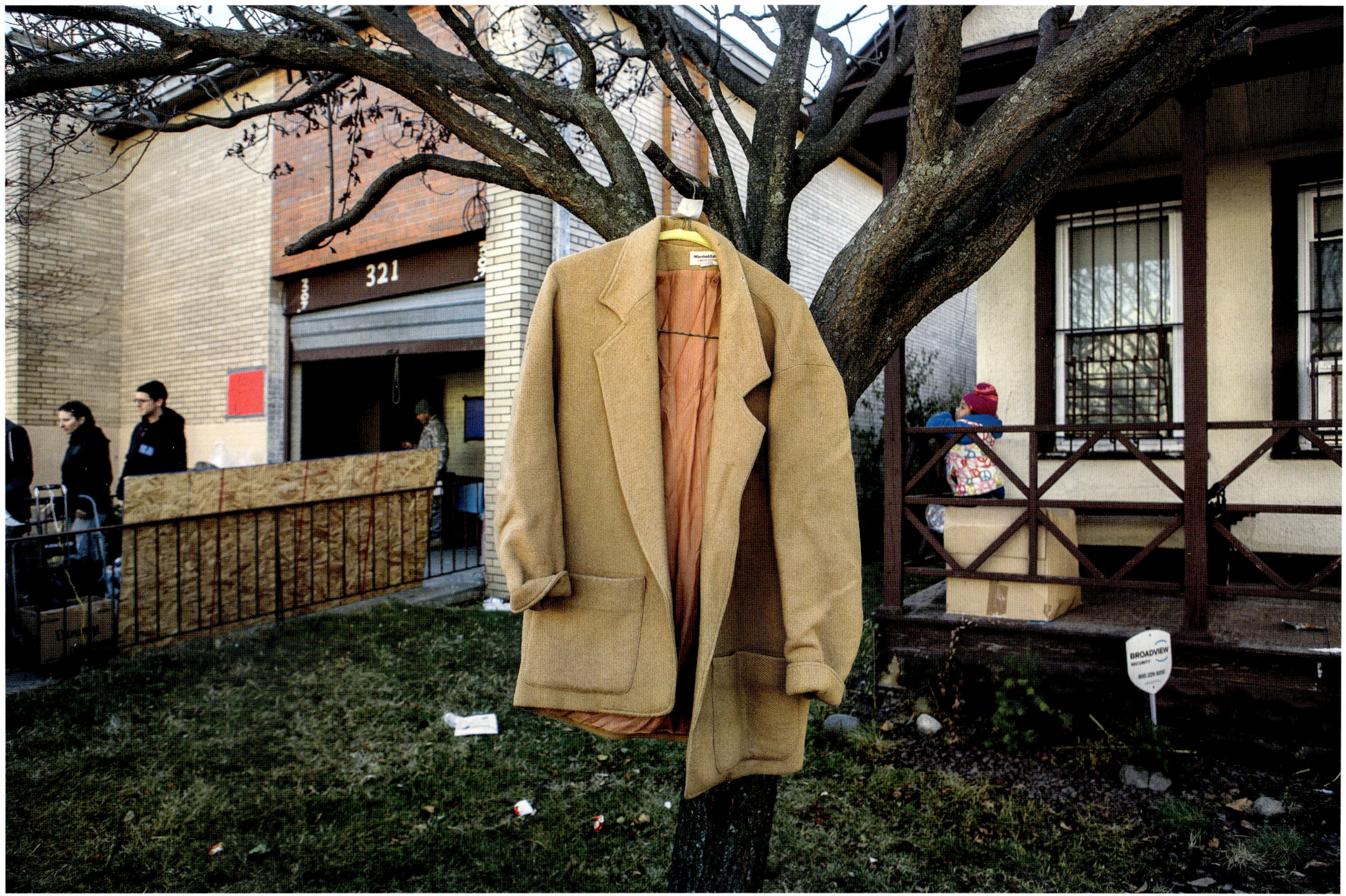

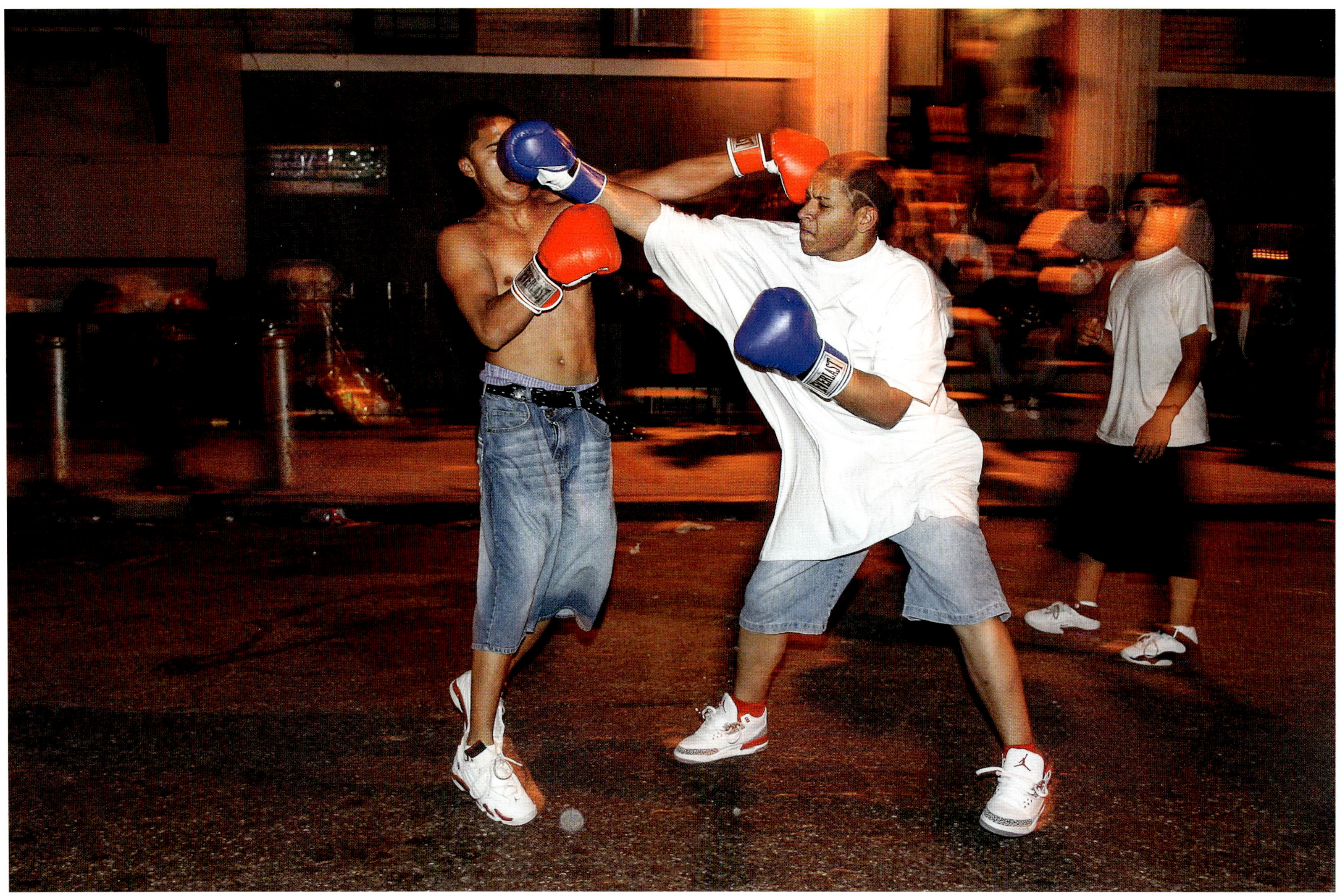

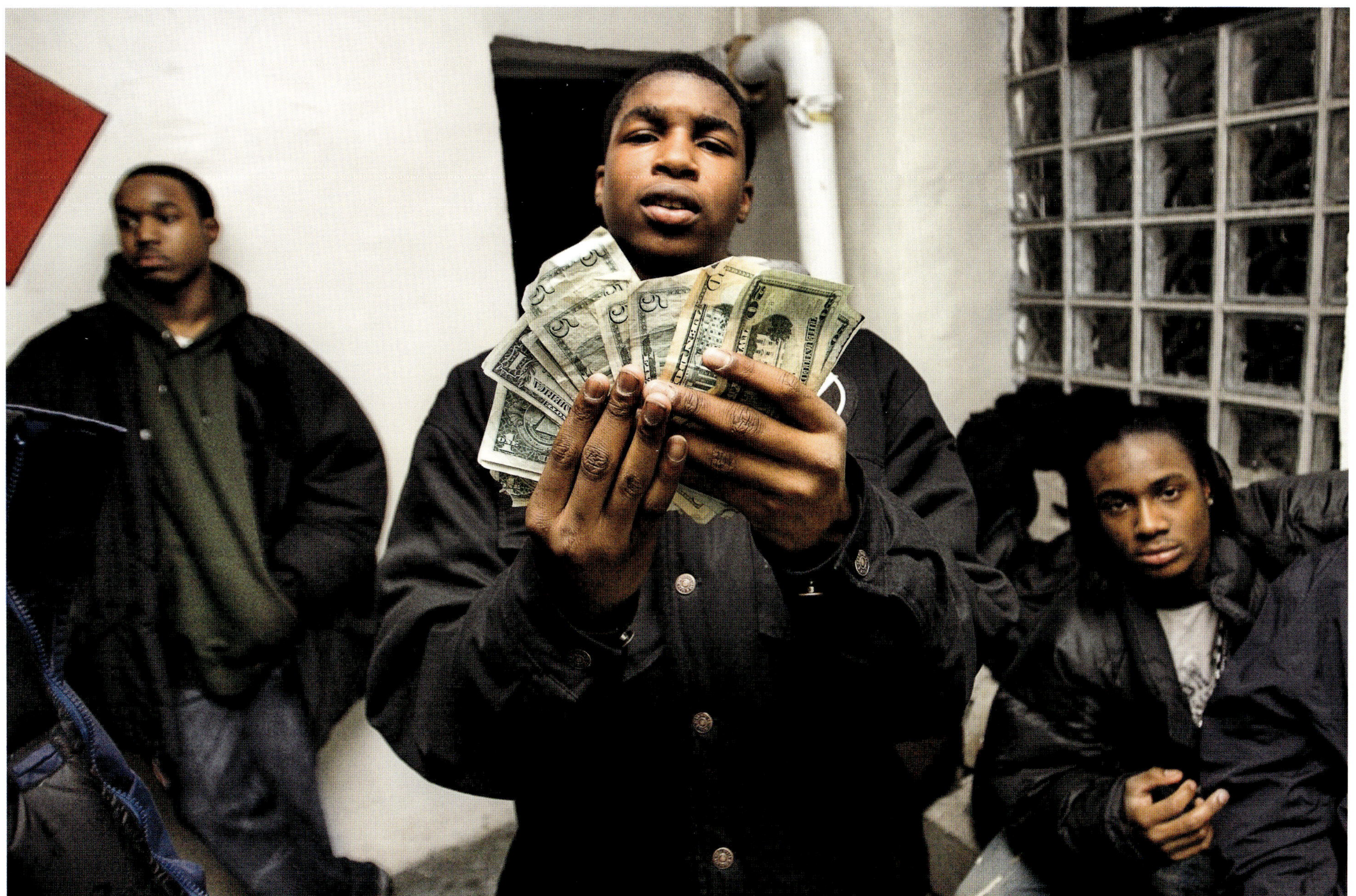

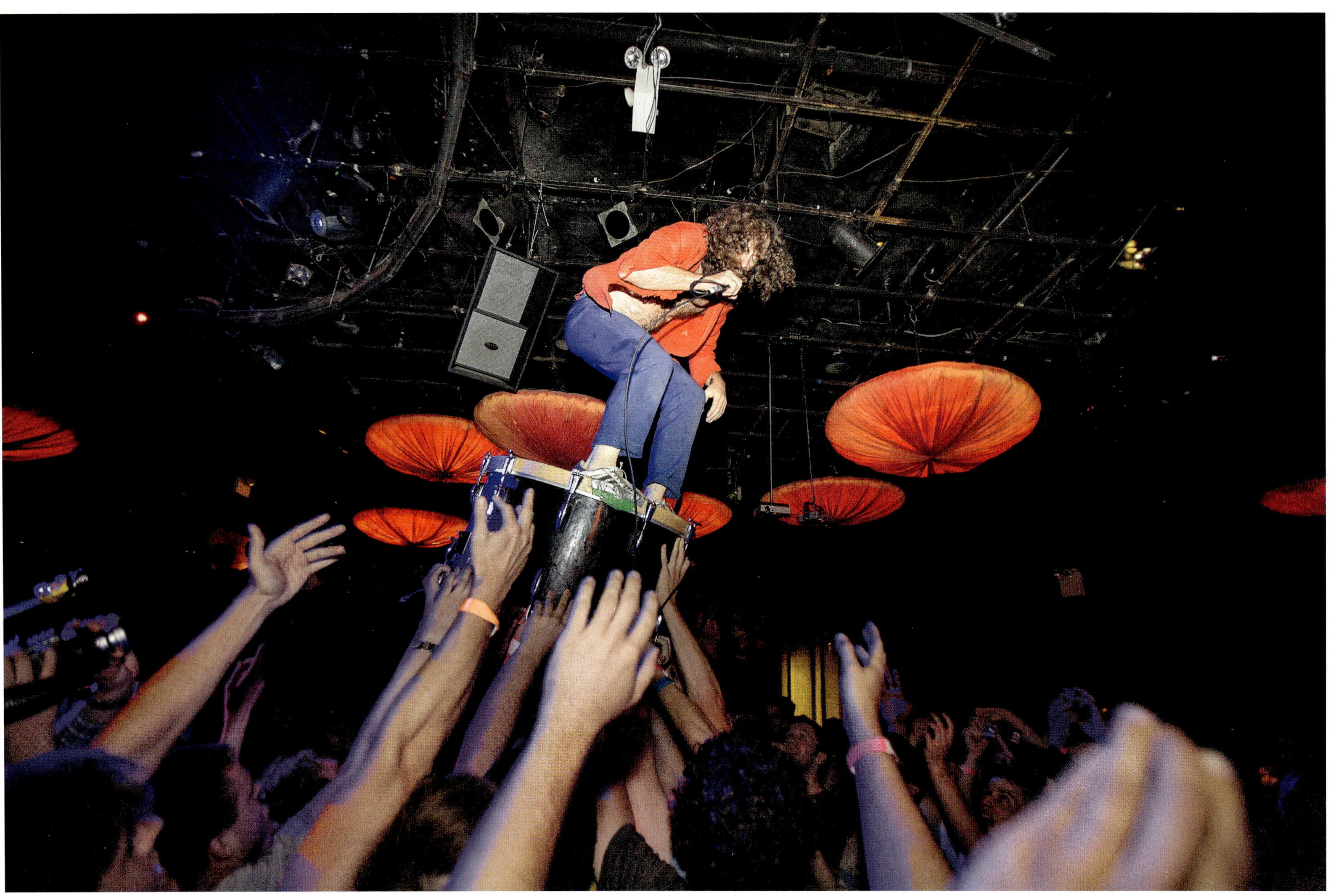

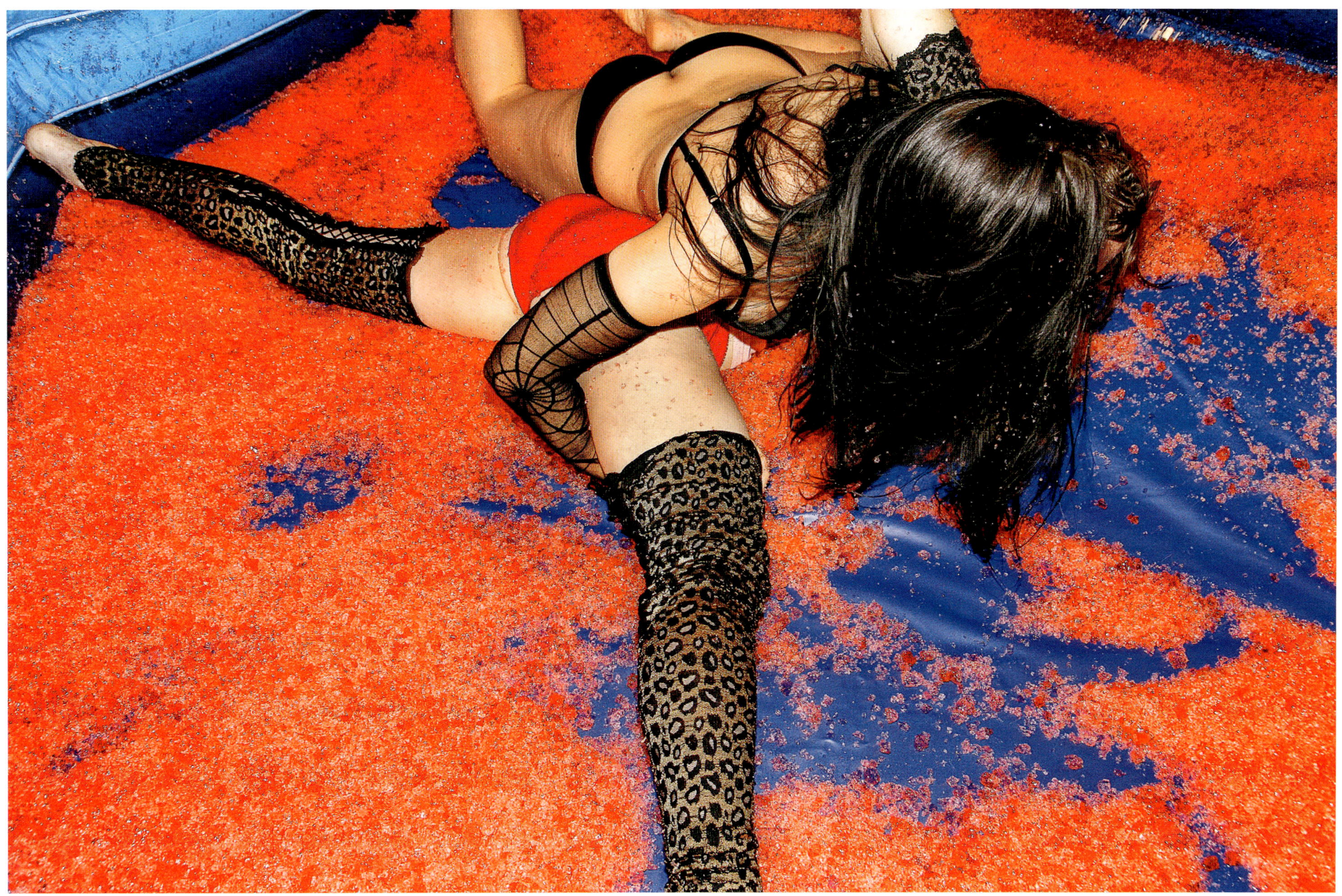

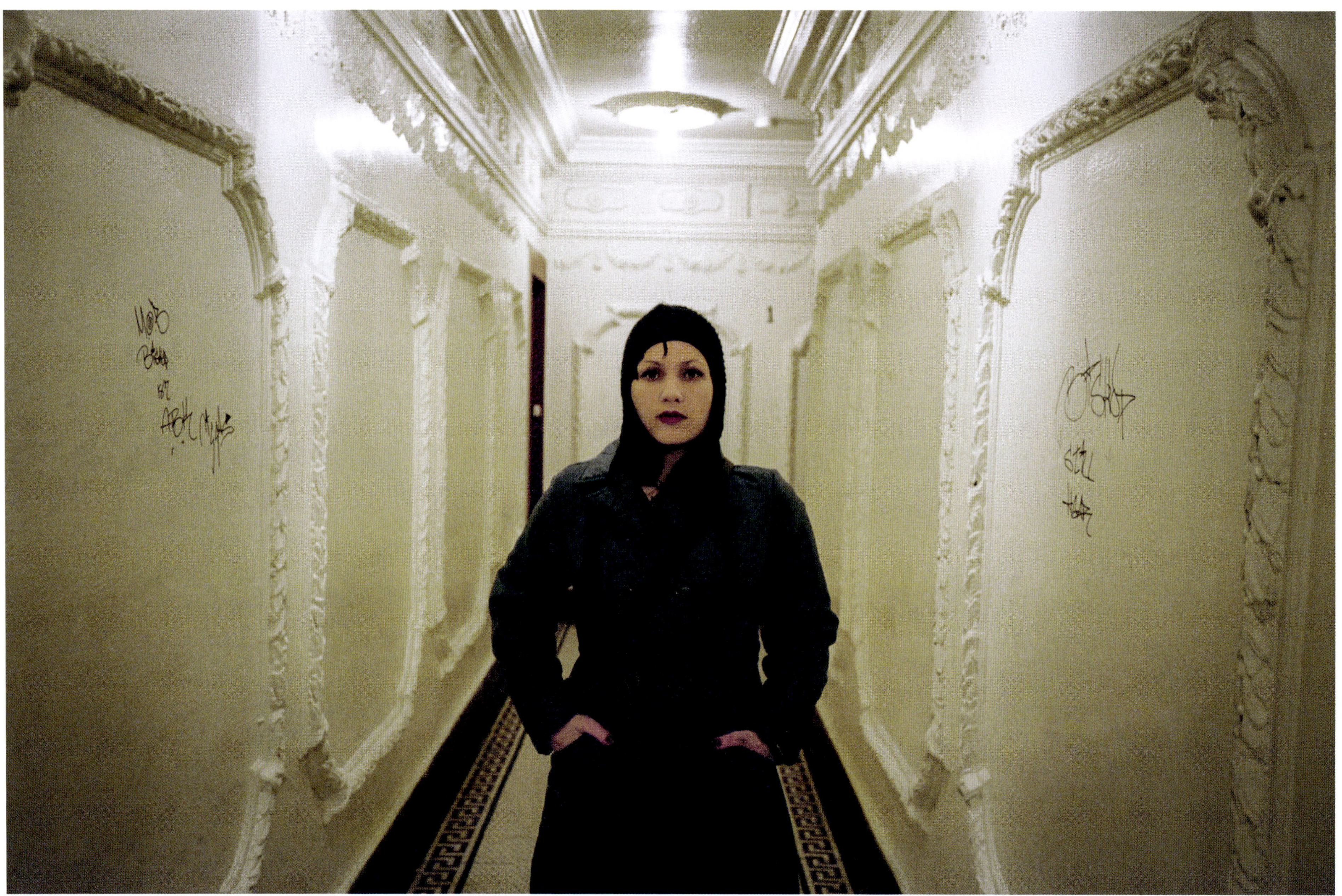

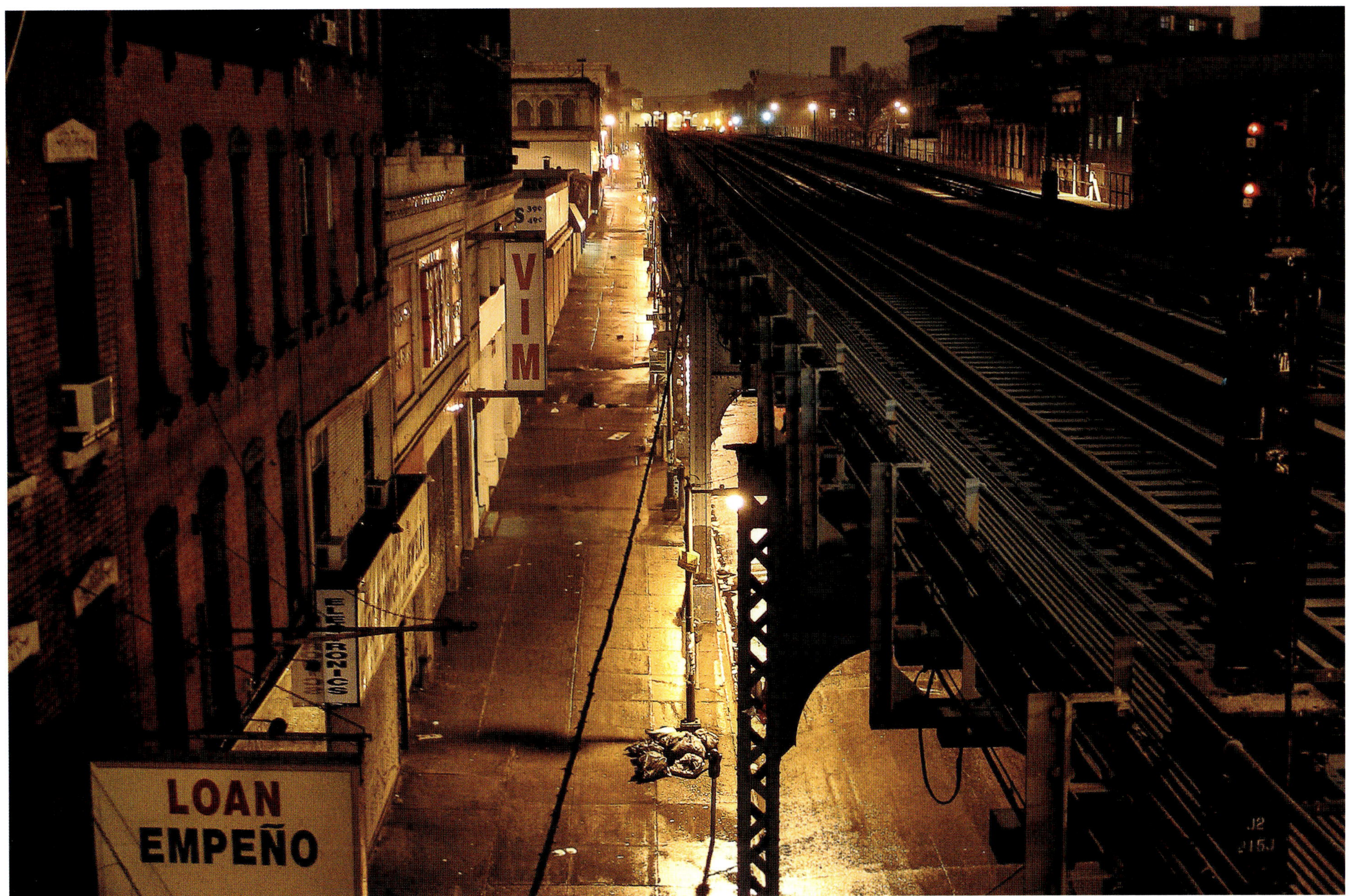

VIM
ELECTRONICS
LOAN
EMPEÑO

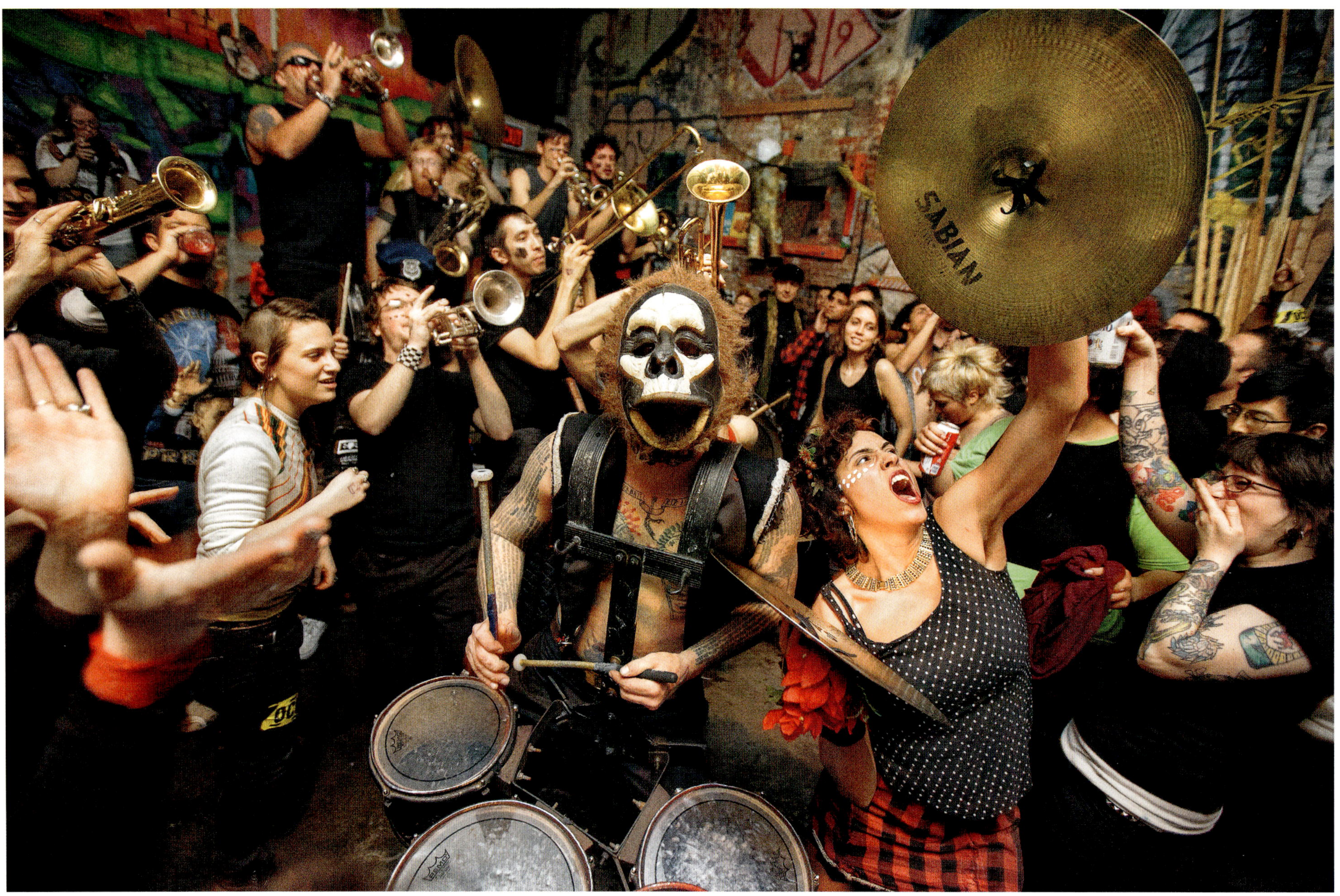

A FERAL UNDERGROUND PARADISE
COLIN MOYNIHAN

Looking back at the 1990s in New York City, it now seems perfectly obvious that the decade was a transitional period. That ten year stretch connected two distinctly different times: the New York of the 1980s, in which adrenaline and anxiety levels were high, rent was low, and a wide variety of crime was open and notorious, and the placid 2000s, in which many of the city's rougher and more distinctive edges were smoothed or removed, and parts of New York began to resemble other neighborhoods in other cities.

During the 1990s, gentrification's purchase on the more rebellious and unruly sections of the city, particularly those in Manhattan, went from a toehold to a stranglehold. Some of the most energetic battles of the decade were fought as rearguard actions in places like the Lower East Side. On the blocks below 14th Street, phalanxes of helmeted cops evicted squats, and community gardeners dug defenses into the earth in an effort to stave off bulldozers sent by city agencies to turn plots of land into housing for deep-pocketed renters.

But while gentrification swept through Manhattan like a wave, its effect across the East River, in Brooklyn, was felt initially as little more than a ripple. There, in neighborhoods like Red Hook, Bushwick, Williamsburg, or Gowanus, one could still find shelter without passing a credit check.

Forsaken pockets of these areas had not yet caught the eye of developers, and landlords had not yet sniffed the scent of high rents. Even in the 2000s there were empty factories, lots, and warehouses that formed a post-industrial urban autonomous zone of unregulated gathering spots and performance spaces, where people had the breathing room to create art, play music, and experiment with their surroundings (and their own ways of life).

There was, for instance, the no man's land along the Williamsburg shoreline, accessible through a broken fence. There, reeds grew shoulder-high, punctuated by sculptures made of trash. Self-organized marching bands rehearsed and graffiti writers tagged walls. Adjoining that area were the abandoned hemp factories of the Greenpoint Terminal Market, known to some as the Forgotten City, where flowering trees grew through decaying floorboards and punk bands played secret shows.

Further south, teams wearing white Tyvek suits gathered one summer afternoon on the cobblestone streets beneath the Manhattan Bridge for a condiment war. Participants used squirt bottles, water guns, slingshots, and balloons to hurl mustard, ketchup, and hot sauce in an event that seemed part performance art and part lowbrow food fight.

THERE WAS A NEXUS OF CREATIVITY IN THE BOROUGH IF YOU KNEW WHERE TO LOOK, AND THERE NEARLY ALWAYS SEEMED TO BE THE POSSIBILITY OF SOMETHING NOVEL AND STRANGE— MAYBE EVEN EXQUISITE—RIGHT AROUND THE CORNER.

And to the east, in Bed-Stuy, beer-fueled bicyclists in denim vests congregated each fall on a dead end street for Bike Kill, climbing atop double decker bike frames, then hurtling into collisions while trying to unseat each other with long PVC lances. Afterward, many adjourned to a chicken slaughterhouse-turned-clubhouse where the smell of dead birds sometimes still permeated the air as bands like Japanther and Lightning Bolt performed.

Not all of the art that emerged in Brooklyn in the 2000s was good, not all of the conceptual experiments merited notice, and not all of the bands were worth the price of a ticket. The opposite was true often enough, though, to allow a critical mass of energy to coalesce, attracting new people and ideas. There was a nexus of creativity in the borough if you knew where to look, and there nearly always seemed to be the possibility of something novel and strange—maybe even exquisite—right around the corner.

But passions fade and places are tamed. Market forces set their sights on Brooklyn soon enough. When they did, the changes came even more rapidly than they had in Manhattan, and without the sort of entrenched, grudging opposition and physical barricades that had slowed the gentrification of the Lower East Side.

The Forgotten City burned to the ground in a massive case of arson following the approval of zoning changes to allow luxury condos in an area that had been zoned for commercial buildings. The no man's land nearby was made into a state park where uniformed officers enforce a laundry list of regulations. And at Bike Kill, the jousters now hide their beer cans in paper bags to avoid tickets.

Maybe Brooklyn was never the feral underground paradise that some imagined it to be. Maybe, sometimes, it was. Either way, there was a time in the 2000s when something special was going on there. It was something that did not exist before and may not exist again. You don't have to take it on faith. There are pictures to prove it.

Colin Moynihan is a reporter for the New York Times. *He covers New York City for the Metro section, and has written extensively about bike culture and street life.*

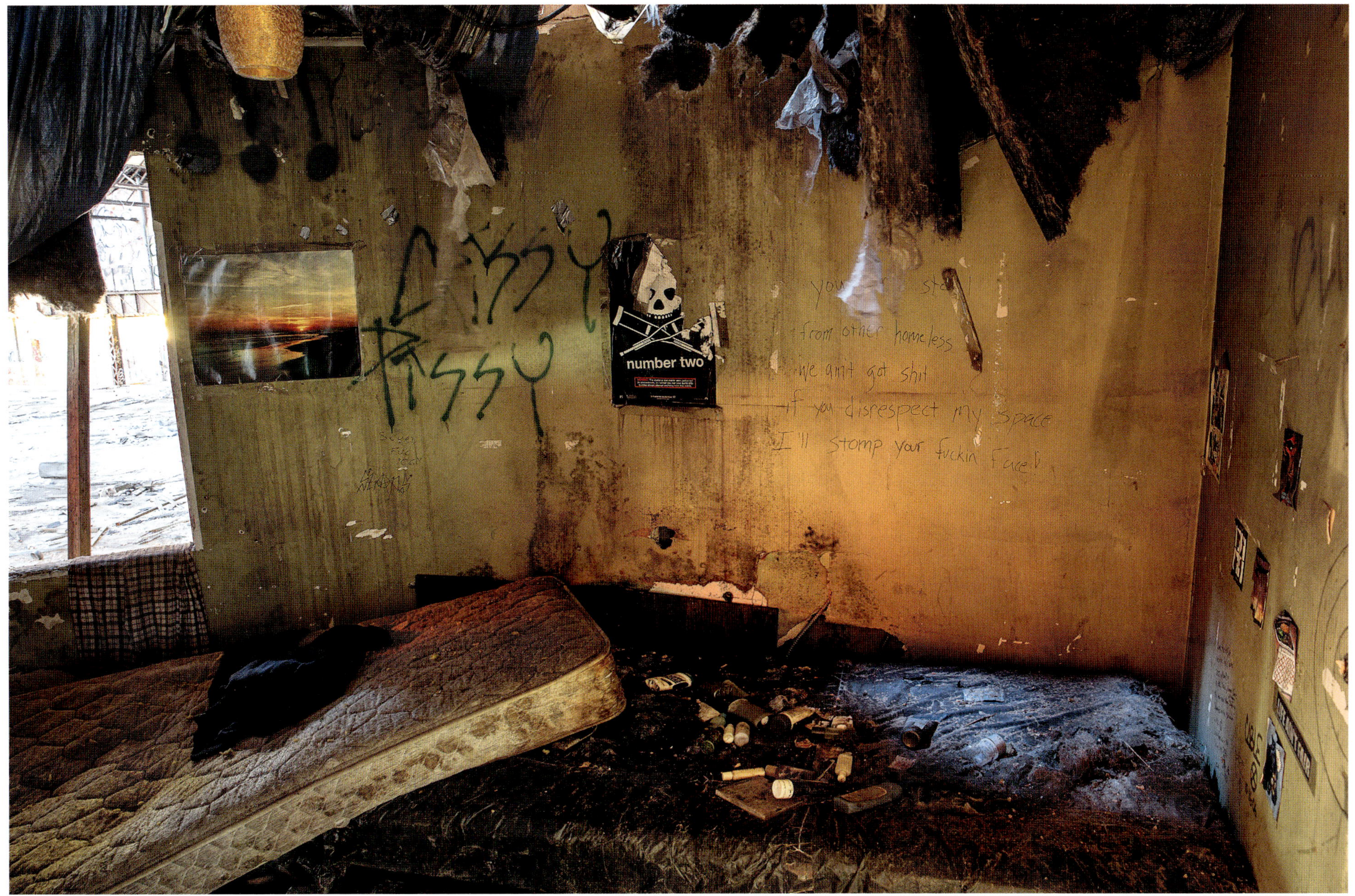
CISSY
PISSY
number two
you can steal
from other homeless
we aint got shit
if you disrespect my space
I'll stomp your fuckin Face!

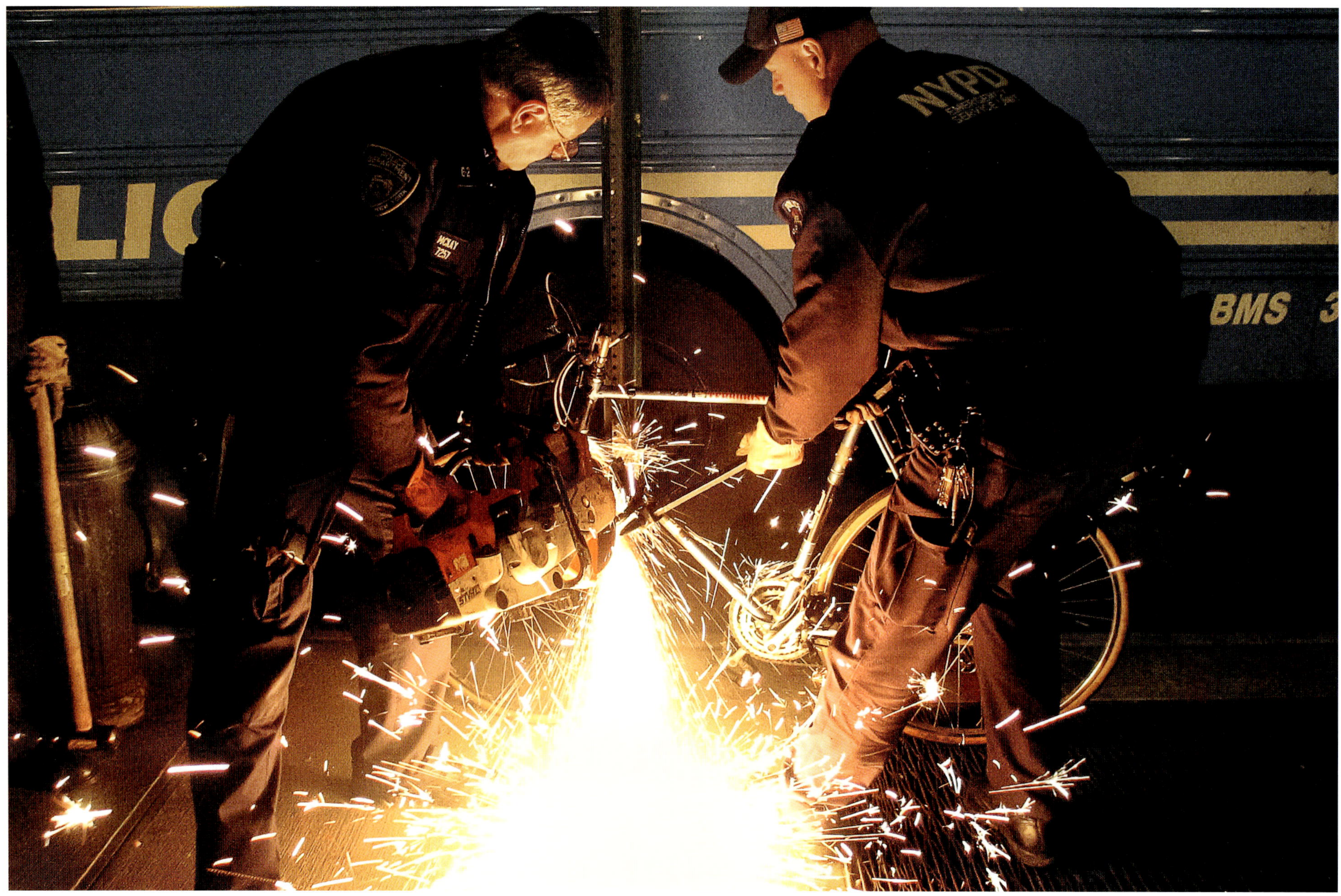

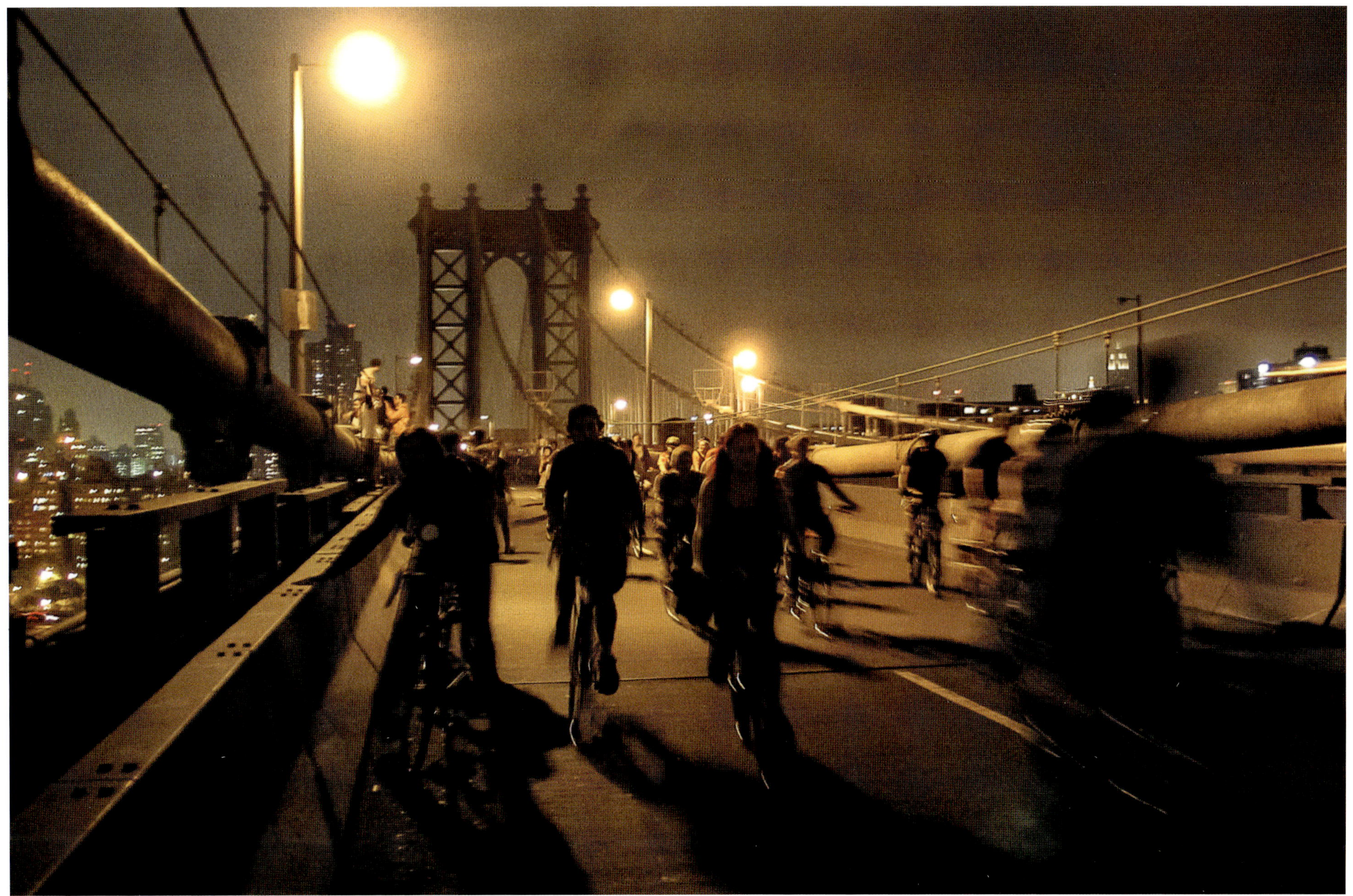

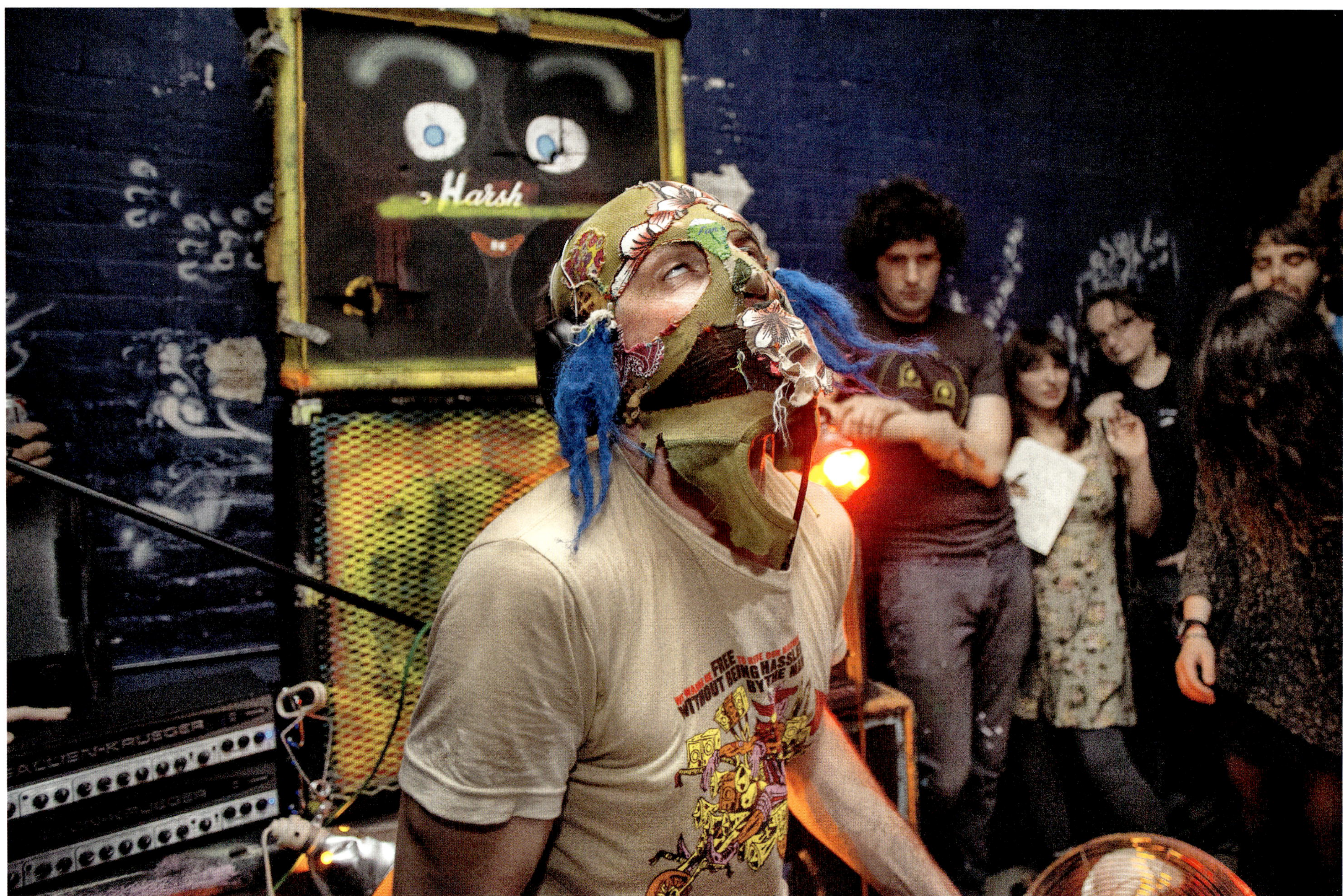
Harsh

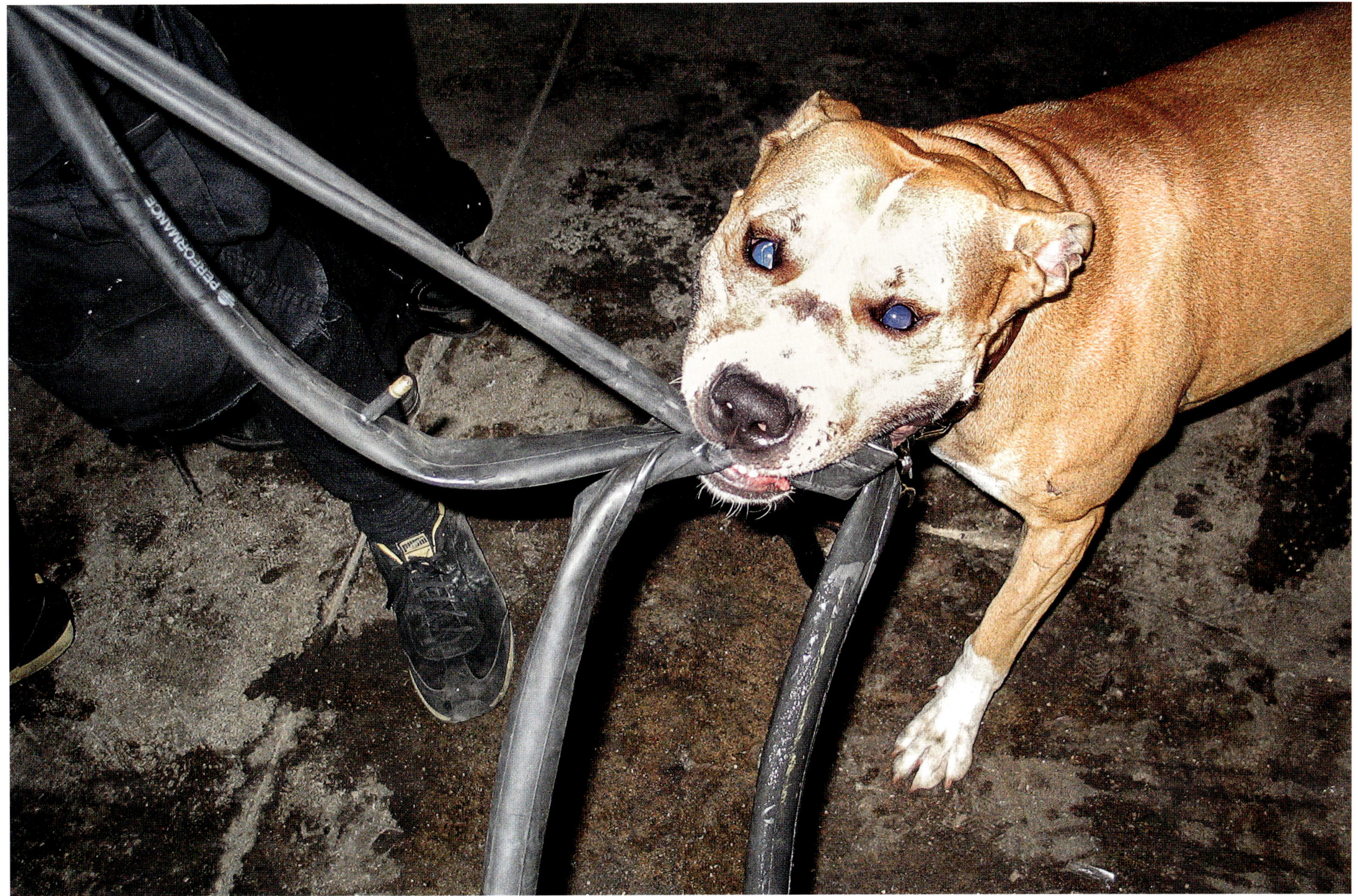

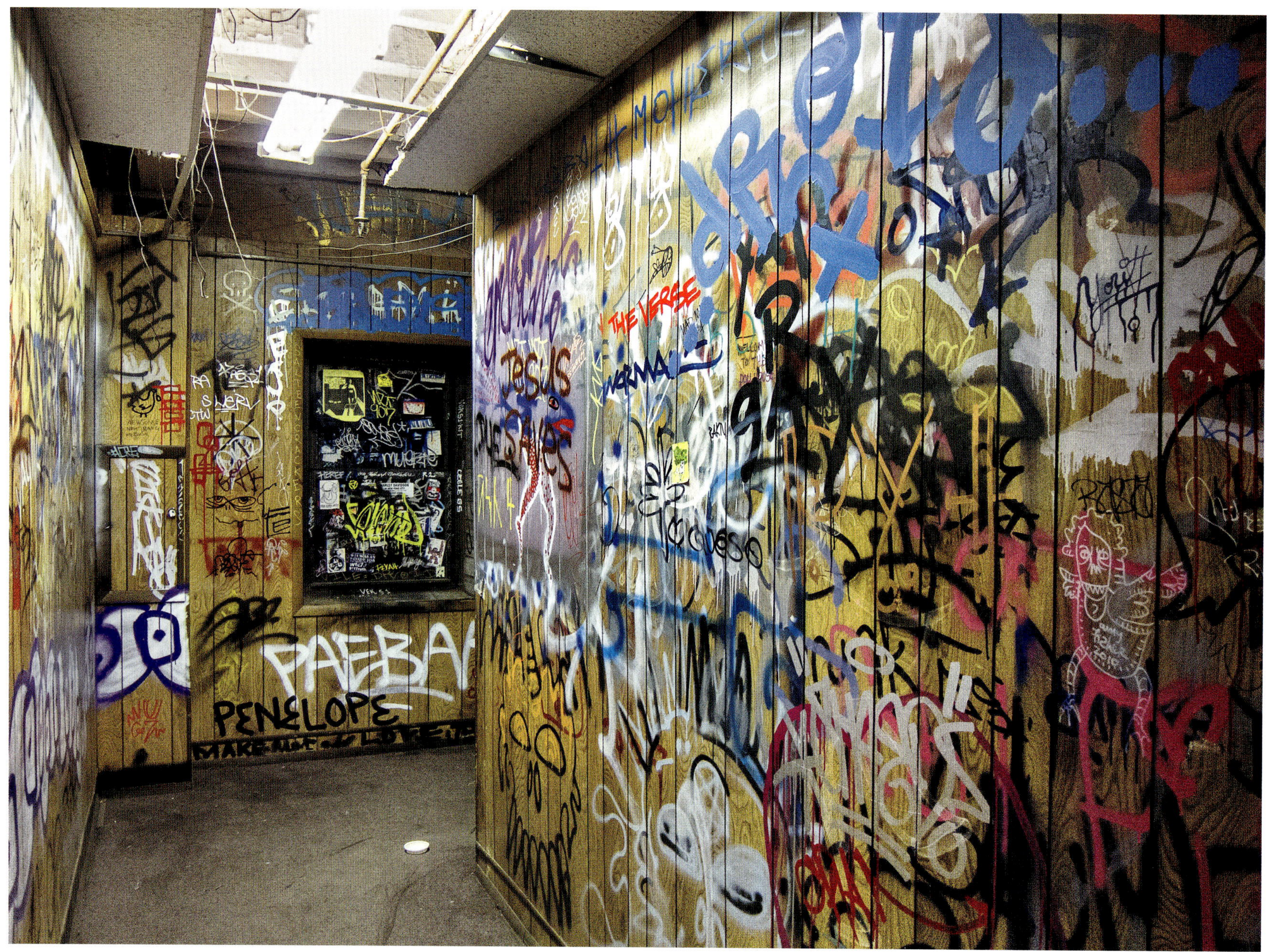

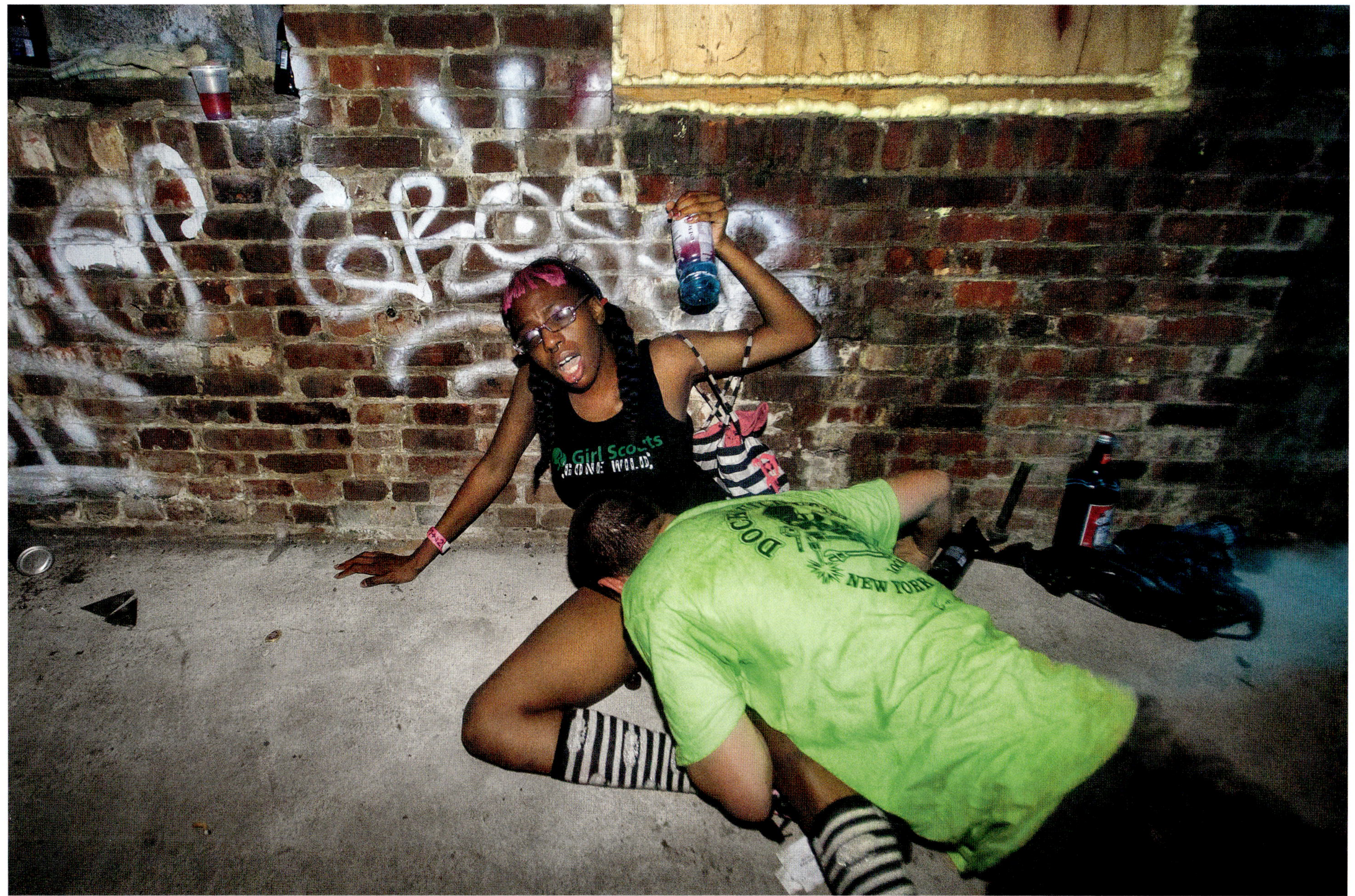

Girl Scouts
GONE WILD
NEW YORK

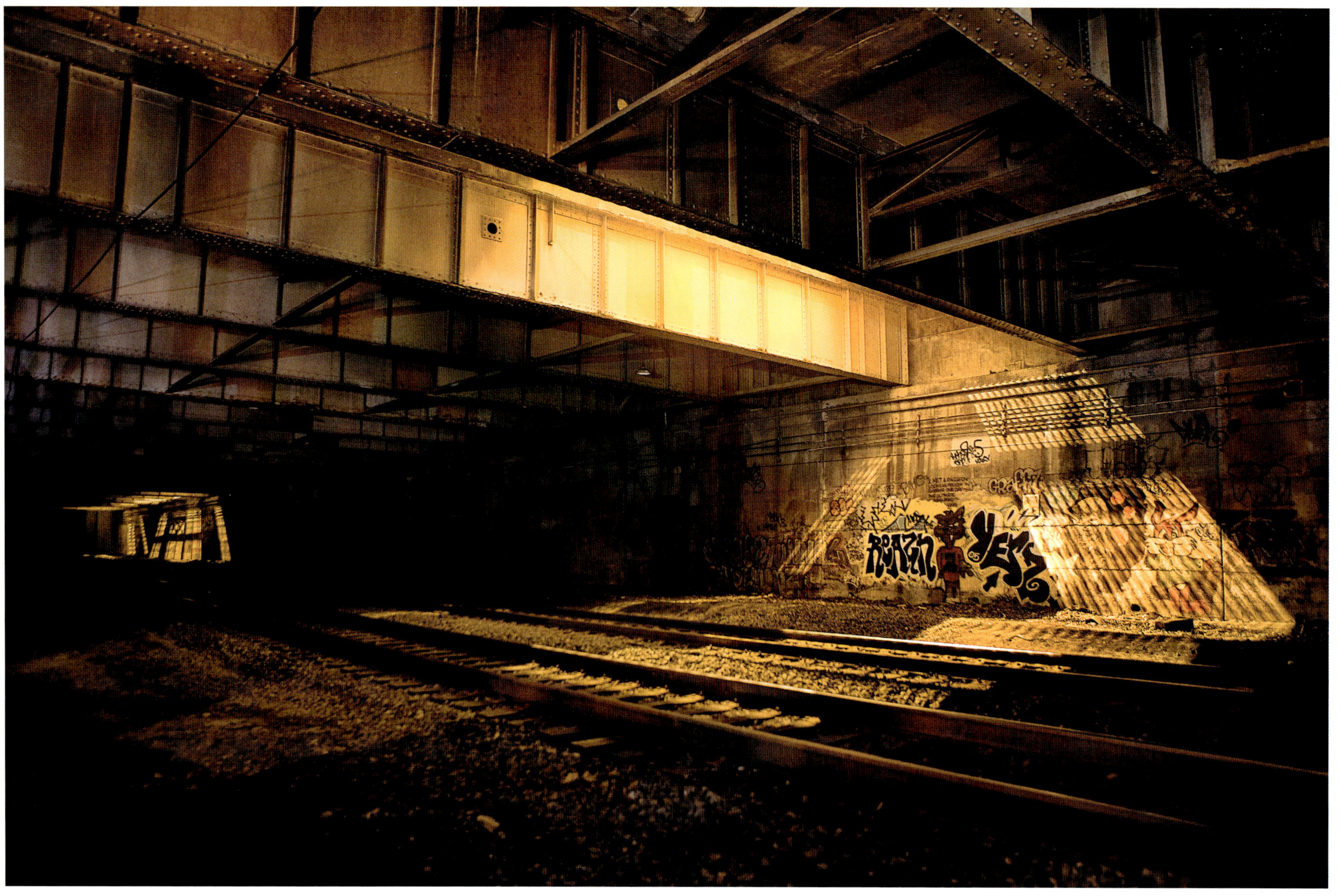

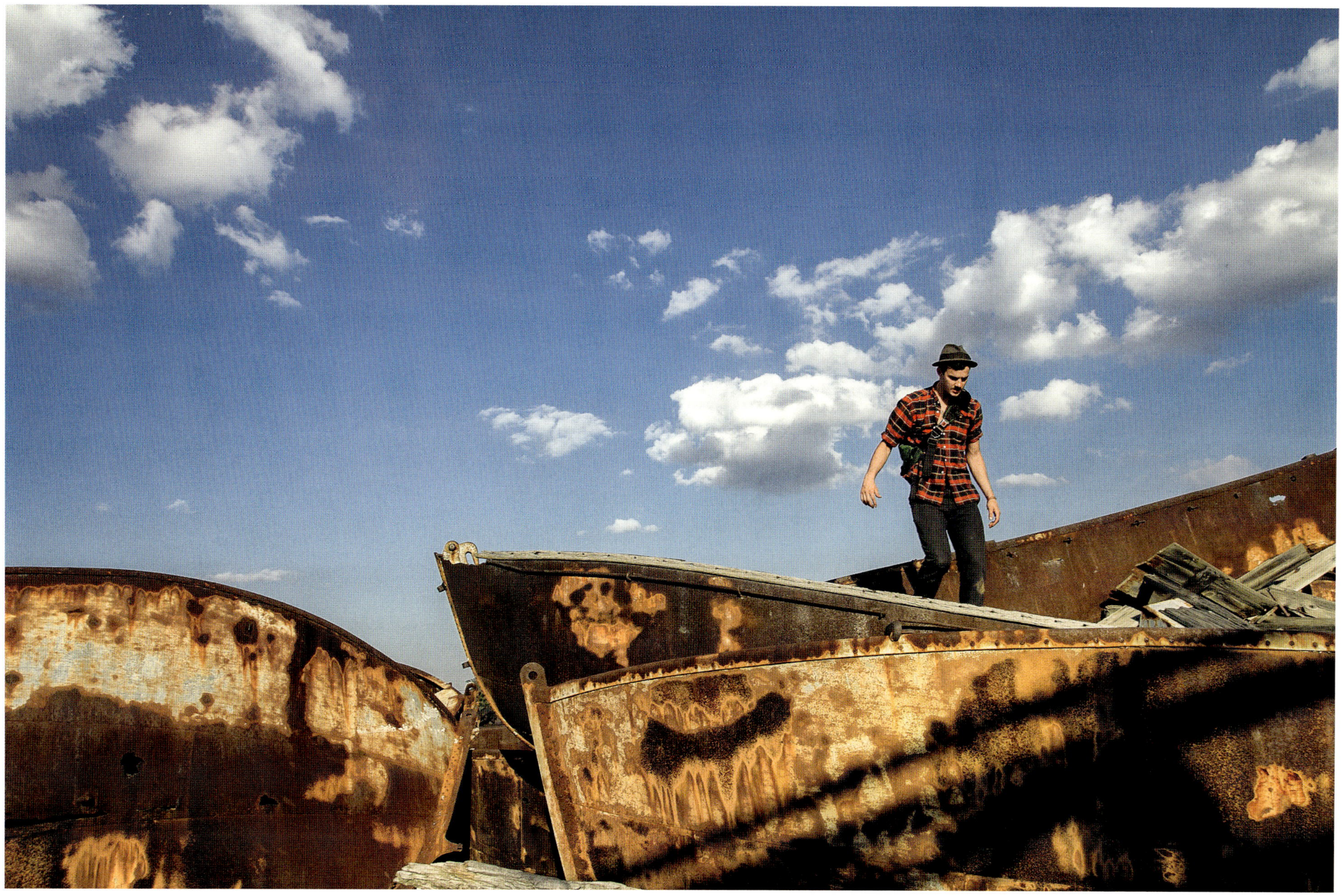

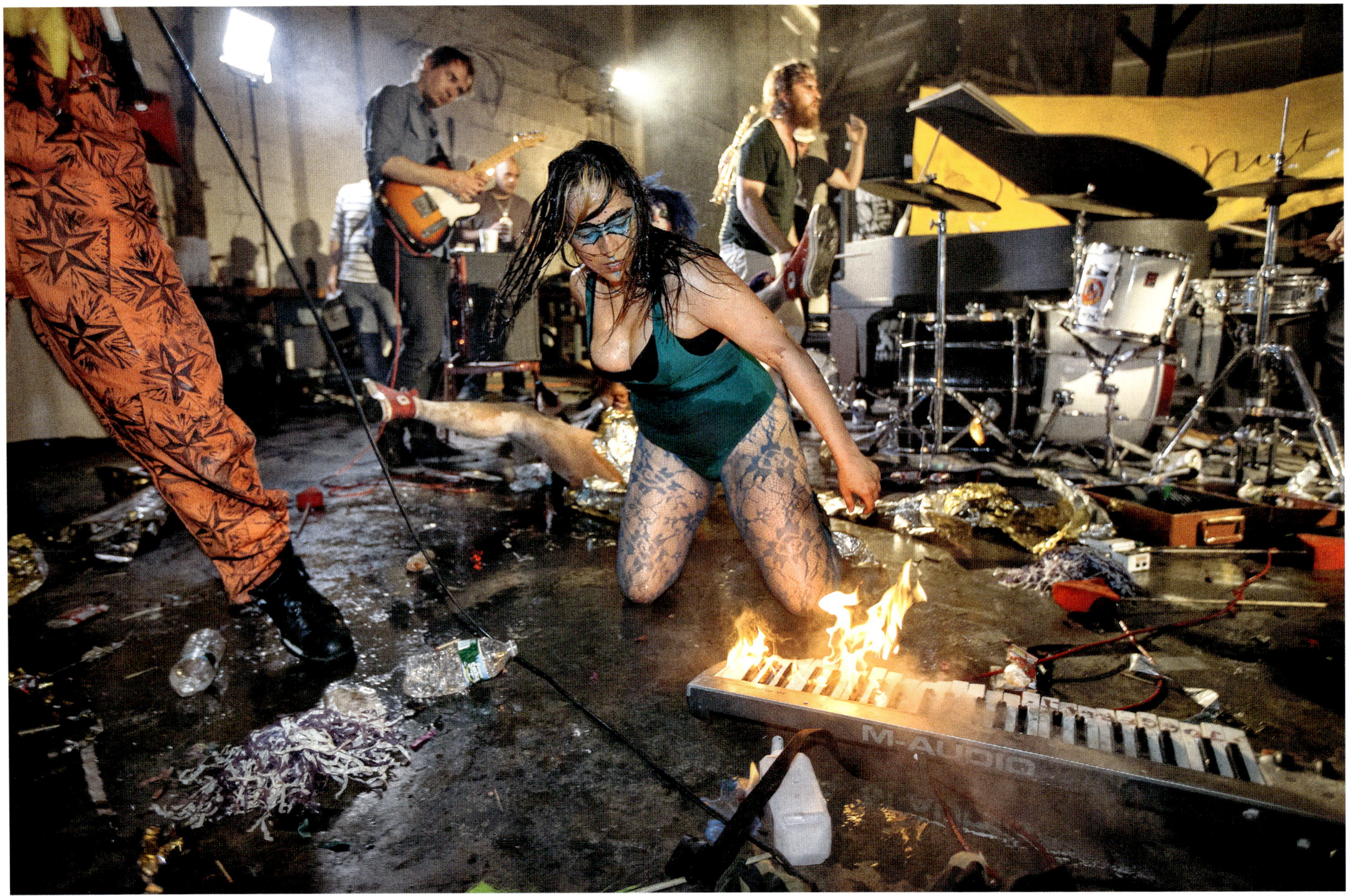

M-AUDIO

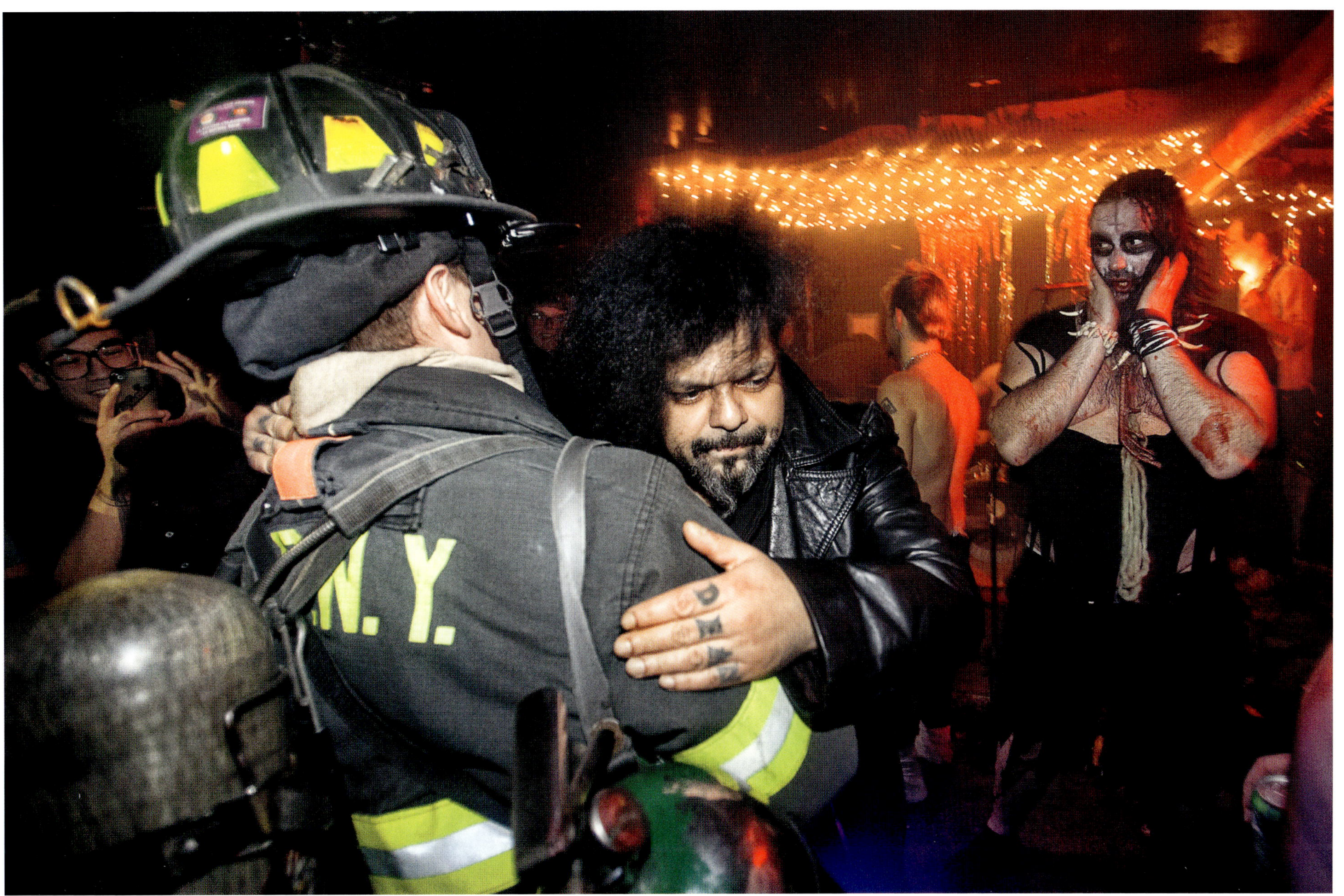

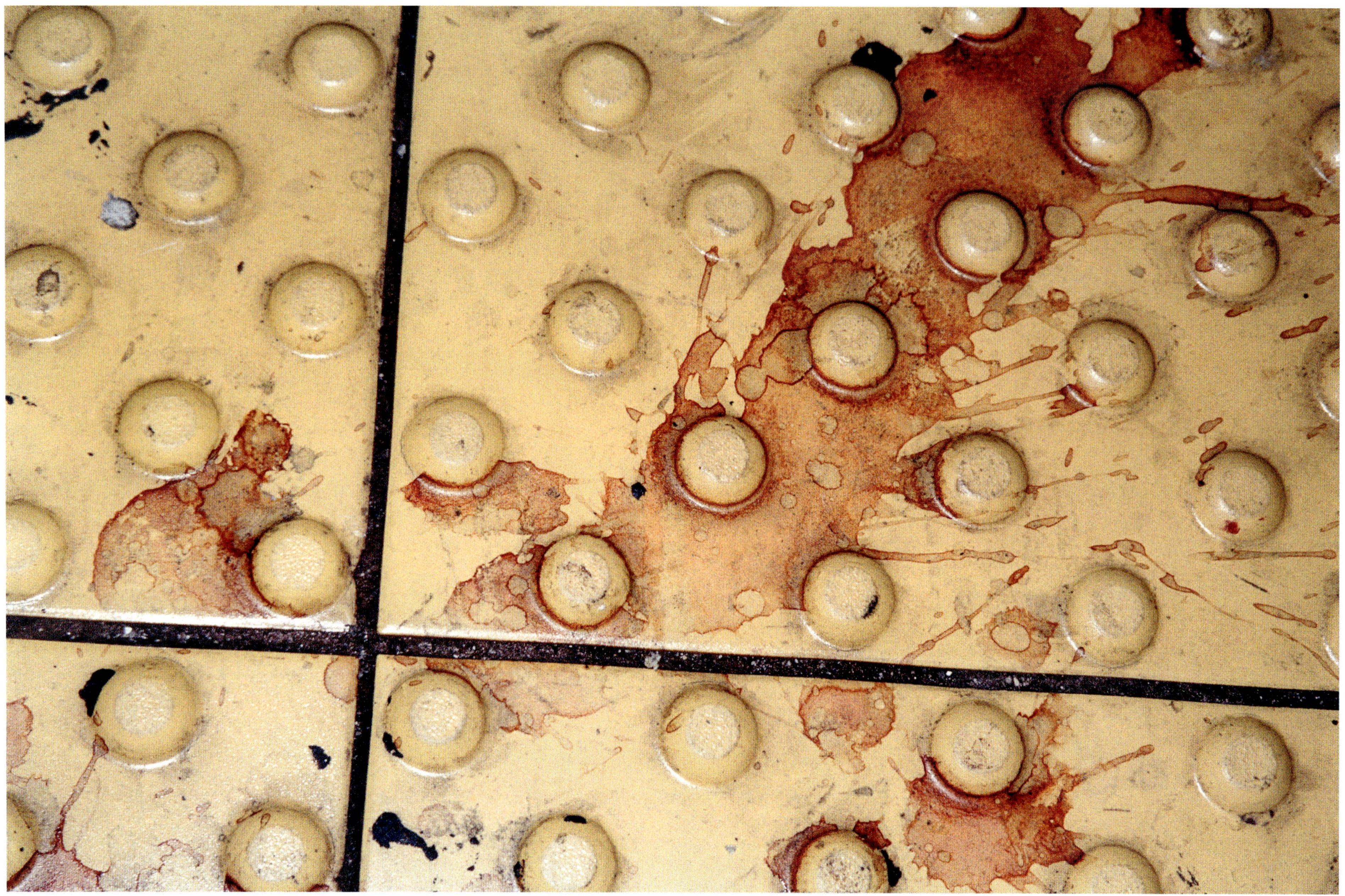

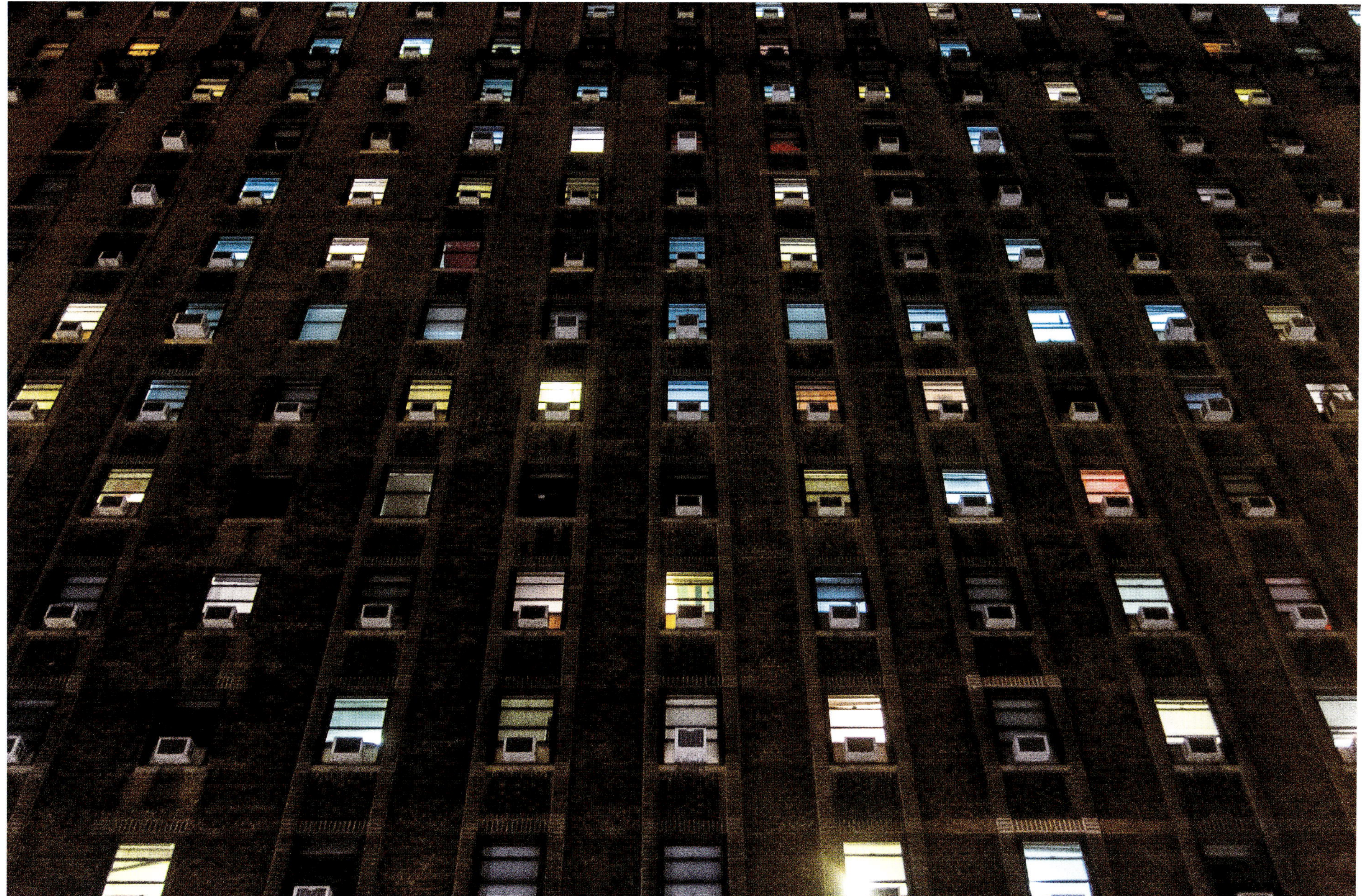

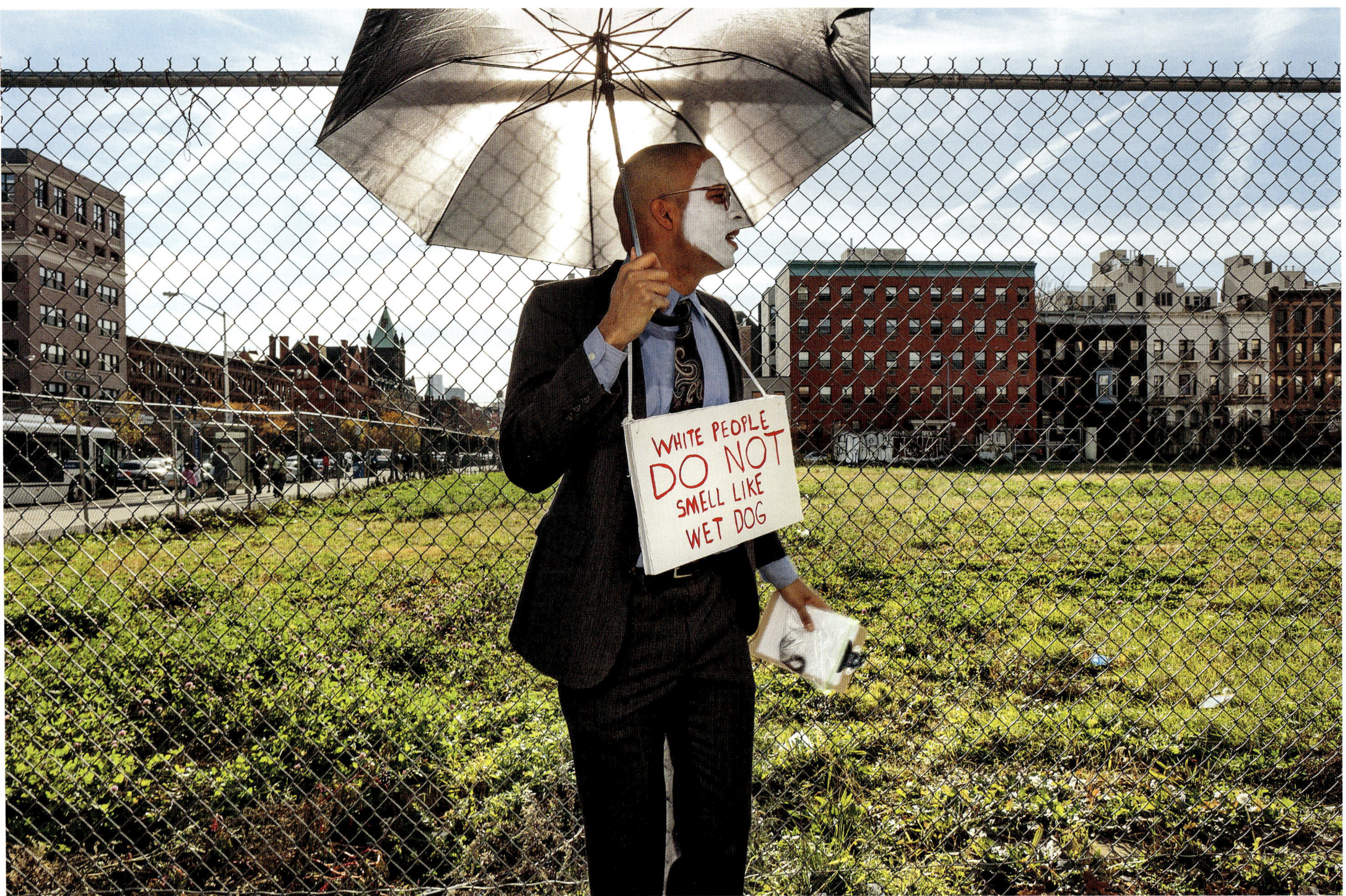
WHITE PEOPLE
DO NOT
SMELL LIKE
WET DOG

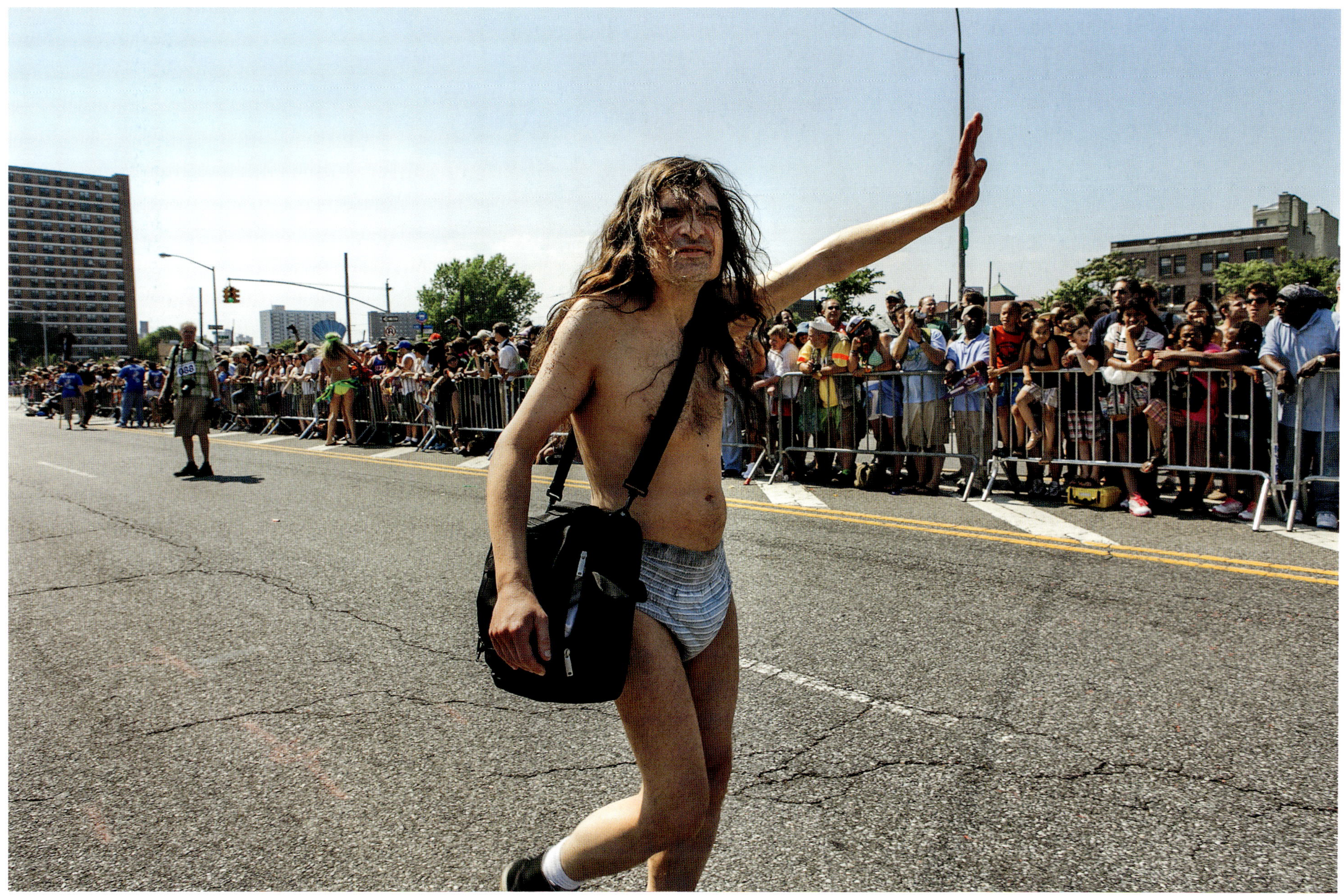

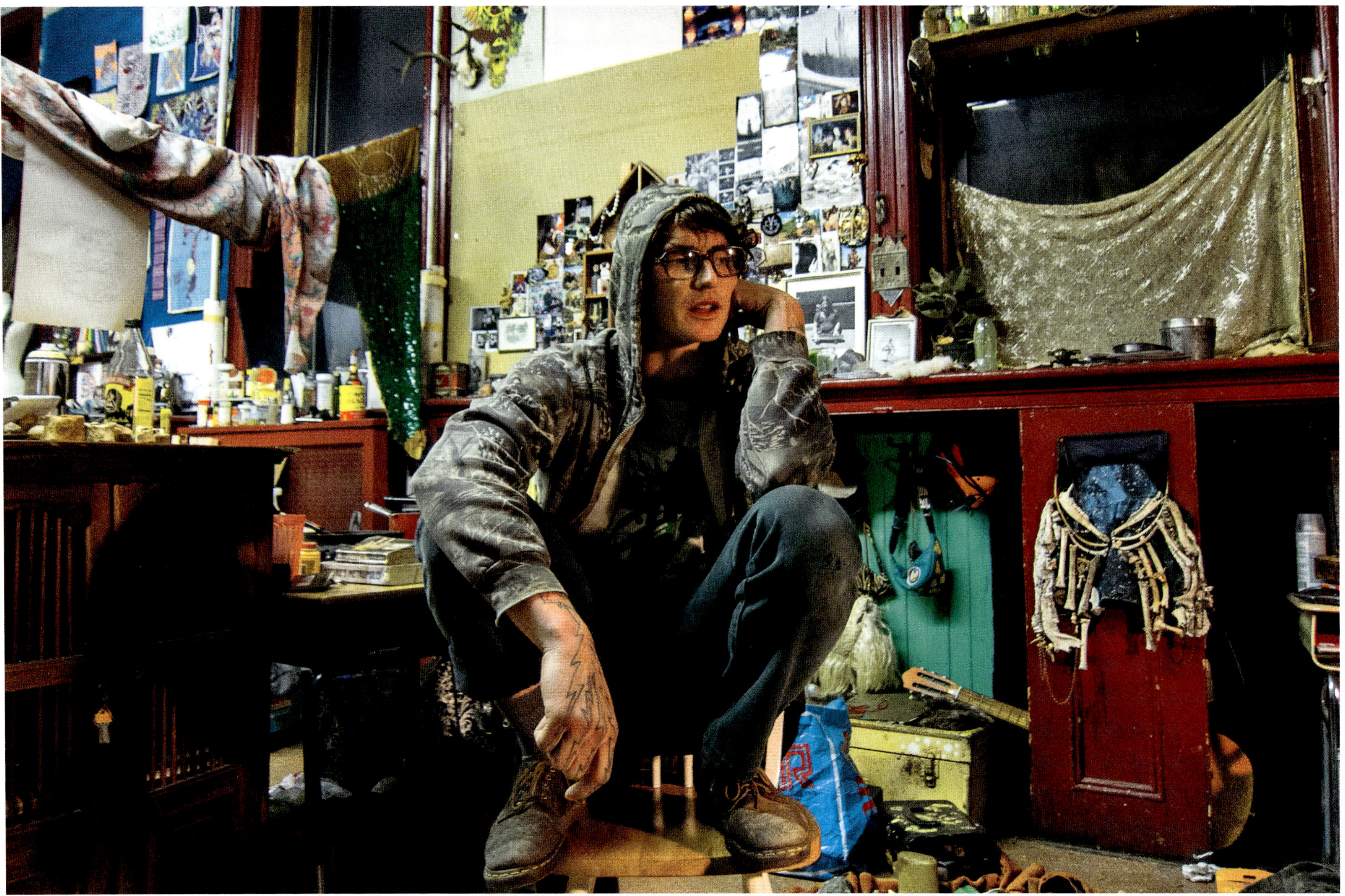

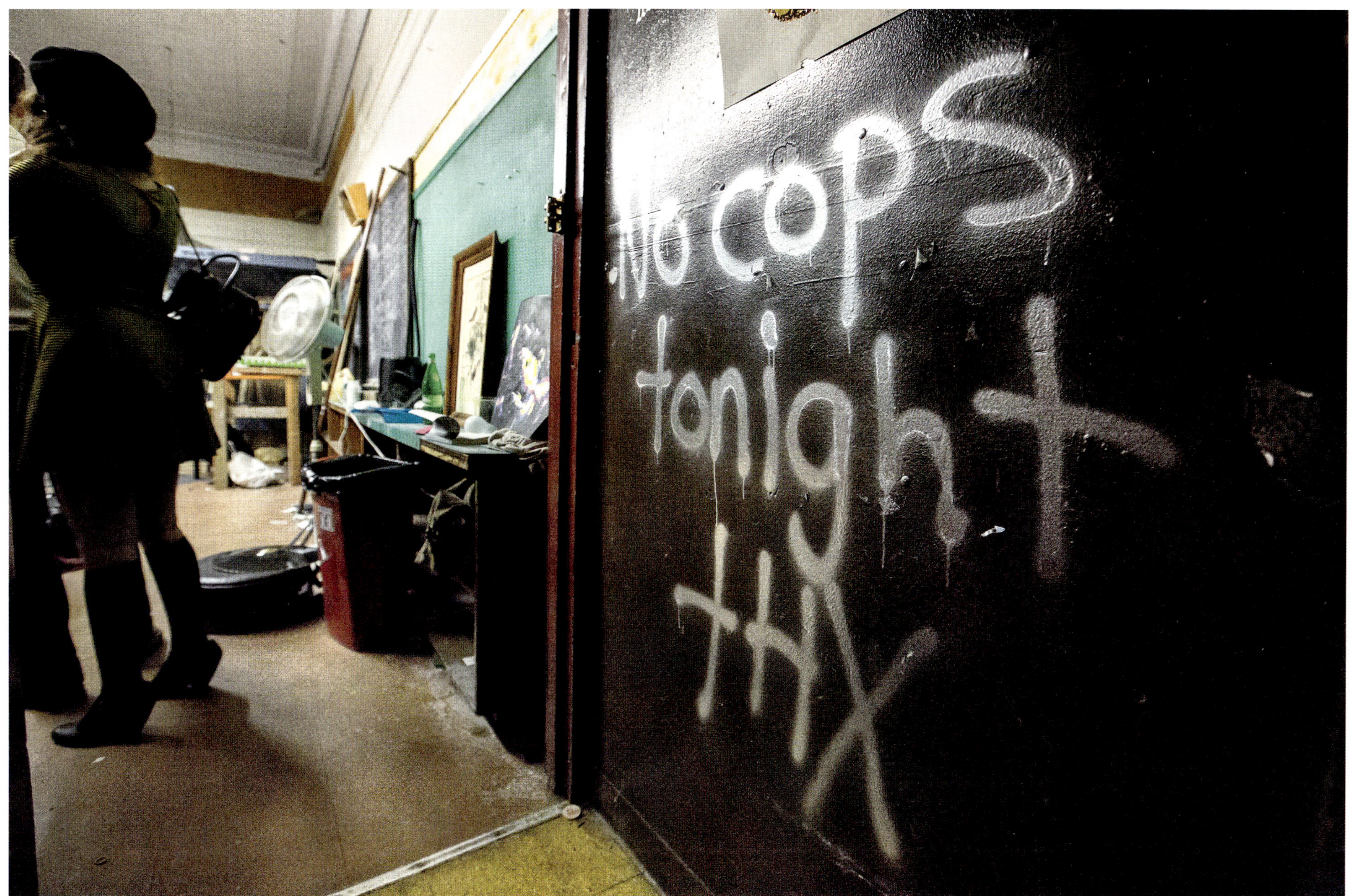
No cops
tonight

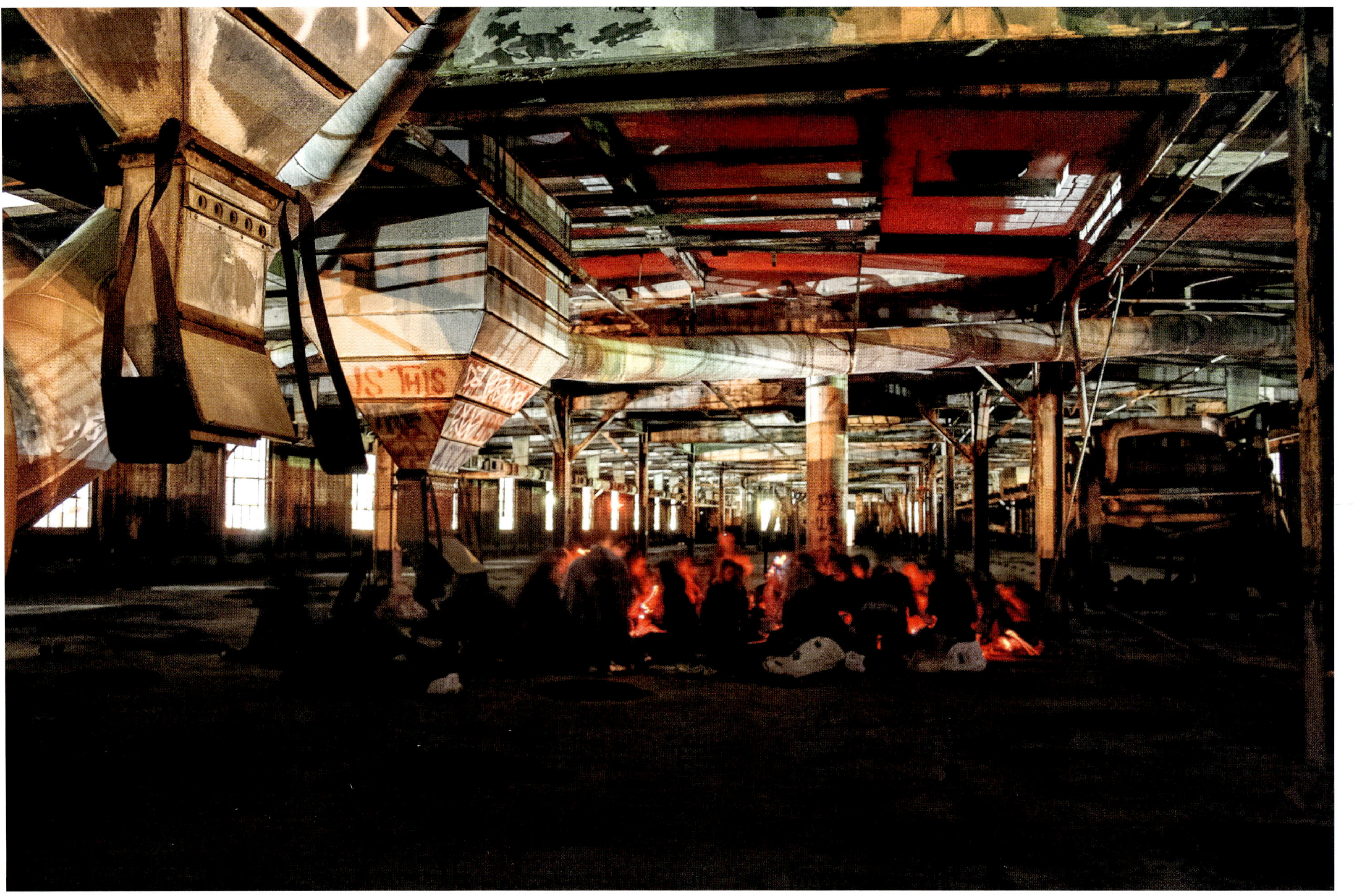

IS THIS

BROOKLYN WAS MORE FUN
STO LEN

With the turn of the century, there came a major shift of focus in the underground art and music scenes in New York from Manhattan to Brooklyn. It was a natural evolution, one spurred on by economics and real estate. When I moved here, I couldn't afford to live on the Lower East Side, so I naturally ended up sleeping on a couch in my friend's kitchen in Greenpoint.

Brooklyn turned out to be way more fun anyhow. It felt freer and rife with possibility. All of a sudden, I wasn't going into Manhattan anymore. I wasn't even going to clubs because the best shows were happening in parking lots, junkyards, warehouses, and people's lofts with names like Rubulad, Mighty Robot, The Woodser, Happy Birthday Hideout, and the Chicken Hut. The bands would be playing in a living room. You immediately felt at home because it *was* actually someone's home, and they were putting on the show because they really cared.

I kept seeing Tod's bald head at all of these good shows, gleaming brightly in a sea of swarming, sweaty bodies, his camera around his neck and flashes going off. Mosh pits got fun again in the early 2000s. Guys and girls were dancing together without the violence that was such a problem in the 1990s. It felt good to move.

But it wasn't just music shows that were happening. The streets were plastered with new street art every day, and communities were converging. Happenings were really happening: a pirate raid on the Staten Island Ferry, a giant condiment war in Dumbo, underwear bike rides, public pillow fights, shopping cart races, secret dinners and plays. Lines and labels were blurred by a lack of pretense.

New York is not an easy place to live. It's expensive, claustrophobic, loud, and polluted—but so many of us stick it out because of the people here. Time is limited because people are so busy; you have to make the most of it. Everyone is working at hyperactive speed, so on any given night something interesting is going on. Sometimes, there are too many things to choose from. The extended community of artists runs deep here, and I think Tod captures it really well.

All of the characters who make up this loose-knit community are attracted to the possibility of living different types of lives; of carving out their own bizarre paths. We inspire each other constantly. If you want to build a crazy-ass boat and live on it, you do it and we'll all try to help you. Dreams become more attainable with a ragtag gang of like-minded buddies who don't think you're nuts. These people are down for it. You say, "Hey,

NEW YORK IS NOT AN EASY PLACE TO LIVE. IT'S EXPENSIVE, CLAUSTROPHOBIC, LOUD, AND POLLUTED—BUT SO MANY OF US STICK IT OUT BECAUSE OF THE PEOPLE HERE.

meet me on this corner, at this time, and we'll throw mayonnaise and ketchup at each other," and people will show up, armed and ready.

Some friends from Richmond, Virginia came to town in a school bus for the first Bike Kill, and we formed a gang called the Dump Trucks. The event was held on a dead end street in Bed-Stuy, and there was an obstacle course with gross, piss-stained mattresses that you had to ride over. It was one of the dirtiest, most lawless events I've ever seen in New York. People lined up on the side of the street and threw full trashcans at you as you rode by them! The party ended with the sound of ambulance sirens. My friends immediately went back to Virginia and started their own version of Bike Kill, called Slaughterama, which still happens today.

I have the memories (mostly), but Tod has the negatives: I've seen them. First, these images started showing up on his blog, Sucka Pants. That was when I realized his photos were really fucking good. I was shocked when he told me he hadn't had an exhibition of his work, and so we promptly organized his first solo show at Cinders, a gallery that I ran with Kelie Bowman in Williamsburg. I was stoked to go through his archive. It's dense. Not only is it an important document of a specific scene as it

was growing, but the photographs are beautifully shot from the point of view of a participant. Tod is right there: in the pit, hopping fences and freight trains, exploring the desolate and the abandoned, capturing wild times and stunningly simple moments alike.

Sto Len is an artist and co-owner of Cinders Gallery with Kelie Bowman. Cinders was founded as an alternative art space in Brooklyn in 2005, and is now a nomadic, project-based non-profit.

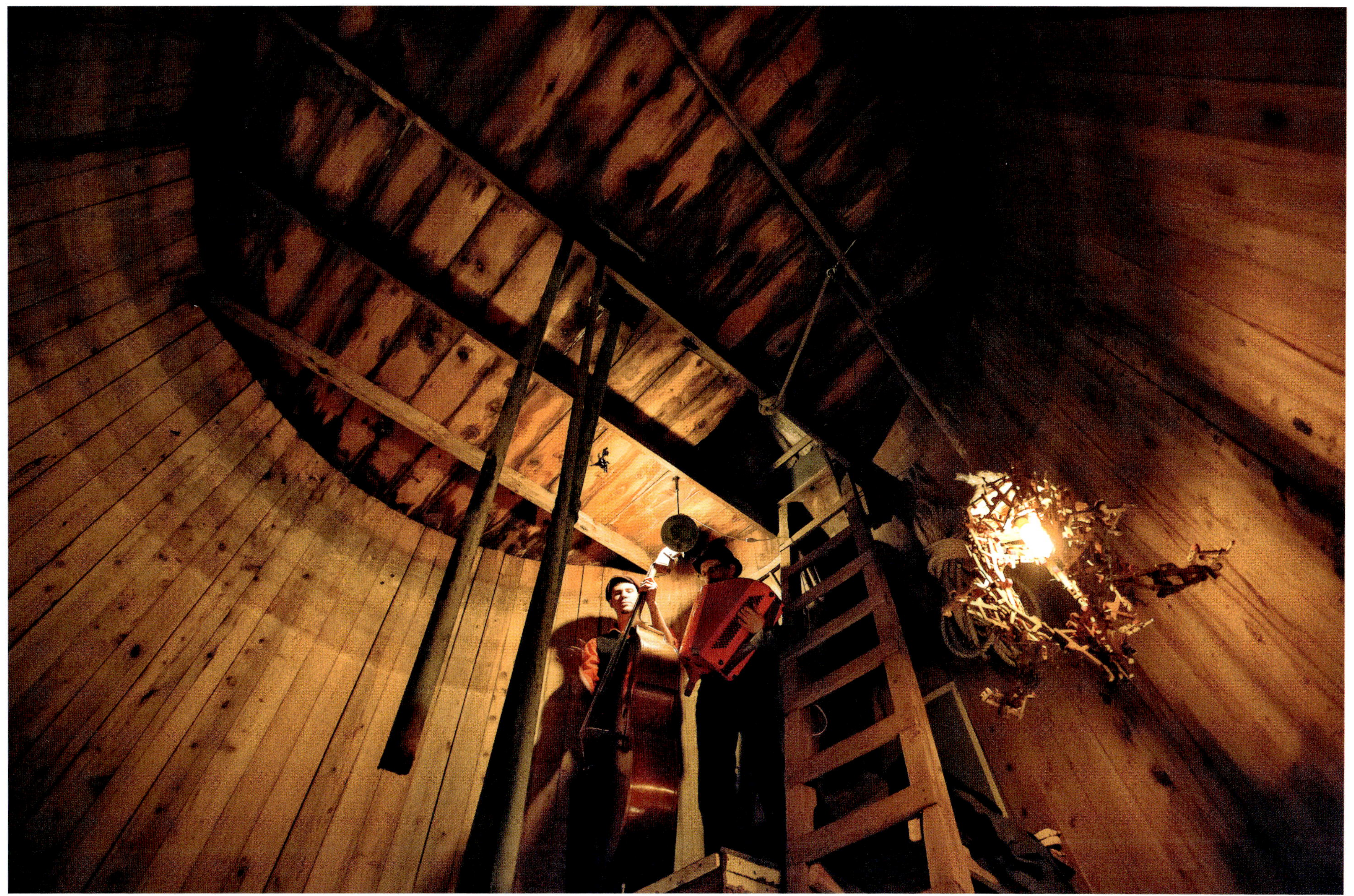

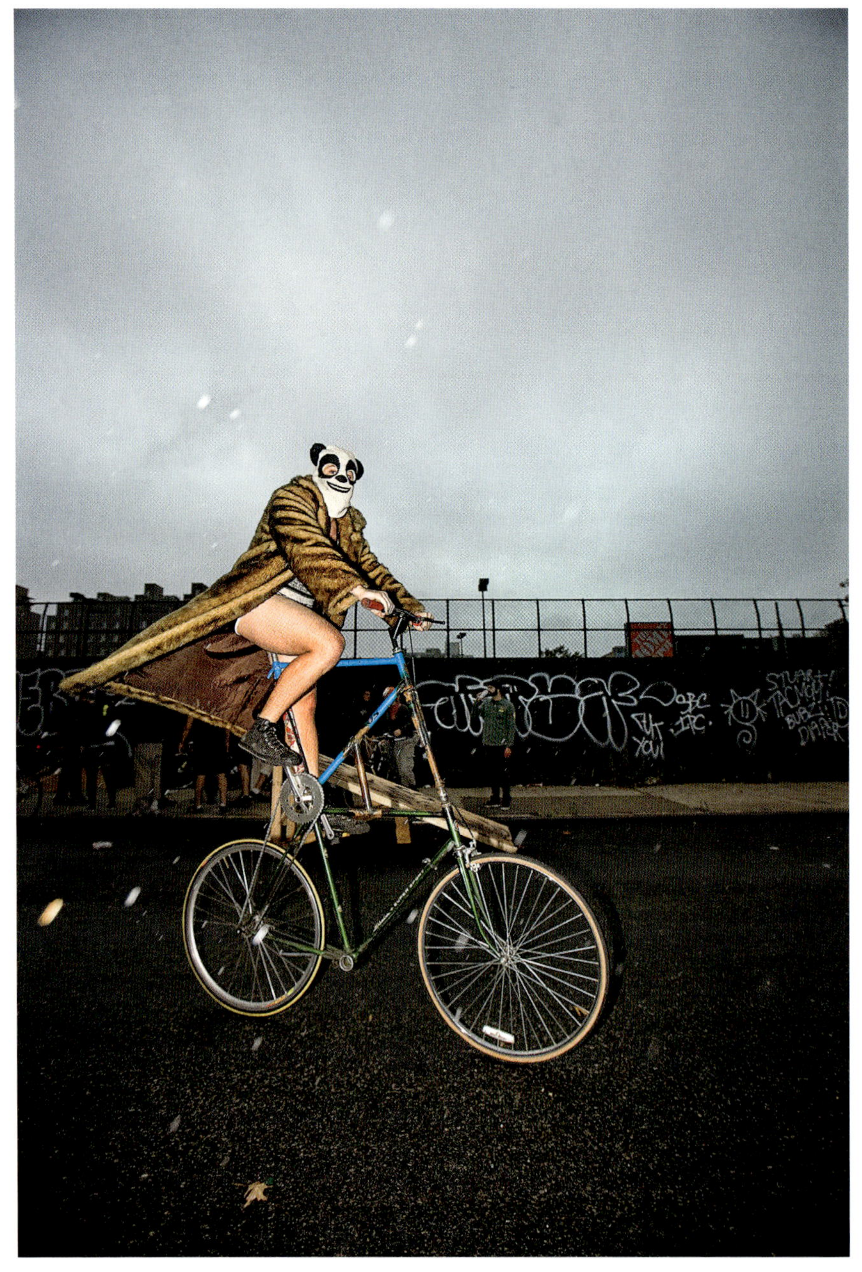

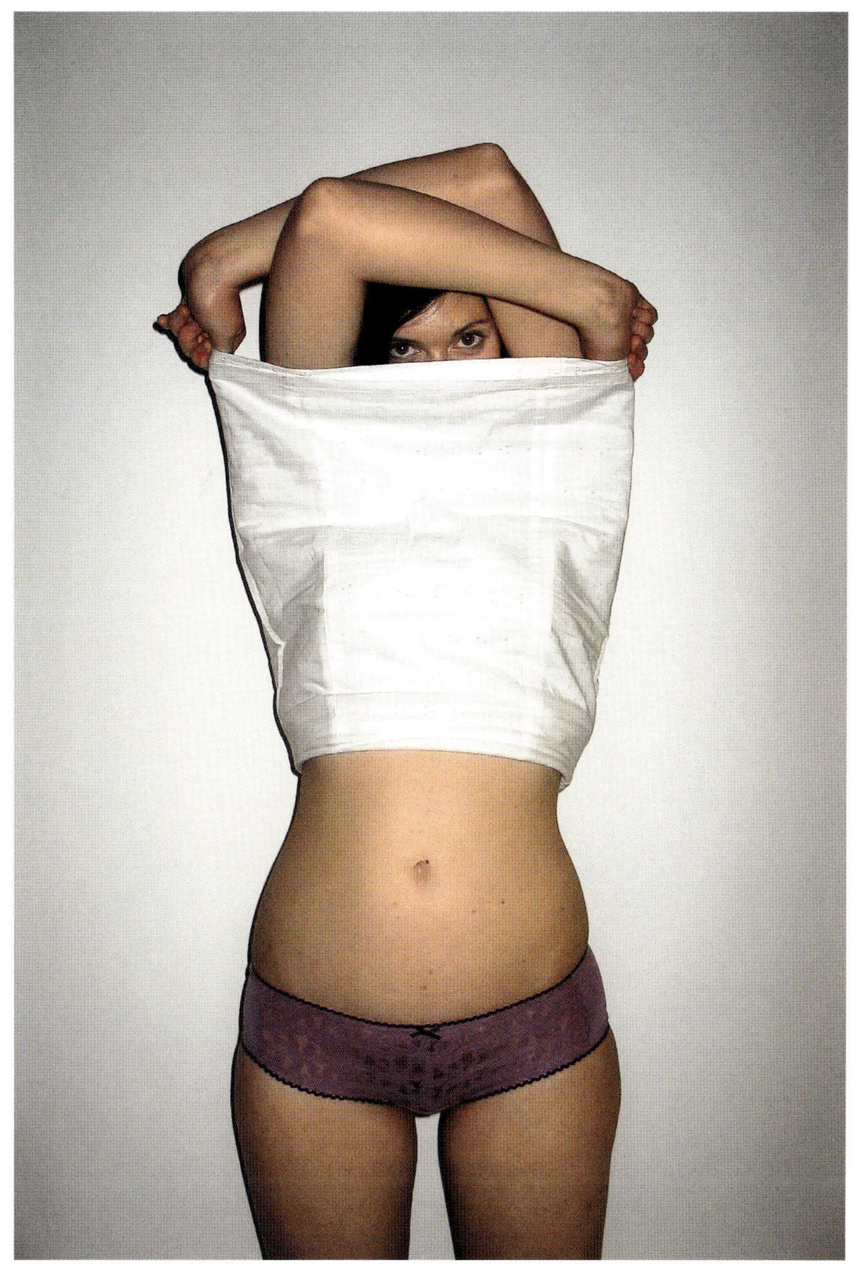

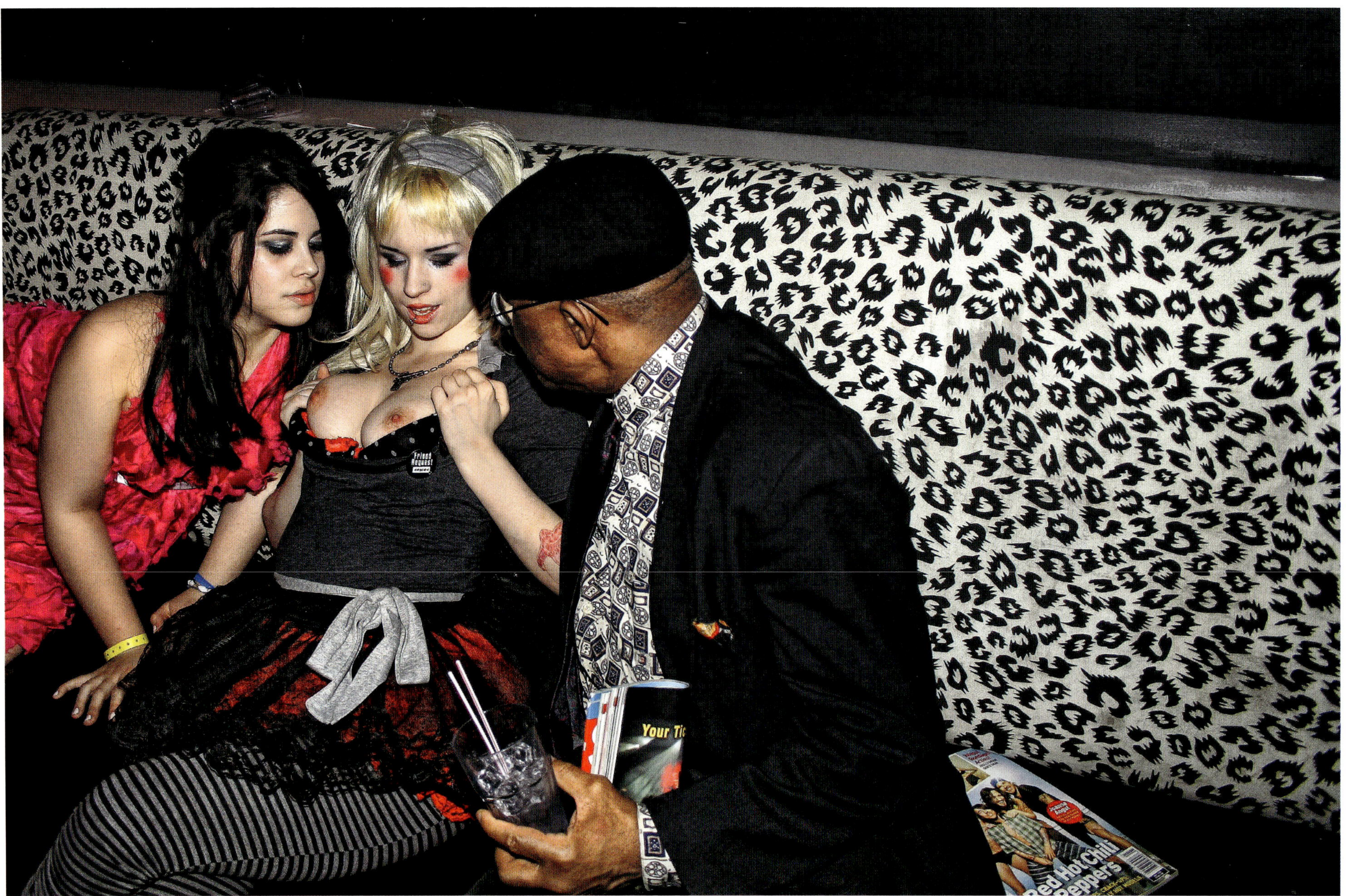

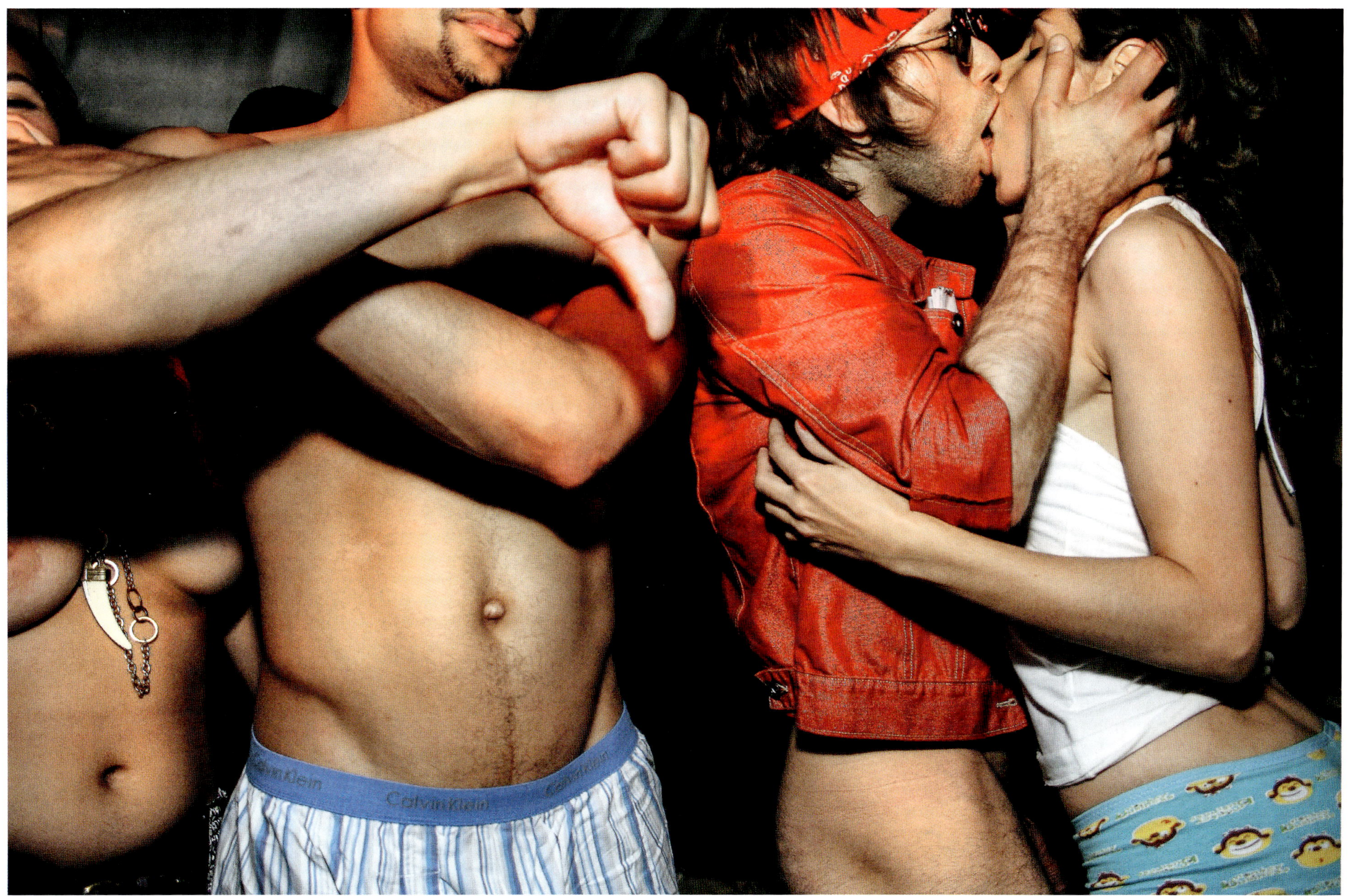

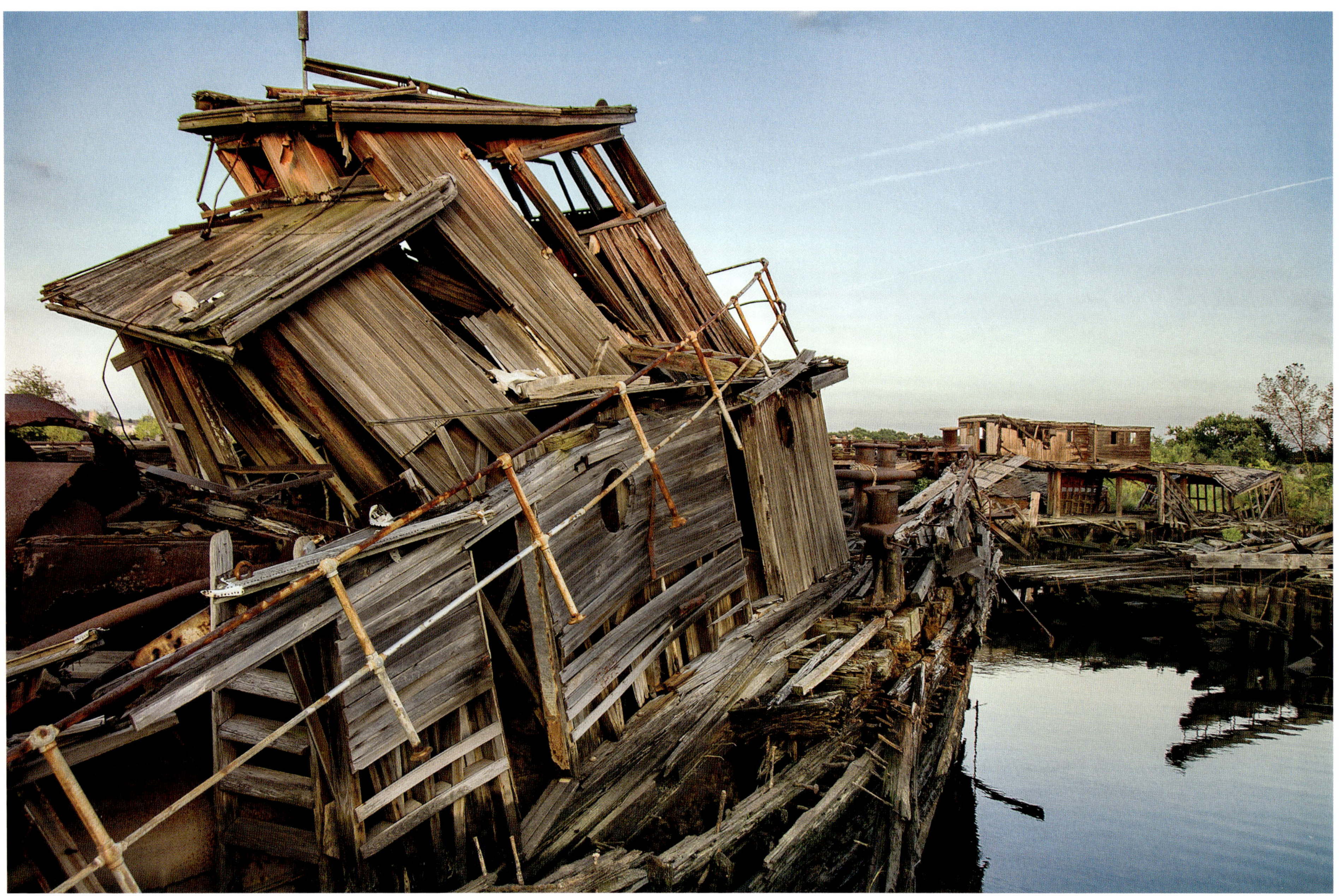

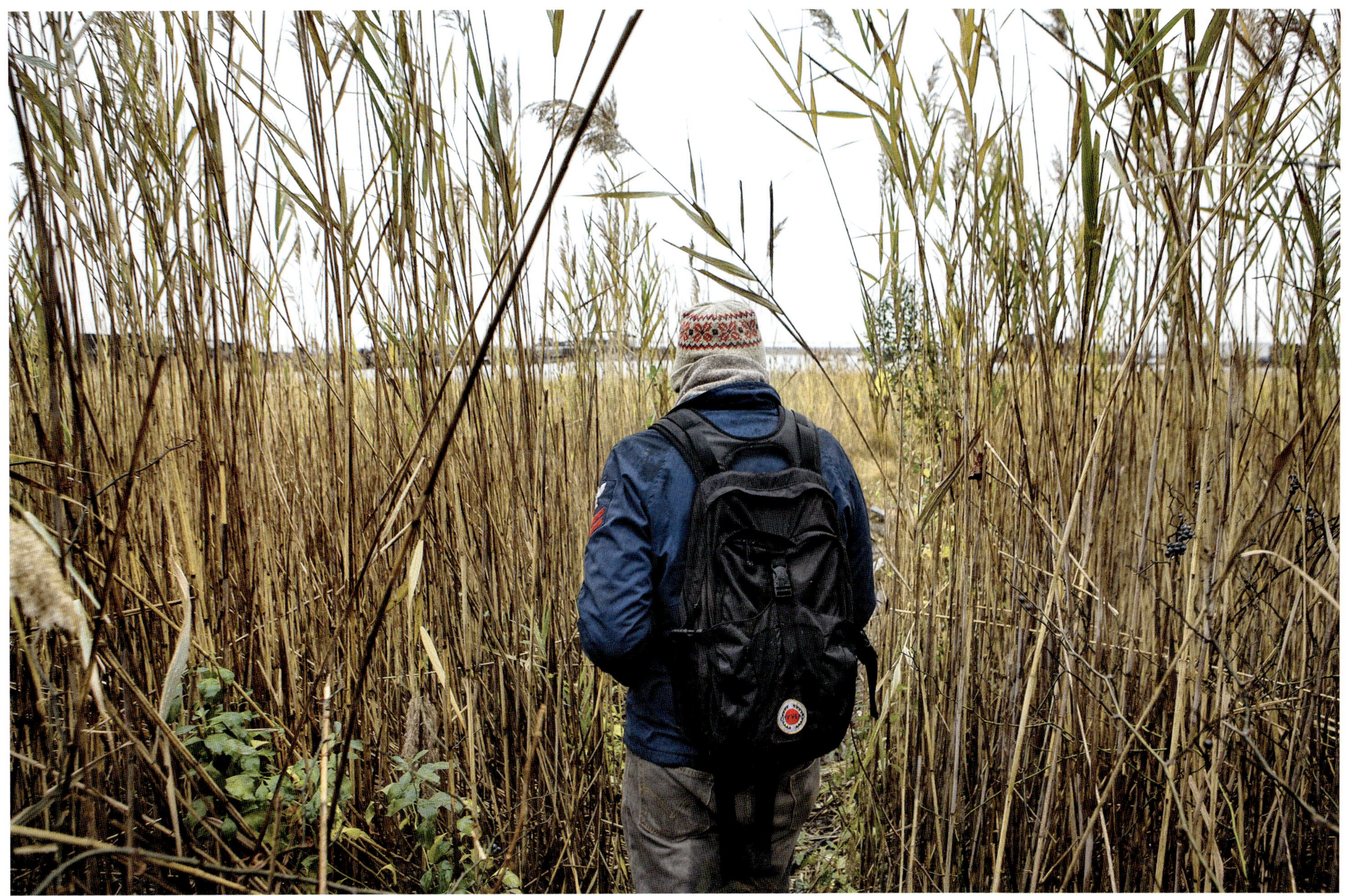

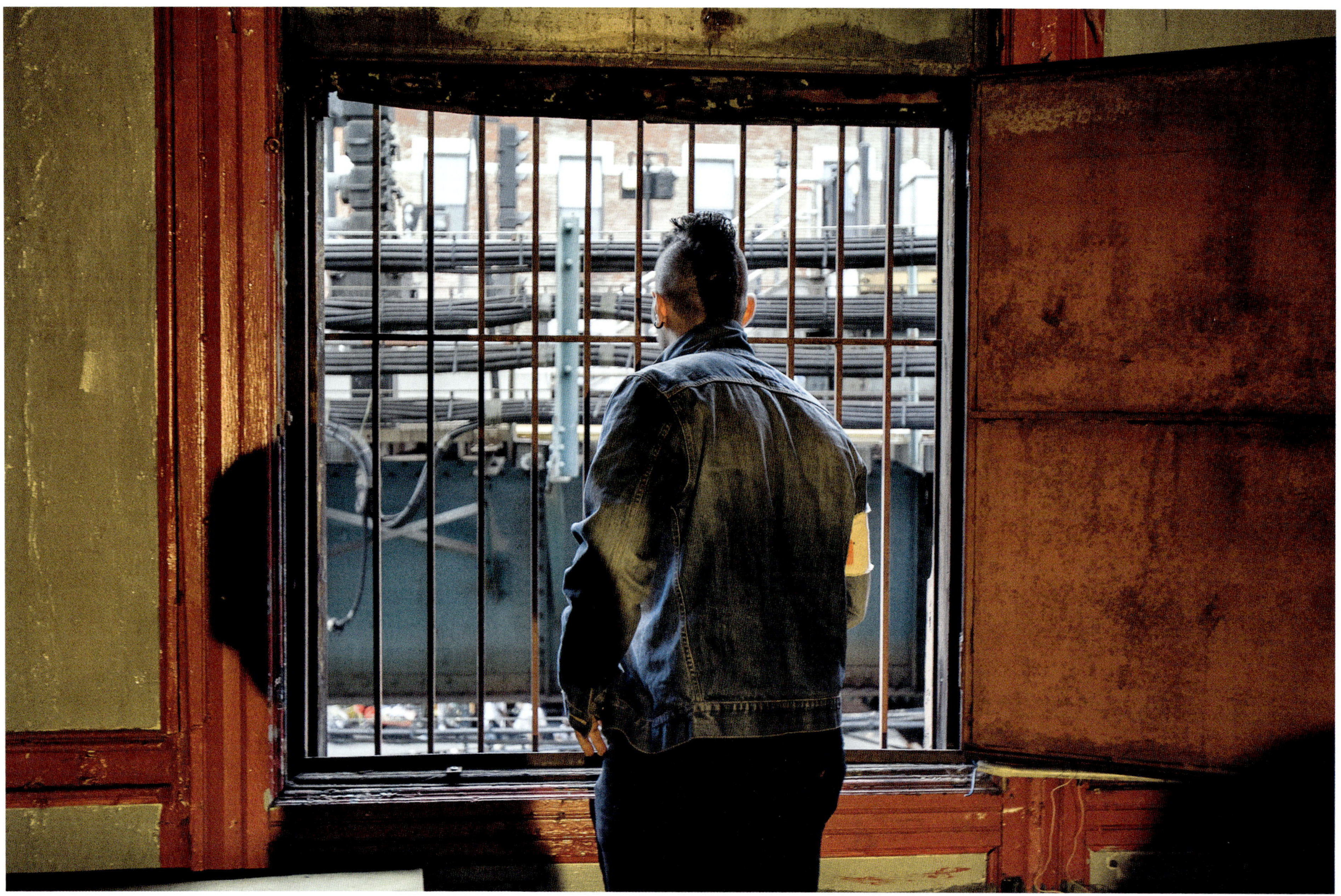

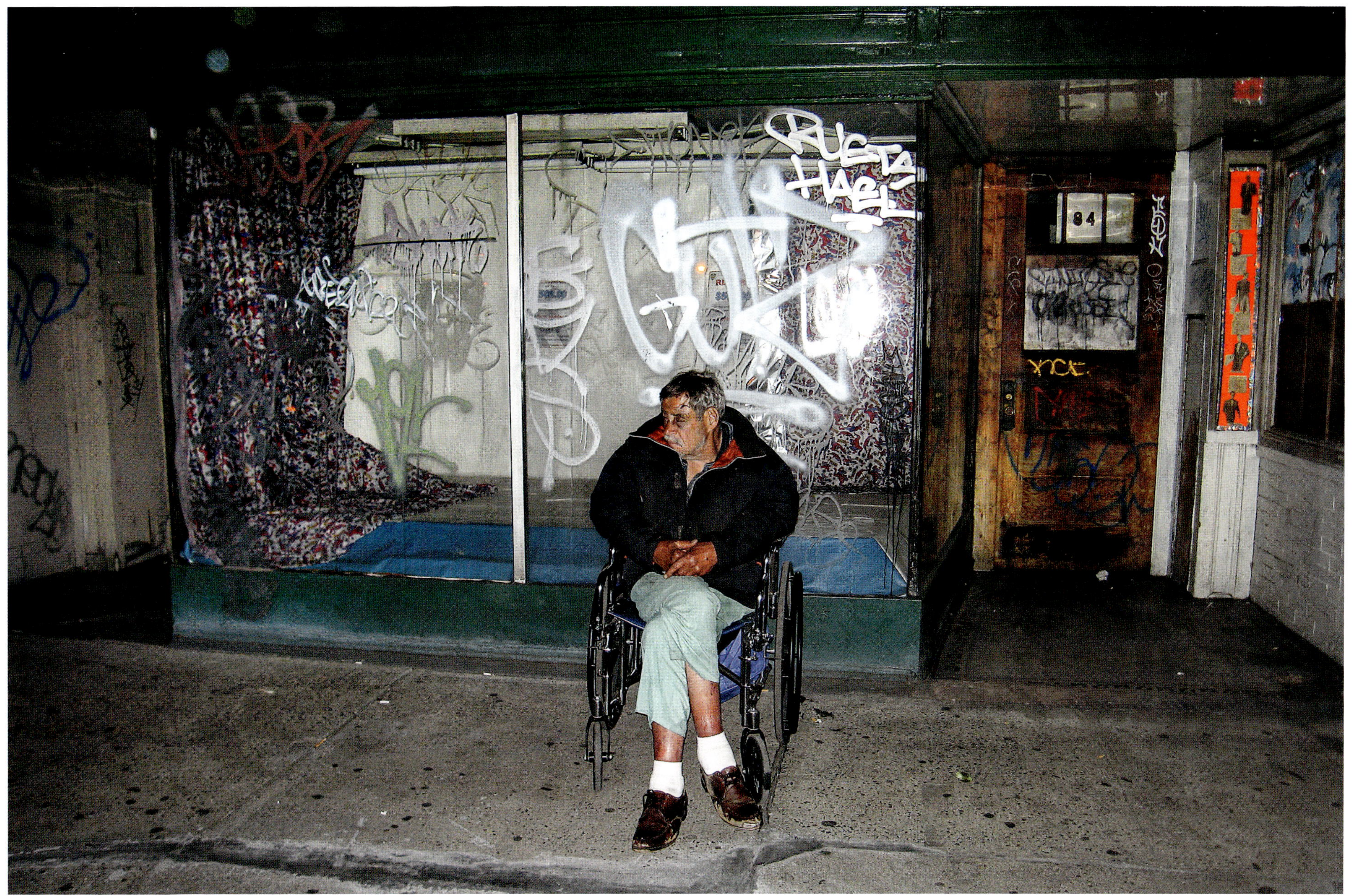

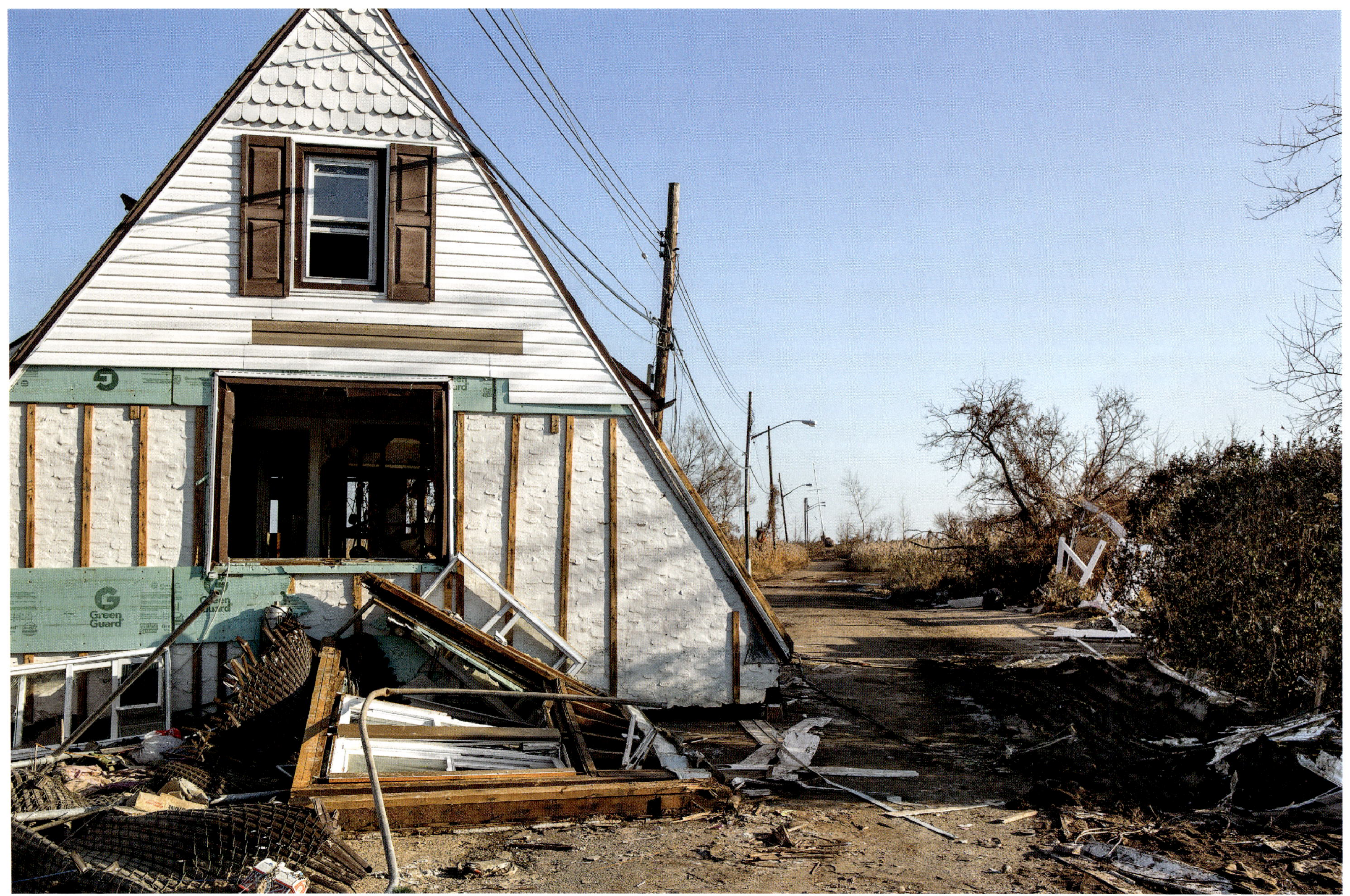

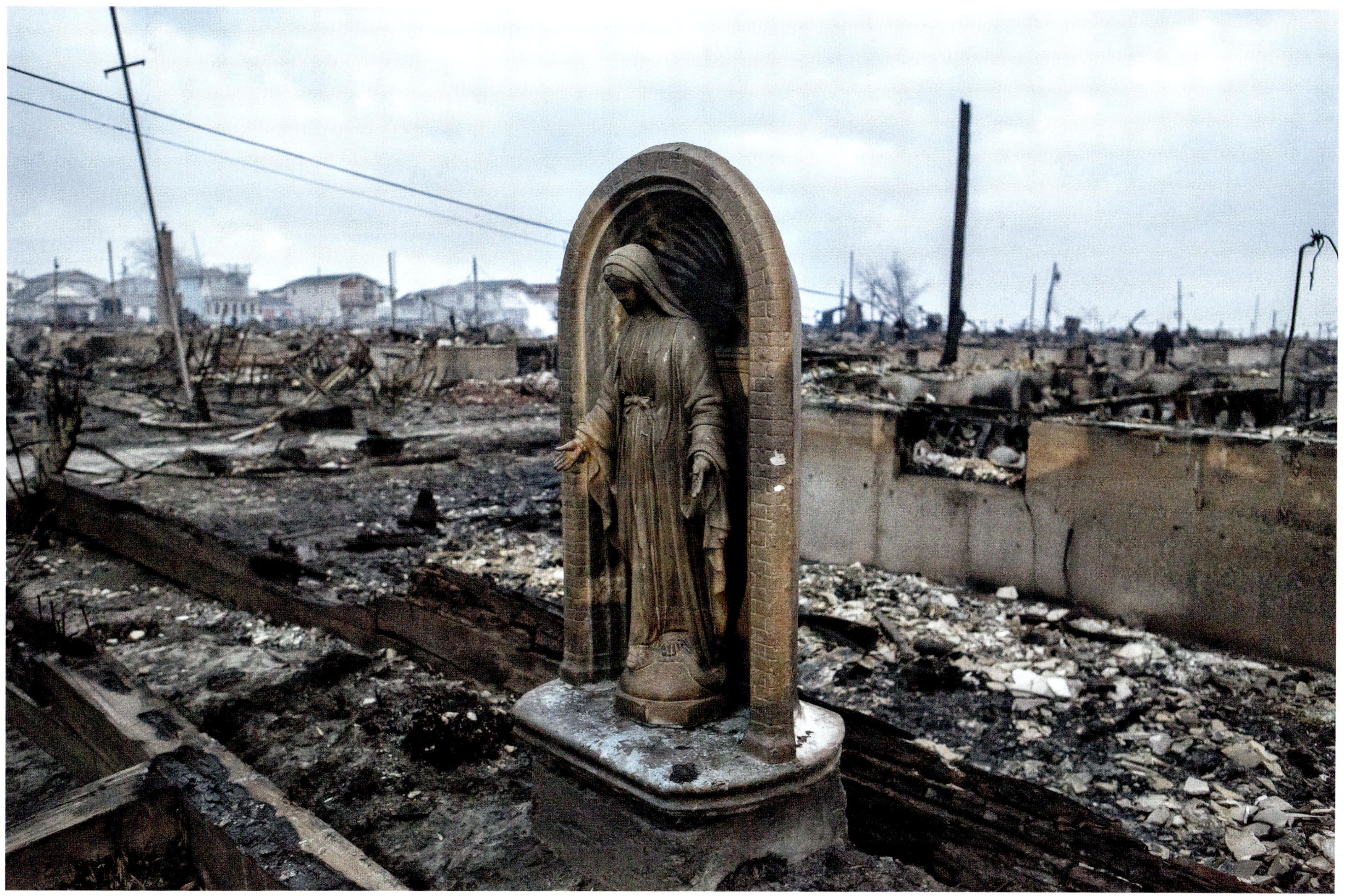

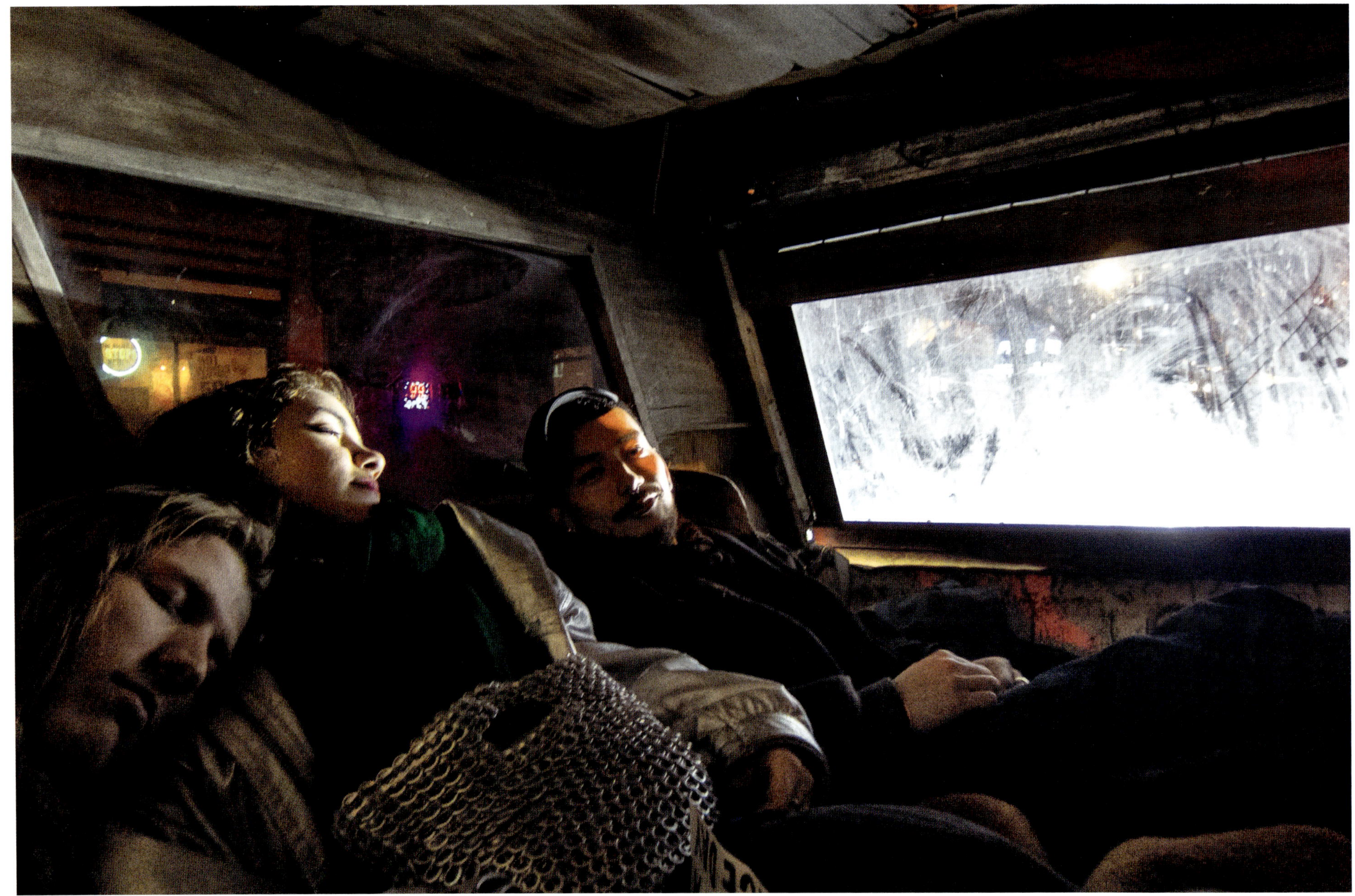

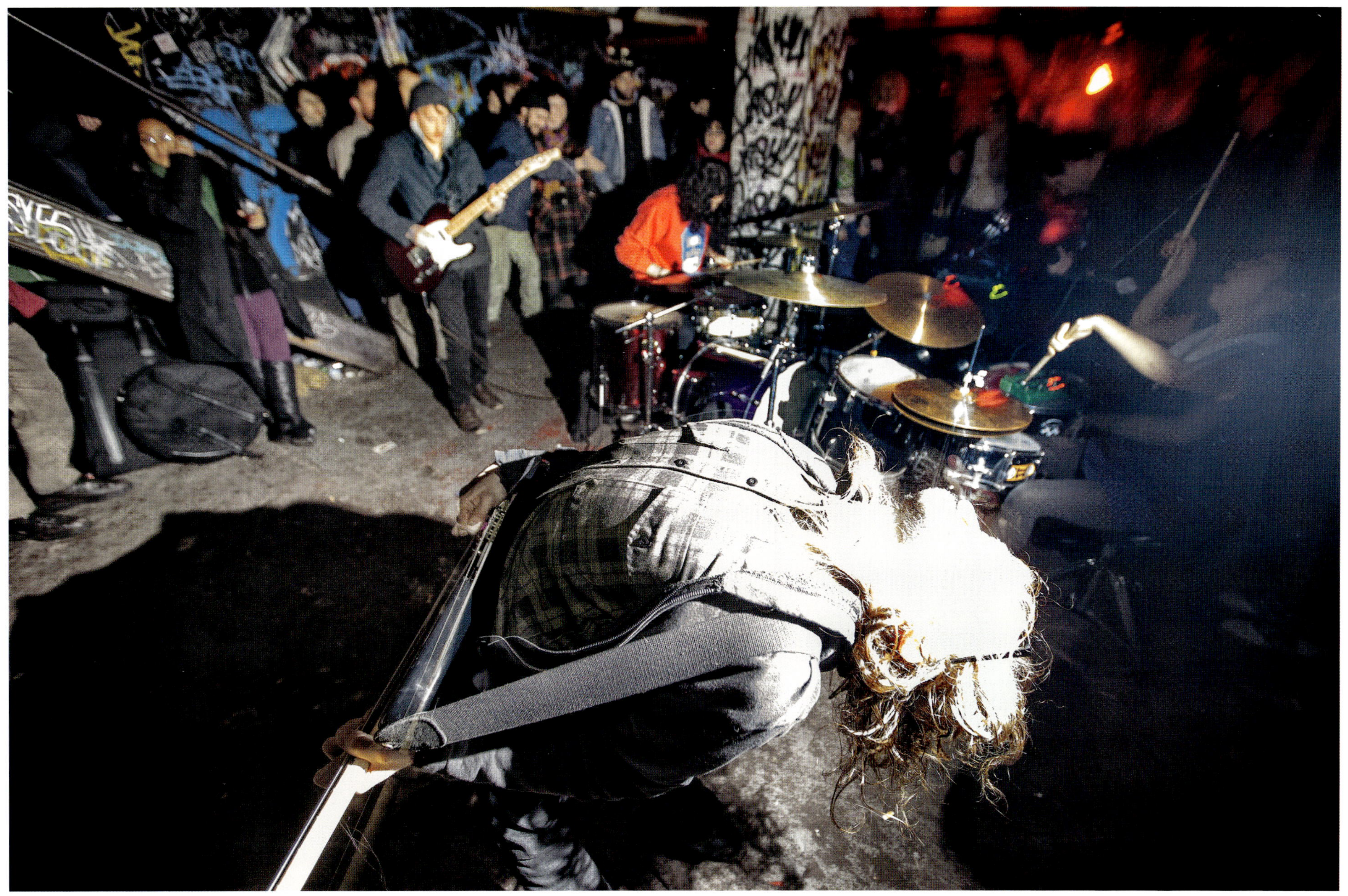

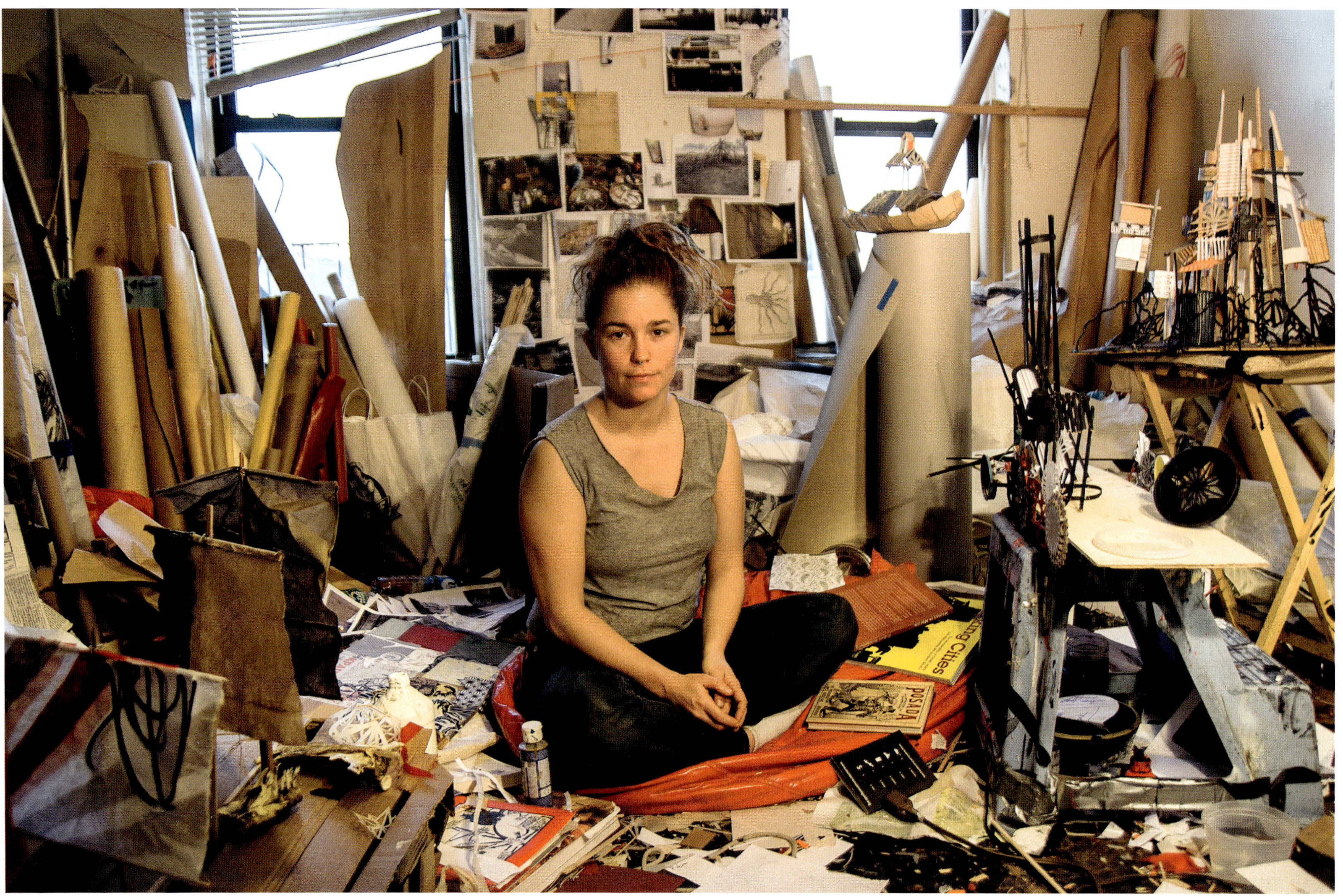

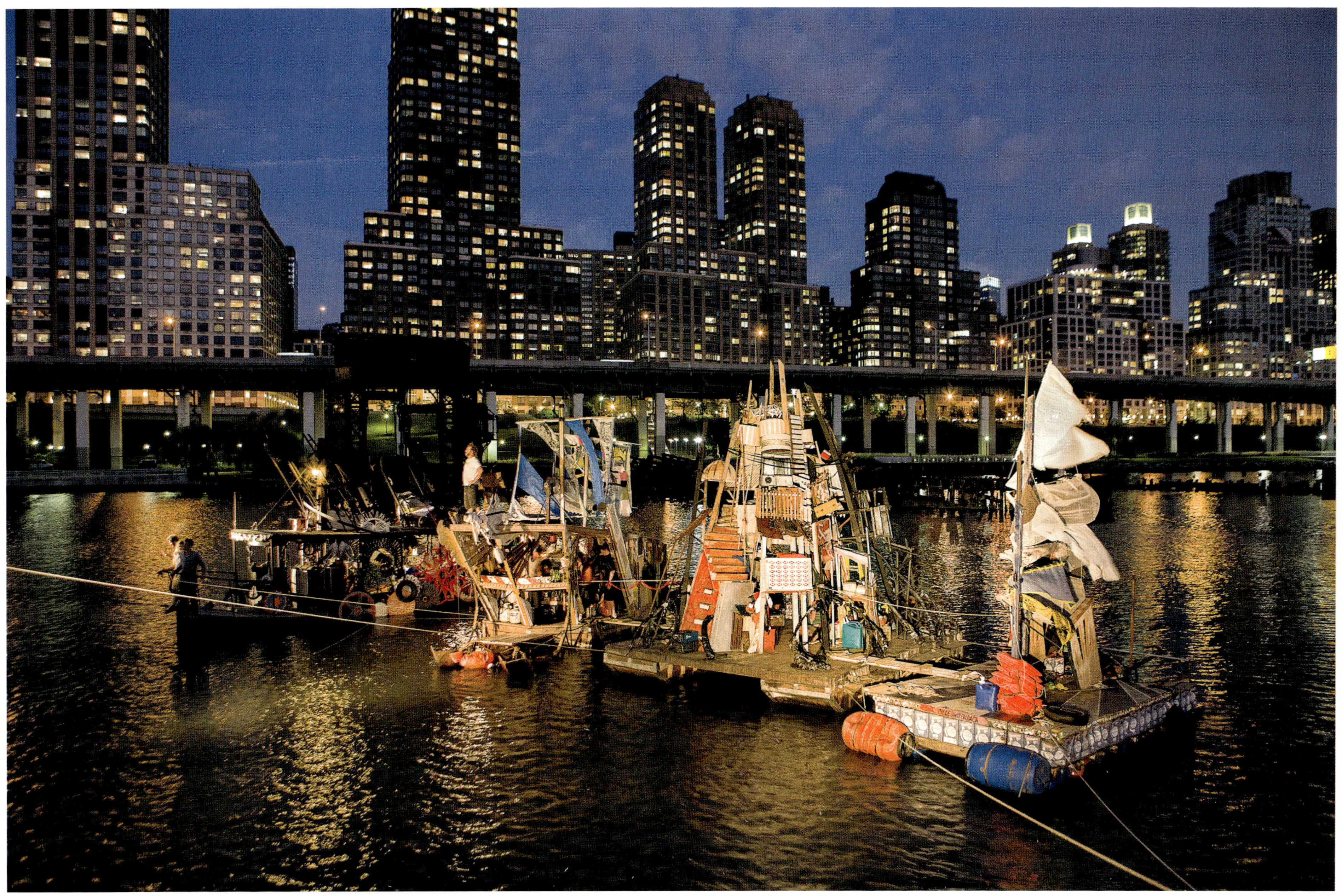

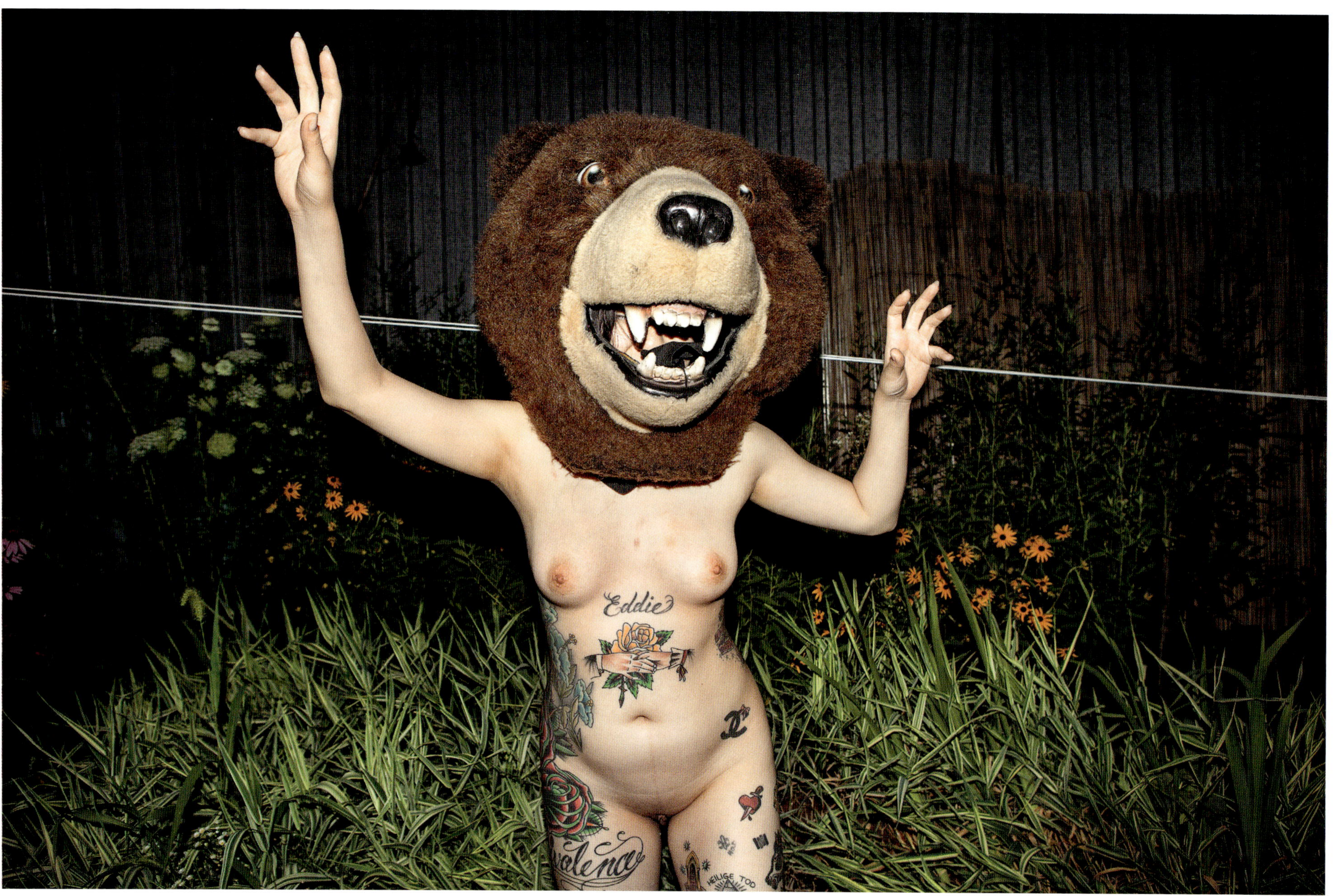

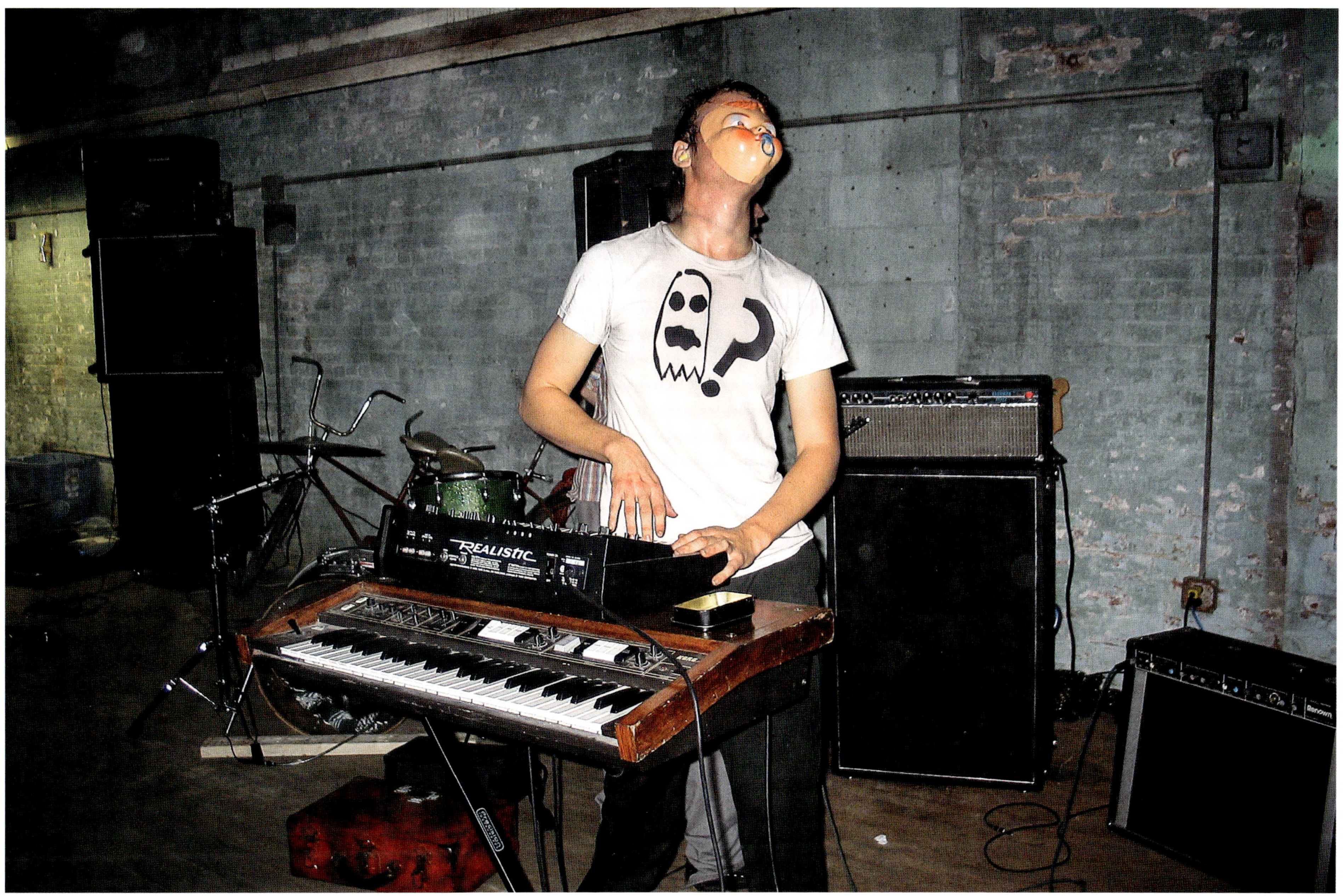
REALISTIC

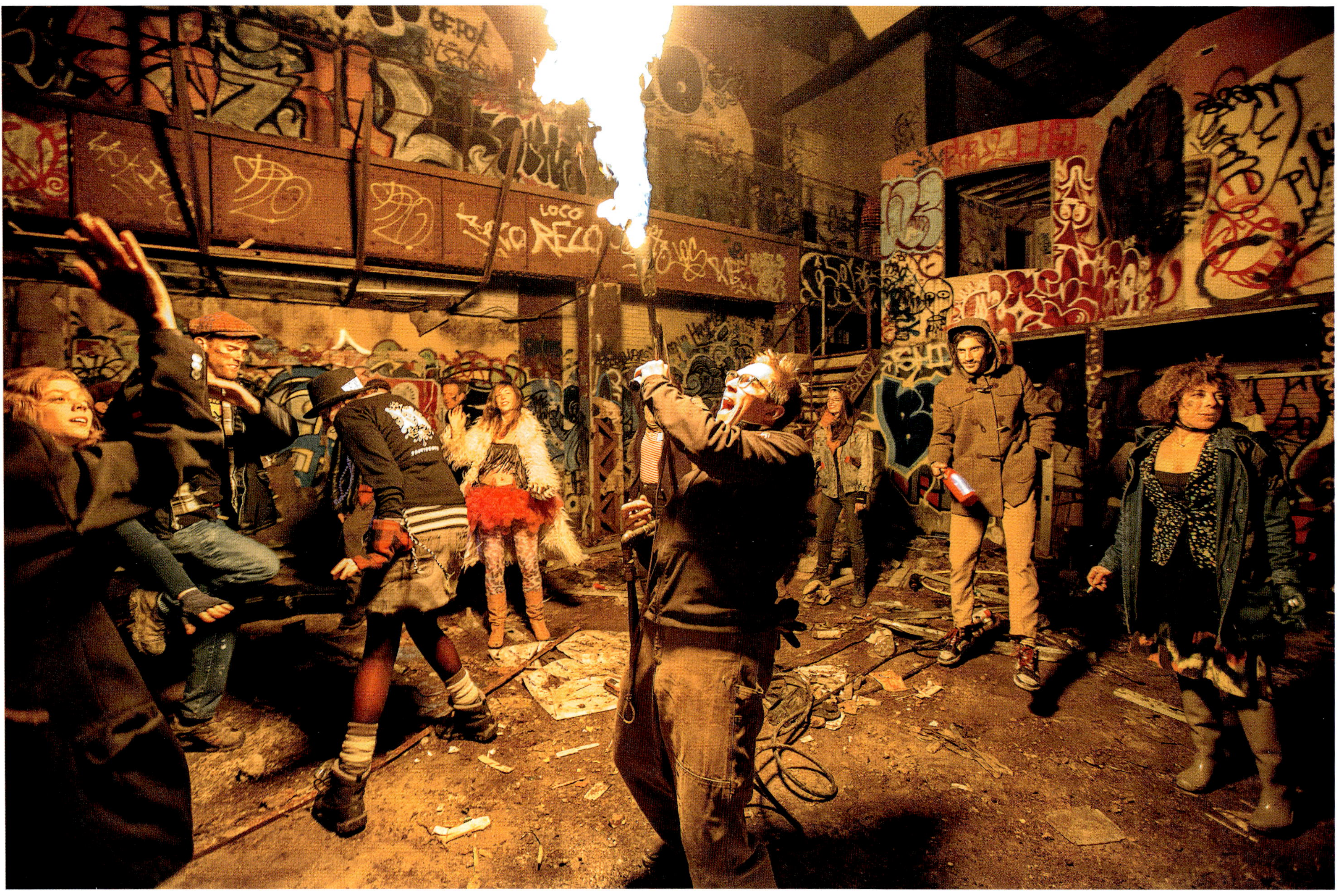

THE CITY ASKEW

BENJAMIN SHAPIRO

If you walk a few miles out of downtown Austin, Texas, east on 6th Street, the lilting live oak trees and free clinics fade into cut-rate fast food chains, gas stations, check cashing centers, and finally to a cracked soup of urban decay. Out there, nestled on a slight bank between burnt-out buildings, there's a crumbling split-level called the Shit Pit. It's the home base for the Austin contingent of a grimy, post-apocalyptic crust punk cycling unit called the Skid Marxxx. That's where I first met Tod Seelie.

The first time I went to the Shit Pit, I saw a parade of atrocities: a gang of 12-year-olds destroying a burning car with skateboards. A punk on PCP trying to jump over that car and stumbling into the jagged glass of its broken windshield, cutting her knee to the cap as she gaped around wild-eyed, screaming, "You can see my bone! You can see my bone!" A particularly brutal mosh pit, presided over by eardrum-rupturing metal bands with no public address system save for an oversized bullhorn, through which singers barked lyrics over the sludge. I saw a sealed paint can flung out of the pit knock a friend of mine out cold, while

frenzied crusties jumped off the roof with lit roman candles and set their own shed on fire. I also saw a bald bulldog with a bushy handlebar mustache and a camera in the middle of it all, and that was Tod.

This was my first impression of him, and it's stuck even after working as his editor for two years in New York. He's a man who has made it his business to poetically document communities and spaces on the fringes of society, elements forced to stitch themselves to each other as they reject, or are rejected by, everyone else. Throughout his career, Tod has consistently given his subjects room to be effortlessly themselves, caught in fleeting moments of flux between the frenetic chaos and soul-annihilating boredom of modern life.

Tod's travelled as much as anyone can, and he brings these ideas with him when he returns to New York. He sees the city askew, from the inside out. Tod is a habitual presence at the most offbeat spots, biking through desolate streets and

trawling corners of lofts and basements in cut-off denim and an oversized backpack. Having honed his technical prowess to a fine point, he has amassed a striking collection of mini-dramas, a vision of urban life shot while climbing around subway tracks, crouching behind speakers, or floating through the East River. The timing and lyricism with which he captures the unseen vibrancy of these neglected spaces would be impossible were he not so effortlessly, stubbornly, and touchingly brave.

Benjamin Shapiro is a regular contributor to The New Yorker, *a film programmer at Spectacle Theater in Williamsburg, and an editor at* VICE, *where he runs their music website Noisey. He has played drums for bands including Pop. 1280, The Fugue, Asobi Seksu, and Scary Mansion.*

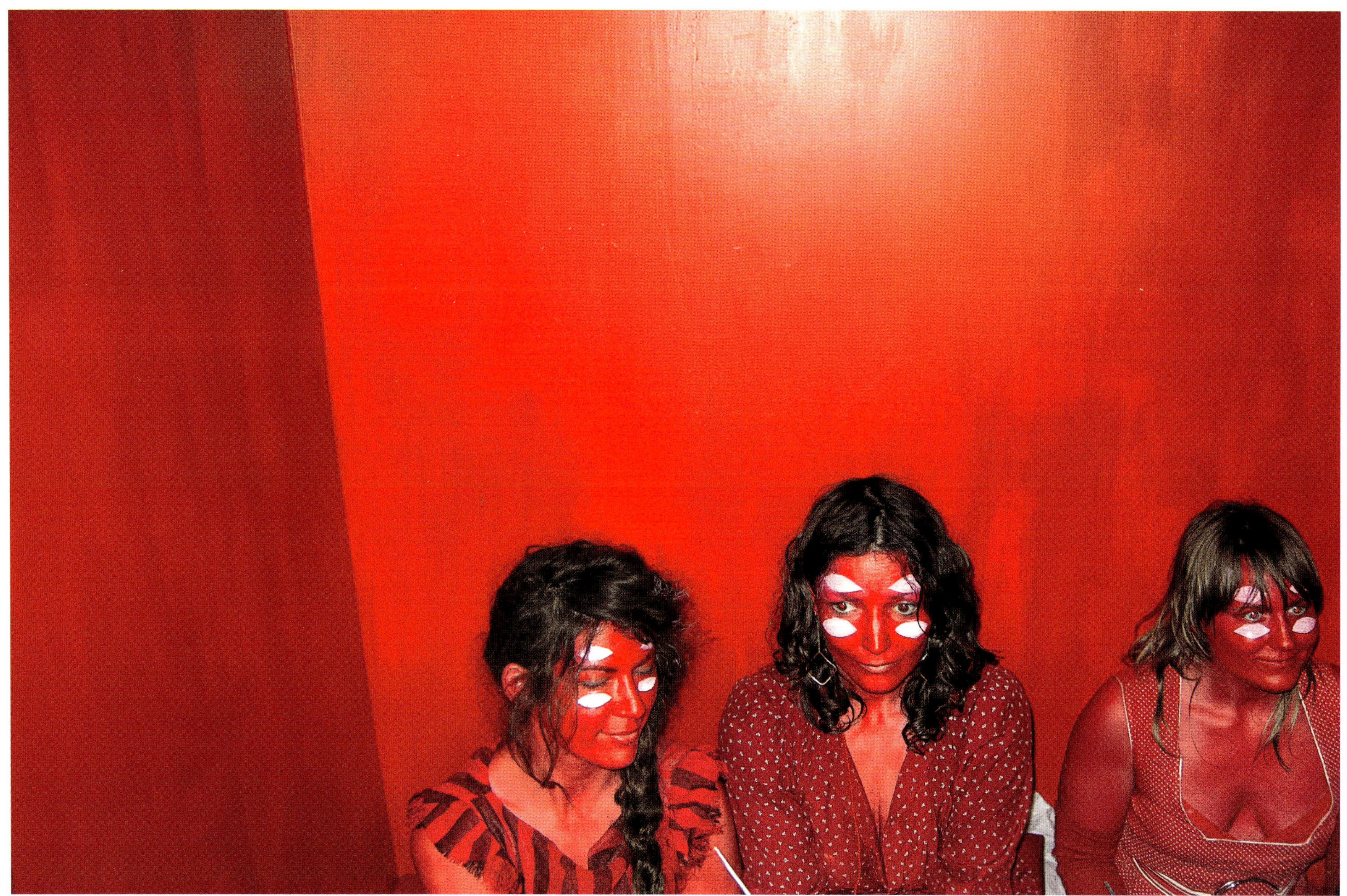

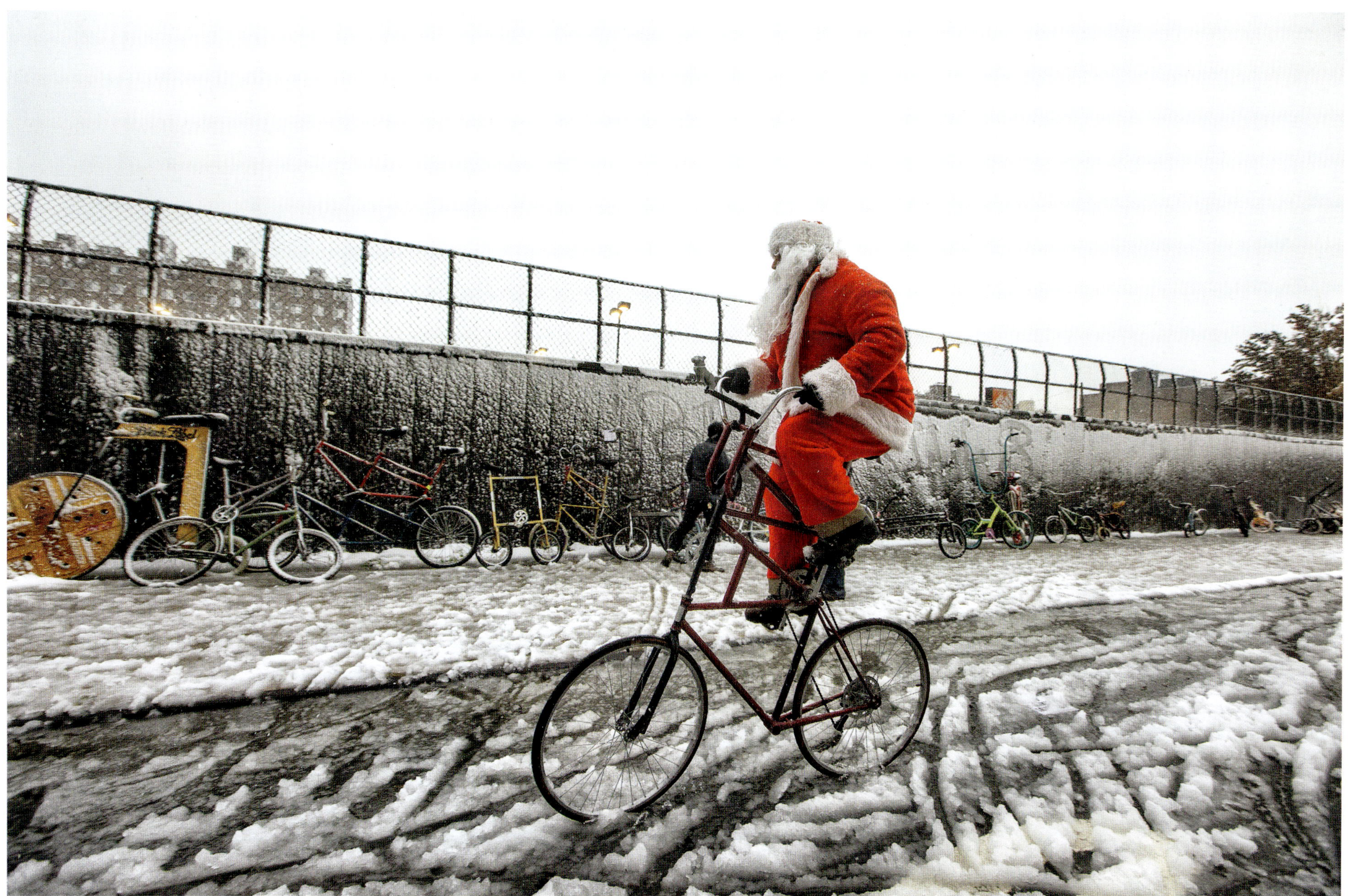

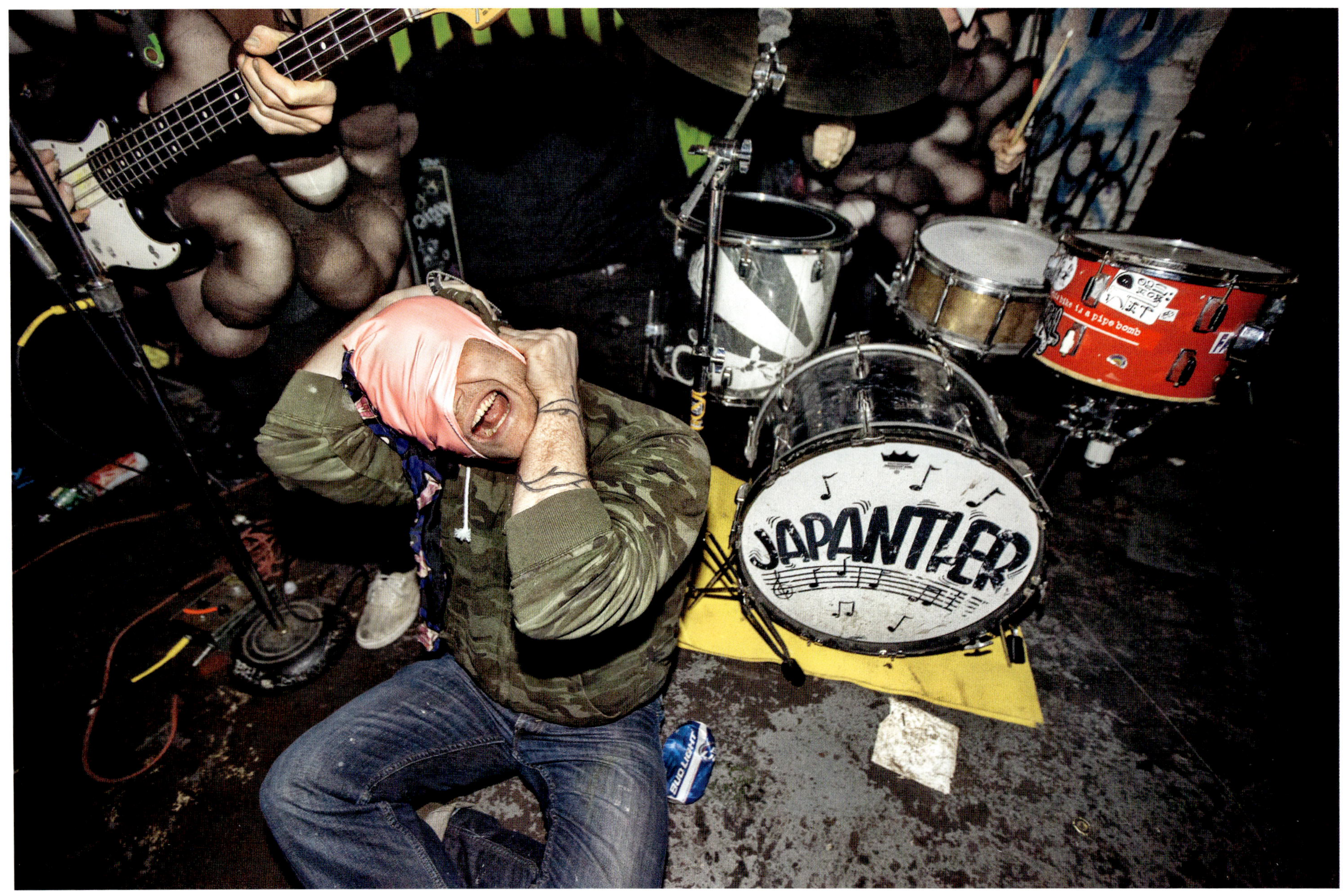

JAPANTHER

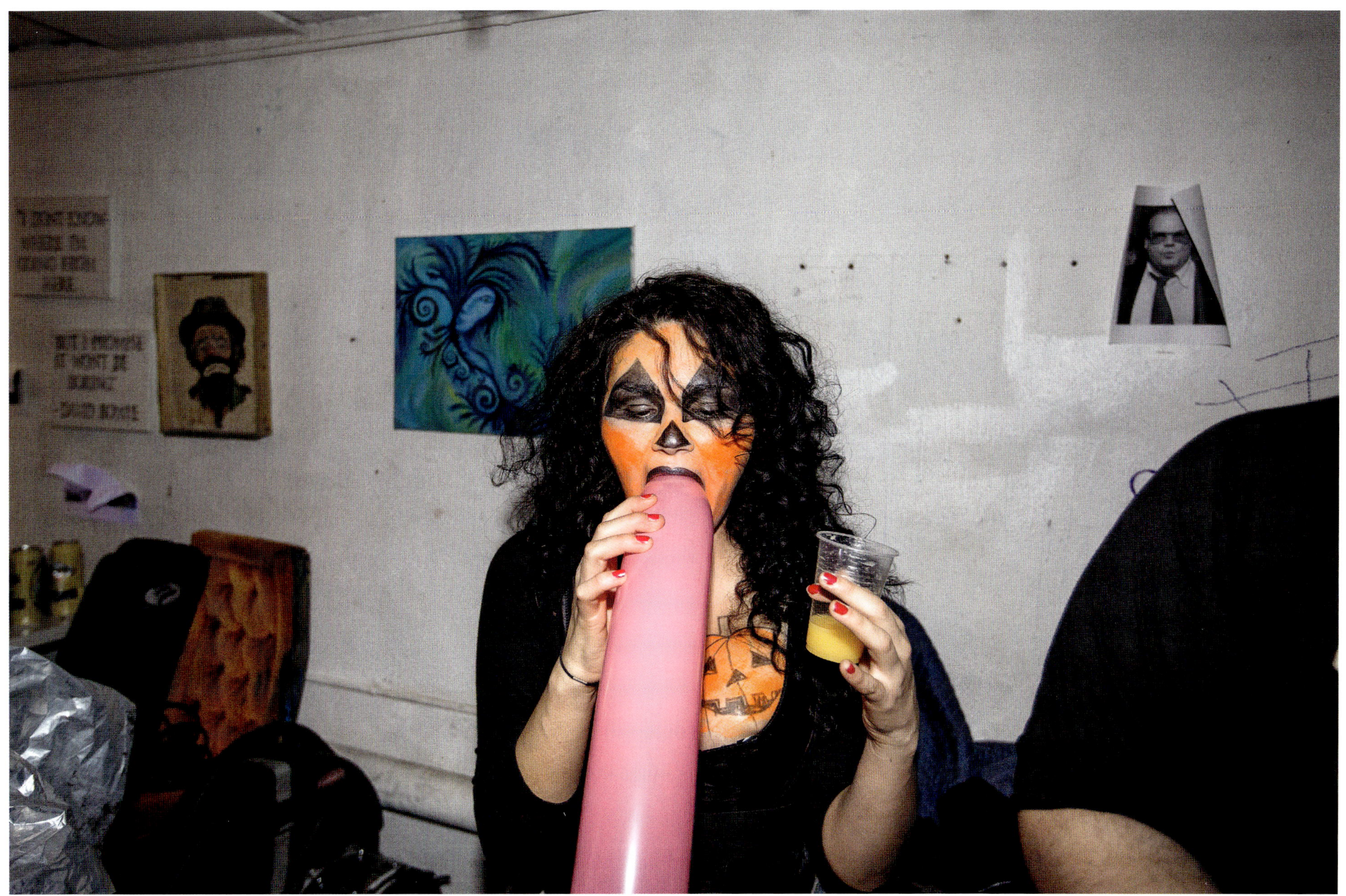

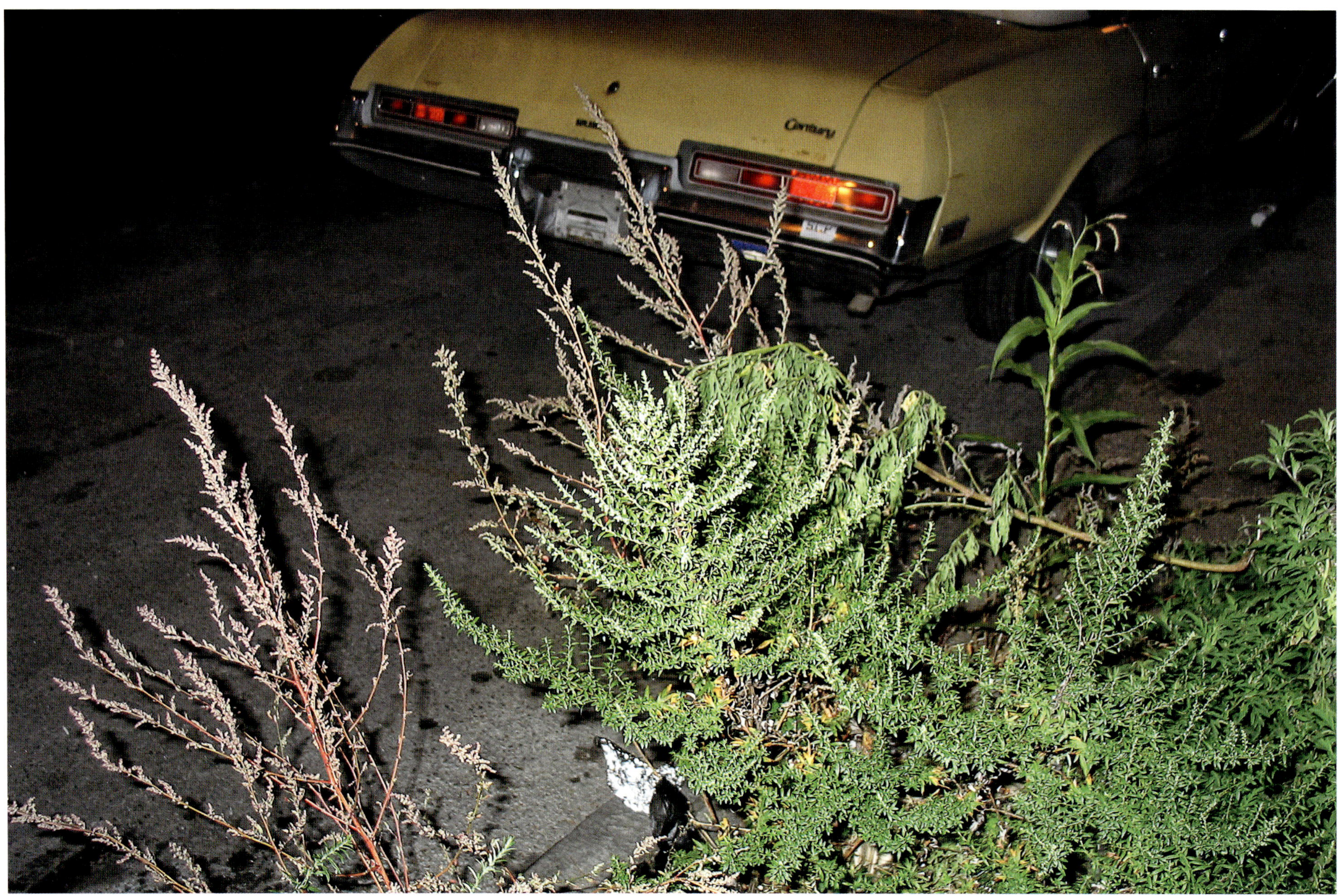

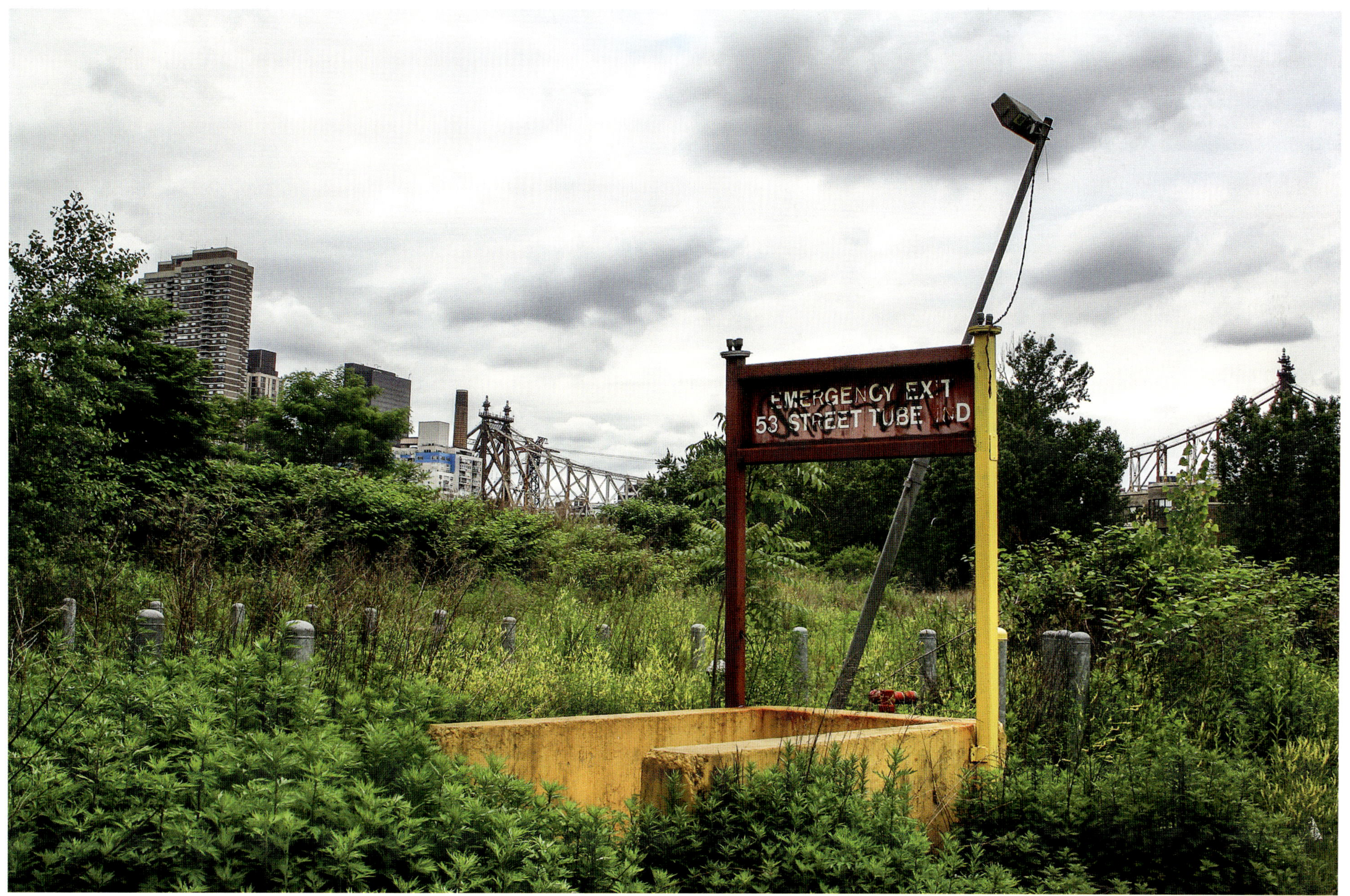

EMERGENCY EXIT
53 STREET TUBE IND

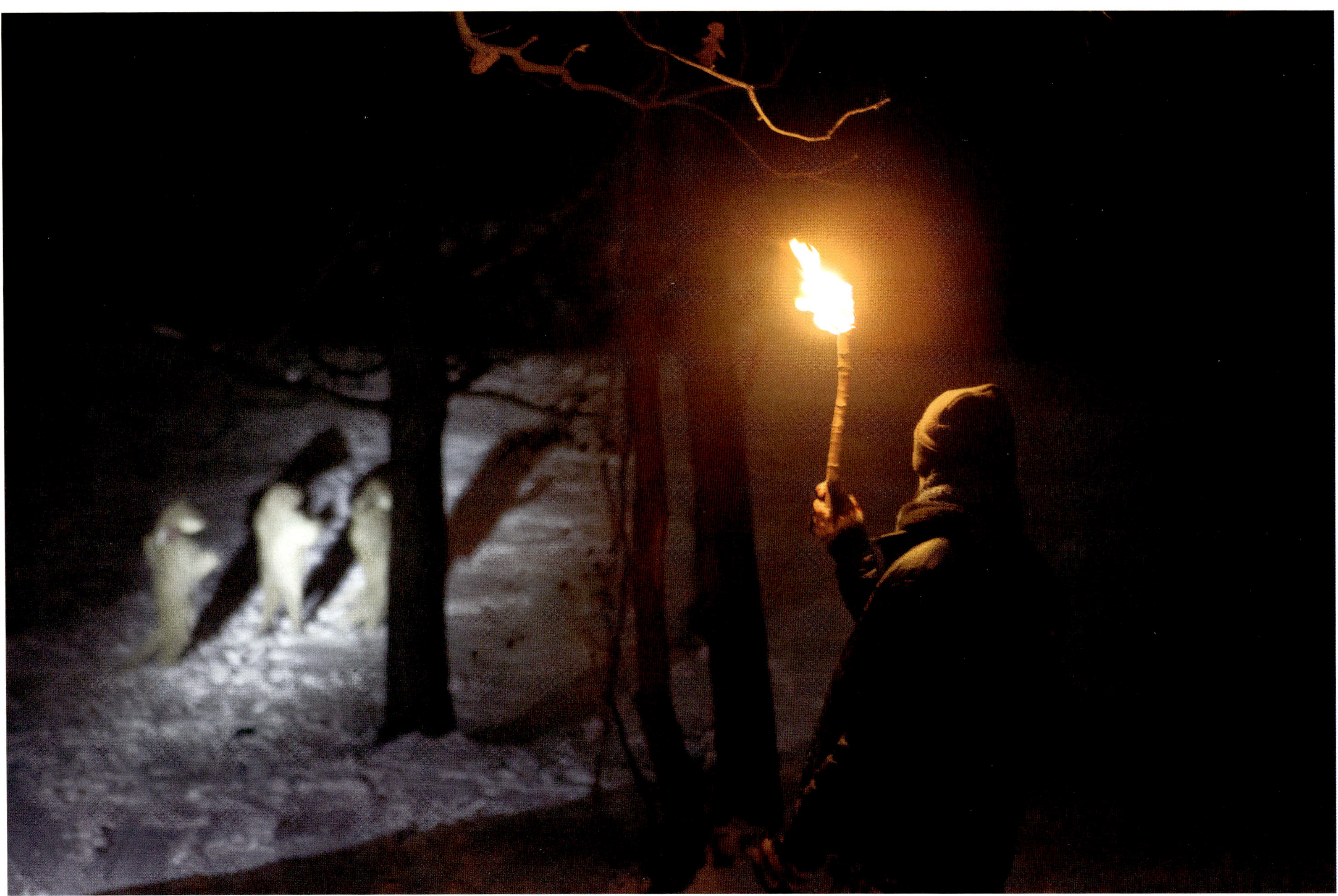

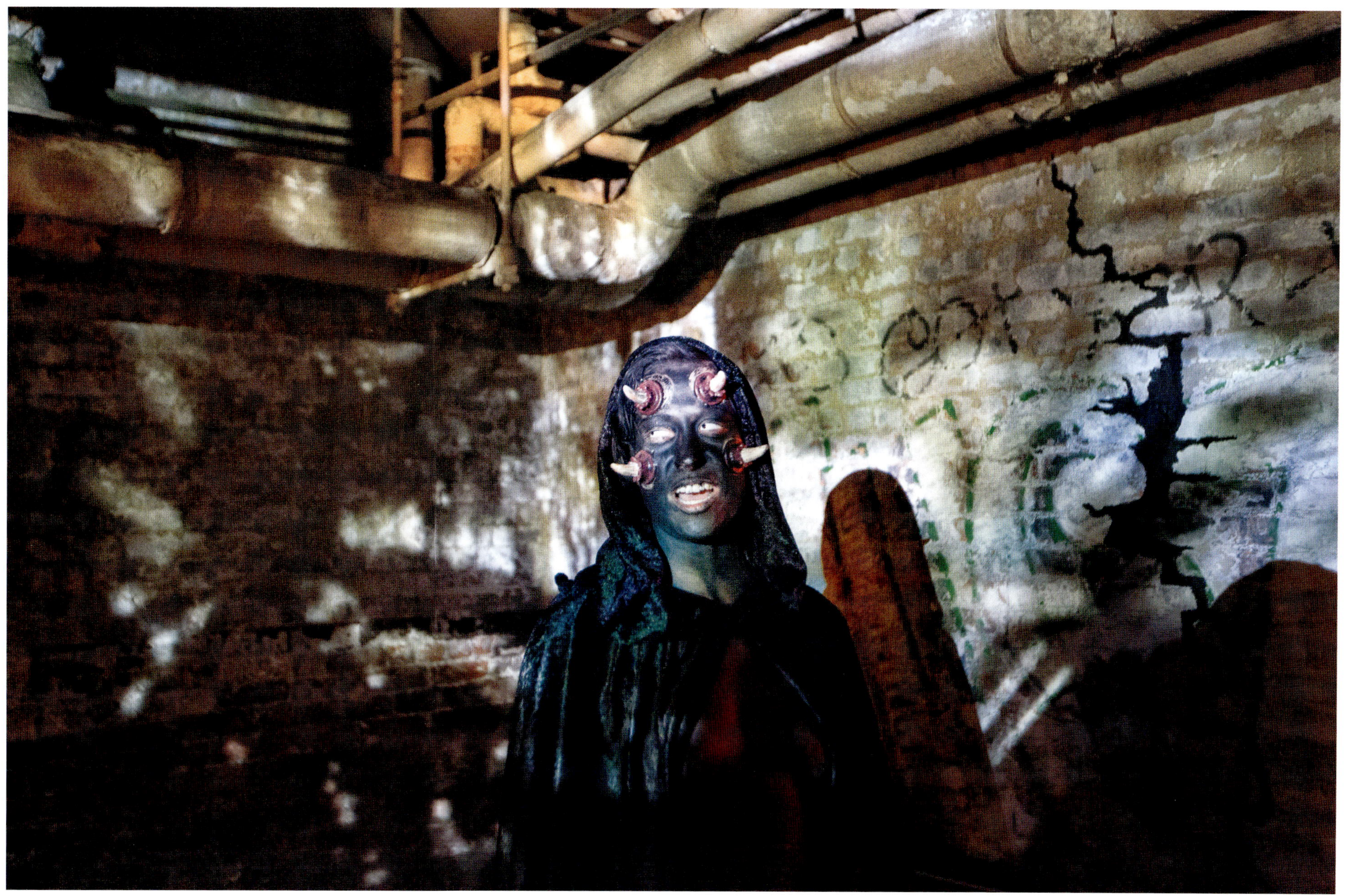

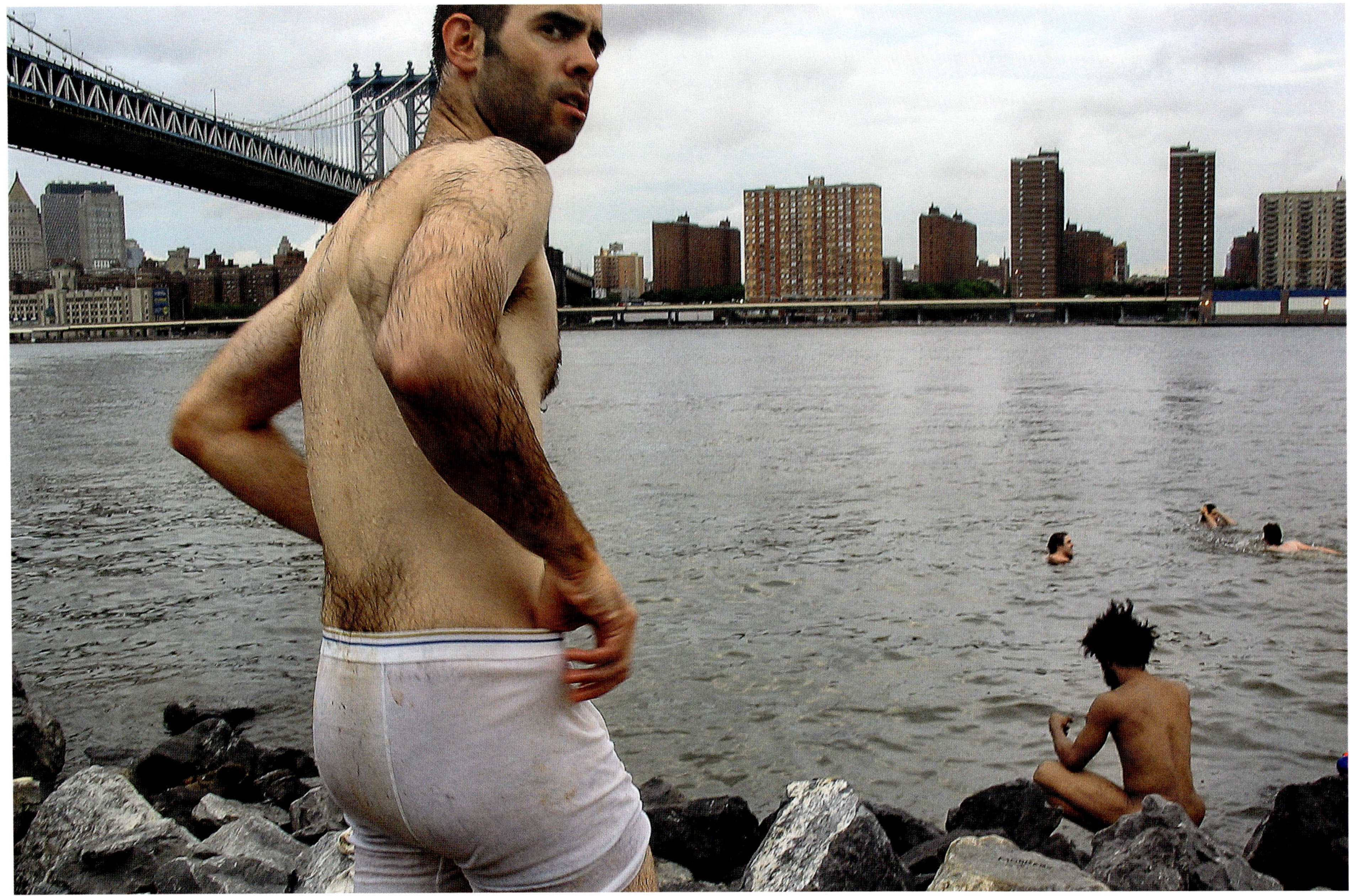

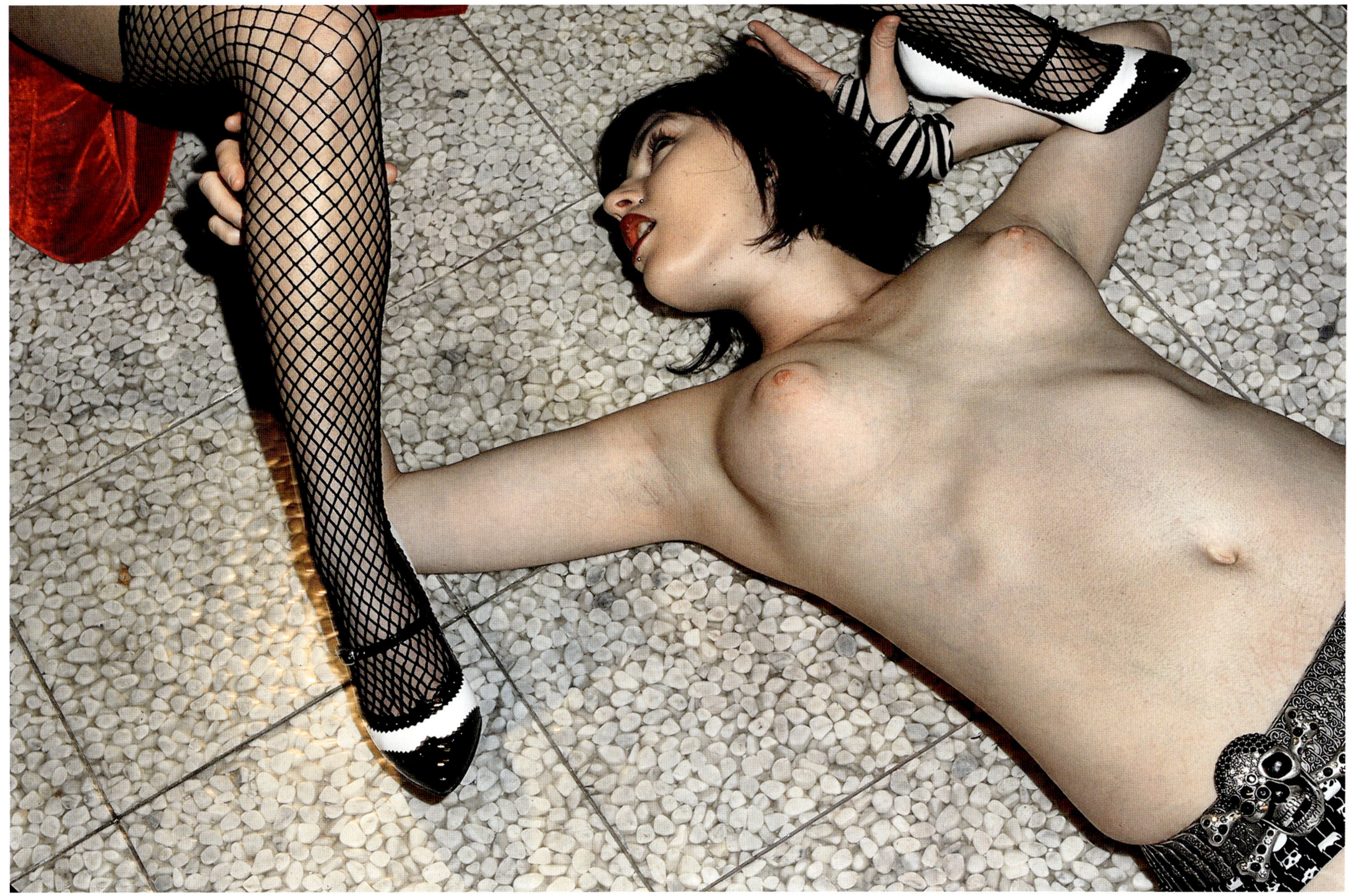

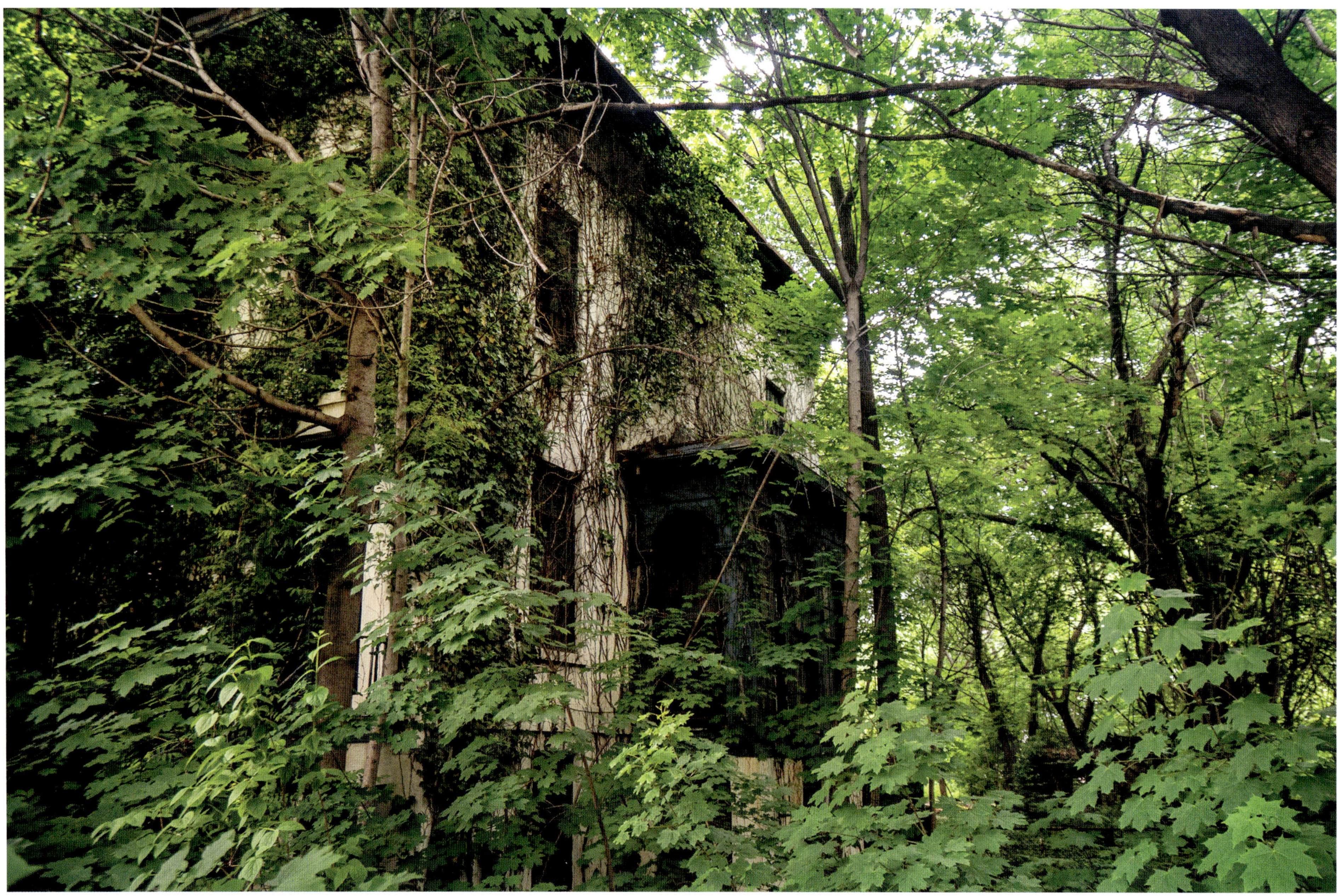

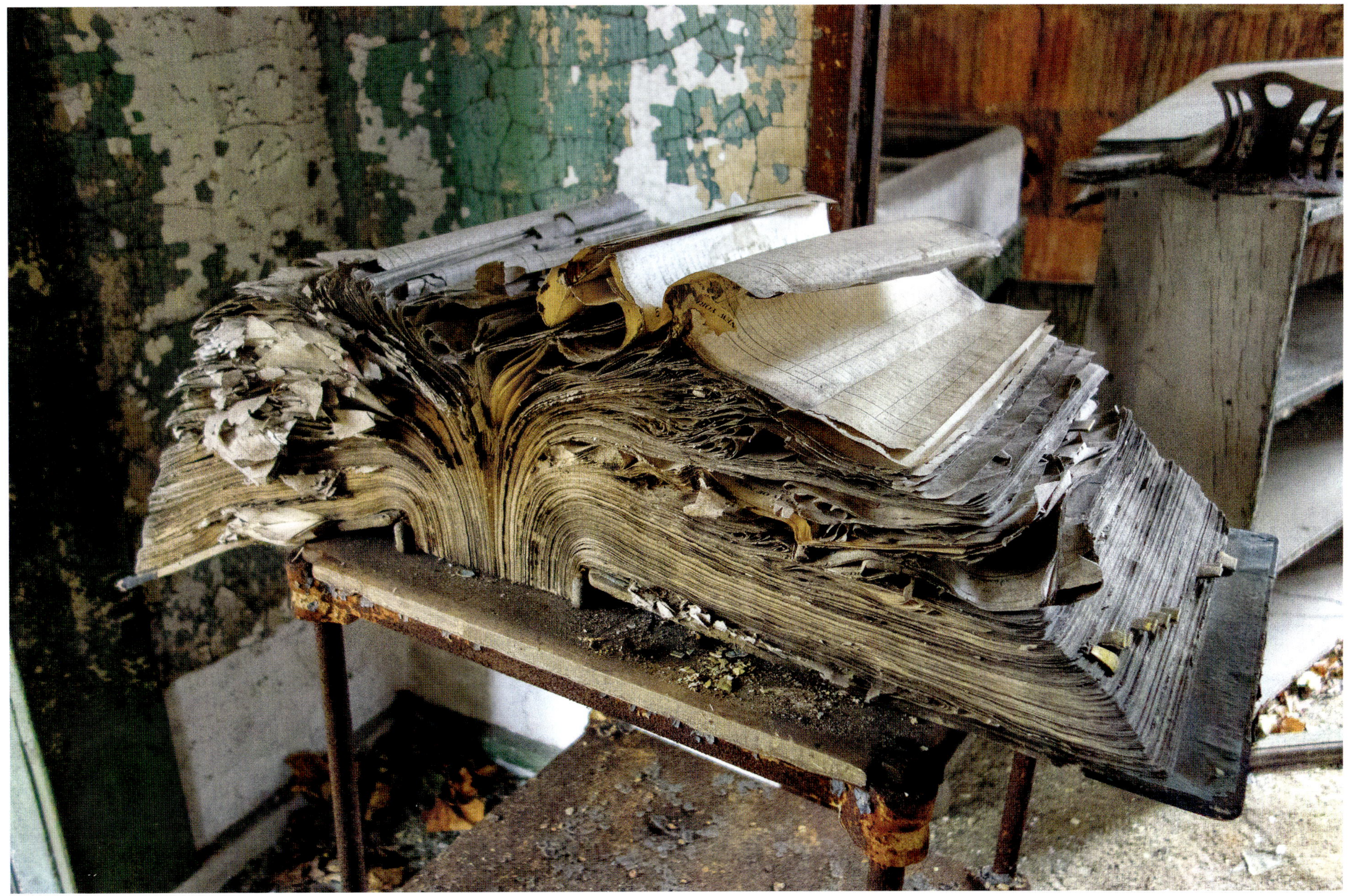

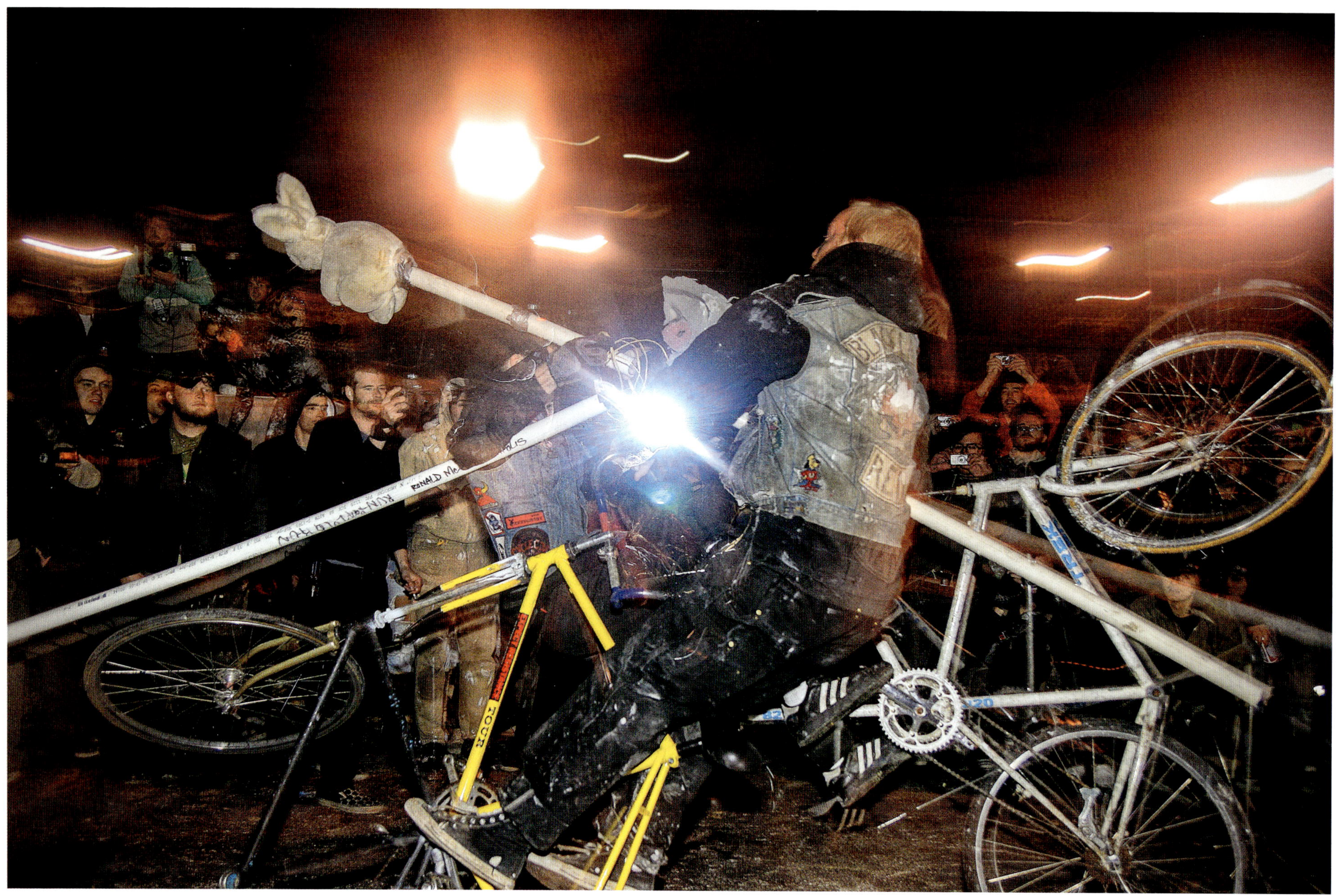

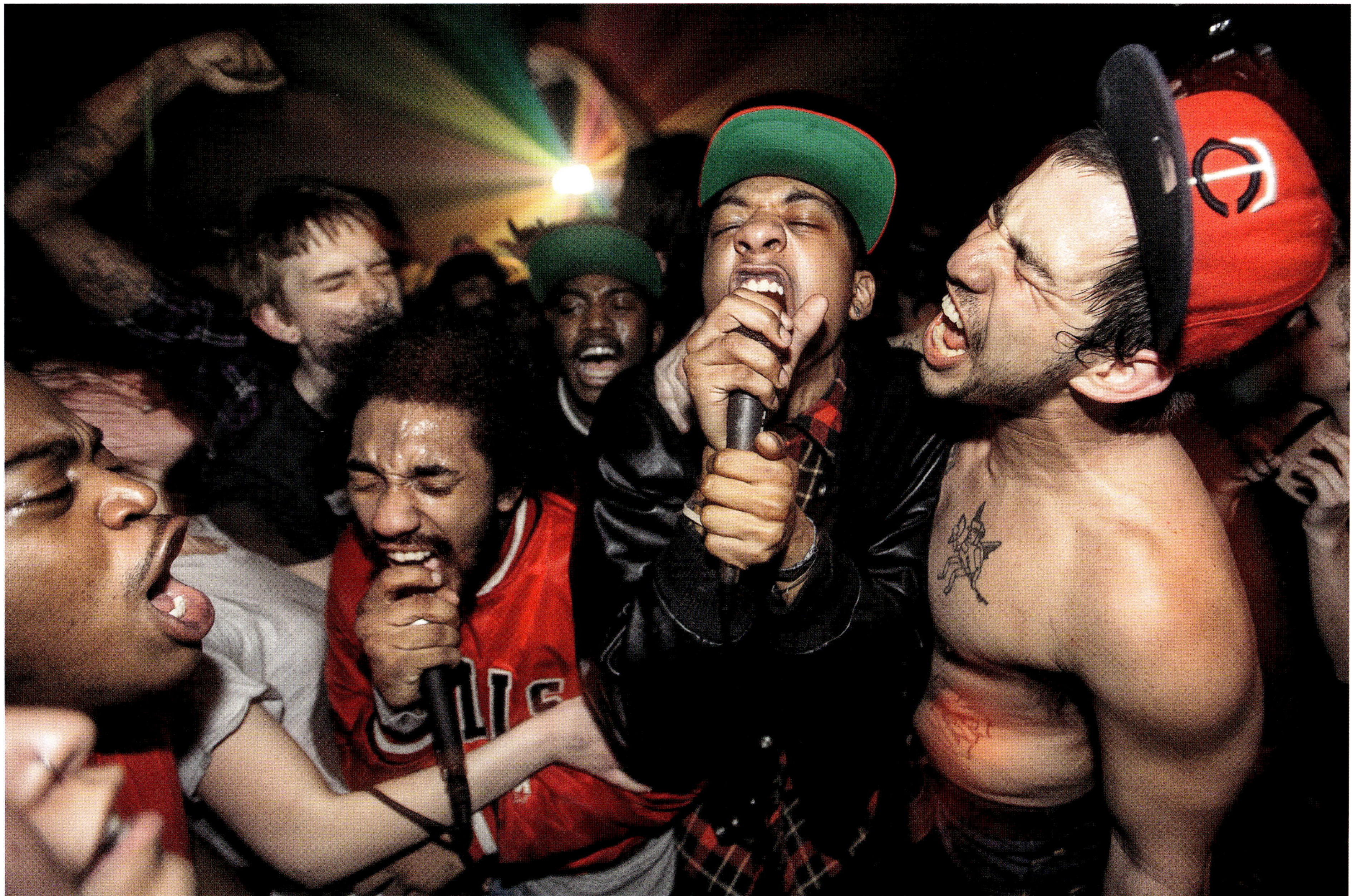

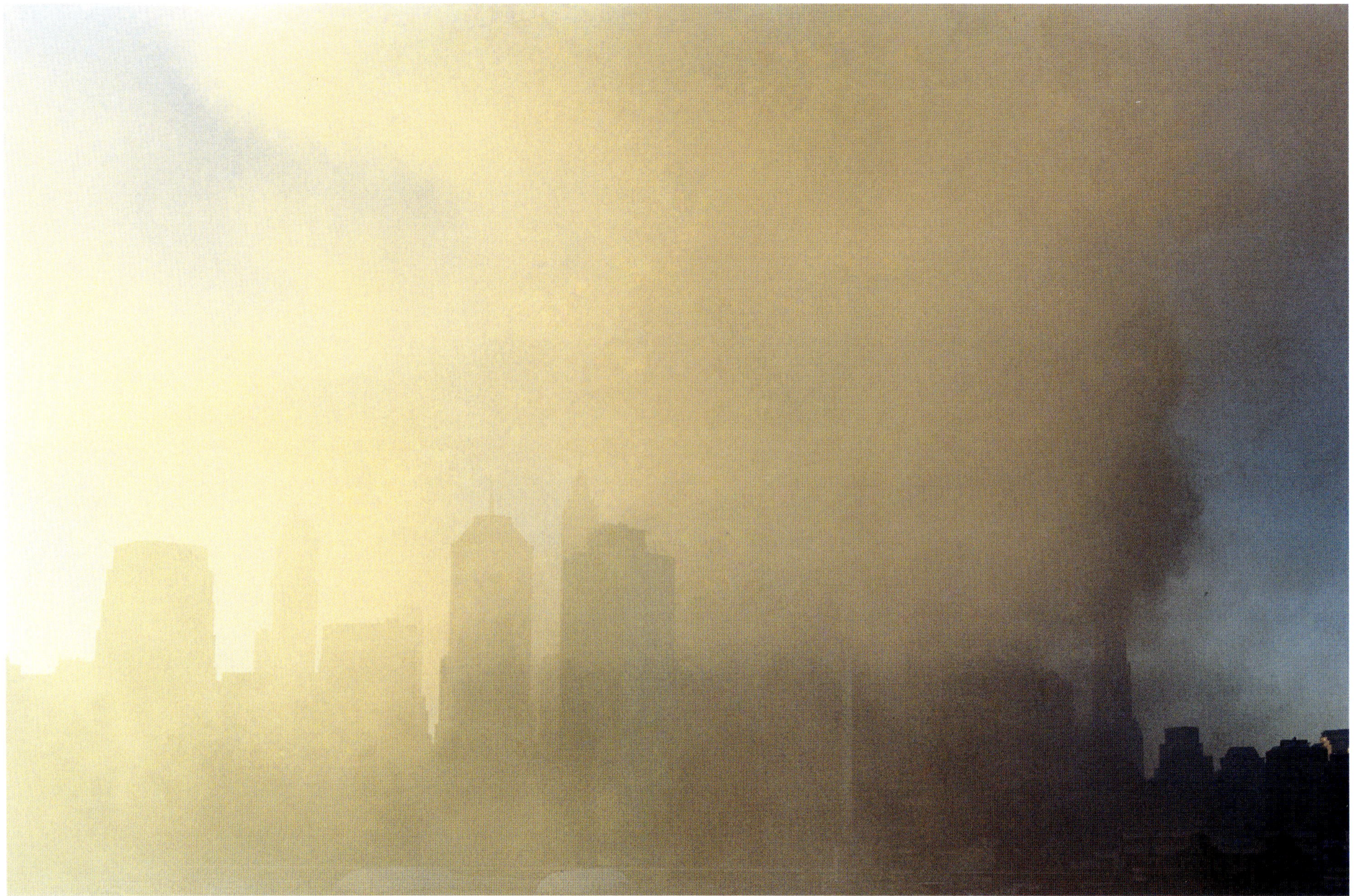

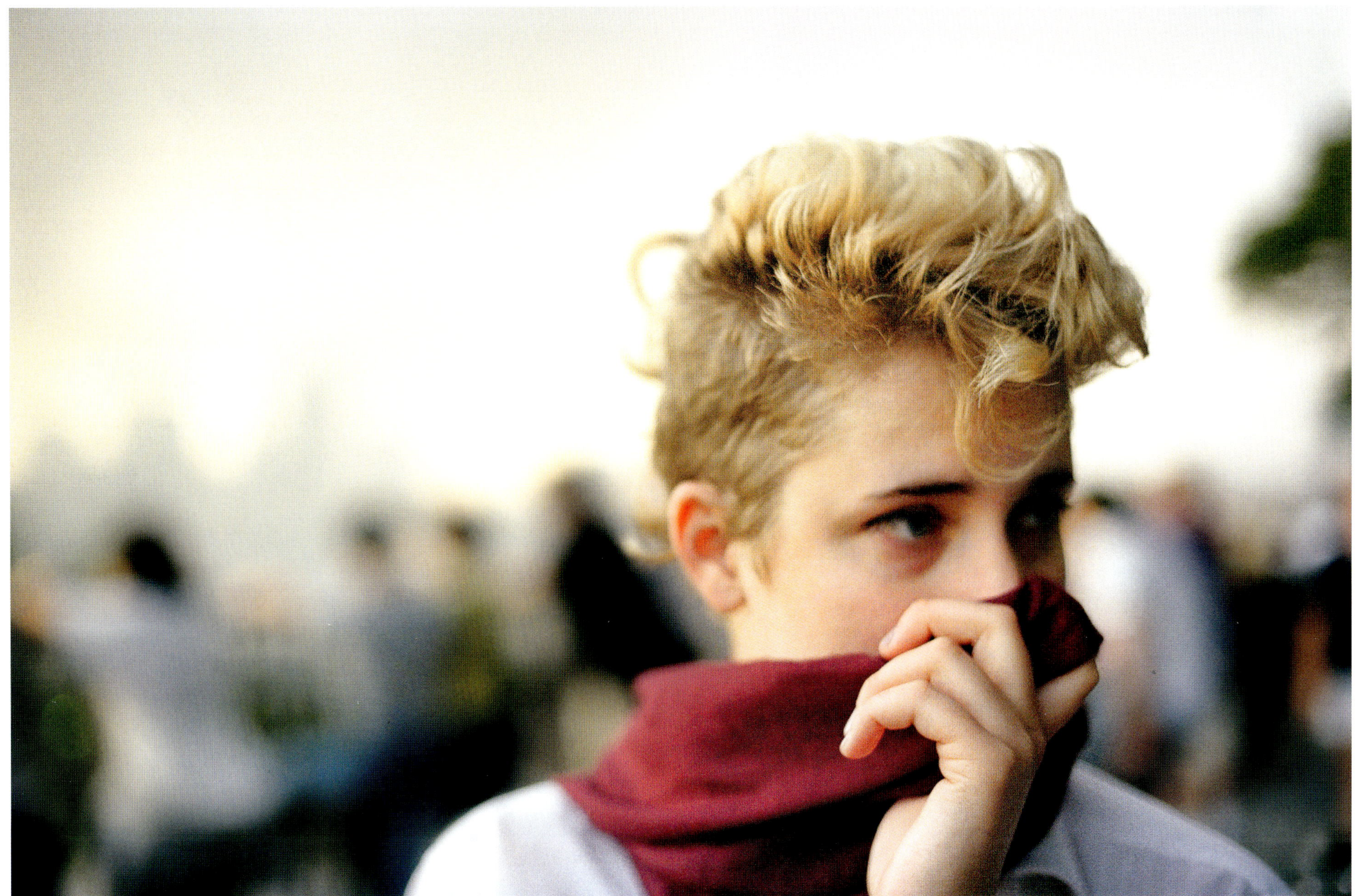

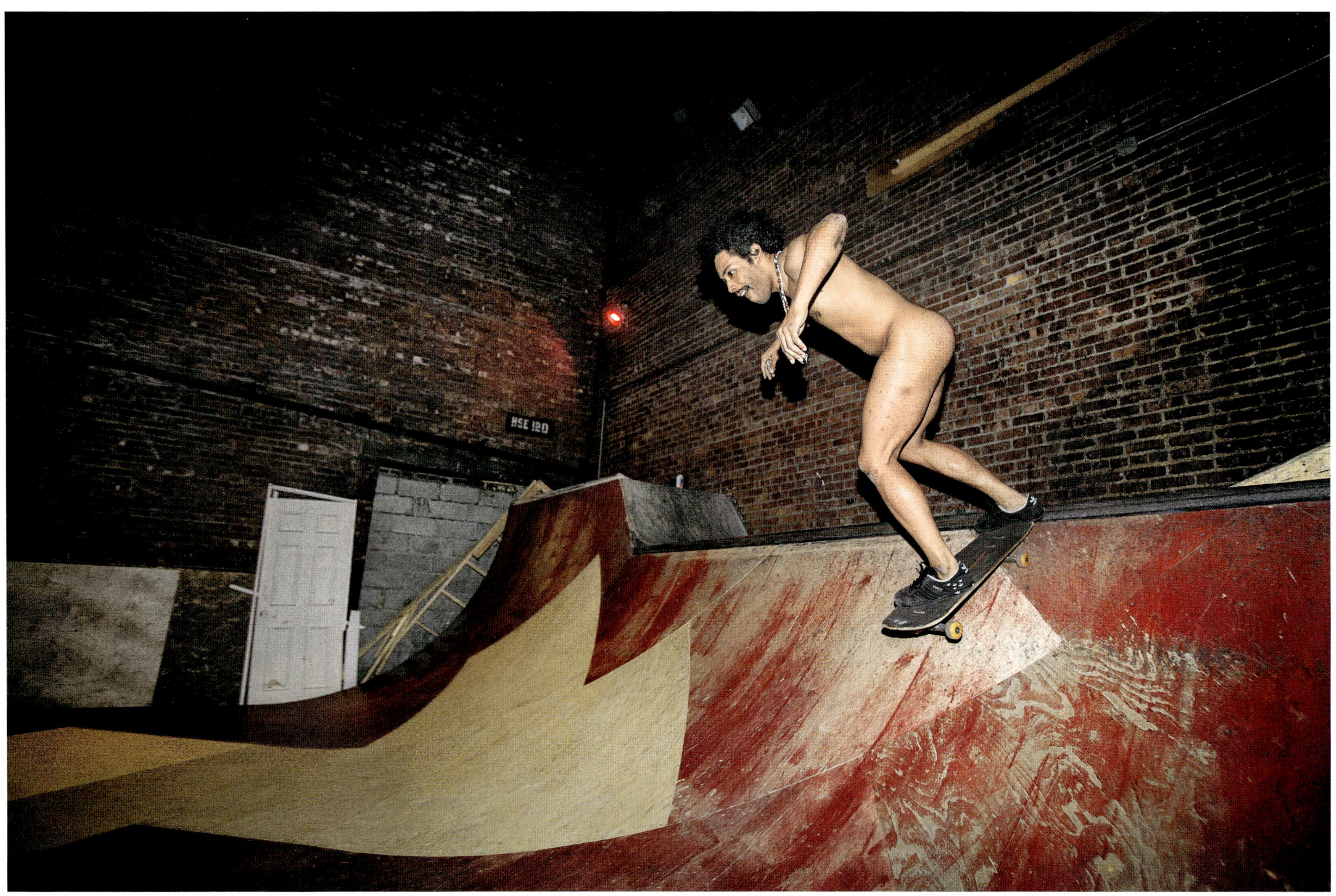
HSE 120

PORTALS TO ANOTHER WORLD
EVAN PRICCO

A photographer can capture the mood of a time period by accident. But when he or she is an active, full-throttle participant within a particular scene, it's *really* noticeable. I get the feeling these people don't come around too often.

I remember watching Woody Allen's *Midnight In Paris* and wishing I had lived in an era that appreciated certain artistic qualities in a more honest and true way. I do think, at the same time, we all come to some sort of agreement in our heads that the period in which we live is the most important to have ever existed. Tod Seelie's photography happens to exist during a time when mass communication and the Internet deliver large audiences at the click of a button. Some would say this is an advantage; I say it's bullshit. It means you have to work harder, think differently, and find ways to convey the world around you in an authentic manner. You have to take people to another world, let them enter as if with a secret code word, and transport them to a place that is not their own. You have to be a bit of a conduit, and find the special things in life that take on new meaning so someone far away can feel part of it all.

There is a concept of magic I'm thinking of, something powerful at play. I always think of that kid in Romania, or Singapore, or Brazil, who sees a certain collection of photos, a living, breathing way of life distant from their own, and wonders, "What is going on here? I want to see more."

When I was younger, this happened by looking at books on subway graffiti and skate culture. I used to get the feeling there were like-minded creative people out in the world doing *things*, profound and at times silly, that spoke to me. It was my portal to where I wanted to go and who I could be. The other day, I looked through Tod Seelie's photos and got that same feeling; these were portals. There is something happening in this world, and I like it.

The New York artists who have lived and produced work there outside of the Chelsea scene, the ones who floated down the Mississippi, who squatted in West Oakland, who settled in New Orleans, have come to represent something over the past ten years. Of course, there will be those whose art will stand the test of time for decades to come, but there have been very few people to document this bohemian underground scene so eloquently. I think the world should be frozen just so we can get a glimpse of this magic.

Evan Pricco is Editor-in-Chief of Juxtapoz Art and Culture Magazine. *He lives and works in San Francisco, California.*

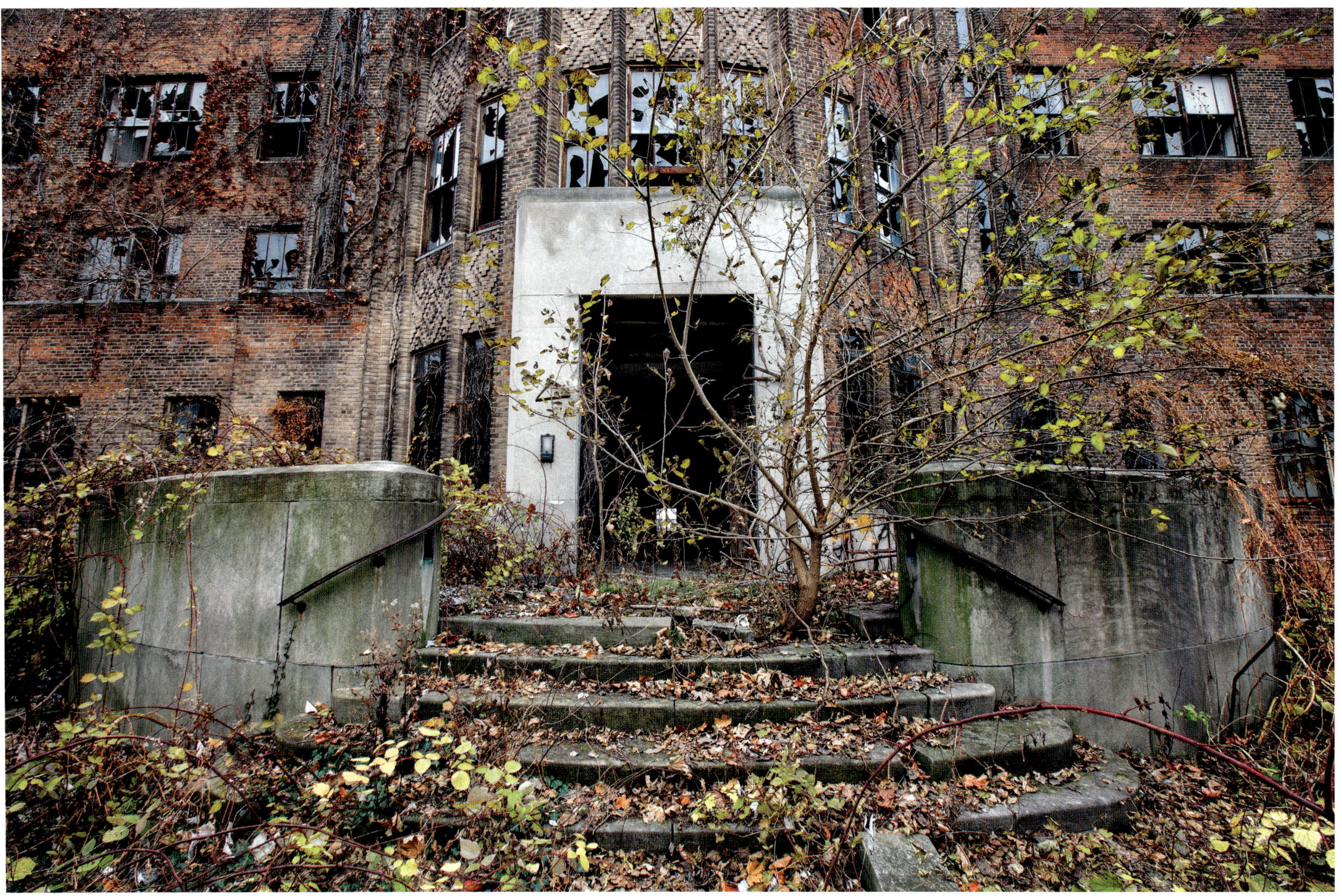

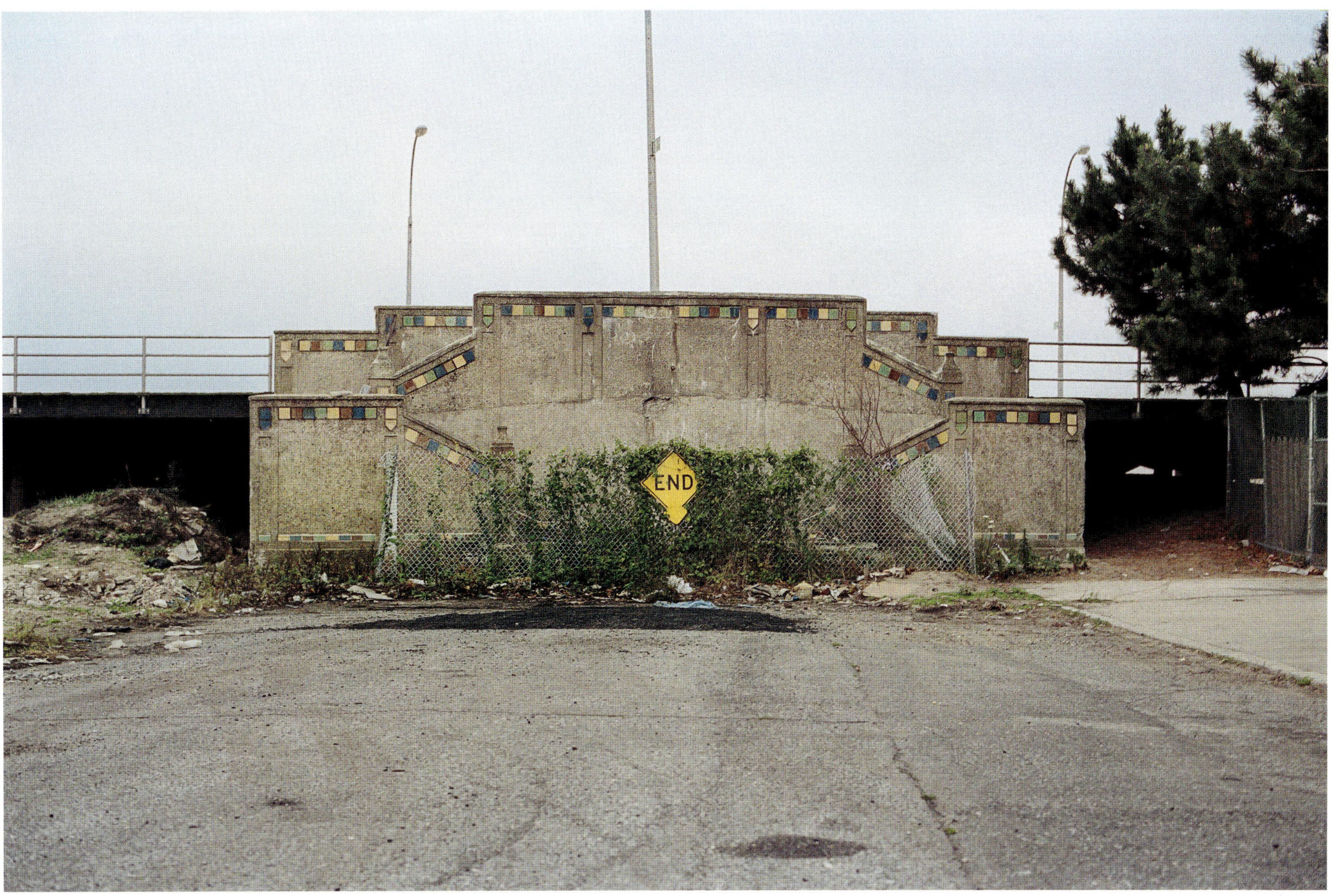
END

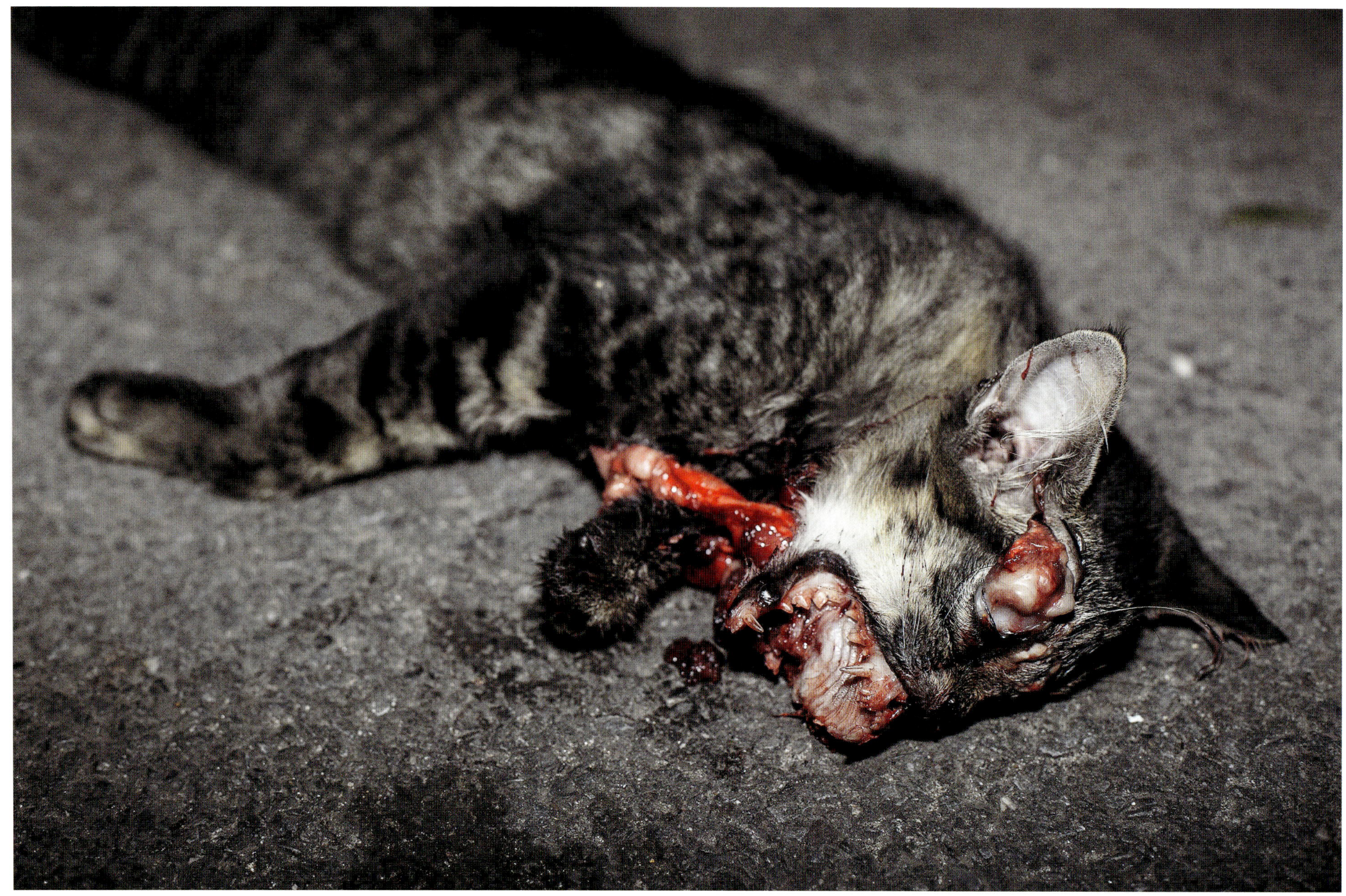

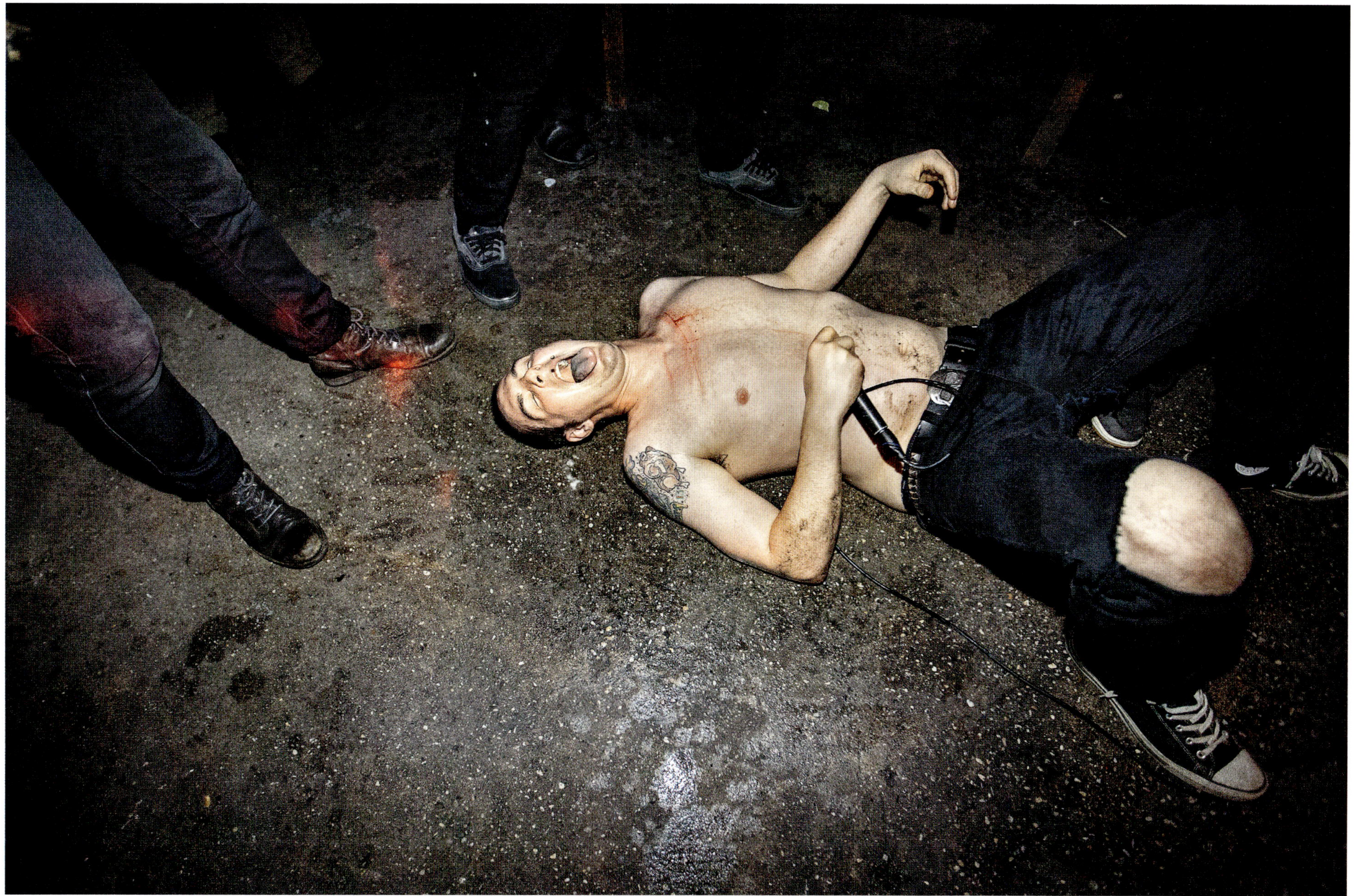

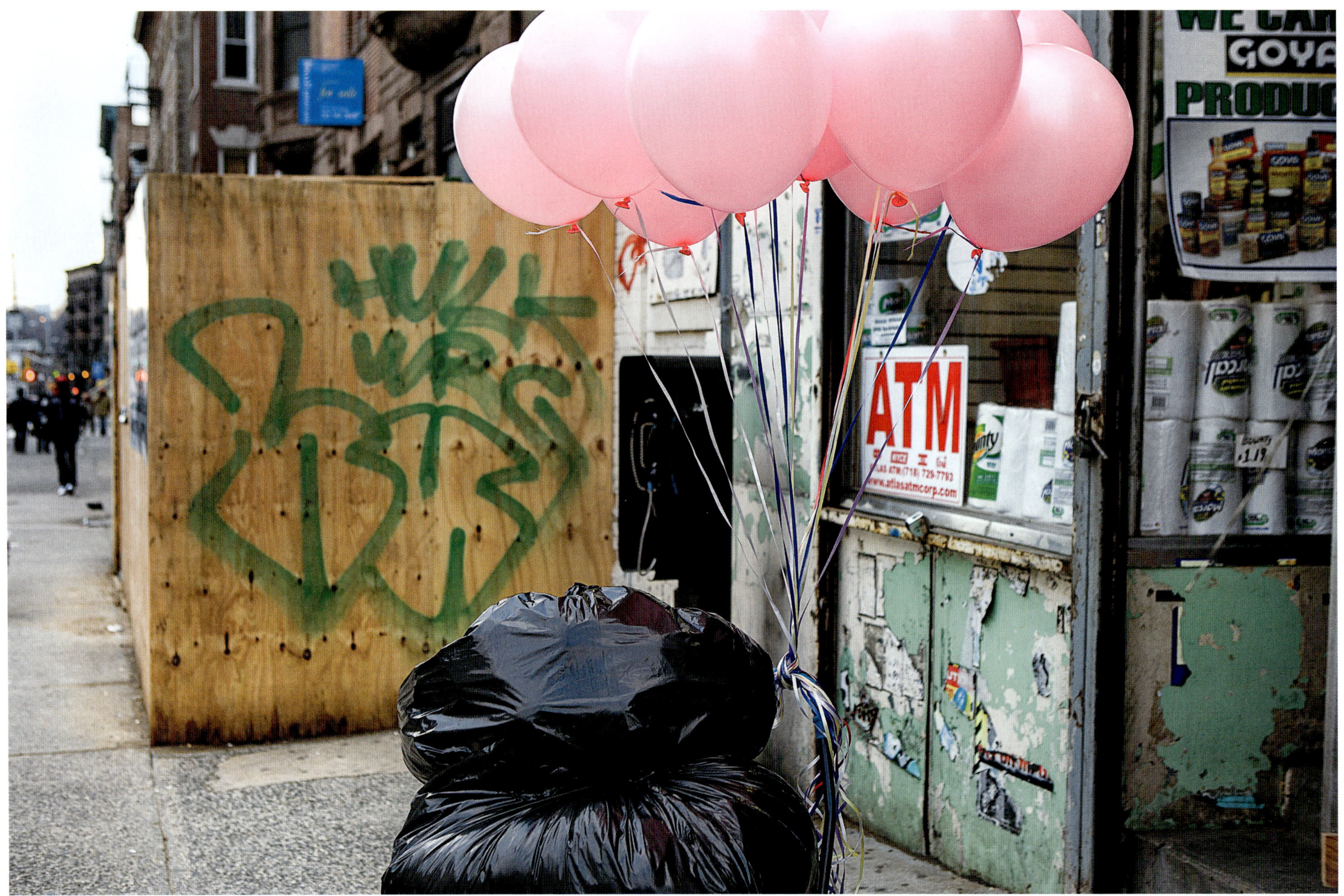

WE CA
GOYA
PRODUC
ATM
LAS ATM (718) 729-7793
www.atlasatmcorp.com

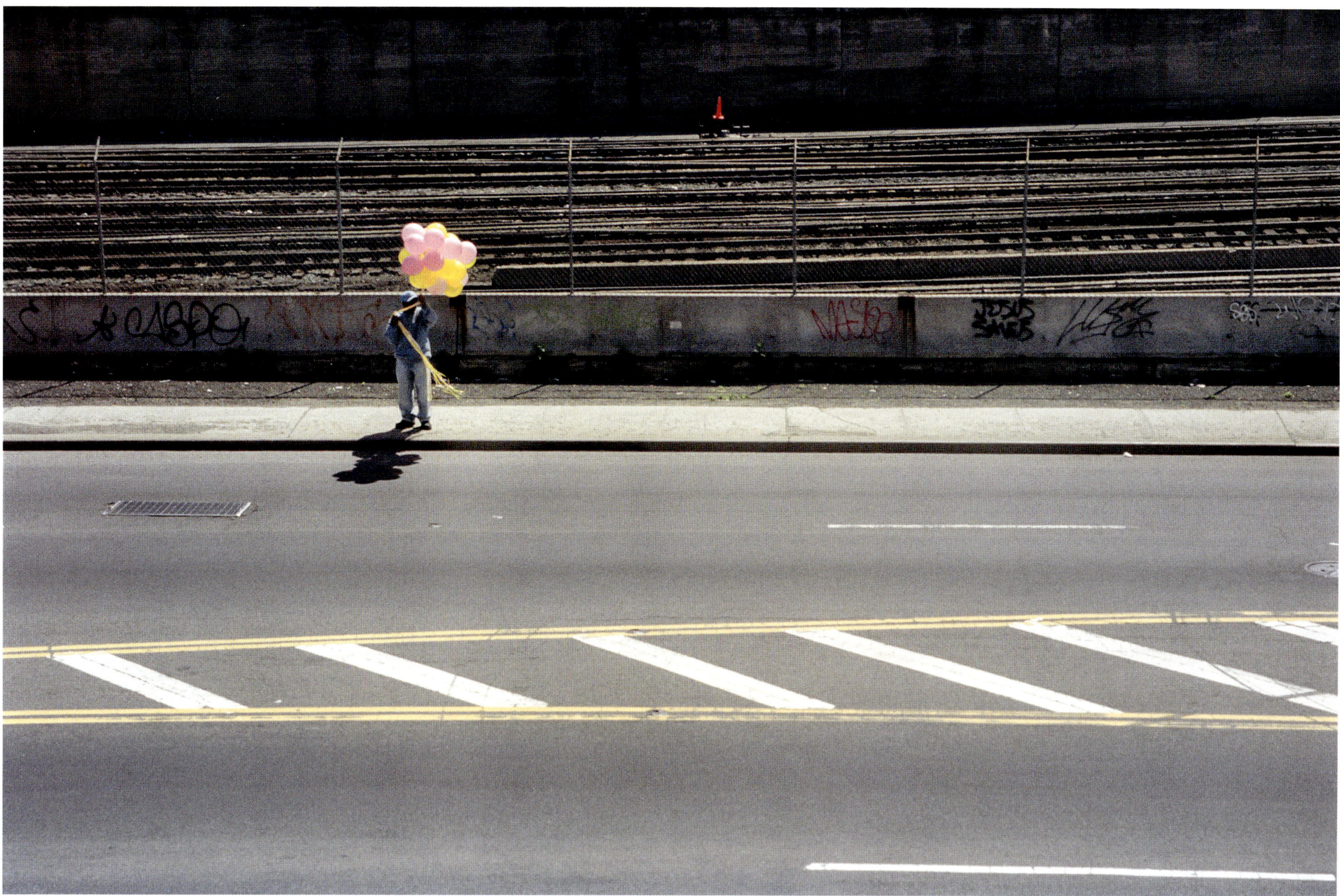

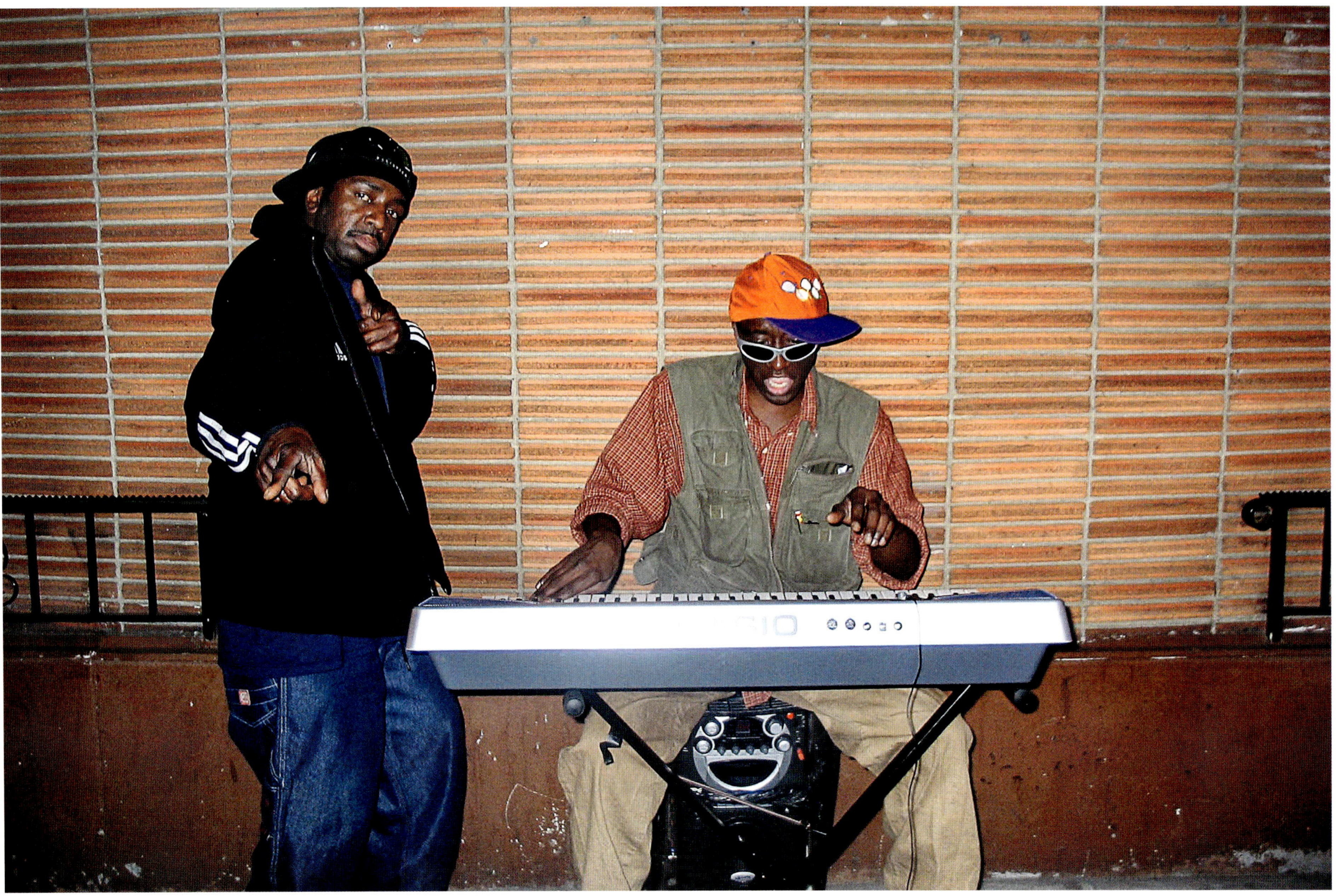

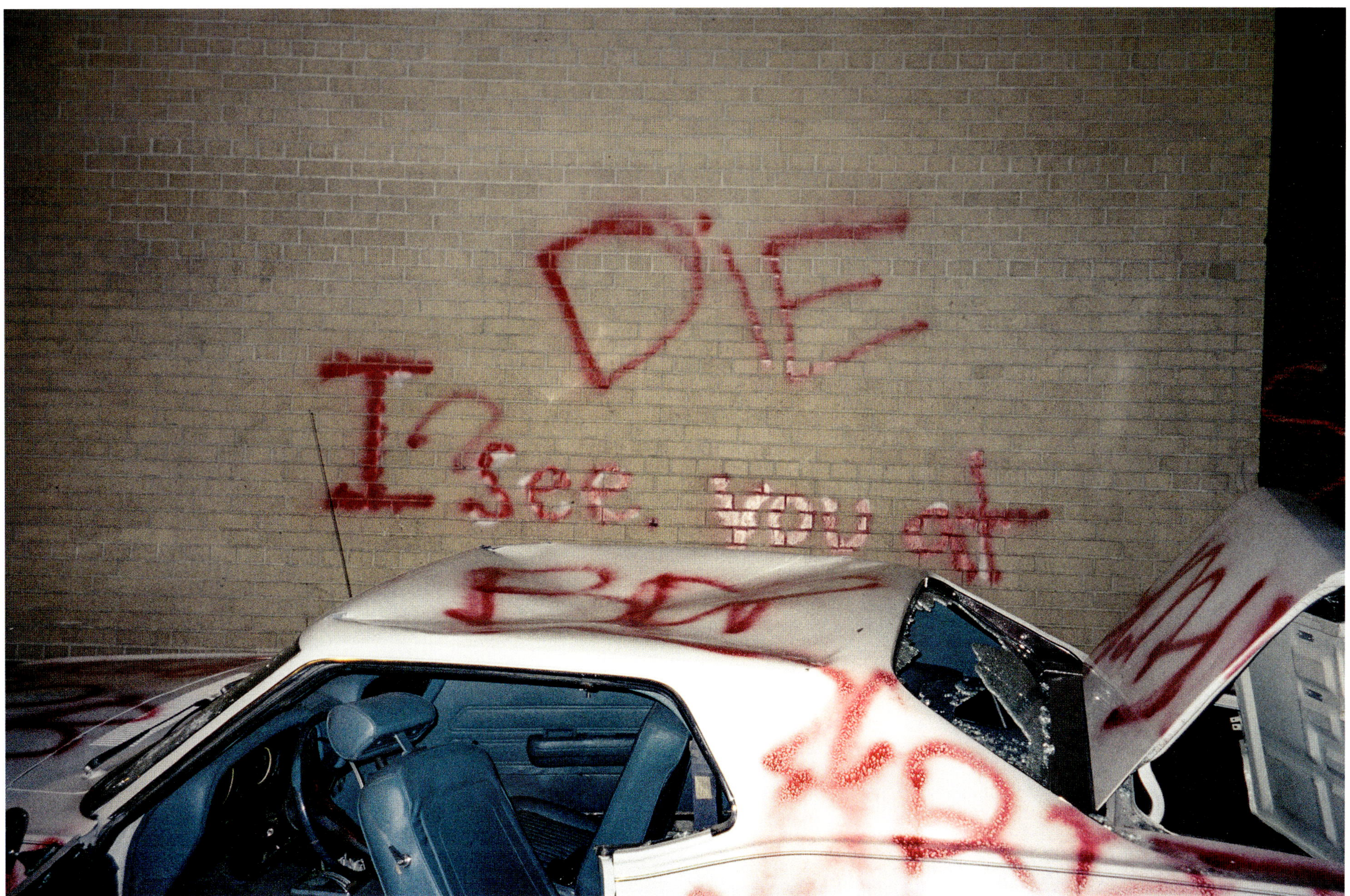
DIE
I see you at

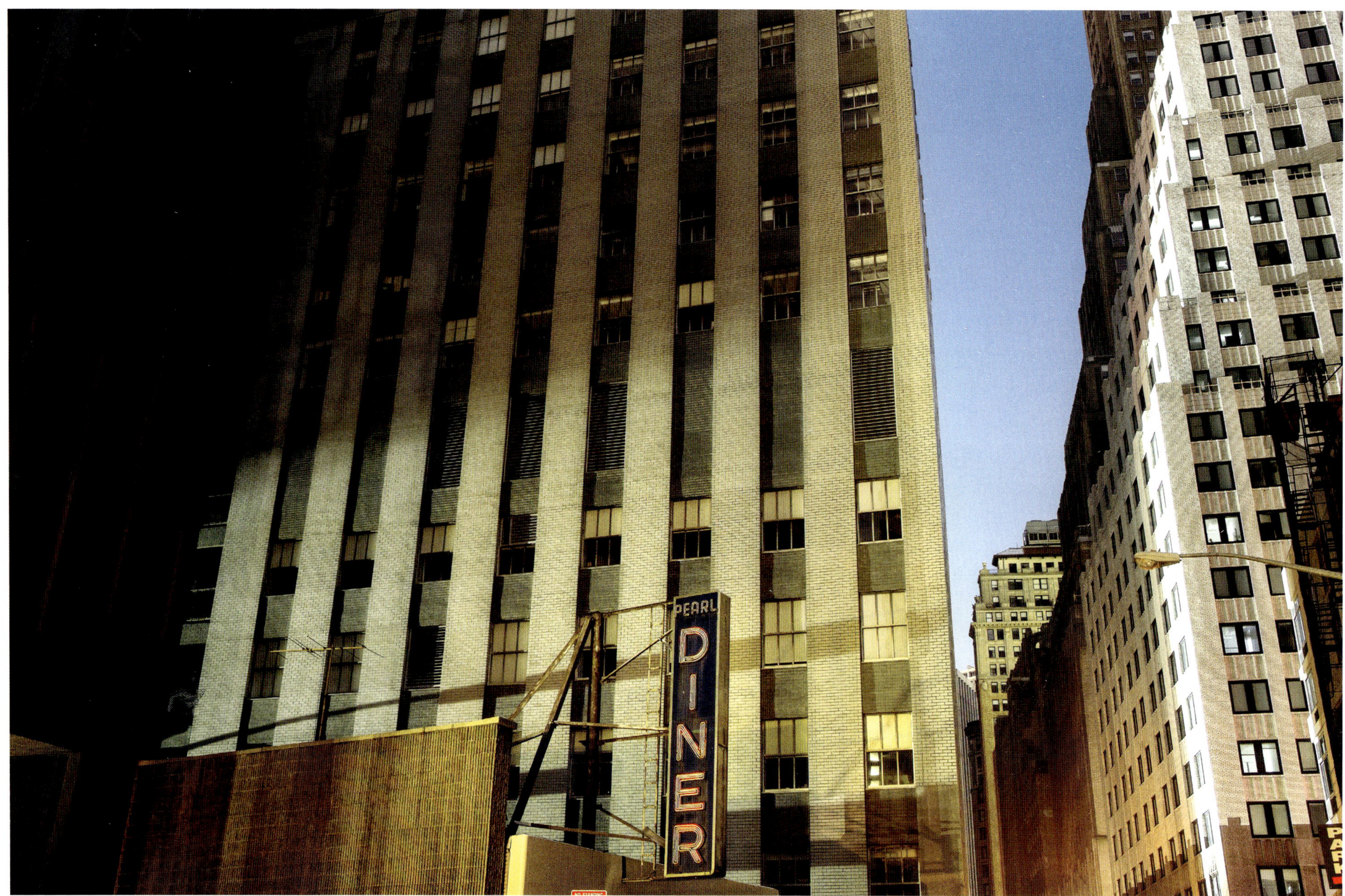

PEARL
DINER

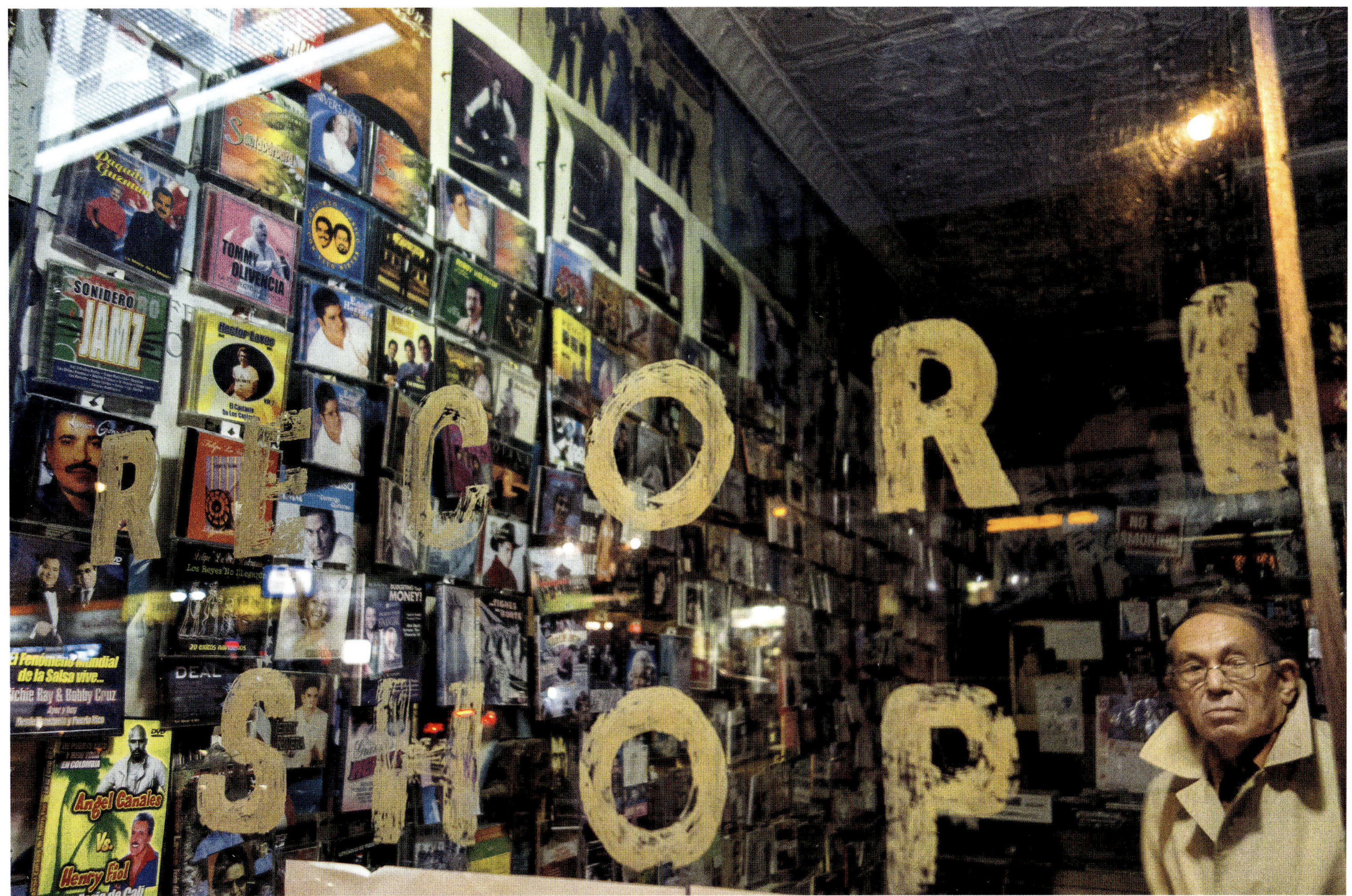

RECORD SHOP

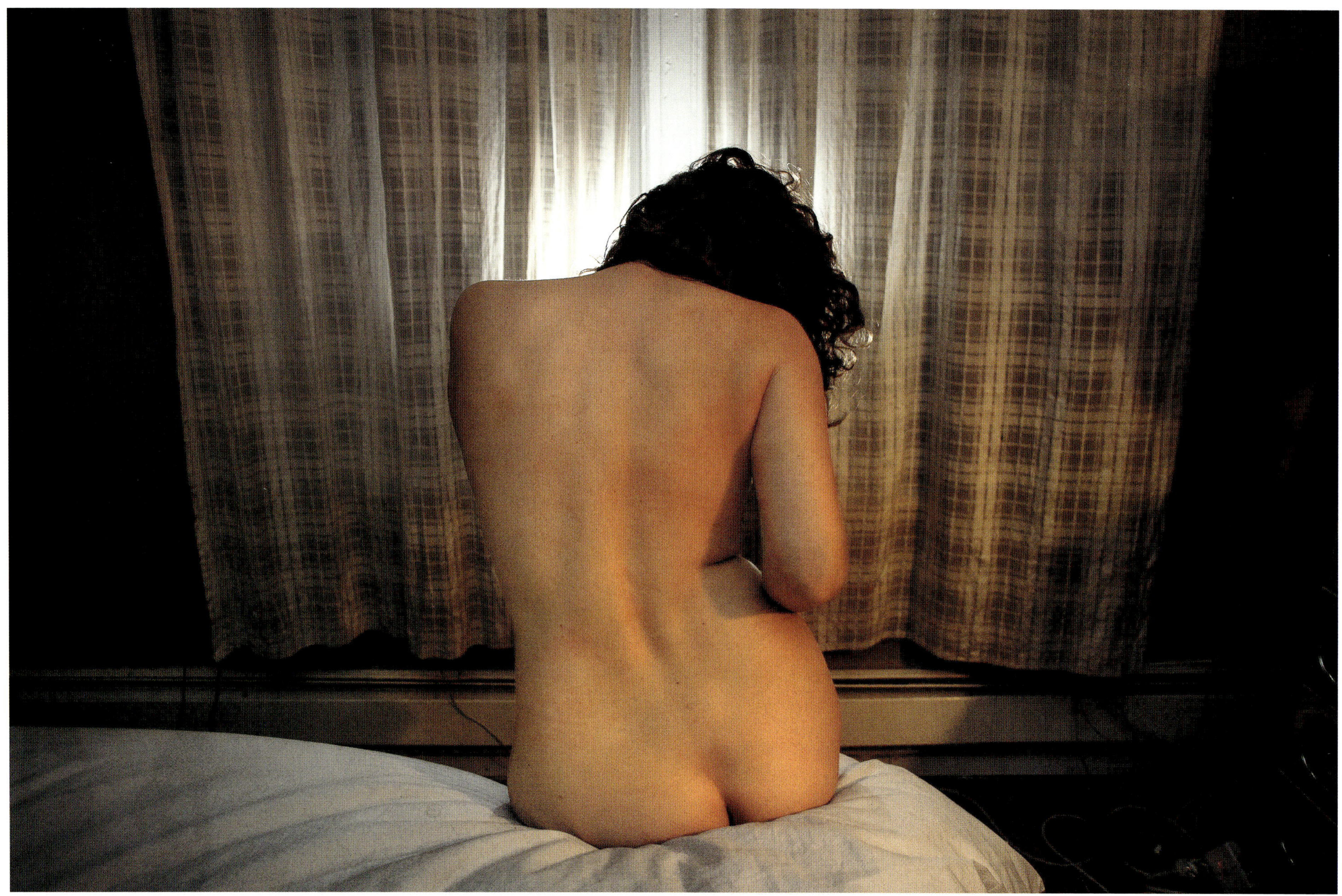

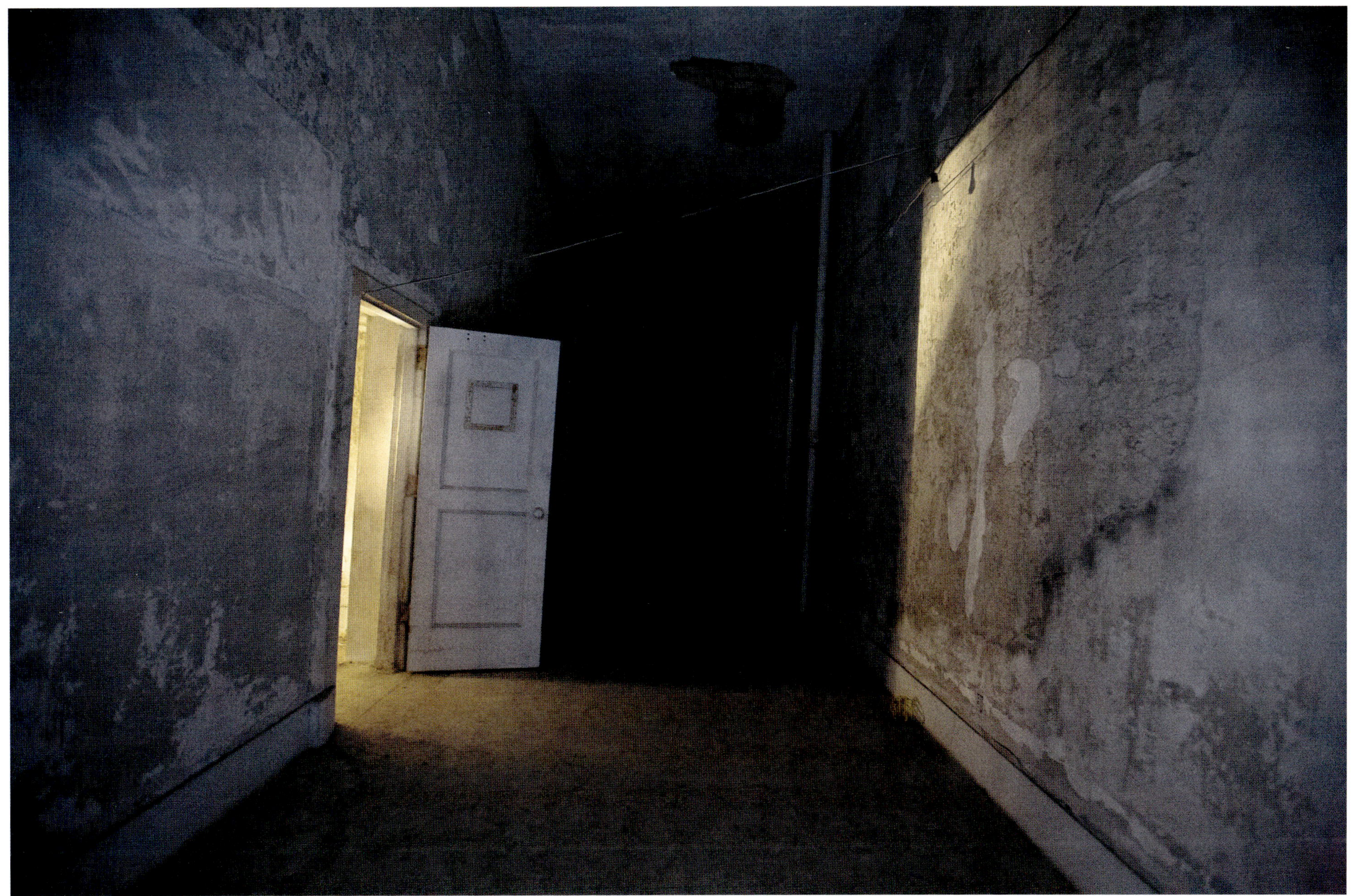

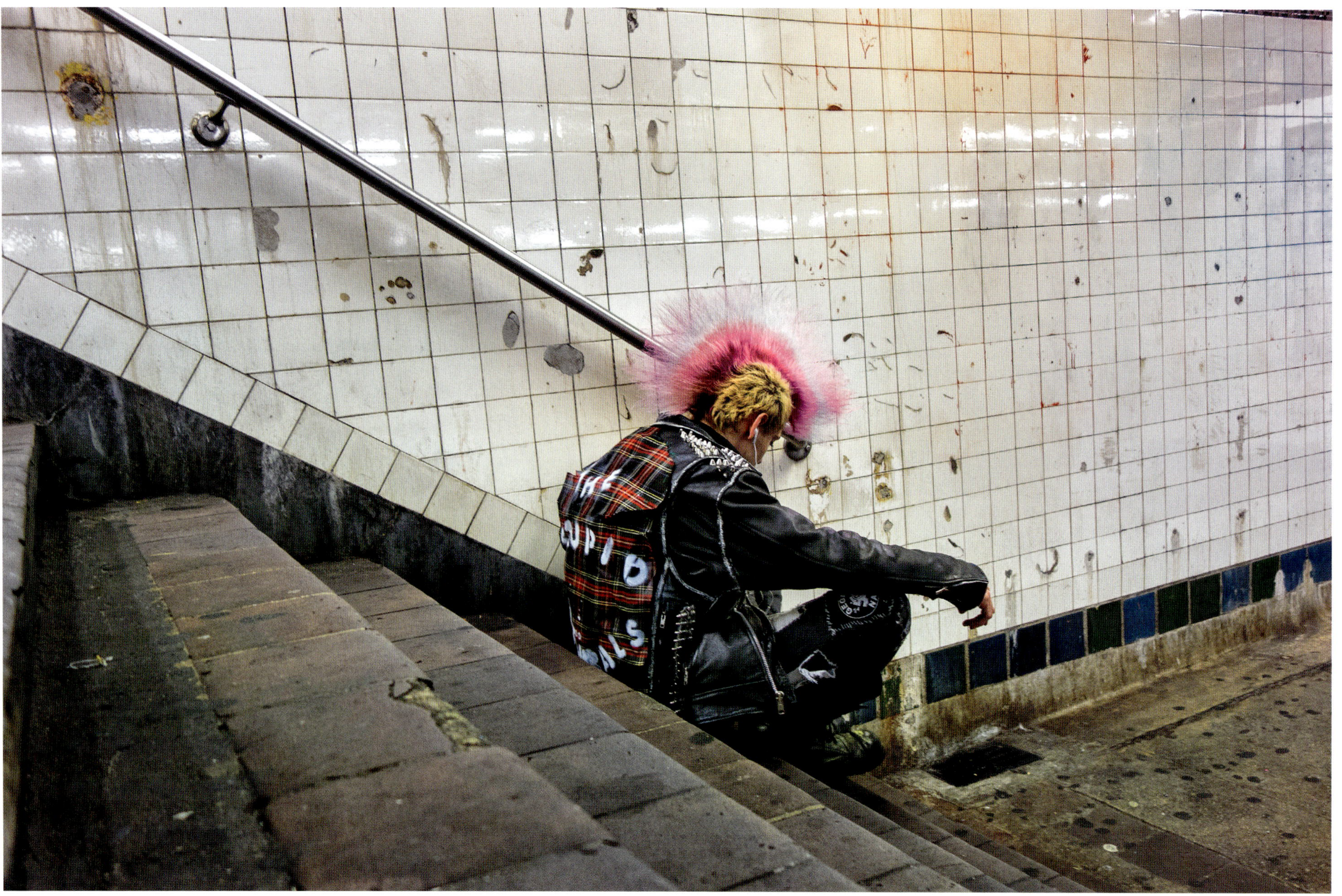

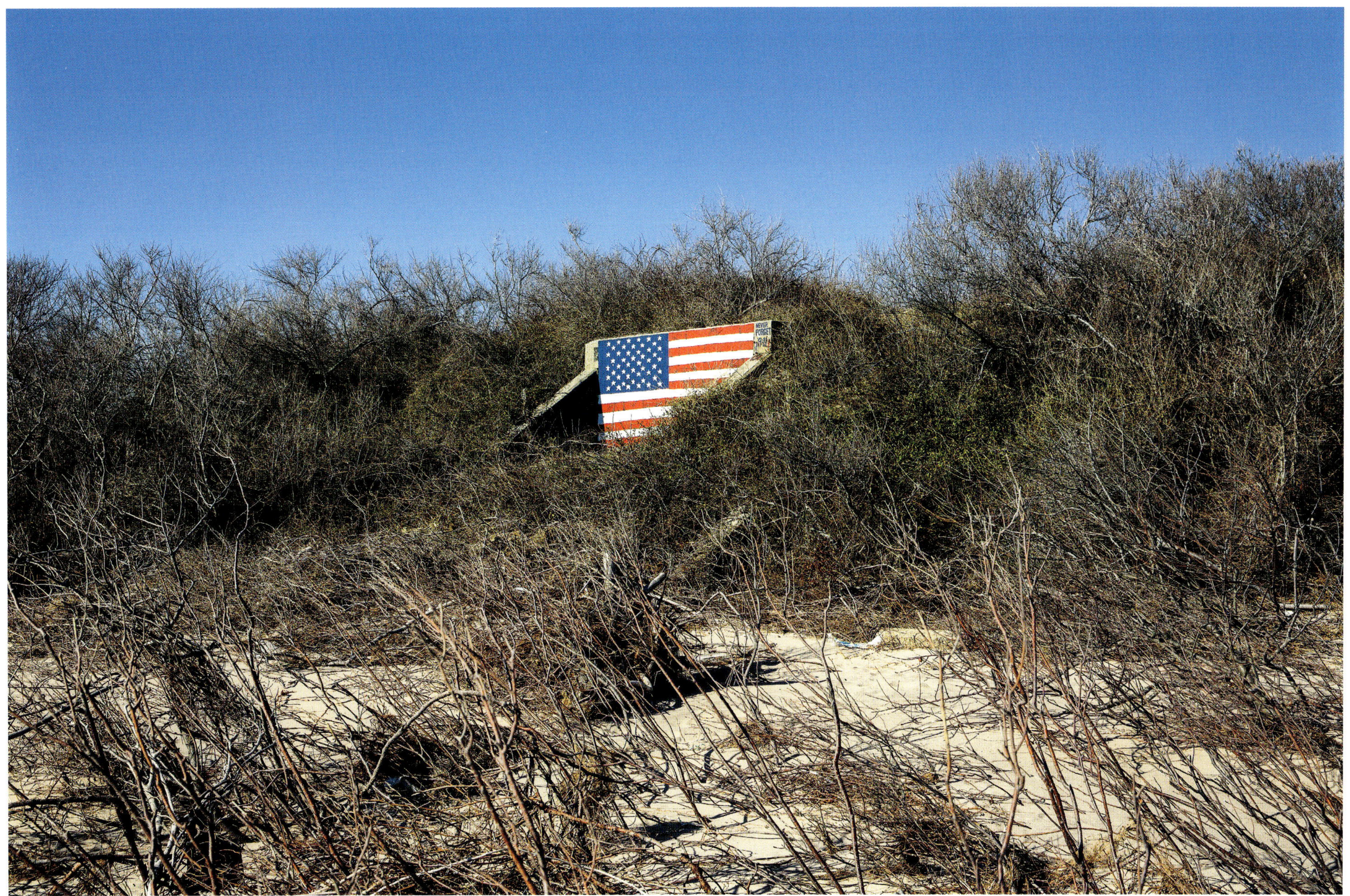

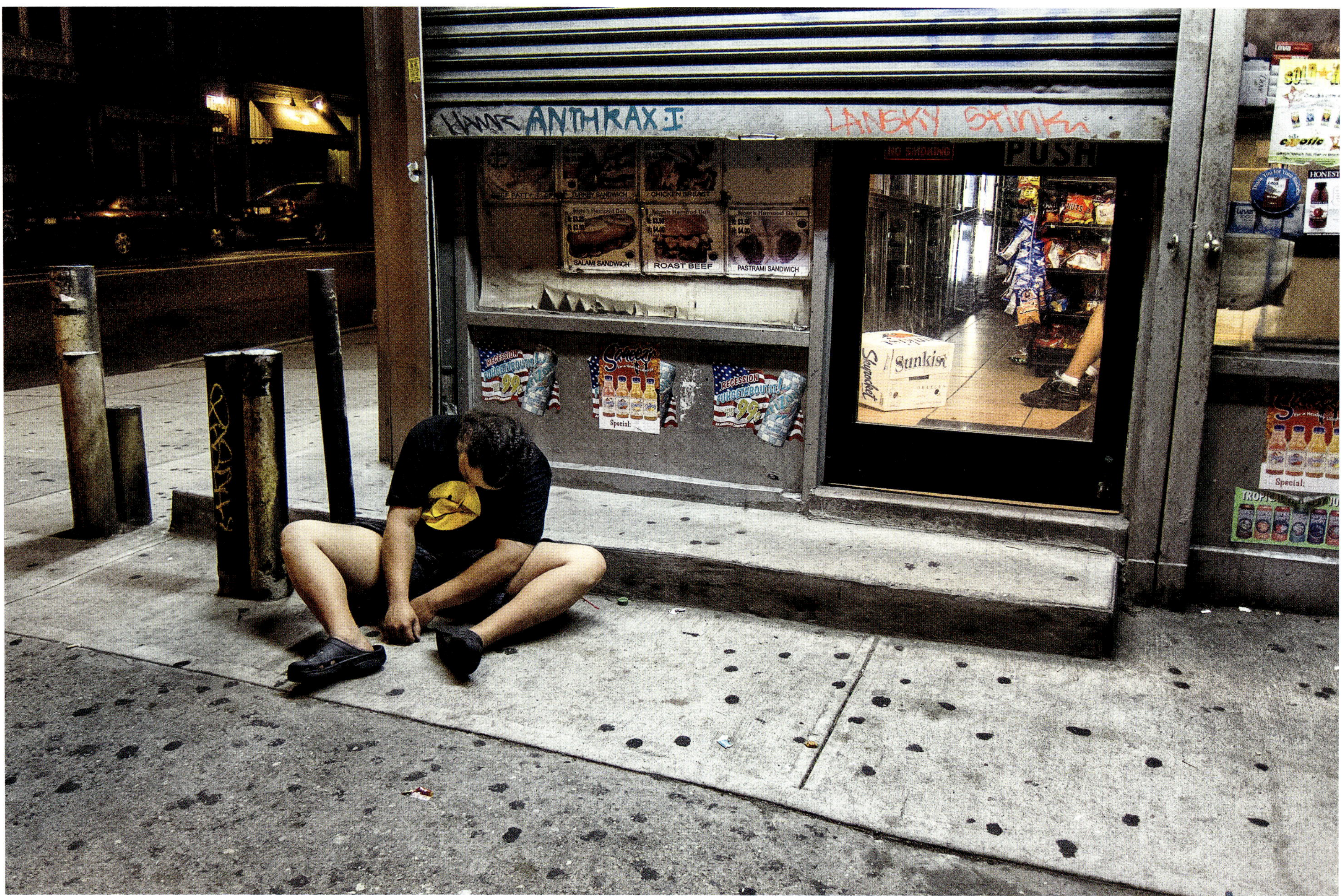

ANTHRAX I
LANSKY STINKS
PUSH
NO SMOKING
TURKEY SANDWICH
CHICKEN BREAST
SALAMI SANDWICH
ROAST BEEF
PASTRAMI SANDWICH
RECESSION
99
Special
Sunkist

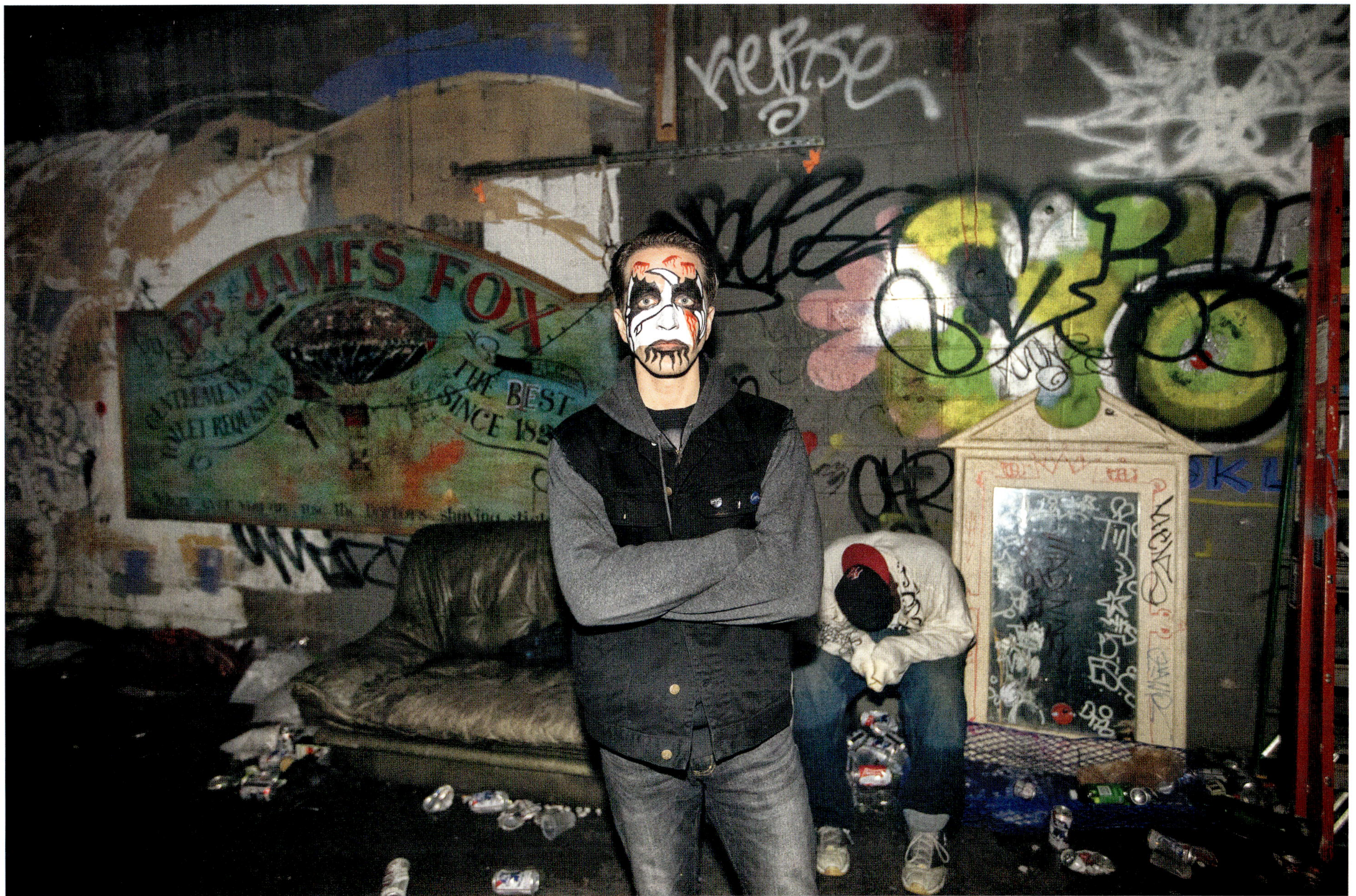

DR JAMES FOX
GENTLEMENS
TOILET REQUISITES
THE BEST
SINCE 188

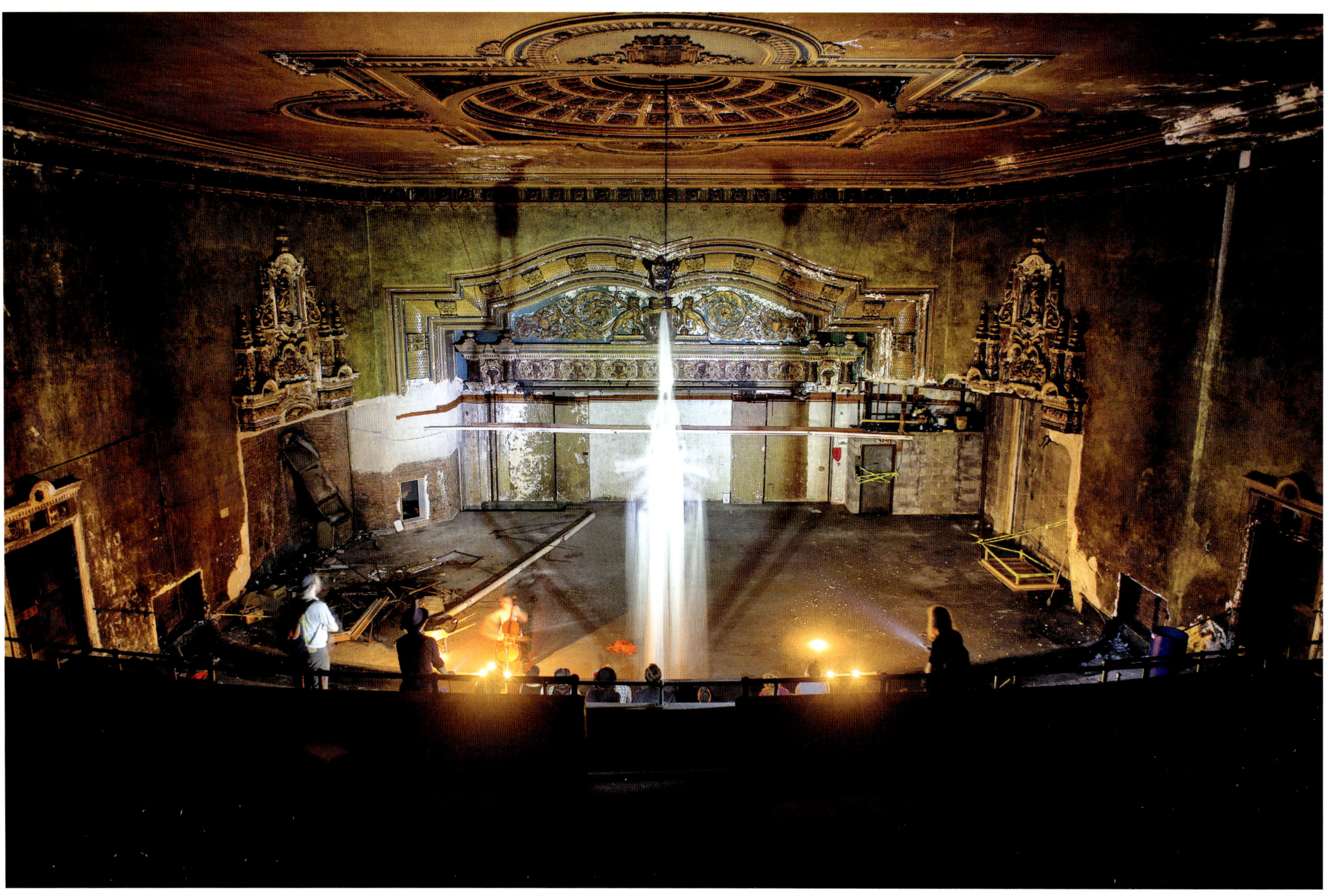

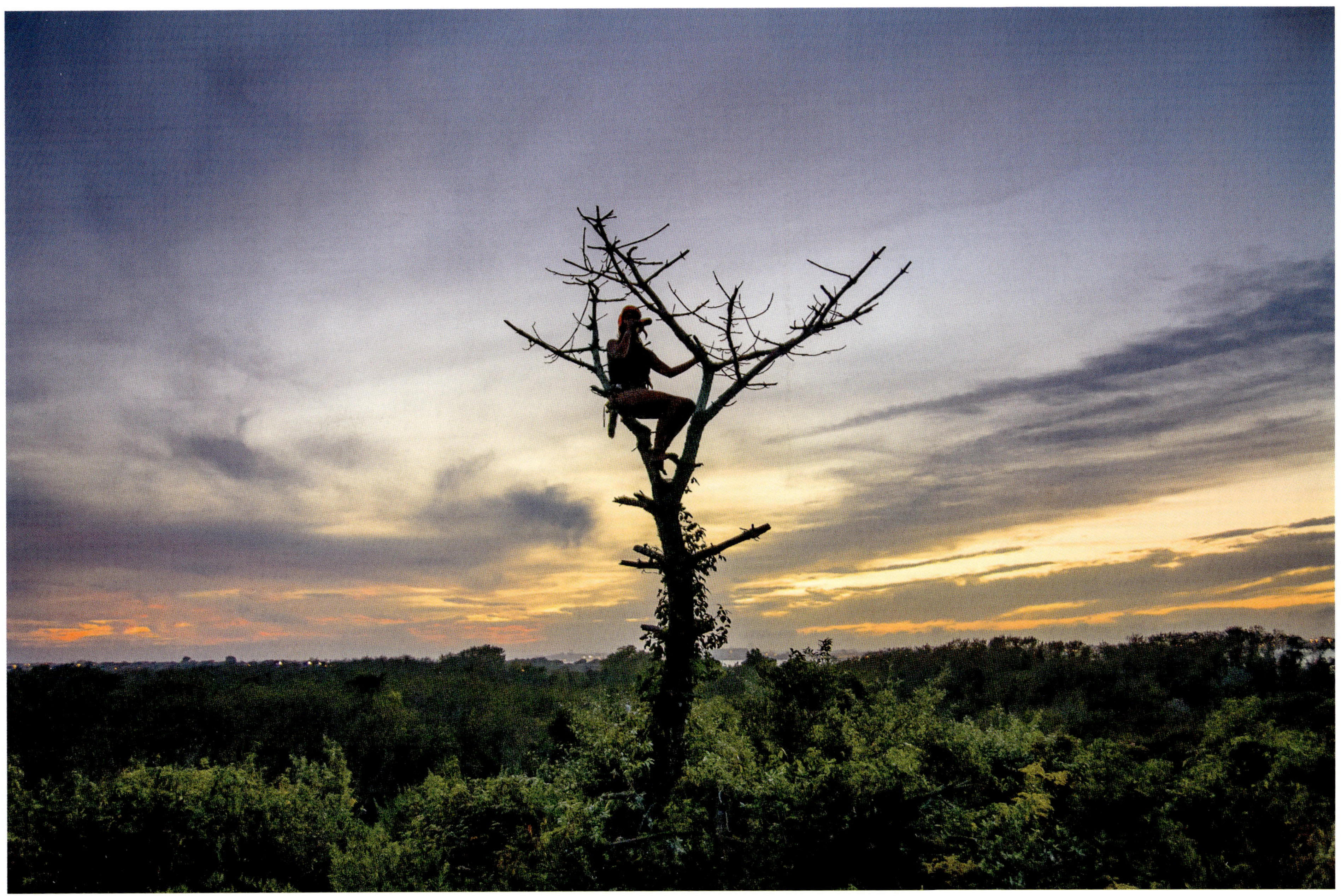

CAPTIONS

Page 6: Double rainbow, Bed-Stuy, Brooklyn, 2002.

Page 10: Callie W. crowd surfing during a Spank Rock show at Bodega, Bushwick, Brooklyn, 2009.

Page 13: The three rafts of the Swimming Cities Voltron together for a swimming party in the Hudson River near the George Washington Bridge, 2008.

Page 14: Crowd dancing on a rooftop during a Fourth of July party, Bushwick, Brooklyn, 2006.

Page 15: Burning car outside of my apartment, Bushwick, Brooklyn, 2007.

Page 16: Lego character running as part of the Idiotarod shopping cart race, Gowanus, Brooklyn, 2008.

Page 17: Solo dancing girl at an apartment show, Greenpoint, Brooklyn, 2007.

Page 18: Timothy Treason and Martina make out on the floor during a party at the Chicken Hut, Bed- , Brooklyn, 2008.

Page 19: A bouncer strangles a partygoer at the opening of The Delancey, Lower East Side, Manhattan, 2004.

Page 20: Broken rungs, Hart Island, Bronx, 2012.

Page 21: Setting up for a Secret Dinner in the Freedom Tunnel, Manhattan, 2007.

Page 22: Vogue dance battle at Escuelita, Manhattan, 2012.

Page 23: Partygoer at Happy Valley, Manhattan, 2006.

Page 24: Lisa's naked arch in my apartment, Bed-Stuy, Brooklyn, 2003.

Page 25: Porkchop straddling the third rails, Staten Island, 2004.

Page 26: Sleeping on the Bowery, Manhattan, 2003.

Page 27: Discarded cabinet outside of my apartment, Bed-Stuy, Brooklyn, 2003.

Page 28: Destroying a car at Bike Kill, Bed-Stuy, Brooklyn, 2005.

Page 29: Preparing to joust at Bike Kill, Bed-Stuy, Brooklyn, 2012.

Page 30: Monica in the tugboat graveyard, Staten Island, 2008.

Page 31: Monotonix performing at Market Hotel, Bushwick, Brooklyn, 2008.

Page 32: The raft Alice rounding the southern tip of Manhattan, 2008.

Page 35: Callie C. in Miss Cuttenclip with Ellery and Orien at the opening of her Swimming Cities solo exhibition at Deitch Projects, Long Island City, Queens, 2008.

Page 36: 1964 New York World's Fair pavilion, Flushing Meadows, Queens, 2007.

Page 37: Ceiling of an abandoned theater, East Village, Manhattan, 2012.

Page 38: Dead rats in a circle on the sidewalk, Bushwick, Brooklyn, 2003.

Page 39: Sex swing and dartboard in a basement sex club, Park Slope, Brooklyn, 1999.

Page 40: Blackface Jesus, Manhattan, 2006.

Page 41: Kissing couple at a Rated X party in the basement of Scenic, East Village, Manhattan, 2006.

Page 42: Ian H. steering with his feet, Floyd Bennett Field, Queens, 2010.

Page 43: Just Friends Day camping trip, Floyd Bennett Field, Queens, 2010.

Page 44: Nathan climbing the ladder to a rooftop water tower, Chelsea, Manhattan, 2013.

Page 45: Rooftops of Chinatown, Manhattan, 2010.

Page 46: World Trade Center, Manhattan, 2000.

Page 47: Security guards attempt to block photography of George W. Bush and Dick Cheney portraits in a federal building, Lower Manhattan, 2003.

Page 48: Paulie Anne in her bedroom, Crown Heights, Brooklyn, 2012.

Page 49: Light pollution in an abandoned grain terminal, Red Hook, Brooklyn, 2006.

Page 50: Right after being punched at a loft party, East Williamsburg, Brooklyn, 2006.

Page 51: Street fight, East Williamsburg, Brooklyn, 2005.

Page 52: Matt & Kim performing at a loft show, East Williamsburg, Brooklyn, 2006.

Page 54: Japanther performing on a street corner powered by a lamppost, Dumbo, Brooklyn, 2002.

Page 55: Reilly with a black eye, Fort Greene, Brooklyn, 2002.

Page 56: The Chicken Hut, Bed-Stuy, Brooklyn, 2012.

Page 57: Nick C-T. riding the boot bike at Bike Kill, Bed-Stuy, Brooklyn, 2007.

Page 58: Costumed racer at the Idiotarod shopping cart race, Manhattan, 2006.

Page 59: Union Square pillow fight, Manhattan, 2006.

Page 60: Couple making out at a tofu wrestling event, East Williamsburg, Brooklyn, 2010.

Page 61: Basement dance party, Harlem, Manhattan, 2007.

Page 62: Masked organizers of Corporation X at the start of the Idiotarod shopping cart race, East Williamsburg, Brooklyn, 2010.

Page 63: Blackout caused by Hurricane Sandy, Lower Manhattan, 2012.

Page 64: Devil grabbing Alex, Bed-Stuy, Brooklyn, 2010.

Page 65: Ian H. and Jen at the Floridian Diner, Marine Park, Brooklyn, 2009.

Page 66: Trash pile of Hurricane Sandy debris at Jacob Riis Park, Far Rockaway, Queens, 2012.

Page 67: Crowd surfer at a warehouse show, East Williamsburg, Brooklyn, 2008.

Page 68: Balloons spilling out of a window at The Silent Barn, Bushwick, Brooklyn, 2013.

Page 69: Matching ladies at 14th Street, Manhattan, 2013.

Page 70: Hanging mannequin in the abandoned Bat Cave, Gowanus, Brooklyn, 2013.

Page 71: Dawn of Humans performing at a basement show, Bushwick, Brooklyn, 2013.

Page 72: Jousting at Bike Kill, Bed-Stuy, Brooklyn, 2010.

Page 74: Jogyo performing in a basement, East Williamsburg, Brooklyn, 2012.

Page 75: Booty dancing at a party at the Chicken Hut, Bed-Stuy, Brooklyn, 2010.

Page 76: UFO graffiti obscured by vines, Red Hook, Brooklyn, 2012.

Page 77: Ian H. with spray can at Fort Tilden, Far Rockaway, Queens, 2009.

Page 78: One-shoe stage diving at a warehouse show, Bushwick, Brooklyn, 2009.

Page 79: Hubert and Greg on the surf bike at Bike Kill, Bed-Stuy, Brooklyn, 2012.

Page 80: Catherine at her flooded house after Hurricane Sandy, Far Rockaway, Queens, 2012.

Page 81: Swim party in the Hudson River as the Swimming Cities fleet approaches New York City, 2008.

Page 82: Broken bench, Far Rockaway, Queens, 2013.

Page 83: Parked car, East Williamsburg, Brooklyn, 2008.

Page 84: Mosh pit at 285 Kent, Williamsburg, Brooklyn, 2012.

Page 85: Moisture performing at a basement apartment show, Bushwick, Brooklyn, 2012.

Page 86: Heavy boxing bag in a vacant lot, Bushwick, Brooklyn, 2006.

Page 87: Traffic light, Midtown, Manhattan, 2012.

Page 88: DJ dancing at a basement party, East Williamsburg, Brooklyn, 2012.

Page 89: Performance art in a vacant convent, Greenpoint, Brooklyn, 2011.

Page 90: Woman at Coney Island, Brooklyn, 2011.

Page 91: Boardwalk destroyed by Hurricane Sandy, Far Rockaway, Queens, 2012.

Page 92: Ian V. in a subway tunnel, Brooklyn, 1999.

Page 94: View of Manhattan from the top of the Williamsburg Bridge, 2011.

Page 95: Atlantic Avenue Tunnel, Brooklyn, 2009.

Page 96: Partygoer at Luke & Leroy, West Village, Manhattan, 2007.

Page 97: Julia at ABC No Rio, Lower East Side, Manhattan, 2000.

Page 98: Surf-bike racing at Bike Kill, Bed-Stuy, Brooklyn, 2007.

Page 99: Flame chopper at Bike Kill, Bed-Stuy, Brooklyn, 2008.

Page 100: Exploring abandoned buildings, Navy Yard, Brooklyn, 2008.

Page 101: Derek at an art show in an abandoned building, East Williamsburg, Brooklyn, 2009.

Page 102: Sidewalk boombox, Harlem, Manhattan, 2008.

Page 103: Abandoned loveseat in front of a children's mural, Bed-Stuy, Brooklyn, 2000.

Page 104: Drying clothes at an encampment, Far Rockaway, Queens, 2012.

Page 105: Overcoat hanging in a tree at a Hurricane Sandy relief center, Far Rockaway, Queens, 2012.

Page 106: Amateur street boxing, East Williamsburg, Brooklyn, 2006.

Page 107: Showing me the money at a basement party, Harlem, Manhattan, 2007.

Page 108: Monotonix performing at Club Exit, Greenpoint, Brooklyn, 2008.

Page 109: Jell-O wrestling, Lower East Side, Manhattan, 2007.

Page 110: Melissa in her hallway, Bed-Stuy, Brooklyn, 2003.

Page 111: JMZ subway tracks, Bushwick, Brooklyn, 2006.

Page 112: What Cheer? Brigade performing at C-Squat, Alphabet City, Manhattan, 2012.

Page 115: Squatted bedroom in the Bat Cave, Gowanus, Brooklyn, 2013.

Page 116: NYPD cutting locks to confiscate bicycles during arrests at a Critical Mass ride, Flatiron District, Manhattan, 2005.

Page 117: Critical Mass ride taking over the Manhattan Bridge, 2003.

Page 118: Black Pus performing at Death By Audio, Williamsburg, Brooklyn, 2012.

Page 119: A dog attacks a bicycle tube at the Chicken Hut, Bed-Stuy, Brooklyn, 2003.

Page 120: Graffitied hallway, Bed-Stuy, Brooklyn, 2011.

Page 121: Going down at a party, Bed-Stuy, Brooklyn, 2010.

Page 122: The Freedom Tunnel, Upper West Side, Manhattan, 2007.

Page 123: Tony Bones climbing on rusted ship hulls in the tugboat graveyard, Staten Island, 2008.

Page 124: Juggernut performing at The Gowanus Ballroom, Gowanus, Brooklyn, 2012.

Page 125: FDNY arrives after a fire alarm at a Juggernut show in the basement of Cake Shop, Lower East Side, Manhattan, 2011.

Page 126: Dried blood on a subway platform, Brooklyn, 2000.

Page 127: Windows, Kips Bay, Manhattan, 2012.

Page 128: Performance art by Nate Hill, Harlem, Manhattan, 2011.

Page 129: Mermaid Parade, Coney Island, Brooklyn, 2010.

Page 130: Brodie in a vacant school, Bushwick, Brooklyn, 2012.

Page 131: Graffiti in a vacant school, Bushwick, Brooklyn, 2012.

Page 132: Secret Dinner in an abandoned grain terminal, Red Hook, Brooklyn, 2006.

Page 135: Matt and Yoni perform in the Night Heron water tower speakeasy, Chelsea, Manhattan, 2013.

Page 136: Panda in an overcoat on a tall bike at Bike Kill, Bed-Stuy, Brooklyn, 2008.

Page 137: Lisa lifting her dress, Williamsburg, Brooklyn, 2004.

Page 138: Partygoer flashing at Happy Valley, North of Madison Square Park, Manhattan, 2006.

Page 139: Amateur Hot Body Contest at a Rated X party, West Village, Manhattan, 2008.

Page 140: Tugboat graveyard, Staten Island, 2008.

Page 141: Exploring the shoreline, Staten Island, 2007.

Page 142: Ryan at the window of Market Hotel, Bushwick, Brooklyn, 2008.

Page 143: Sleeping in a wheelchair, East Village, Manhattan, 2006.

Page 144: House destroyed by Hurricane Sandy, Staten Island, 2012.

Page 145: Breezy Point destroyed by fire during Hurricane Sandy, Far Rockaway, Queens, 2012.

Page 146: Riding home in the back of a truck, Manhattan, 2012.

Page 147: BEEF performing at a basement show, East Williamsburg, Brooklyn, 2012.

Page 148: Callie C. in her studio, Gowanus, Brooklyn, 2008.

Page 149: The rafts of the Swimming Cities fleet moored off the West 70th Street Pier, Upper West Side, Manhattan, 2008.

Page 150: Sarah in a bear head, East Williamsburg, Brooklyn, 2011.

Page 151: Black Feelings performing at the Chicken Hut, Bed-Stuy, Brooklyn, 2003.

Page 152: Myric with a flamethrower at a party in the Bat Cave, Gowanus, Brooklyn, 2013.

Page 154: Serra, Adriana, and Vanessa in an art installation, Bushwick, Brooklyn, 2011.

Page 155: Santa Claus on a tall bike at Bike Kill, Bed-Stuy, Brooklyn, 2011.

Page 156: Fan on the floor during a Japanther basement show, East Williamsburg, Brooklyn, 2012.

Page 157: Jacquelyn preparing before a performance by Juggernut at a basement show, Bushwick, Brooklyn, 2012.

Page 158: Curbside weeds and car, Williamsburg, Brooklyn, 2003.

Page 159: Emergency exit, Roosevelt Island, 2006.

Page 160: Snow Migration performance, Staten Island, 2011.

Page 161: Demon in the basement of a vacant convent during an art installation, Greenpoint, Brooklyn, 2011.

Page 162: Nick H. and Porkchop after swimming in the East River to clean up from the Condiment War in Dumbo, Brooklyn, 2003.

Page 163: Pixie Pearl on the floor at a party, Manhattan, 2007.

Page 164: Abandoned naval housing, Navy Yard, Brooklyn, 2012.

Page 165: Inventory logbook in an abandoned house, North Brother Island, Bronx, 2012.

Page 166: Tall bike jousting at Bike Kill, Bed-Stuy, Brooklyn, 2006.

Page 167: Ninjasonik performing with members of Cerebral Ballzy at The Shank, Williamsburg, Brooklyn, 2009.

Page 168: View of lower Manhattan from the Brooklyn waterfront on September 11, 2001.

Page 169: Laura covering her nose, Brooklyn waterfront, September 11, 2001.

Page 170: Porkchop skateboarding at the Autumn Bowl, Greenpoint, Brooklyn, 2009.

Page 172: Abandoned hospital, North Brother Island, Bronx, 2012.

Page 173: Dead end at the boardwalk, Coney Island, Brooklyn, 2001.

Page 174: Roadkill cat outside of my apartment, Bushwick, Brooklyn, 2009.

Page 175: Igor of Fucking Bullshit at Lit Lounge, East Village, Manhattan, 2011.

Page 176: Balloons on a cart, Harlem, Manhattan, 2008.

Page 177: Man with balloons, Atlantic Yards, Brooklyn, 2002.

Page 178: Street performers, East Village, Manhattan, 2008.

Page 179: Trashed car with a spraypainted message, Dumbo, Brooklyn, 2000.

Page 180: Blackout caused by Hurricane Sandy, Lower Manhattan, 2012.

Page 181: Record store and its owner, East Williamsburg, Brooklyn, 2013.

Page 182: Rebecca on the bed, Prospect Heights, Brooklyn, 2009.

Page 183: Hallway in abandoned naval housing, Navy Yard, Brooklyn, 2008.

Page 184: Punk on subway stairs, Brooklyn, 2012.

Page 185: American flag mural on an abandoned bunker, Far Rockaway, Queens, 2013.

Page 186: Passed out in front of a bodega, Bed-Stuy, Brooklyn, 2010.

Page 187: Warehouse party, East Williamsburg, Brooklyn, 2011.

Page 188: Aerial performance in an abandoned theater, East Village, Manhattan, 2012.

Page 189: Monica drinking in a tree at Fort Tilden, Far Rockaway, Queens, 2008.

ACKNOWLEDGEMENTS

I would like to express my deep gratitude to everyone who has ever let me take their picture, to my family for their support, to my friends for inviting me to their parties, to all the bands and venues for the years of guest list spots, and to my fellow artists and adventurers for helping keep NYC the crazy place that it is. This book (and many more memories) would not exist without you. Thank you.

I would also like to thank everyone who helped me wrangle this book into existence: Jeff Stark for his unwavering support over the years, his insightful words, and his dedication; Ali Gitlow for taking a chance on an unknown photographer and sticking by me through the growing pains of a first book; and all the writers for helping me tell a much better story. Thanks to N. D. Austin and Dan Glass for their abandoned building expertise; Todd Chandler, Lauren Melodia, Christina Ray, and Sharilyn Neidhardt for giving me great feedback on image sequencing and selection; Malena Seldin, Marina Galperina, Serra Victoria Bothwell Fels, and Nicole Tourtelot for supporting me at various stages in this process; and Aaron Silverstein for his legal expertise and patience. Finally, thanks to Paulie Anne Duke for suffering through many late nights, acting as a third eye when my own eyes were exhausted. I am infinitely grateful to all of you.

© Prestel Verlag, Munich · London · New York, 2013.
© for the photographs by Tod Seelie.
© for the texts by the individual contributors.

Front cover: Myric with a flamethrower at a party in the Bat Cave, Gowanus, Brooklyn, 2013.

Prestel Verlag, Munich
A member of Verlagsgruppe Random House GmbH

Prestel Verlag
Neumarkter Strasse 28
81673 Munich
Tel. +49 (0)89 4136-0
Fax +49 (0)89 4136-2335

www.prestel.de

Prestel Publishing Ltd.
14–17 Wells Street
London W1T 3PD
Tel. +44 (0)20 7323 5004
Fax +44 (0)20 7323 0271

Prestel Publishing
900 Broadway, Suite 603
New York, NY 10003
Tel. +1 (212) 995-2720
Fax +1 (212) 995-2733

www.prestel.com

Library of Congress Control Number: 2013938623

British Library Cataloguing-in-Publication Data: a catalogue record for this book is available from the British Library; Deutsche Nationalbibliothek holds a record of this publication in the Deutsche Nationalbibliografie; detailed bibliographical data can be found under: http://dnb.d-nb.de

Prestel books are available worldwide. Please contact your nearest bookseller or one of the above addresses for information concerning your local distributor.

Editorial direction: Ali Gitlow
Editorial assistance: Eve Dawoud, Luna Schmidt
Design and layout: Bags of Joy
Production: Friederike Schirge
Origination: Reproline Genceller, Munich
Printing and binding: TBB, a. s., Banská Bystrica
Printed in Slovakia

Verlagsgruppe Random House FSC® N001967

The FSC-certified paper Profisilk has been supplied by Igepa, Germany

ISBN 978-3-7913-4855-1

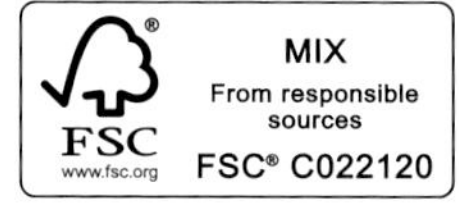